Client-Centered Therapy and the Person-Centered Approach: New Directions in Theory, Research, and Practice

Client-Centered Therapy and the Person-Centered Approach: New Directions in Theory, Research, and Practice

Edited by

Ronald F. Levant
John M. Shlien

PRAEGER SPECIAL STUDIES • PRAEGER SCIENTIFIC

New York • Philadelphia • Eastbourne, UK
Toronto • Hong Kong • Tokyo • Sydney

Library of Congress Cataloging in Publication Data
Main entry under title:

Client-centered therapy and the person-centered approach.

Bibliography: p.
Includes index.
1. Client-centered psychotherapy.   I. Levant, Ronald F.
II. Shlien, John M.   [DNLM: 1. Nondirective therapy.
WM 420 C636]
RC481.C54   1984   158'.3   84-6832
ISBN 0-03-070761-7 (alk. paper)

Published in 1984 by Praeger Publishers
CBS Educational and Professional Publishing
A Division of CBS, Inc.
521 Fifth Avenue, New York, NY 10175 USA

456789   052   987654321

Printed in the United States of America
on acid-free paper

Contents

v

Part Two: Developments in Practice

A Individual Psychotherapy

B Family Therapy and Enhancement

C Clinical Supervision

D Large Groups

Part Three:
Wider Applications of the Person-Centered Approach

Acknowledgments

The author and publisher wish to acknowledge the following sources for permission to quote throughout:

Josef Breuer and Sigmund Freud, *Studies on Hysteria,* New York: Basic Books, 1957. Copyright © 1957 by Basic Books. Reprinted by permission.

Jimmy Carter, *Keeping Faith,* New York: Bantam, 1982. Copyright © 1982 by Jimmy Carter. Reprinted by permission.

Moshe Dayan, *Breakthrough,* New York: Knopf, 1981. Copyright © 1981 by Random House. Reprinted by permission.

Lucy Freeman, *The Story of Anna O,* New York: Walker, 1972. Copyright © 1972 by Walker & Co. Reprinted by permission.

Sigmund Freud, *A General Introduction to Psychoanalysis* (Vol. 1), New York: Liveright, 1935. Copyright © 1935 by Liveright. Reprinted by permission.

Sigmund Freud, *An Autobiographical Study,* London: Hogarth, 1948. Copyright © 1948 by Hogarth. Reprinted by permission.

Sigmund Freud, *Collected Papers* (Vol. 3), New York: Basic Books, 1959. Copyright © 1959 by Basic Books. Reprinted by permission.

Ernest Jones, *The Life and Work of Sigmund Freud* (Vol. 1), New York: Basic Books, 1953. Copyright © 1953 by Basic Books. Reprinted by permission.

R.D. Laing, *The Politics of the Family,* New York: Pantheon, 1969, 1971. Copyright © 1969, 1971 by Random House. Reprinted by permission.

Janet Malcolm, "Annals of Scholarship. Trouble in the Archives—I," *The New Yorker,* Dec. 5, 1983, pp. 59–152. Reprinted by permission; © 1983 Janet Malcolm. Original in *The New Yorker.*

Carl Rogers, *Client-Centered Therapy*, Boston: Houghton Mifflin, 1951. Copyright © 1951 by Houghton Mifflin in the United States and Constable and Co. in the United Kingdom. Reprinted by permission.

Carl Rogers, *On Becoming a Person*, Boston: Houghton Mifflin, 1961. Copyright © 1961 by Houghton Mifflin in the United States and Constable and Co. in the United Kingdom. Reprinted by permission.

Carl Rogers, *Carl Rogers on Personal Power: Inner Strength and Its Revolutionary Impact*, New York: Delacorte, 1977. Copyright © 1977 by Delacorte. Reprinted by permission.

Carl Rogers, *A Way of Being*, Boston: Houghton Mifflin, 1980. Copyright © 1980 by Houghton Mifflin in the United States and Constable and Co. in the United Kingdom. Reprinted by permission.

Acknowledgments for lengthy extracts appear in text.

The authors would also like to acknowledge the efforts of numerous individuals in providing suggestions and in developing many fine prospecti and manuscripts, which, because of space limitations could not be included in the book. They would also like to acknowledge with gratitude the efforts of Richard Osborne, who contributed excellent editorial assistance, and of Marina Mihalakis, who provided consistently good administrative and secretarial support.

Contributors

David Barnard, Ph.D.
Assistant Professor
Institute for the Medical Humanities
University of Texas, Medical Branch
Galveston, Texas

Godfrey T. Barrett-Lennard
Fellow and Director
The Centre for Studies in Human Relations
Perth, Australia

Jerold D. Bozarth, Ph.D.
Professor and Chairman
Department of Counseling and Human Development Services
University of Georgia
Athens, Georgia

Desmond S. Cartwright, Ph.D.
Professor
Department of Psychology
University of Colorado
Boulder, Colorado

Robert C. Fuller, Ph.D.
Associate Professor
Department of Religious Studies
Bradley University
Peoria, Illinois

Eugene T. Gendlin, Ph.D.
Professor
Department of Behavioral Sciences
Committee on Methodology of Behavioral Research
University of Chicago
Chicago, Illinois

Rodney K. Goodyear, Ph.D.
Associate Professor
Counseling and Student Personnel Services Program
Kansas State University
Manhattan, Kansas

Mary Jane Graham
Research Assistant
Department of Psychology
University of Colorado
Boulder, Colorado

Bernard G. Guerney, Jr., Ph.D.
Professor of Human Development
Pennsylvania State University
University Park, Pennsylvania

Harold Hackney, Ed.D.
Associate Professor
Department of Counseling and Personnel Services
Purdue University
West Lafayette, Indiana

Ronald F. Levant, Ed.D.
Clinical Associate Professor
Program in Counseling Psychology
Boston University
Boston, Massachusetts

Germain Lietaer, Ph.D.
Professor
Counseling Centrum
Catholic University
Leuven, Belgium

Dave Mearns
Lecturer in Social Psychology and Counselling
Jordanhill College of Education
Glasgow, Scotland

John McLeod, Ph.D.
Lecturer in Psychology
The Polytechnic
Wolverhampton, England

Maureen Miller O'Hara, Ph.D.
Resident Fellow
Center for Studies of the Person
La Jolla, California

Laura N. Rice, Ph.D.
Professor
Department of Psychology
York University
Downsview, Ontario, Canada

Carl R. Rogers, Ph.D.
Resident Fellow
Center for Studies of the Person
La Jolla, California

William R. Rogers, Ph.D.
President
Guilford College
Greensboro, North Carolina

David Ryback, Ph.D.
Clinical Psychologist
Atlanta, Georgia

Julius Seeman, Ph.D.
Professor
Department of Psychology and Human Development
George Peabody College for Teachers
Vanderbilt University
Nashville, Tennessee

John M. Shlien, Ph.D.
Professor
Program in Counseling and Consulting Psychology
Harvard Graduate School of Education
Cambridge, Massachusetts

Neill Watson, Ph.D.
Associate Professor
Psychology Department
College of William and Mary
Williamsburg, Virginia

John Keith Wood, Ph.D.
Director
Center for Studies of the Person
La Jolla, California

1 Introduction

John M. Shlien
Ronald F. Levant

PROBLEMS

Volumes such as this appear every decade or so. In such a periodic review, recurring issues persist. One is the continuing debate on human nature: good or evil? This tends to be a "projective" question: answers come from knowledge of self as well as conjecture about others, which may explain some of the durability and intensity of the debate. Here we take another look at it.

Client-centered theory is generally identified with the optimistic position, in which human nature is basically good: good when enlightened, good when free, or ultimately good. Whether human nature is ultimately good is an evolutionary question; we may not know until the world ends, by which time it would not matter. Whether it is basically good must be determined on the evidence of all that appears in human behavior. Evil must be taken into account. Rogerians are not blind fools, but neither do they want to turn the world over to the cynics, who already have the advantage of appearing to be the more realistic. Why so? That advantage is all too easy. Cynicism takes its scornful ease at the expense of idealism's efforts. Pessimists can't be disappointed or accused of bad judgment in case of failure. They hold a defensive position.

It is worthwhile to examine this position. First, that which we call evil (like that which we call violence) is that which hurts. Definitions of what hurts (and is therefore evil) depend considerably upon our vulnerability or resistance to pain, as well as to others' intent to do injury.

"Harmless folk" are not considered evil. It appears, then, that the stronger need less protection, can bear more vulnerability, can afford idealism or dare to sacrifice for it. Cynicism comes from weakness, not realism. It is weakness in the face of pain, and since realism is a "survival concept," pain is wrongly credited with more realism than is pleasure. To take the cynic's position is to feed on that wrong-headedness. In short, the world hangs together, as much as it does, because of what good there is in human nature.

The cynic doubts this logic, knowing as he does that people are motivated by reward and punishment. If true, what's the reward for goodness? Where is the reward in giving instead of taking? The answer makes sense only at a certain level of moral judgment. The answer is that virtue is its own reward. "Virtue is its own reward?" It is beyond the comprehension of any cynic and not easily grasped by every idealist. The admiration of virtue is more than the pleasure of giving. It is a thing in itself. It is not the opposite of the position "Making life hell for others is my greatest pleasure," either, and evil cannot be its own reward unless you can admire evil for itself—not for its style. There is really not much to be said for cynicism, except that it is self-protective. It may not subscribe to evil, but it denies good, it makes a false claim to realism, and its arguments are not especially sound.

At the same time, those who would use client-centered theory to support an idealistic view make a mistake when they point to our reliance upon the "growth motive." It is not the same thing. Growth is a "positive" force, but it is neither good nor evil in a moral sense. Client-centered theory is *hospitable* to the idea of goodness; client-centered *therapy* has witnessed goodness produced at choice points in successful outcomes; but neither the theory *nor* the therapy can be held to prove the essential goodness of human nature.

Some changes in currents of thought lead us to a balanced perspective. People are capable of both good and evil, obviously. It is not clear that either one is naturally predominant. The first newer perspective is *interaction*. No longer does anyone argue for heredity or environment exclusively. Neither does one base an argument on humanity's hypothetical nature in isolation from social interaction. It is partly a question of what we, with *our* natures, do to, for, and with the person(s) whose "human natures" are in question.

A second perspective is that of adjustable balance. There is no philosophical absolute, nor is any individual totally good or bad. Each one carries a double-entry moral ledger sheet, and the balance can change.

We are basically both good and bad, much as it is now commonly recognized that all are somewhat female or male. It is a matter of proportion. If good and evil are matters of behavior (how else would we know them?) as well as of hypothesized nature, behavior can and does change. Where evil was, there good can be. Who is evil can become good. That is what matters, rather than "nature." That change is something to which experience in client-centered therapy *can* testify. It need not be a fundamental assumption about nature, but only a working assumption about ways of being. What is fundamentally assumed is the *potential to change*. That is unequivocal. It underlies all belief in growth, education, and therapy. The change could be in any direction, but the prediction is that it will be in a positive direction. Does that guarantee a positive "basic nature"? It does not. Unpredictability is one of our happily held assumptions about life and freedom. The establishing of certain conditions—such as a nourishing environment—has a predictable, encouraging, but not controlling, effect.

The "flying circus" debates, such as Skinner (Rogerian man is determined to feel free) vs. Rogers (Skinnerian man is free to feel determined) have run their course. It may be that the debaters of the human nature issue should take their quest elsewhere. Client-centered therapy allows for everything but tries to promote the best. That is an uphill struggle and a risk, at a constant disadvantage. Effortless gravity is on the side of evil. Evil can always have the last word, wiping out opposition (because death is so final) where good must allow for a continuation of all possibilities. That is where client-centered therapy may have appeared to take a side on the human nature question, for it does choose life. It *is* on the side of life.

Questions about Futures

There are some questions about the characteristics and characters of this movement that might influence its future. Where is its current vitality? Is its center fading or only moving? At one time, it was in the universities. Research of the particular sort that met the needs of the blossoming system of therapy and the quantitative-experimental conventions of the institutions was the object and source of great energy. The theory needed development. The therapy needed outcome evaluation. Impact and respectability were gained thereby. Audio and, later, film recordings were made. They were lauded forms of leadership. Now everyone does it. The research that once seemed such a proud achievement is also now a commonplace, and a source of criticism as well: no such research ever proves to anyone's satisfaction the absolutely irrefutable value and effectiveness of any psychotherapy.

In the beginning there was a wave of enthusiasm and a whole-hearted embracing of the fundamental ideas, at least for the purpose of a whole-hearted research. There was novelty, opportunity, a point of view that provided a welcome alternative and that appeared to be the democratic-egalitarian form of freedom and individuality in the field of mental health. The attitude was one of sincere commitment.

There is relatively little such commitment now. Students entering the field have a dazzling range of choices, presented in forceful competition. All claim to have some effectiveness and validity. How is one to choose? The general response is one of "synthesis," "integration," "matching method to client needs and therapist's preference." There are some examples in this volume.

The result is an eclecticism that tends to preclude the fully informed, fully invested commitment to any single mode. It leads toward incorporation of any chosen feature into the pragmatic mainstream of "whatever works." At least two problems stem from this. One is that "pure forms" will disappear. Aside from nostalgia for classical types, the problem is that eclectics cannot test "what works" because there will be confounded factors and effects. Research tends to come from a rather valiant belief and effort to confirm or deny a point. Those who use many methods will probably never discover *what* works, if they can study in a disciplined way whether anything is working at all. Research in this subject should (in order to have a fair chance of success) use only the most skillful and competent practitioners of a pure form. Neither the form nor the competence seems likely without the commitment. It is a formula for decline.

Cohesion and Dispersion

Another factor is the urge of the practitioner (explicitly including those in this school of thought and in this volume) to be unique, find some expression of originality, develop some virtuosity. Rogers says they should; he does; it is reasonable in the service of progress and self-enhancement. The problem is one of centrifugal effect. There is no "central committee"; no organization, formal or informal; and no stable center of information, communication, or membership. Subscribers to this system of thought may often recognize each other partly for what they are not (not behaviorists, nor psychoanalytic, etc.) though there are certain characteristics they and the system share.

For one, there are deliberately set limits to the power, authority, and status of the client-centered therapist. The therapist is always considered in relationship to the client; the relationship is one of service. The term "empowering" is fashionable among those who feel they can bestow power. The intent is laudable in the interests of equalizing, so long as it is not demeaning in its magnanimity, and it is their *own* power they give. Rogers puts it a bit differently—the client-centered therapist "never takes power away" (1977, xii). It is not an act of grace, but one of genuine respect.

Other orientations describe the therapist's role as "surgeon," "scientist," "commander-in-chief," and, of course, doctor, with all that these imply about management and knowing best. Superiority is evident and considered necessary for the successful outcome of the operation, the battle "for the sake of the patient." The quite different role of the client-centered therapist is one of companion, fellow traveler, gardener—not servant, though serving, and certainly not master.

While these egalitarian modes have individual appeal for personal and political reasons, the renunciation of superior power is absolutely required by the implications of a central point *in the theory*. That is, the client is the very source, as well as criterion, of health and progress.

This is implicit in reliance on the growth motive as the prime cause. It states: (1) growth is a natural process; (2) the essential healing comes from within. The surgeon, then, may remove diseased tissue but cannot claim to grow the healthy tissue. Some think that Rogers brought an agriculturalist's leanings to his theory. Perhaps, though each of us, however citified, knows that farmers do not grow the corn; they may plant and cultivate, but the corn grows itself. It grows even where there are no farmers. So it is not a mistake when Rogerian therapy is called "homeopathic." This supercilious accusation was made in scorn, but it is true and a compliment. While these growth analogies may help the reader to understand the theory's base, they have a limit. Rogers means for the growth to lead to self-understanding, made possible because of a self-reflexive consciousness plants do not possess. The overall point is that this *theory*, independent of fair-mindedness or humility, dictates that the role of the therapist is to assist in another's inherent process.

Though power is limited, there are no limits to the possible levels of artistry, skill, and craft. But these are generally private performances. In the more public roles, Rogerians do not make the most of them. Our research, for instance, is not characterized by the "flash of genius." Not the sort that captures the imagination. Rather it is the painstaking collection and analysis of data, with some excitement, but without the glory of the instant revelation. When Rogers and his collaborators were preparing to publish the research in *Psychotherapy and Personality Change* at the University of Chicago, the dean of the division took note of the fact that it had been richly funded by prestigious sources (such as Rockefeller, NIMH) and that it was in keeping with the highest standards of respectable research, rules of evidence, etc. He went on to remind the faculty senate of the occasion on which Freud's discoveries had been called by some scoffing Viennese colleagues "a sort of scientific fairy tale." "What we need," said the dean, "are more scientific fairy tales." He was wrong—we are suffocating from too many—but he was correct in realizing that this was not what he would get from the client-centered scientist. For a world wanting to be startled with revelations, such "rigorous research" is disappointing and pedestrian.

So it goes. In client-centered writing, you do not find the literary flair, historical and mythological allusions, not the arcane; seldom the exotic or even erotic. No Ratman, or Wolfman—just homely Mr. Lin, or Mrs. Oak. Never called brilliant, or clever; occasionally eloquent but more often admired as lucid, plain-spoken, sensitive. The overall tone is more than mundane, but far less than glamorous. Not that either style has any bearing on truth or value. It does have some bearing on who is attracted to this orientation.

The "dispossessed" rarely choose the Rogerian approach, though well they might, since it offers at once the dignity for others that they seek for themselves. Usually, though, if they have any opportunity to choose at all, more authoritarian orientations seem to suit better. Power, not the renunciation of it, may be the initial goal of the powerless. On the other hand, neither is this viewpoint a favored choice of the rich, aristocratic, elite, sophisticated. It lacks hauteur. We have known a few wealthy adherents, sometimes Quakers who are discreet about money and costliness but who have a quiet passion for friendly persuasion. Nor is this for those foaming with ambition. Rogers once said that those seeking fame and fortune would have more success if they did not attach themselves to him.

That leaves the middle class—not to be confused with second class, for many are as intelligent as can be found. But not arch, not wily, not artful. Middle class, or déclassé, and middle American in culture. Mild-mannered, unassuming, not weak, and, in fact, stronger than some more aggressive sorts, but able to bear their vulnerabilities. Students at the University of Chicago once made up a caricature regarding the problem of "what is in the black box": Freud said he would pry it open through symbolic analysis; Skinner said there was nothing in it; and Rogers said that it wasn't polite to ask.

For reasons besides the inherent force and appeal of its ideas, this native movement spread rapidly in response to opportunities now disappearing. First, there was the Veteran's Administration, expanded on so vast and sudden a scale that training and employment became available for more psychologists than existed. In VA hospitals, psychologists who began providing adjunct services to psychiatry (testing; vocational counseling) soon began to fill the gaps caused by shortages of psychiatrists. Thus they became "clinicians" doing "psychotherapy." Second, universities received a flood of graduate students and began to train many for those vacant professional positions in psychology. Student counseling centers were installed in dozens of colleges and universities, creating additional demand for graduates from training centers in universities. Client-centered therapy was well positioned to prepare candidates to fill these vacancies. Doctoral graduates could immediately enter senior academic and clinical positions. It was a multiplier effect. Third, the field of pastoral counseling had long been seeking a way to enable its ministry to combine theology and psychological therapeutics. (See Chapter 18.) Freud had declared that religion had no place in psychoanalysis, and some religionists replied in kind. Rogers, who had personal connections with liberal Christian theology, offered a practical alternative that enabled the field of pastoral counseling to grow through psychological instruction in the denominational seminaries.

As this is written, the situation is reversed. Vacancies in the psychological professions are fewer, and the production of doctoral level psychology graduates far exceeds the demand. Private practice is the self-employment solution often chosen, and all forms of psychotherapy are soon to be in harsh competition with the medical profession and each other—a situation somewhat foreign to the origins of the movement.

Finally, there are two other perennials.

One is the challenge forever thrown to the permissive philosophy. What would you do if (your child is crossing a busy street, suicide is contemplated, etc.)? Emergency is a real problem, and one does what one must according to the acceptable limits of risk, which depend a good deal on strength and vulnerability as well as long-term effects. There is a special debating tactic in such challenges: take one step not in keeping with your philosophy, and you lose the whole of it. Such a challenge appears in Chapter 14, where Hackney and Goodyear (p. 295) (themselves not of a client-centered persuasion, but participating in a comparative study of supervisors including Rogers) note that Rogers did not address the issue of "vicarious liability" for ultimate welfare of supervisee's clients, citing the *Tarasoff* case of the threatened homicide as the instance of emergency. The basic answer comes from the lawyer-philosopher Roscoe Pound: "Hard cases make bad laws." We recognize that if all practice is geared to safeguards against extremes, it is the ruination of the open society. Curfews do reduce crime, but when emergency rules, democracy dies. It is an authoritarian strategy for control, not necessarily based on the welfare of the client as first consideration but on the fault-free status of the therapist. It remains a problem, and it is everyone's. The costs and benefits need to be weighed and reweighed constantly and for each particular instance.

The second is a means/ends problem. Some who use techniques abhorrent to client-centered therapists justify intrusive or domineering ways as being for the ultimate good of the client. Interestingly, some who hold client-centered philosophy in contempt borrow its techniques (such as reflection, tentative understandings) to open up the client in early sessions for deeper probes later. The client-centered position recommends its own way throughout, holding with John Dewey that "Means are ends at lower levels." One never knows when the "end" arrives. Really, the end is, for this moment, right now. It is not only that, as Martin Luther King put it, "We cannot achieve moral ends by immoral means," but that the immoral means is at that very instant an immoral end. It may be the only end your client will ever experience. It is simply inimical to client-centered therapy to act on a "You may not like or understand this now but you will thank me for it later" basis, not only for the sake of consistency, but especially because "means are ends at lower levels," and we do not assume the opportunity of a hypothetical forever.

Here we turn to a description of the contents.

INTRODUCTION TO THE PRESENT VOLUME

Carl Rogers's theories of personality and therapy have had a major influence on the mental health and counseling professions, both in the United States and abroad. Since the 1950s, the basic hypotheses of the approach have been applied to an expanding array of issues other than mental health, including such diverse fields of human interaction as family life, administration, education, medicine, business and industry, government and politics, community organization, religion and spirituality, and art and creativity.[1] Throughout the entire period of the development and expansion of the client-centered approach, increasing numbers of people became involved in various aspects of the work, some becoming major foci of activity themselves (e.g., Gordon, 1970; Gendlin, 1981a). This expansion was in keeping with Rogers's basic outlook and with his personal style. He did not lay claim to sole ownership of the approach and disdained the idea of creating a doctrine or a school of followers.

In the early 1970s two anthologies of "new directions" and "innovations" in client-centered therapy appeared, containing the work of the major lights of this tradition of thought and practice (Hart & Tomlinson, 1970; Wexler & Rice, 1974). While both volumes were significant sources of current and emergent work in client-centered therapy, it has been 10 years since the last one appeared, and much has happened since then.

There have been several major developments in the client-centered approach in the last decade (see Lietaer, 1981, for an extensive bibliography of this literature). These developments fall roughly into two sets, one concerned with the mental health field (client-centered therapy), and the second concerned with the extensions to other fields (the person-centered approach).

Client-Centered Therapy

In the domain of client-centered therapy, developments have occurred in the areas of research, theory, and practice.

Research. One troubling development occurred in the area of research. Until the mid-1970s, there was considerable support for Rogers's (1957a) hypothesis regarding the necessary and sufficient conditions for psychotherapy, or at least for the association of the facilitative conditions (empathy, congruence, and unconditional positive regard) with therapeutic outcome (cf. Bergin, 1966, 1971). Yet by the late 1970s Parloff, Waskow, and Wolfe concluded: "Evidence for the hypothesis that judged accurate empathy, warmth, and genuineness of the therapist represent the 'necessary and sufficient' conditions of effective treatment has become increasingly clouded" (1978, p. 273; see also Bergin & Lambert, 1978; Mitchell, Bozarth, & Krauft, 1977). This clouding of the empirical status of the client-centered hypothesis was based in part on critiques of some of the original studies conducted at the University of Chicago and the University of Wisconsin, and in part on new studies conducted by researchers who do not share the client-centered theoretical orientation (e.g., Sloane, Staples, Cristol, Yorkston, & Whipple, 1975). This literature has demanded re-examination from a client-centered perspective, and this task is undertaken by Neill Watson in Chapter 2 of the present volume. After careful review, Watson concludes that Rogers's hypotheses have never been put to adequate test—not in the more favorable early studies, nor in the recent less favorable ones. From this point of view, reviewers were in error both then and now, and neither research methodology nor outcome evaluation have much to be proud about. It can only be said that no firm negative proof exists, and that no psychotherapy has yet had its basic theory validated empirically, even though some support exists for a modest degree of efficacy in many therapies.

Theory. Theory has been a lively area in the 1970s and early 1980s. There have been several lines of development. The first is, in some respects, associated with the apparent fall in empirical stature of the client-centered hypothesis, in that it has involved a re-examination of the facilitative conditions from workers both inside and outside of the client-centered tradition. This re-examination has focused on empathy (Hackney, 1978; Corcoran, 1981; Troemel-Ploetz, 1980) and its clinical embodiment in the technique of reflection (Judge, 1979), and on unconditional positive regard (Schmitt, 1980). The exquisitely reasoned chapter by Germain Lietaer (Chapter 3) and the following one by Jerold Bozarth (Chapter 4) are the most recent representatives of this trend. Both have cogent supportive critiques of some aspect of theory and technique. Bozarth supports Rogers's critical view of the skill-training uses of reflection, and of the great significance of empathic understanding. At the same time, he moves beyond reflection to more idiosyncratic ways on several grounds: that empathy has many modes of expression, some verifiable; that Rogers exceeds reflective techniques himself; that the self-actualizing tendency is a value for the therapist's development as well as the client's; and that strict adherence to the single mode "restricts the potency" of the therapist. Some press for originality, not necessarily a client-centered version of "wild analysis," is in evidence.

Another line of theoretical development has been the continued expansion and refinement of Eugene Gendlin's (1981a) experiential psychotherapy, a trend started when Gendlin's (1962) volume *Experiencing and the Creation of Meaning* provided the most systematic treatment, from a client-centered perspective, of the concept of experience only sketchily developed in Rogers's (1959b) otherwise elegant statement of theory. Rogers's thoughts about "organismic valuing of experience" were bound to lead to some expression of body-awareness practices. They are clearly evident in Gendlin's matured and most recent formulation of his approach (Chapter 5).

A third line of theoretical development has been to enlarge aspects of client-centered theory by considering them in relationship to other theories. The 1974 volume (Wexler & Rice, 1974) provided the first glimpse of this trend, emphasizing client-centered theory in relation to cognitive psychology (Anderson, 1974; Wexler, 1974; Zimring, 1974). Recent publications have been concerned with examining client-centered theory in relation to the psychoanalytic self-psychology of Heinz Kohut (Stolorow, 1976), learning theory (Martin, 1972), and paradoxical psychotherapy (Troemel-Ploetz, 1980). Not all these efforts are entirely on the mark, and some are misguided. But taken as a whole, they represent a stage in the maturing (or at least aging) of the approach, one in which some concern is toward synthesis and reconciliation of differences among theories, and some is toward separation and new identities. We may see more of this two-directional trend, having come to the point of the "third (and perhaps fourth) generation," i.e., productions of students of Rogers's students. The chapter by Desmond Cartwright and Mary Jane Graham (Chapter 6) continues the trend begun in the Wexler and Rice volume, using a cognitive model to examine the client-centered construct of the self-concept in relation to Erikson's ego-psychological construct of identity. Continuing in a similar spirit, veteran Julius Seeman's chapter (Chapter 7) broadens and universalizes Rogers's construct of the fully functioning person by considering a broad scope of theory and research on optimal human functioning, with reference to psychoanalytic ego psychology, as well as to the work of Abraham Maslow, Marie Jahoda, Brewster Smith, and Robert White. John Shlien's chapter (Chapter 8) examines a classical feature of psychoanalysis, "transference" from a client-centered "literalist" (Shlien, 1970) viewpoint, and traces its origins historically and functionally to the precious central factor in most therapies, understanding. His argument completely contradicts the idea that therapeutic behavior and situation do not account for transference, and he suggests that the invention and maintenance of the concept are due to a failure of nerve.

Practice. There have been some interesting changes in emphasis in the writings on practice over the past decade. The Wexler and Rice (1974) volume placed some emphasis on encounter groups and group therapy, reflecting the popularity of those modalities in that period (Bebout, 1974; Beck, 1974). The reader will find almost no discussion of small groups in the present volume. This is a reflection of the diminishing interest in encounter groups over the decade of the 1970s and of the rise of other modalities of therapy, particularly family therapy. It also reflects the direction taken in the person-centered workshops, in which the use of encounter groups became part of the process of large group work.

There are still some continuities with past productions. Laura Rice continues her description of the evocative function of therapist empathy, presenting (Chapter 9) a model of the client's tasks in therapy. Like Bozarth, she also moves toward a personal brand of response, geared to her work/task vs. emotional/interpersonal division, assuming that cognition and affect are processed through different systems. The 1974 Wexler and Rice volume included a chapter concerned with integrating client-centered therapy and Gestalt therapy (Cochrane & Holloway, 1974), a concern again taken up in the present volume by Maureen Miller O'Hara (Chapter 10). This is a topic that raises important issues with regard to holism in theory and directivity in practice.

We mentioned the increasing interest in families and family therapy. Perhaps the earliest example of this trend is Rogers's chapter, "The Implications of Client-Centered Therapy for Family Life," which appeared in *On Becoming a Person* (1961). Rogers's own interest in marriage and the family continued in a book on couple relationships (1972) and two chapters on marriage and the family in a more recent book (1977). This trend was also represented in articles in the 1970 anthology (Hart & Tomlinson, 1970) on the application of client-centered principles to family therapy (Raskin & van der Veen, 1970) and to skills-training preventive and developmental programs (Gordon, 1970; Guerney, Guerney, & Andronico, 1970). The latter trend showed considerable development in the last decade (cf. Levant, 1978a, 1983 for reviews). Client-centered family therapy has been slower in developing (Levant, 1978b). Part of the problem lies in the difficulty in integrating such seemingly opposite orientations as phenomenology and systems theory. Despite this, there are many clinicians and counselors working with families from a client-centered orientation.[2]

Interest in families is represented here in three chapters. In Chapter 11, G. Barrett-Lennard tackles the problem of integrating phenomenology with structural and systemic concepts through an examination of the effects of different family constellations on the relationship possibilities and on the lived experience of family members. In Chapter 12, Ronald Levant compares two approaches to the construction of a theoretical bridge between persons and systems, one informed by psychoanalytic theory, and the other from a client-centered perspective. Finally, Bernard Guerney, Jr. (in Chapter 13) provides an update on his Relationship Enhancement program, covering both practice and evaluative research, and touching on the influence of client-centered theory. Like several other authors whose work appears in this volume, Guerney's theoretical orientation is eclectic, with client-centered therapy existing alongside other orientations, such as social-learning theory. In some ways this addresses one of the purposes of this book, which is to represent the client-centered tradition as a large extended family, with main lineages as well as collaterals. We have tried to sample the major representatives of current thought and practice that have been significantly influenced by Carl Rogers and his theories.

One of the notable gaps is a lack of any work on child therapy. It may be that some of the enormously competent workers in this area do not take time away from practice to write. There is little in the literature beyond that of Axline. Further, in this first volume, space limitations prevented contributions from many without whom representation is certainly incomplete. Thomas Gordon, for example, has influenced literally hundreds of thousands through his Effectiveness Training programs. Carl Rogers regretted omission of the work of Reinhard and Anne-Marie Tausch (her unfortunate death delayed their contribution) since they and colleagues at the University of Hamburg have done more research in our school of thought than any person or group in the world. We would also have included work from Douglas Blocksma, William Coulson, Gerard Haigh, Nathaniel Raskin, Ferdinand van der Veen, Fred Zimring, Richard Farson, Natalie Rogers, Gerald Goodman, William Perry, to name only 10 of 100 on our list.

A third area that is included in our consideration of practice is the topic of clinical supervision. Supervision has been a major focus of research and writing in counseling psychology over the past decade, yet surprisingly little has been written on supervision from a client-centered perspective. The chapter by Harold Hackney and Rodney Goodyear (Chapter 14) attempts to fill this gap, using as their basic datum a transcript of Carl Rogers supervising the work of one of the co-authors.

Finally, we mentioned the virtual disappearance from the scene of encounter groups qua encounter groups, and their incorporation into the large group work that has characterized certain thrusts of the person-centered approach. This evolution, and the nature of large group work is discussed in Chapter 15 by John Keith Wood (unfortunately reduced due to page limits), which serves thereby as a bridge from the domain of client-centered therapy to the domain of the person-centered approach.

The Person-Centered Approach

The person-centered approach was conceived to accommodate the expansion of client-centered therapy beyond its original boundaries of counseling and mental health (Rogers, 1979). This relabeling recognized the increasing emphasis given to working with a wide range of people, few of whom would define themselves as "clients" seeking therapy. Early representatives of this trend can be found in Rogers's (1951) book, *Client-Centered Therapy*, in Gordon's chapter on leadership and administration, and Rogers's on student-centered teaching. These continued with (for example) Richard Farson's work at the Western Behavioral Sciences Institute on business and industry, and Rogers's continuing work on education (1969). It was in the late 1960s and 1970s that the focus widened to include such diverse fields as medicine and health care; religion and spirituality; art and creativity; research and epistemology; the psychology of secrecy; and community organization, politics, and intergroup and international tensions and relations. This final area became the concerted interest of Carl Rogers and his associates in La Jolla from about the mid-1970s to the present (Rogers, 1977, 1979, 1980). It was this focus on community organization, politics, intergroup and international tensions and relations that was served by the development of the large group or "person-centered workshop" approach.

Coincident with the development of the person-centered approach has been the emergence of growing international interest in client-centered therapy. This has been stimulated, in part, by the establishment of European Facilitator Development Institutes and other workshops in countries such as England, Scotland, Holland, Belgium, Germany, Italy, Sweden, Switzerland, and South Africa. The development in some places has been so extensive that, for example, there are now at least four distinct approaches to client-centered therapy in Germany (D. Tscheulin, personal communication, December 7, 1982). In addition, there has been one European conference (Lietaer, 1981) and one worldwide conference held recently. The worldwide conference occurred in the summer of 1982 in Mexico City and included participants from the United States, Europe, Latin America, and Asia. The present volume includes selections from a few of those authors from around the world.

Six selections in the present volume sample the wider applications of the person-centered approach. The topics of education and administration are merged in Chapter 16, in which William Rogers develops a framework, supplemented by personal example, for a person-centered approach to higher-educational administration. In Chapter 17, David Barnard discusses an emergent approach to the re-evaluation of the nature of the doctor-patient relationship in medicine and health care delivery. Robert Fuller's chapter (Chapter 18) examines the profound influence of Carl Roger's theories and methods in religion and pastoral counseling. In Chapter 19, Dave Mearns and John McLeod develop a person-centered approach to conducting research, one that achieves validity at several more levels than does the currently ascendant positivist-empiricist approach. John Shlien reports (in Chapter 20) on his studies in the psychology of secrecy, first presented at the 1981 annual meeting of the American Psychological Association. Finally, in Part Four (Chapter 21), Carl Rogers with David Ryback present a thought-provoking discussion of the issue of nuclear war and its possible prevention, based on experience with antagonistic interests and sometimes hostile—to-the-death—groups where he has been a facilitator, and on President Carter's Camp David conference. This is not another "Why War," but a hopeful though sobering set of ideas on how wars can be prevented through that same personal understanding first tested in the therapeutic relationship.

NOTES

1. Rogers's theories of personality and of therapy are discussed in Rogers (1959b) and Rogers (1942b, 1951, 1957a), respectively; the foundational empirical research is presented in Rogers & Dymond (1954) and summarized in Cartwright (1957). The extensions of client-centered therapy into the areas mentioned are discussed in Rogers (1951, 1961, 1969, 1972, 1977, 1980), Hart & Tomlinson (1970), and Wexler & Rice (1974). For an excellent biography of Carl Rogers, see Kirschenbaum (1979); a lively history of the client-centered/person-centered approach can be found in Barrett-Lennard (1979a); and a bibliography of Rogers's work (complete until early 1980) can be found at the end of Rogers (1980).

2. Indeed, a recent survey of 600 clinical members of the American Association of Marital and Family Therapy found that Rogers was the third most influential theorist, ranking ahead of such family therapy notables as Murray Bowen, Salvador Minuchin, and Jay Haley (Sprenkle, Keeney, & Sutton, 1982).

2 The Empirical Status of Rogers's Hypotheses of the Necessary and Sufficient Conditions for Effective Psychotherapy

Neill Watson

Rogers began the development of the theory and practice of client-centered therapy on the basis of his observations of his relationships with clients in individual psychotherapy (Rogers, 1942b, 1951). Research on this phenomenological approach to therapy followed. Empirical verification of its effectiveness was a focus of the early studies (Rogers & Dymond, 1954). With the publication of Rogers's theory of the necessary and sufficient conditions for effective therapy (Rogers, 1957a, 1959b), research on client-centered therapy began to focus on the hypothesized mechanism of therapy (e.g., Barrett-Lennard, 1962; Halkides, 1958; Rogers, Gendlin, Kiesler, & Truax, 1967). Over the past 25 years there has been a substantial amount of research on the theory of the mechanism of effective therapy from a client-centered perspective.

Is there now empirical evidence of the validity of Rogers's theory of the necessary and sufficient conditions for constructive personality change in a client? A number of reviews have been concerned with the empirical status of this theory (Bergin & Lambert, 1978; Gurman, 1977; Lambert, De Julio, & Stein, 1978; Marshall, 1977; Meltzoff & Kornreich, 1970; Mitchell, Bozarth, & Krauft, 1977; Orlinsky & Howard, 1978; Parloff, Waskow, & Wolfe, 1978; Rachman & Wilson, 1980; Shapiro, 1976; Truax & Mitchell, 1971). The present review develops conceptual and methodological criteria to evaluate the research on Rogers's theory. These criteria are also used to evaluate the methods of the previous reviews of this research.

THE HYPOTHESES

Rogers hypothesized that six conditions are necessary and sufficient for constructive personality change in the client:

1. Two persons are in psychological contact.
2. The first, whom we shall term the client, is in a state of incongruence, being vulnerable or anxious.
3. The second person, whom we shall term the therapist, is congruent or integrated in the relationship.
4. The therapist experiences unconditional positive regard for the client.
5. The therapist experiences an empathic understanding of the client's internal frame of reference and endeavors to communicate this experience to the client.
6. The communication to the client of the therapist's empathic understanding and unconditional positive regard is to a minimal degree achieved. (Rogers, 1957a, p. 96)

Rogers stated the hypotheses as testable, cause-effect propositions:

If these six conditions (as operationally defined) exist, then constructive personality change (as defined) will occur in the client.

If one or more of these conditions is not present, constructive personality change will not occur.

If all six conditions are present, then the greater the degree to which Conditions 2 to 6 exist, the more marked will be the constructive personality change in the client. (Rogers, 1957a, p. 100)

The omission of Condition 1 in the last hypothesis deserves comment. In an extended explanation of these conditions, Rogers stated that the first condition "specifies a minimal relationship, a psychological contact," without which the remaining five conditions would have no meaning (Rogers, 1957a, p. 96). Conditions 2 through 6 describe the characteristics of that relationship. If Conditions 2 through 6 are operationally defined and shown to be present, then it follows that Condition 1 is present. Condition 1, then, does not require its own operational definition separate from those for the remaining conditions.

For the purpose of empirical validation, it is important to note the roles of the client and the therapist in establishing Conditions 2 through 6. Condition 2, the client's incongruence, is brought to the relationship by the client. Conditions 3 through 5, the therapist's congruence, unconditional positive regard, and empathy, are provided by the therapist. Condition 6 exists if the client perceives the therapist's unconditional positive regard and empathy. Though Rogers does not state explicitly in his article (Rogers, 1957a) that the client must also perceive the therapist's congruence, this condition is implied in his later theoretical statement of the interrelationship among the therapist-provided conditions: congruence on the part of the therapist is a precondition for the therapist's experience of unconditional positive regard and empathy toward the client (Rogers & Truax, 1967). It seems reasonable to the present author to make a similar hypothesis about the experience of the client: the client's perception of the therapist's congruence is a precondition for the client's perception of the therapist's unconditional positive regard and empathy. If the client perceives the therapist as ungenuine, then the client will not perceive the therapist as communicating the other two conditions. It follows from this hypothesis that the client's perception of the therapist's congruence is one of the necessary and sufficient conditions for effective therapy.

The empirical validation of Rogers's hypothesis requires the demonstration of a causal relationship between all of the conditions, present together, and constructive personality change in the client. In the present review, research on Rogers's hypotheses is evaluated in terms of its conceptual and methodological rigor.

CONCEPTUAL AND METHODOLOGICAL CRITERIA

Conceptual rigor refers to the consistency of the method used to test Rogers's (1957a, 1959b) hypotheses with the hypotheses in their phenomenological context. Three criteria of conceptual rigor can be identified: testing the hypotheses as stated, the face validity of the operational definitions, and the source of the ratings of the therapist-provided conditions.

Testing the Hypotheses as Stated

The criterion of testing the hypotheses as stated refers to whether a study includes all of Conditions 2 through 6 in researching the relationships between the conditions and client improvement. According to the hypotheses, if one of the conditions is absent, then no client improvement will occur. If no client improvement occurs, then it is impossible to demonstrate a causal relationship between any of the other conditions and client improvement. Thus, if one of the conditions is absent, no relationship is predicted between any of the other conditions and client improvement. In order for the hypothesized causal relationships to be demonstrated empirically, all of the conditions must be present, to some degree, in at least some of the therapist-client dyads under study.

Studies that do not include incongruent clients are not adequate tests of the hypotheses, since relationships between the therapist-provided conditions and outcome are not predicted in the absence of client incongruence. Analog studies of therapy are presumably not likely to include incongruent participants in the role of client, since these participants are not seeking therapy. If an analog study does not obtain significant relationships between the therapist-provided conditions and outcome, the null finding could be the result of the absence of the condition of client incongruence. For this reason, analog studies are not regarded in the present review as adequate tests of Rogers's hypotheses, unless they assess the incongruence of the "clients."

A study of an actual therapy situation may well include a substantial number of clients who are not incongruent. The presence of these clients, for whom no personality change is predicted, would attenuate the strength of the relationships between the therapist-provided conditions and outcome if these clients perceived moderate or high levels of the therapist-provided conditions. In support of this point, there is evidence that less incongruent clients perceive higher levels of the therapist-provided conditions (Stoler, cited in van der Veen, 1970). A study that adequately tests Rogers's hypotheses must assess client incongruence and be designed to demonstrate that the therapist-provided conditions are related to outcome for incongruent clients but not for clients who are not incongruent.

Face Validity of the Operational Definitions

In terms of face validity, the operational definitions employed in a study should be tied directly to the concepts of the hypothesized conditions as defined by Rogers (1957a, 1959b). Operational definitions of related concepts, such as therapist warmth, may not be face valid measures of one of the conditions as defined by Rogers. For example, the measurement of therapist warmth is not an adequate operational definition of unconditional positive regard if the measure does not focus on the conditionality of the warmth. The measurement of therapist unconditional positive regard requires recognition that some therapists may be more distant than others in their styles. The central issue in this respect is not whether one therapist is more distant, that is, less warm, than another, but whether a therapist's distance varies with the content of the client's experience. This distinction is made in several items of the Unconditionality of Regard Scale of the Barrett-Lennard Relationship Inventory; for example, "He (the therapist) always responds to me with warmth and interest—or always with coldness and disinterest" (Barrett-Lennard, 1962, p. 34). The unconditionality of the regard is essential to the construct. Studies that employ operational definitions of questionable face validity are not considered in the present review to be adequate tests of Rogers's hypotheses.

Client Ratings of Therapist-Provided Conditions

A third criterion of the conceptual rigor of research on Rogers's hypotheses concerns the source of the ratings of the therapist-provided conditions. Rogers explicitly stated that the therapist-provided conditions must be perceived by the client in order for constructive personality change to occur (Rogers, 1957a, 1959b). From a phenomenological perspective, only the client has direct access to his or her own perceptions in the process of self-reflection; unless the client gives a self-report, other persons must infer the client's perceptions indirectly from other overt behavior. From this standpoint, adequate assessment of the therapist-provided conditions requires that the client be the source of the ratings. Previous reviewers have made a similar argument for using the client's self-report (Gurman, 1977; Parloff et al., 1978), though only one reviewer has applied this criterion systematically in drawing conclusions about empirical research on Rogers's hypotheses (Gurman, 1977).

A number of studies have relied on judges' ratings of the therapist-provided conditions from tape recordings of therapy sessions (e.g., Truax, Altmann, Wright, & Mitchell, 1973; Truax, Wittmer, & Wargo, 1971). The seminal investigators who developed this method have discussed Rogers's hypotheses from the point of view of a behavioral paradigm (Truax, 1966a, 1968; Truax & Carkhuff, 1967a). These reformulations of the hypotheses suggest that these investigators did not construe their research from the perspective of the phenomenological paradigm that forms the context for Rogers's hypotheses. The research that is based on judge ratings of the therapist-provided conditions is irrelevant from the phenomenological perspective of Rogers's hypotheses. Regardless of a judge's perceptions, if a client does not perceive the conditions, then the hypothesized conditions for effective therapy do not exist.

If judge ratings were highly correlated with client ratings of the therapist-provided conditions, then the argument above, based on conceptual considerations, would be moot from the point of view of empirical findings. High correlations between the two types of ratings would suggest that they are interchangeable. However, research has shown that the two types of ratings are not highly correlated. Though four studies have found significant correlations between client and judge ratings of one or more of the therapist-provided conditions (Burstein & Carkhuff, 1968; Caracena & Victory, 1969; Hill, 1974; Rogers et al., 1967), the failure of seven other studies to confirm these findings (Bozarth & Grace, 1970; Bozarth, Mitchell, & Krauft, 1976; Fish, 1970; Hansen, Moore, & Carkhuff, 1968; Kurtz & Grummon, 1972; McWhirter, 1973; Truax, 1966b) has led previous reviewers to conclude that there is not reliable agreement between client and judge ratings (Gurman, 1977; Parloff et al., 1978). Since research indicates that judges and clients do not agree on the presence of the therapist-provided conditions, from the point of view of conceptual rigor, client ratings of these conditions are the only ones that are relevant to tests of Rogers's hypotheses.

The use of client ratings of the therapist-provided conditions has implications for another aspect of the methodology of correlational studies of Rogers's hypotheses. If client ratings of these conditions are correlated with client ratings of outcome, there may be a bias toward inflated correlations because of shared method variance. Correlations between these two sets of client ratings also present a problem of ambiguity in the interpretation of significant results. A plausible alternative to the interpretation that supports Rogers's hypotheses is the interpretation that clients who rate their experience in therapy as beneficial also rate their therapists positively (see Parloff et al., 1978). In order to avoid these problems of shared method variance and ambiguity of interpretation, client ratings of the therapist-provided conditions should be related to outcome measures from other sources, such as judges or therapists. Though client ratings of outcome are problematic in correlational studies, they still have value. If relationships are not obtained between client ratings of the therapist-provided conditions and client ratings of outcome in a study that is otherwise conceptually and methodologically sound, it can be concluded that Rogers's hypotheses are not supported.

Therapist-Provided Conditions as Causal

Most of the research on the relationship between the hypothesized conditions and therapy outcome has been correlational research based on naturalistic observations (e.g., Barrett-Lennard, 1962; Kurtz & Grummon, 1972). In correlational research that meets the criteria discussed in the present review, positive results are necessary for establishing the validity of Rogers's hypotheses, since null findings contradict the hypotheses. However, positive results in such correlational studies are not sufficient evidence, because they are subject to ambiguity of interpretation, even when outcome is not rated by clients. Correlations between the therapist-provided conditions rated by clients and therapy outcome rated by another source may be interpreted to mean that the clients who perceive the conditions are the ones who benefit from therapy, rather than that the conditions are provided by the therapist. These two interpretations, it should be noted, are compatible with each other and are both consistent with Rogers's hypotheses. However, Rogers (1957a, 1959b) clearly hypothesized that the therapist provides the conditions of congruence, unconditional positive regard, and empathy. Unequivocal evidence that these conditions are provided by the therapist requires a path analysis or an experimental design. A method that preserves, as much as possible, the natural situation of therapy enhances the external validity of the results. For this reason, artificial manipulations of the levels of the therapist-provided conditions should be avoided. An example of an experiment with high external validity is the random assignment of incongruent clients to groups and the groups to each of several therapists. The independent variable is the individual therapist. The dependent variables are the therapist-provided conditions rated by the clients and therapy outcome rated by multiple sources. If the therapists are found to differ in levels of the therapist-provided conditions, and if corresponding differences are found among therapists in level of outcome, then the results provide unequivocal evidence that therapists who are perceived by clients as providing higher levels of the therapist-provided conditions produce better outcomes in therapy. An experiment, then, can unambiguously support Rogers's hypotheses that the therapist provides the interpersonal conditions for effective therapy.

Adequate Ranges in Reliable Measures of Hypothesized Conditions

In order to obtain relationships between the hypothesized conditions and the outcome of therapy, there must be an adequate range of scores for each of the conditions. If the ranges of these scores are truncated, then the probability of accepting the null hypothesis when it is false is increased. Studies that do not include a sufficient range of scores for the hypothesized conditions are not considered adequate tests of Rogers's hypotheses.

Methodological rigor in research on Rogers's hypotheses also requires that the measures of the hypothesized conditions be reliable. Unreliable measures bias the results against support for Rogers's hypotheses by increasing measurement error. Gurman (1977) reviewed studies of the reliability of the Barrett-Lennard Relationship Inventory (Barrett-Lennard, 1962), one of the most frequently used measures of client perceptions of the therapist-provided conditions. The mean split-half reliabilities, based on 14 studies, are: Congruence, .88; Regard, .91; Unconditionality, .74; and Empathy, .84 (Gurman, 1977). The mean test-retest reliabilities, based on 10 studies, are: Congruence, .85; Regard, .83; Unconditionality, .80; and Empathy, .83 (Gurman, 1977). Research that uses the Barrett-Lennard Relationship Inventory, or an instrument with known comparable reliability, is considered in the present review to meet the criterion of reliability of the measures of the therapist-provided conditions.

Adequate Outcome Measures

Another methodological consideration in studies of the relationship between the hypothesized conditions and outcome of therapy is the adequacy of the outcome measures. A reliable instrument should be used to measure outcome. When outcome is measured by administering the instrument before and after therapy, the raw difference score should not be used to index improvement. Raw difference scores are correlated as much as –.71 with the scores on the pretest (Fiske, 1971) because of statistical artifacts. One of these artifacts is a ceiling effect, in which high scores on the pretest cannot improve as much as low scores. Another artifact is the statistical phenomenon of regression to the mean, in which extreme scores on the pretest are more likely than middle-range scores to change in the direction of the mean on the posttest (Campbell & Stanley, 1963). This statistical artifact tends to inflate any upward changes from pretest to posttest for low scores on the pretest and to depress any upward change for high scores on the pretest. The result is that low scores show the most change from pretest to posttest and that high scores show the least change. The effect of these artifacts can be corrected by using a regression transformation to yield a change score that is independent of the pretest score (Bereiter, 1963).

What are the implications for research on Rogers's hypotheses if uncorrected raw difference scores are used to measure outcome? In correlations between ratings of the hypothesized conditions and uncorrected difference scores, bias toward significant results due to the statistical artifacts would exist only if clients with low scores on the pretest (whose uncorrected difference scores are higher because of the artifacts) gave higher ratings of the therapist-provided conditions than the other clients, and/or clients with high pretest scores (whose uncorrected difference scores are lower because of the artifacts) gave lower ratings of the conditions. However, empirical evidence indicates that the reverse is the case. Stoler (cited in van der Veen, 1970) found that clients who were less disturbed—that is, who had higher scores on the pretest—gave higher ratings of the therapist-provided conditions. Therefore, correlational studies that use uncorrected difference scores would be biased against significant results. Even in the absence of this evidence, it would be reasonable to expect that the statistical artifacts exert no systematic bias and that they work against obtaining significant correlations by increasing measurement error. This conclusion differs from that of previous reviewers, who have assumed, without stating a rationale or citing empirical support, that the use of uncorrected difference scores biases the results toward significant positive correlations (Gurman, 1977; Parloff et al., 1978). In the present review, then, the use of uncorrected difference scores in correlational studies is considered to bias results against support for Rogers's hypotheses.

Summary of Criteria

In summary, several conceptual and methodological criteria of adequate research on Rogers's hypotheses can be identified: testing the hypotheses as stated, face valid measures of the hypothesized conditions, the client as the source of the ratings of the therapist-provided conditions, reliable ratings of the hypothesized conditions and of outcome, and sufficient range in levels of the conditions provided by the therapists. Positive results in correlational studies are necessary, but not sufficient, evidence for the validity of the hypotheses. An experimental design or a path analysis is required in order to provide evidence that is sufficient for the conclusion that the therapist provides the conditions of congruence, unconditional positive regard, and empathy. The present review asks whether any studies meet these criteria and form a basis for drawing conclusions about the validity of Rogers's hypotheses. The review is concerned only with studies of individual counseling or psychotherapy, as this was the modality on which Rogers's theory focused.

STUDIES EMPLOYING CLIENT RATINGS OF THERAPIST-PROVIDED CONDITIONS

Table 2.1 presents studies of the relationship of client perceptions of the therapist-provided conditions to outcome in individual counseling and psychotherapy. Several analog studies in this area (Colistro, 1979; Hill, Snyder, & Schill, 1974; Jones, 1969; Stanley, 1967; Zauderer, 1968) are not included, because one of the hypothesized conditions, an incongruent client, is not likely to be present. As discussed above, in the absence of an incongruent client, Rogers's hypotheses predict no therapeutic change and, therefore, no relationship between therapist-provided conditions and outcome. A second reason for excluding these studies is the questionable generalizability of their results to actual therapy situations. Only research conducted in actual therapy situations is considered in this review.

Several other studies of client perceptions of the therapeutic relationship are not included in this review, because they used measures that the author evaluates as not face valid measures of the conditions defined by Rogers. Grigg and Goodstein's (1957) study of the client's perception of closeness to the therapist and Libo's (1957) study of the client's attraction to the therapist did not address the therapist's regard. Sapolsky's (1965) measure of empathy, the correspondence between a client's self-description and the client's rating of how the therapist would describe him, did not address the therapist's understanding of the client's experience during therapy. Saltzman, Luetgert, Roth, Creaser, & Howard (1976) used client ratings of the mutual openness and understanding between client and therapist, rather than ratings of the therapist's contribution of these conditions. However, the Saltzman team (1976) used a face valid measure of unconditionality of regard that is considered below.

Only level of regard is measured in Board's (1959) study of the client's perception of being liked by the therapist, and in Lorr's (1965) and Martin and Sterne's (1976) studies of client perceptions of acceptance by the therapist. Although client ratings of the level of therapist regard are not considered in the present review to be a satisfactory operational definition of Rogers's concept of unconditional positive regard, the results of these studies are reviewed, as a matter of empirical interest, together with the results of the Level of Regard Scale in studies that used the Barrett-Lennard Relationship Inventory.

The Truax Relationship Questionnaire (Truax & Carkhuff, 1967a) was used to measure client perceptions of therapist-provided conditions in several studies (Anthony, 1972; Athay, 1974; Sloane, Staples, Cristol, Yorkston, & Whipple, 1975; Truax, Leslie, Smith, Glenn, & Fisher, cited in Truax & Carkhuff, 1967a). Because the Nonpossessive Warmth Scale of this instrument includes several items that address the unconditionality of the therapist's regard, the Scale is considered by the author to be a face valid measure of this construct.

The results of the studies listed in Table 2.1 are presented below in categories defined by the source of the outcome evaluation: the client, the therapist, or an external judge (or other external criterion). Many studies fall into more than one category. Within each category, the results for each of the hypothesized conditions are discussed.

Client as Source of Outcome Evaluation

In this category, only two studies (Barrett-Lennard, 1962; Strupp, Fox, & Lessler, 1969) assessed all the hypothesized conditions: client incongruence, therapist congruence, therapist unconditional positive regard, and therapist empathy. Strupp, Fox, and Lessler (1969) found that all the conditions were correlated with posttherapy client ratings of

TABLE 2.1. Studies of Client Perceptions of the Relationship and Outcome in Individual Therapy

Author	Population	Therapists' Orientation, Experience	Therapy Length	Conditions Assessed	Outcome Sources and Measures[a]	Significant Results per Outcome Source
Anthony (1972)	high school students (n=40)	counseling, exp. (n=20)	?	C,U,E (TRQ)	Cl: satisfaction	Cl: C,U,E
Athay (1974)	high school students (n=150)	counseling, exp. (n=50)	?	C,U,E (TRQ)	Cl: improvement, semantic differential Th: improvement	Cl: C,U,E Th: none
Barrett-Lennard (1962)	university counseling center clients (n=29)	client centered, inexp. (n=21)	7 to 96 sess., x̄=33	I,C,U,R,E (B-LRI)	Cl: combined pre-post Q-sort, Taylor MA, MMPI-D Th: combined pre-post adjustment and post change	Cl: I,C,U,R,E Th: C,U,R,E
Board (1959)	m. h. clinic outpatients (n=101)	supportive therapy, exp. (n=57)	6 mos. minimum	R (liked by Th)	Cl: success Th: success	Cl: R Th: R

28

Study	Client population	Therapist	Sessions	Scale	Measure	Results
Cain (1973)	university counseling center clients (n=101)	?, exp. (n=18)	?	C,U,E	Cl: helpfulness Th: helpfulness	Cl: C,U,E Th: C,U,E
Feitel (1968)	university clinic outpatients (n=35)	?, inexp. (n=27)	5 sess. minimum	C,U,R,E (B-LRI)	Ex: supervisor's ratings of success	Ex: U,R,E
Fretz (1966)	college students (n=17)	counseling, inexp. (n=17)	7 sess.	C,U,R,E (B-LRI)	Cl: satisfaction Th: satisfaction	Cl: C,R,E Th: C,R,E
Kalfas (1974)	m. h. clinic outpatients (n=?)	?, ? (n=?)	"brief therapy"	E	Cl: self-concept	Cl: none
Kiesler et al. (1967)	hospitalized schizophrenics (n=12)	dynamic, client centered, exp. (n=12)	$\bar{x}=74$ sess.	C,U,R,E (B-LRI)	Cl: pre-post Q-sort, MMPI Th: change Ex: pre-post ward behavior; days out hosp.	Cl: none Th: none Ex: none
Kurtz & Grummon (1972)	university counseling center clients (n=31)	mixed, exp. & inexp. (n=31)	4 to 27 sess., $\bar{x}=12$	E (B-LRI)	Cl: pre-post self-concept, MMPI Th: improvement	Cl: E Th: E

TABLE 2.1. (*continued*)

Author	Population	Therapists' Orientation, Experience	Therapy Length	Conditions Assessed	Outcome Sources and Measures[a]	Significant Results per Outcome Source
Lesser (1961)	university counseling center clients (n=22)	?, exp. (n=11)	3 to 12 sess.	E	Cl: pre-post Q-sort	Cl: none
Lorr (1965)	VA clinic outpatients (n=523)	?, exp. (n=?)	3 mos. to 10 yr.	R (acceptance) E (understanding)	Cl: improvement Th: improvement	Cl: R,E Th: R,E
Martin & Sterne (1976)	psychiatric inpatients (n=143)	eclectic (supportive therapy), exp. (n=?)	$\bar{x}$=90 days	R (acceptance) E (understanding)	Cl: MMPI, Katz AS-S$_2$ Ex: assessor ratings of disturbance	Cl: R,E Ex: none
McClanahan (1974)	university counseling center clients (n=83)	personal adjustment counseling, exp. (n=11)	3 to 8 sess.	C,U,R,E (B-LRI)	Cl: satisfaction	Cl: C,U,R,E

Saltzman et al. (1976)	university counseling center clients (n=91)	eclectic & dynamic, exp. (n=19)	1 to 116 mdn=19	U	Cl: improvement Th: improvement	Cl: none Th: U
Sloane et al. (1975)	m. h. clinic outpatients (n=60)	psychoanalytic & behavioral, exp. (n=6)	$\bar{x}$=13.7 sess.	I,C,U,E (TRQ)	Ex: assessor pre-post target symptoms	Ex: none (strong tendencies for C,U,E)
Strupp et al. (1969)	university clinic outpatients (n=122)	dynamic, exp. (n=79)	25 sess. minimum	I,C,U,R,E	Cl: change Ex: clinician rating of file data	Cl: I,C,U,R,E Ex: I,C,U,R,E
Tausch et al. (Gurman, 1977)	outpatients (n=10)	client-centered, exp. (n=5)	?	C,U,R,E (B-LRI)	Cl: change	Cl: C,E
Truax et al. (Truax & Carkhuff, 1967a)	vocational rehab. clients (n=219)	vocational counseling, exp. (n=?)	?	C,U,E (TRQ)	Ex: work quality, dependability	Ex: C,U,E

Note. I = client incongruence, C = therapist congruence, U = unconditionality of regard, R = level of regard, E = empathy, Cl = client, Th = therapist, Ex = external judge, TRQ = Truax Relationship Questionnaire, B-LRI = Barrett-Lennard Relationship Inventory.
[a]Measure is posttherapy only, unless indicated as pre-post.

change. Barrett-Lennard (1962) found that all the conditions were correlated with pre-posttherapy difference scores on a combined measure of Q-sort, Taylor Manifest Anxiety Scale, and MMPI D Scale.

Seven studies assessed only the therapist-provided conditions with the Barrett-Lennard Relationship Inventory (Fretz, 1966; Kiesler, Klein, Mathieu, & Schoeninger, 1967; McClanahan, 1974; Tausch, Sander, Bastine, & Friese, cited in Gurman, 1977), with the Truax Relationship Questionnaire (Anthony, 1972; Athay, 1974), or with another measure (Cain, 1973). Four of these studies found correlations between all of the therapist-provided conditions and client posttherapy ratings of satisfaction (Anthony, 1972; McClanahan, 1974), improvement and semantic differential (Athay, 1974), and helpfulness (Cain, 1973). Fretz (1966) obtained relationships between the conditions, except for unconditionality of regard, and posttherapy client satisfaction. Tausch and co-workers (cited in Gurman, 1977) found that congruence and empathy, but not unconditionality of regard or level of regard, were correlated with client posttherapy ratings of change. Kiesler and associates (1967) obtained no relationships between any of the therapist-provided conditions and pre-posttherapy change scores on the Q-sort or the MMPI.

Two studies assessed only level of regard and empathy, finding correlations between these two conditions and client posttherapy ratings of improvement (Lorr, 1965) and posttherapy scores on the MMPI and the Katz Adjustment Scale–S2 (Martin & Sterne, 1976).

Three studies assessed only empathy, one study obtaining correlations between empathy and pre-posttherapy differences in self-concept and MMPI scores (Kurtz & Grummon, 1972). Two of these studies obtained no relationships between empathy and posttherapy self-concept (Kalfas, 1974) or pre-posttherapy change in Q-sort (Lesser, 1961).

Saltzman and co-workers (1976) assessed only unconditionality of regard, finding no relationship between it and posttherapy client ratings of improvement. Board (1959) assessed only level of regard, which was related to posttherapy client ratings of success.

To summarize the results of the studies with the client as the source of the outcome measure, only two of the 15 studies assessed all the hypothesized conditions, including client incongruence. The results of these two studies support Rogers's hypotheses, obtaining correlations between each condition and outcome. Over all the studies, each condition, with the exception of unconditionality of regard, was related to outcome much more frequently than not. Client incongruence was related to outcome in both studies in which it was included. Therapist congruence was related to outcome in eight of the nine studies in which it was included. Empathy was related to outcome in 11 of 14 studies. Unconditionality of regard was related to outcome in only six of 10 studies. Level of regard was related to outcome in seven of nine studies. In studies that used client ratings of outcome, then, the results were reliable across studies for all the hypothesized conditions except unconditionality of regard.

Therapist as Source of Outcome Evaluation

In this category, five studies assessed the three therapist-provided conditions with the Barrett-Lennard Relationship Inventory (Barrett-Lennard, 1962; Fretz, 1966; Kiesler et al., 1967), with the Truax Relationship Questionnaire (Athay, 1974), or with another measure (Cain, 1973). Two of these studies obtained relationships between all the therapist-provided conditions and posttherapy ratings of helpfulness by the therapist (Cain, 1973) and a combined measure of pre-posttherapy change in ratings of adjustment and posttherapy ratings of change by the therapist (Barrett-Lennard, 1962). The results of the study by Barrett-Lennard (1962) were all significant only when client perceptions of the relationship were assessed at the fifth interview; when client perceptions were assessed at termination, only congruence and empathy were related to outcome, though there was a strong tendency toward significance for level of regard. Fretz (1966) obtained relationships between the therapist-provided conditions and therapist satisfaction, except for unconditionality of regard. Neither Kiesler and associates (1967) nor Athay (1974) found relationships between any of the three conditions and posttherapy improvement ratings by therapists.

Lorr (1965) assessed only level of regard and empathy, finding correlations between each condition and posttherapy ratings of improvement by the therapist. Saltzman and co-workers (1976) assessed only unconditionality of regard and obtained a relationship between it and posttherapy ratings of improvement by the therapist. Kurtz and Grummon (1972) assessed only empathy, which was correlated with posttherapy ratings of improvement by the therapist.

In summary, none of the studies that used therapist ratings of outcome assessed all the hypothesized conditions. None included the condition of client incongruence. The results for the therapist-provided conditions varied in the reliability of findings across studies. Empathy was related to outcome in five of the seven studies in which it was assessed. Congruence was related to outcome in three of five studies. Unconditionality of regard was related to outcome in three of six studies. Level of regard was related to outcome in four of five studies. In the studies that used therapist ratings of outcome, then, positive findings were reliable across studies for empathy and level of regard, but not for congruence or unconditionality of regard.

External Source of Outcome Evaluation

In this category only two studies assessed all the hypothesized conditions, including client incongruence (Sloane et al., 1975; Strupp et al., 1969). Strupp, Fox, and Lessler (1969) found that client ratings of each of the conditions were correlated with independent clinicians' ratings of outcome based on case files. However, Sloane and associates (1975) found no relationships between any of the conditions and pre-posttherapy ratings of target symptoms by independent assessors, though strong tendencies toward significance were obtained for the therapist-provided conditions.

Three studies assessed only the therapist-provided conditions with the Barrett-Lennard Relationship Inventory (Feitel, 1968; Kiesler et al., 1967) or with the Truax Relationship Questionnaire (Truax et al., cited in Truax & Carkhuff, 1967a). Truax and co-workers (cited in Truax & Carkhuff, 1967a) obtained correlations between each of the therapist-provided conditions and ratings of clients' work quality and dependability by vocational training staff. Feitel (1968) found relationships between therapist-provided conditions, except congruence, and supervisors' ratings of successful outcome. However, Kiesler and associates (1967) found no relationships between any of the therapist-provided conditions and pre-posttherapy staff ratings of ward behavior or percentage of time out of the hospital.

Martin and Sterne (1976) assessed only level of regard and empathy, finding no correlations with an independent interviewer's posttherapy ratings of disturbance.

To summarize the results of the studies that used an external source for the outcome evaluation, only two studies included all the hypothesized conditions, including client incongruence. The results of only one of these two studies support Rogers's hypotheses, obtaining correlations between each condition and outcome. Over all the studies, positive findings were not reliable. Client incongruence was related to outcome in one of two studies. Therapist congruence was related to outcome in only two of five studies. Unconditionality of regard was related to outcome in only three of five studies. Empathy was related to outcome in only three of six studies. Level of regard was related to outcome in only two of four studies. In the studies that used an external outcome criterion, then, the findings were not reliable for any of the hypothesized conditions.

DISCUSSION

The present review located no studies that adequately tested Rogers's hypotheses. Of 19 studies of the client's perception of the therapeutic relationship, only three assessed all of the hypothesized conditions, including client incongruence (Barrett-Lennard, 1962; Sloane et al., 1975; Strupp et al., 1969). However, these three studies were correlational in design, failing to address the issue of the hypothesized conditions as causal factors. Only one study addressed the issue of causality, doing so with a path analysis (Colistro, 1979); however, this was an analog study that assessed only empathy and used only the analog client as the source of the outcome evaluation. It is noteworthy that the design of the study by the Sloane group (1975), involving random assignment of 10 clients to each of six therapists, would permit an experimental test of the therapist-provided conditions as causal factors. However, the data were not analyzed in a manner that tested whether these are causal factors as stated in Rogers's hypotheses. Neither this study, nor any other study in the present review, was undertaken for the explicit purpose of testing Rogers's hypotheses of the necessary and sufficient conditions as causal factors in effective therapy.

Correlations between the hypothesized conditions and outcome, as discussed above, are necessary but not sufficient evidence for Rogers's hypotheses. In studies that used client evaluations of outcome, the results were reliable across studies for all the hypothesized conditions except unconditionality of regard. Though the results of these studies provide qualified support for the hypotheses, the correlations obtained are potentially confounded with method variance and with a halo effect in the client ratings of both the conditions and the outcome.

Relationships between client-rated conditions and outcome rated by another source are also required as correlational evidence for Rogers's hypotheses. In studies that used therapist evaluations of outcome, positive findings were reliable across studies for empathy and level of regard, but not for congruence and unconditionality of regard. In studies that used an external source of evaluation, the findings were not reliable for any of the hypothesized conditions. To summarize, Rogers's hypotheses are not consistently supported by the results of correlational studies in which outcome is evaluated by a source other than the client.

However, the absence of predicted correlations in these studies does not unequivocally refute Rogers's hypotheses. Most of the studies do not report data, which were available in many instances, that are necessary for drawing the conclusion that the results refute the hypotheses. The necessary data include the means and variances of the hypothesized conditions, the strength of the nonsignificant relationships, and the demonstration of client incongruence. The importance of each of these pieces of information is discussed below.

Most of the studies in this review do not report the means and variances of the hypothesized conditions. These data are necessary in order to evaluate whether the results of a correlational study refute Rogers's hypotheses. If a hypothesized condition is not correlated with outcome, the absence of the correlation could be due to a truncated range in the measure of the hypothesized condition. If the range is truncated, and if the mean score is high for the hypothesized condition, then the absence of the predicted correlation does not refute the hypotheses. Because the published reports typically did not include means and variances, the present review does not conclude that the absence of predicted correlations refutes Rogers's hypotheses.

Most of the studies in this review did not report correlations if they were not significant at $p < .05$. Knowledge of the strength of nonsignificant correlations would make it possible to perform a meta-analysis of the results. In a meta-analysis, the nonsignificant correlations from a number of studies may become significant when considered together. The method of the present review is a "box score" of significant correlations versus nonsignificant correlations. With the box score method, the conclusion is that the correlational evidence does not support, though it does not clearly refute, Rogers's hypotheses. However, if the necessary information were made available, the method of meta-analysis might lead to a conclusion that the correlational evidence supports the hypotheses.

Rogers hypothesizes that an incongruent client is one of the necessary conditions for effective therapy. As discussed above, it follows from the hypotheses that the inclusion of clients who are not incongruent in a study attenuates the strength of the correlations between the therapist-provided conditions and outcome. Only three studies even assessed client incongruence (Barrett-Lennard, 1962; Sloane et al., 1975; Strupp et al., 1969). Of these three studies only the Barrett-Lennard (1962) study tested the correlations between the therapist-provided conditions and outcome for a subgroup of clients who were demonstrably incongruent, obtaining the predicted correlations. (However, Barrett-Lennard followed this procedure only for client-rated outcome and not for therapist-rated outcome.) The absence of predicted correlations in other studies could be due to the inclusion of clients who were not incongruent.

The studies included in the present review met the criteria of using face valid measures of the therapist-provided conditions in actual counseling or therapy situations. However, all these studies failed to fulfill other criteria for an adequate study of Rogers's hypotheses. As discussed above, none addressed the issue of causality, and only three assessed all of the hypothesized conditions. Many studies in the review also failed to meet other criteria, such as reliability of the measures of the hypothesized conditions or adequacy of the outcome measures. The reliability of the measures of client perceptions of the hypothesized conditions is unknown for a majority of the studies in the review. The Barrett-Lennard Relationship Inventory (Barrett-Lennard, 1962), an instrument of known and acceptable reliability (Gurman, 1977), was used in only seven studies (Barrett-Lennard, 1962; Feitel, 1968; Fretz, 1966; Kiesler et al., 1967; Kurtz & Grummon, 1972; McClanahan, 1974; Tausch et al., cited in Gurman, 1977). Lesser (1961) reported evidence of the internal consistency, though not the test-retest reliability, of the empathy scale that he employed. The present author could not locate published research on the psychometric properties of the Truax Relationship Questionnaire (Truax & Carkhuff, 1967a), which was used in four studies (Anthony, 1972; Athay, 1974; Sloane et al., 1975; Truax et al., cited in Truax & Carkhuff, 1967a). The remaining studies in Table 2.1 did not report the reliability of the instruments employed (Board, 1959; Cain, 1973; Kalfas, 1974; Lorr, 1965; Martin & Sterne, 1976; Saltzman et al., 1976; Strupp et al., 1969). Many of the researchers in this area, then, have not been concerned with the reliability of their measures of the hypothesized conditions.

The adequacy of the outcome measures employed in most of the studies in Table 2.1 is questionable. Measures of satisfaction or help-fulness lack face validity as measures of client change in several studies (Anthony, 1972; Cain, 1973; Fretz, 1966; McClanahan, 1974). The reliabilities of most of the outcome measures are unknown, with the exception of measures employed by Barrett-Lennard (1962), Kiesler and co-workers (1967), Kurtz and Grummon (1972), Lesser (1961), Martin and Sterne (1976), and Sloane and associates (1975). More-over, a majority of the studies employ posttherapy measures only. As Garfield (1980) argues, posttherapy outcome measures do not ade-quately assess the extent of change over the course of therapy; pre-posttherapy outcome measures are essential for assessing change. Only five studies reviewed here employed pre-posttherapy outcome mea-sures (Barrett-Lennard, 1962; Kiesler et al., 1967; Kurtz & Grummon, 1972; Lesser, 1961; Sloane et al., 1975). In order to avoid bias against significant correlations due to statistical artifacts, pre-posttherapy dif-ference scores must be corrected by a regression transformation to make them independent of pretherapy test scores, as discussed above. Only one of the five studies employing pre-posttherapy change scores made this statistical correction (Sloane et al., 1975). The inadequacy of the outcome measures that are typically employed is a major problem in the research on Rogers's hypotheses.

In summary, the present review of client perceptions of the thera-peutic relationship did not locate any studies that adequately test Rogers's hypotheses. The issue of the causality of the hypothesized conditions has never been addressed in a study that assessed all the hypothesized conditions in an actual therapy situation. The correla-tional studies do not reliably support the hypotheses. However, because of the inadequacies of these studies, it is not reasonable to conclude that the hypotheses have been refuted.

PREVIOUS REVIEWS

Research on the relationship between the hypothesized conditions and outcome in therapy has been the subject of several previous reviews (Bergin & Lambert, 1978; Gurman, 1977; Lambert et al., 1978; Mar-shall, 1977; Meltzoff & Kornreich, 1970; Mitchell et al., 1977; Orlinsky & Howard, 1978; Parloff et al., 1978; Rachman & Wilson, 1980; Shapiro, 1976; Truax & Mitchell, 1971). The present review differs in method from previous reviews in several respects. A major difference is that the present review systematically evaluates the research evidence from the point of view of Rogers's hypotheses of the necessary and sufficient conditions, which include client incongruence. Meltzoff and Kornreich (1970) note parenthetically that in many studies of Rogers's hypotheses "the clients seem in no way vulnerable" (p. 394). However, these authors do not apply this criticism subsequently in their review. Parloff, Waskow, and Wolfe (1978) state that the purpose of research in this area should be to test whether "*three* specific conditions are necessary and sufficient" (p. 251, emphasis added), failing to recognize that Rogers also hypothesized the necessity of client incongruence. Researchers and reviewers typically have not addressed Rogers's hypotheses as he stated them.

The present review focuses exclusively on studies of individual therapy, whereas only one of the previous reviews (Gurman, 1977) distinguished between studies of individual therapy and studies of group therapy in evaluating the research. This distinction is crucial to drawing conclusions that are specific to a particular modality of therapy.

The present review is concerned only with studies of client perceptions of the therapeutic relationship. Most of the previous reviews either considered only studies employing judge ratings of the relationship (Marshall, 1977; Mitchell et al., 1977; Shapiro, 1976; Truax & Mitchell, 1971) or did not distinguish between studies employing client perceptions and studies employing judge ratings in drawing conclusions (Bergin & Lambert, 1978; Lambert et al., 1978; Meltzoff & Kornreich, 1970; Rachman & Wilson, 1980). Three previous reviews (Gurman, 1977; Orlinsky & Howard, 1978; Parloff et al., 1978) distinguished between client perceptions and judge ratings of the therapeutic relationship in evaluating the research evidence. However, two of these three reviews (Orlinsky & Howard, 1978; Parloff et al., 1978) did not distinguish between studies of individual and group therapy. The review by Gurman (1977), then, is the only review that both focused on studies of client perceptions and distinguished between individual and group therapy in drawing conclusions. In these respects the present review is most similar to Gurman's review.

However, the method of the present review differs from that of Gurman's (1977) review in other important respects. First, Gurman did not consider client incongruence as one of the necessary and sufficient conditions. In regard to this consideration, the present review excludes the analog studies that were included in Gurman's review

(Carmichael, 1970; Jones, 1969; Stanley, 1967; Zauderer, 1968). Second, the present review exercises a more stringent criterion for the face validity of measures of the hypothesized conditions, excluding several studies that Gurman included (Bown, 1954; Grigg & Goodstein, 1957; Libo, 1957; Sapolsky, 1965). Third, unlike Gurman's review, the present review distinguishes between sources of the outcome rating—client, therapist, or external judge—in drawing conclusions.

As a result of the differences in method between the present review and Gurman's review, the conclusions of each contrast sharply. Gurman (1977) concluded that "there exists substantial, if not overwhelming, evidence in support of the hypothesized relationship between patient-perceived therapeutic conditions and outcome in individual psychotherapy and counseling" (p. 523). The present review concludes that, because of its inadequacies, the research neither supports nor refutes the hypotheses.

CONCLUSION

Though there is a substantial amount of research on Rogers's hypotheses of the necessary and sufficient conditions for effective therapy, none of the studies meet all of the conceptual and methodological criteria for rigorous research on this topic. Researchers have not carefully followed the logic of the hypotheses in designing studies and interpreting the results. A central shortcoming is the inattention to major conceptual criteria: employing client ratings of the therapist-provided conditions, including all the hypothesized conditions, and addressing the issue of causality. A large number of studies have used judge ratings of the therapist-provided conditions, which are irrelevant to the hypotheses as Rogers stated them, and neglected client perceptions of the relationship, which are essential to a test of the hypotheses. The studies that have focused on client perceptions of the relationship typically have not included all of the hypothesized conditions, thereby not testing the hypotheses as propositions of a *set* of necessary and sufficient conditions. Moreover, studies of client perceptions have not addressed the issue of the hypothesized conditions as causes of outcome. After 25 years of research on Rogers's hypotheses, there is not yet research of the rigor required for drawing conclusions about the validity of this important theory.

3   Unconditional Positive Regard: A Controversial Basic Attitude in Client-Centered Therapy[1]

Germain Lietaer

Unconditional positive regard is probably one of the most questioned concepts in client-centered therapy. Both within and without client-centered therapy this basic attitude has not always been welcomed in an unconditionally positive way. In my view, part of this ambivalence is related to the fact that Rogers did not elaborate on this basic attitude or at least did not go into detail regarding its problems. These problems include the following: (1) There is a potential conflict between genuineness or congruence on the one hand, and unconditionality on the other; (2) It is a rare person and a rare time in which the constancy of acceptance can be provided by any therapist for any client. Thus, while unconditionality is not impossible, it is improbable; (3) Unconditionality calls upon the therapist for a devoted self-effacing that often leads to a compensatory reaction in which confrontation becomes a form of self-assertion. The questions and the difficulties with regard to this basic attitude came more distinctly to the foreground as client-centered therapy became more relationship-centered, and as the genuineness of the therapist—which implies among other things feedback and confrontation—became more prominent. My involvement in this issue came about through my own practice and through my experiences with trainees who presented me with their struggles with this basic attitude. This provided an impetus for me to reflect on some of the theoretical and clinical aspects of unconditional positive regard.

After first giving a preliminary definition of the concept I will point out the importance of it in the therapeutic process. Third, I will briefly consider some criticisms of this concept. Fourth, I will provide a more precise definition of the essence of this basic attitude. Finally, using this more elaborate definition as a frame of reference, I will deal in more detail with some of the limitations and difficulties in experiencing and communicating this basic attitude and with the way in which confrontal interventions may be integrated into a climate of acceptance.

PRELIMINARY DEFINITION OF UNCONDITIONAL POSITIVE REGARD

Unconditional positive regard is a multidimensional concept. In the clinical descriptions of this basic attitude one can distinguish different components, which are interrelated to a certain degree, but which are specific enough on their own to be dealt with separately (see, among others, Barrett-Lennard, 1962; Rogers, 1957a, 1959a, 1961, 1962; Rogers & Truax, 1967; Rogers & Wood, 1974; Truax & Kiesler, 1967; Truax & Mitchell, 1971, pp. 315–317; Vandevelde, 1977). Also, in the empirical, factor analytic research, this basic attitude seems to be composed of a number of relatively independent dimensions (Barrett-Lennard, 1978; Gurman, 1977, pp. 508–514; Lietaer, 1976), namely: positive regard, nondirectivity, and unconditionality. It is mainly the dimension of unconditionality that will be discussed at length.

Positive regard refers to the affective attitude of the therapist toward his client: the extent to which he values his client and welcomes his coming, believes in his potentialities and engages him in a nonpossessive way. This attitude is also called "caring" or "nonpossessive warmth."

Nondirectivity—a dimension more accurately termed "client-centeredness"—refers mainly to an attitude of respect: to approach the client as a unique and independent person, with the right to live according to his own viewpoint. In contrast to this stands a more paternalistic attitude in which one treats the client from one's own frame of reference. Some aspects of the contrasting paternalistic attitude are: lack of respect for the privacy and the pace of the client, and the intention to mold the client toward one's own patterns of feeling, thinking and behaving.

Finally, *unconditionality* refers to the *constancy* in accepting the client, the extent to which the therapist accepts his client without "ifs."

Unconditional acceptance means that the attitude of the therapist toward his client does not fluctuate as a function of either the emotional state or the behavior of his client, or of the client's attitude toward the therapist, or of what other people think of the client (Barrett-Lennard, 1962, p. 4). Rogers (1961, p. 54) expresses the importance he attaches to this aspect of the helping relationship as follows:

> Still another issue is whether I can be acceptant of each facet of this other person which he presents to me. Can I receive him as he is? Can I communicate this attitude? Or can I only receive him conditionally, acceptant of some aspects of his feelings and silently or openly disapproving of other aspects? It has been my experience that when my attitude is conditional, then he cannot change or grow in those respects in which I cannot fully receive him.

So unconditionality implies, among other things, no judgment from the outside and no approval or disapproval stemming from the frame of reference of the therapist. As Truax and Mitchell (1971, p. 316) tersely put it: "...it does involve an acceptance of what is, rather than a demand of what ought to be." A client of a colleague of mine, who used to write down his therapy experiences, phrased the "unusual side" of this attitude of the therapist as follows: "On the faces of the people who are nevertheless favorably disposed towards me, I always read a norm, or set of expectations, and I feared not to live up to it. On your face, however, from the first conversation on I did not read a norm" (Jennen, 1974, p. 25).

THE FUNCTION OF UNCONDITIONALITY IN THE THERAPEUTIC PROCESS

Why did Rogers attach so much weight to this attitude? What is the importance of this attitude in the therapy process? The answer to this question obviously cannot be viewed apart from the objectives of client-centered therapy and from the way in which we believe we are able to achieve these objectives.

The major aim of client-centered therapy can be very generally described as an attempt to get the experiencing process of the client going again, or to help it function in a richer and more flexible way (Rogers, 1961; Gendlin, 1964). We want to help the client to live through fully, and to integrate, elements of her experience she was not able to face until then. We help the client come to a larger unity with herself, to become "congruent." This means that a continuous zigzag between the more conscious experience of the self and the underlying stream of experience becomes possible. Thus the person becomes less rigid in her manner of experiencing, becomes more open to *all* aspects of her experience, and begins to trust more fully her own experience—in all its complexity, layers, and change—as a valuable guide for a process-like way of living.

In this "journey into self" we try to assist the client by continuously being personally centered on, and responsive to, her experiential world (Gendlin, 1968; Rogers, 1975b). The actual "work" of a client-centered therapist consists mainly in being in touch with, and communicating, the explicit, and, above all, the implicit felt meanings in the message of the client about herself, in what is welling up in myself, and in what is going on between the two of us. Empathy and (more sporadically) self-expression form the most tangible aspects of our contributions as therapists.

What then is the importance of an attitude of unconditionality? Together with the congruence of the therapist, I consider these two attitudes to be the foundation, the deeper-lying fertile soil, necessary to enable the therapist to respond sensitively to the experiential world of the client. They are basic attitudes that are not readily visible in the therapist's interventions, but nonetheless constitute indispensable basic conditions. As a matter of fact, congruence and acceptance are thought to be closely related to one another; they are parts of a more basic attitude of "openness" (Truax & Carkhuff, 1967b, p. 504): openness toward myself (congruence) and openness toward the other (unconditional acceptance). The more I accept myself and am able to be present in a comfortable way with everything that bubbles up in me, without fear or defense, the more I can be receptive to everything that lives in my client. Without this openness, without this acceptance, it is not possible to let the experience of my client unfold, to let it come to life fully; for with a conditional attitude the chances are great that I dare not see certain parts of the client's experience, and that I will minimize or reject some of them.

The importance that Rogers attaches to an attitude of unconditional acceptance must be viewed in the context of his view of the origin of psychological dysfunctions (Rogers, 1959b, 1963a, 1964; Standal, 1954). Indeed, he considers the conditional love of parents and significant others to be the basic source of alienation. In order to retain the love of the people who are important to him, a person internalizes norms that may be contrary to his desires and experience. A disassociation thus arises between what we strive after consciously and our true self; we become alienated from our deeper core. In therapy, then, the attitude of unconditionality of the therapist serves as a "counterbalancing force," as a kind of "counterconditioning" in the corrective experience which the client hopefully has during therapy! As a result of the unconditional acceptance of the therapist, the client gradually feels safe enough to explore himself more deeply, to face aspects that up to that moment had been too threatening or too shameful. So the acceptance by the therapist facilitates self-acceptance and subsequent change. When experiencing a sufficient degree of interpersonal safety, the client dares to let go of his defensive attitude and succeeds in having closer contact with himself. Therefore, an attitude of acceptance does not lead to stagnation, but rather enables evolution of "frozen" aspects of ourselves. Growth and change become possible precisely when we are able to accept ourselves as we are. In this respect the above-mentioned client wrote: "From the beginning I experienced this as if light was shining for the first time on dark chilly spots where nobody had ever come before. It was not cold neon-light but a warm benevolence by which something could start living. It is as if you pass a lamp over all kinds of sore places which then heal and begin to live" (Jennen, 1974, p. 25). At the same time, this absence of external judgment stimulates the client toward more independence and self-responsibility: not what others think or expect, but the individual's own experience becomes the major basis of choices and decisions.

SOME CRITICISMS

At the beginning of this chapter, it was noted that the concept of unconditional acceptance has been heavily criticized both from within and without client-centered therapy. Here is a brief formulation of the most pertinent of those criticisms. (Because some criticisms arise from a misunderstanding of the concept, they are consequently not to the point.)

The learning theorists and behavior therapists tell us that it is naive to believe that unconditionality is possible at all. According to them, selective reinforcement is inevitable. They do not believe, for that matter, that this is bad, at least when the therapist reinforces in a good way, that is, in the direction of more adaptive behavior. In their criticism they refer to the effects of modeling, which they believe occurs in every therapeutic encounter. In particular, they point to research (Murray, 1956; Truax, 1966a) that claims to demonstrate that Rogers does reinforce selectively.

Systems theory stresses that we cannot "not influence"; consequently, "nondirective" therapy is inherently an illusion. There is directive influencing in every therapy session, although one therapist may be more subtle than another.

Within client-centered therapy this attitude of unconditionality has been questioned as well. On the occasion of his work with more seriously disturbed clients (Rogers, Gendlin, Kiesler, & Truax, 1967), Rogers himself wrote that the client often experiences an attitude of unconditionality on the part of the therapist as indifference and that—at least in the first phase of therapy—a more conditional, demanding attitude would probably be more effective in building up a relationship (Rogers, 1959a, p. 186). Through this work with schizophrenics, but also through their experience with encounter groups and under the influence of their contacts with the existential orientation in American psychotherapy, client-centered therapists started to put more emphasis on genuineness and on bringing in one's own experience. In this context, an attitude of unconditionality was sometimes seen as unnecessary self-effacement in the therapeutic relationship, since the client can be helped forward through the feedback with which the therapist confronts him (Rogers et al., 1967; Gendlin, 1967).

These then are some of the criticisms of the concept of unconditional acceptance. They provide reason enough to make an attempt to describe this attitude more precisely.

A MORE PRECISE DEFINITION OF UNCONDITIONALITY

It is important to make a distinction between experience and external behavior—between, on the one hand, all my client's feelings, thoughts, fantasies, desires, and, on the other hand, his actual behavior. Unconditionality refers to my acceptance of his experience. My client ought to experience the freedom to feel *anything* with me; he should sense that I am open to his experience and will not judge it. In behavioristic terms this is a client-centered form of desensitizing. My client will only be able to explore further, and live through more deeply, those experiences which are anxiety provoking when he feels that I am able to be present in a comfortable way. When someone tells me that he is looking forward to the moment that his father is dead, or when a client tells me that she secretly wishes her friend to have a miscarriage, or when someone lets his deep feelings of despair emerge...then it is important that I be able to go along with this experience without indignation or anxiety. Only then is the client able to explore the deeper needs underlying this experience.

This attitude of receptivity toward the inner experiential world of my client does not mean that I welcome all behavior equally. Both within and without the therapeutic relationship there can be specific behaviors of which I disapprove, would like to change, or simply do not accept. Often the person himself does not advocate this behavior; that may be why he came into therapy in the first place. When someone tells me that he never dares to refuse anyone, that he steals, that he withdraws more and more from all relationships, that he has thrashed his child, and so on...then these are behaviors that I—as much as my client— would like to see change. It remains, however, important that I do not merely look at this behavior from the outside, but try to understand it from the perspective of everything that the client experienced in his life (Rogers & Truax, 1967, p. 103). Without approving of it, I accept his behavior as something that is there "for the time being" and go with him into the personal problems that lie behind it. Sometimes, however, it happens that I feel disapproval or irritation toward behavior that my client hardly questions or does not question at all, or that I cannot comply with what the client requests of me. The former situation can lead to confrontations in which I give my client clear feedback about the consequences of his behavior for himself or for others. In the case of difficulties within the therapeutic relationship itself, I can express to her what kind of feelings she stirs in me and what my limits are. For instance, my client might take a very dependent position, be mad at me, want to dominate me, or wish to have a more informal friendship relationship or even a sexual relationship with me. It remains important that she can express and discuss everything that she experiences with respect to me, without my becoming reluctant or rejecting her as a person; but with regard to her behavior, I do confront her with *my* limits.

Unconditionality, then, means *that I keep on valuing the deeper core of the person, what she basically is and can become.* My client must sense that I continue to stand on her side, that I will not let her down in spite of her disquieting fantasies, in spite of her antisocial or self-destructive behavior, or in spite of the difficulties we are having in our relationship.[2] Unconditionality in its optimal form has consequently nothing to do with indifference but rather points to a deep involvement with and belief in the other. It is accepting the other as a person in the process of becoming, through which I confirm her in her potentialities and help her to realize them (Rogers, 1961, p. 55).

My acceptance of my client is something that grows. I cannot force it, but my attitude of understanding him from the inside helps me in it. Truax and Mitchell (1971, p. 315) compare it to reading a good novel: As I continue reading a book I become more and more familiar with the inner world of the main characters and my external judgment fades away. In the same way, in therapy I try to keep in touch with what lies behind the behavior of my client. This is not always easy. Sometimes we cannot "find" each other; sometimes I do not succeed in getting in touch with the inner side of my client but remain stuck on particular behaviors that disturb me. A few moments of personal encounter may weaken my irritation; then I know: "Basically he is different." When, however, this does not occur, I believe that therapy with this client will not be a very successful endeavor. With this I arrive at the topic of the limitations and difficulties in realizing this attitude.

LIMITATIONS AND DIFFICULTIES: SOURCES OF CONDITIONALITY

Like the other basic attitudes that Rogers described, unconditional acceptance is described in ideal terms. We can never attain a total openness to the experiential world of the other, but we can nevertheless try to raise our personal limits. In connection with our own limitations, there are three sources of conditionality: our own vulnerabilities; the repercussions of the other's life on our own life; and, finally, problems that relate to the fundamental objective of therapy, which is to facilitate change in our client.

Therapist Vulnerabilities or Incongruencies

I have already indicated the close tie between congruence and acceptance. Sometimes we cannot let the experience of our clients be fully what it is because of our own personal difficulties. Themes of life with which we have not come to terms, personal needs that interfere with therapy, and our own vulnerabilities and blind spots sometimes cause us to feel threatened and to be unable to respond to certain feelings of our clients in a serene way (Tiedemann, 1976). This seems to me to be an important source of conditionality to which much attention ought to be paid in training programs. Indeed, our own person is the most important tool with which we work. Entering into the experiential world of someone with values totally different from our own, allowing feelings of helplessness and despair, empathizing with peak experiences of happiness, responding in nondefensive ways to strong negative or positive feelings of a client toward us: these are not easy things to do. That is why I feel rather skeptical about "crash-courses" in which the basic client-centered attitudes are trained at a rushed pace. Personal growth and the development of an understanding of the impact our own difficulties have on our therapeutic work are events that can probably only happen thoroughly during a training of longer duration, in which the person of the therapist has a more central position (Lietaer, 1980b).

Conflicts of Interests

Often we cannot fully hear the experience of the other because of what it entails for our own life. This is especially true for real life relationships in which we are interdependent as partners and in which conflicts of interests occur. What my partner experiences can be an obstacle to how I want to live. If my wife is scared to be alone at night, or is jealous, or is afraid of people, or is compulsively orderly, it may be difficult for me to accept and understand her experience. This is because she probably would not expect me "merely" to understand, but also would want me to take it into account in the way we live together. In the therapeutic relationship this problem plays a smaller role because therapist and client are less interdependent in their daily living. How my client feels or what he does usually has no direct repercussions for my own life. The structure of the therapeutic relationship protects me on this point. There is the outer structure: he comes only once or twice a week, at fixed hours. There is also the inner structure, my inner attitude: for in the therapy I have fewer expectations for myself; I mainly want to be occupied with him, to carry *his* process further. This distance, the fact that I am more protected and less self-interested, enables me to be closer and helps me attune myself better to his experience (Lehmann, 1975). That is why parents are at times bad counselors for their growing children. Because of their own needs and expectations, they might not be capable of accepting and understanding their children's evolution toward more independence.

The fact that acceptance is less difficult to experience in a therapeutic relationship than in daily life poses some problems, particularly in the client-centered orientation, where the distinction between professional-therapeutic relationships and real life relationships is less sharply drawn than in other orientations. First and foremost there is the problem of "unfair competition." Sometimes my client finds I understand him much better than his partner does. This can create secondary problems in his or her relationship at home. In this respect, I sometimes wonder if I am not providing my client with an illusory model, something that is many times more difficult to reach in real life relationships. Usually, however, the client himself recognizes that the comparison is invalid, and I do not neglect to underscore this when my client mentions the subject. Also, in groups, especially one-time workshops, the acceptance and understanding of members of the group sometimes forms a painful contrast to the experience of someone in his own relationships. For this reason I strongly prefer the more continuous groups, with their various ups and downs, in which the members have contact between meetings with the people with whom they are actually living. An experience that is rather contrary to the problem of unfair competition is the feeling of "acceptance at a distance," in which the client wonders: "Is your acceptance authentic? What can I do with your acceptance, when you could not live with me after all?" It can indeed happen that I get saddled with that feeling as a therapist, but this seems to me to be only a shabby form of acceptance. Acceptance at its best is not aloof but implies a warm involvement with the other, which is probably fed by a feeling of affinity. Within the structure of a therapeutic relationship this is indeed less difficult, but surely that is no reason for it to be less genuine. In any case such a relationship can be an important source of help for the client: a situation that differs from ordinary life because he can explore "without being disturbed" everything that lives in him, go to the depth of his feelings and draw understanding and strength from them in order to grow.

Selective Reinforcement and the Objective of Therapy

Is acceptance necessarily selective and consequently "conditional" simply because of the objective of therapy, which is to bring about change in the client? Is it true that we are not able and even do not want to be "nondirective," since we hope to have an impact on the life of our client in our role as "change agents"?

One form of directivity and selectivity is abundantly plain and has been readily admitted by Rogers and other client-centered therapists—and that is that we are experience oriented. Not every statement of the client receives equal attention. We always try to shift from the narrative to the feelings, from the theoretical-abstract level to what is concretely lived through. Rogers writes in this sense about his interventions in an encounter group (1970a, pp. 50–51):

> There is no doubt that I am selective in my listening, hence "directive" if people wish to accuse me of this. I am centered in the group member who is speaking, and am unquestionably much less interested in the details of his quarrel with his wife, or of his difficulties on the job, or his disagreement with what has just been said, than in the *meaning* these experiences have for him now and the *feelings* they arouse in him. It is to these meanings and feelings that I try to respond.*

Consequently there is a formal kind of directivity, which amounts to a reinforcement of the client's experience. In addition, we support our client as she evolves toward a more experience-oriented way of living, holds on less tightly to external norms, undertakes actions toward more autonomy, dares to risk herself more personally in relationships—in short, when she changes in the direction of our concept of the "fully functioning person" (Rogers, 1963b).

The question remains, however, whether we also reinforce selectively within experience itself, whether our directivity is also content oriented. Rogers hopes it is not. He believes that he does therapy at its best when every feeling of the client is welcome, when the client is "rewarded" through therapy for *each* expression of herself, whatever the content of the feeling (Rogers et al., 1967, p. 519). Also, when a client secludes herself, for instance, or decides to quit the therapy because she shrinks before everything it might entail, or falls back on former ways of behavior, and so on...in such moments we can help our client best of all by accepting where she finds herself now, by focusing on and exploring more in depth what she experiences *now*. Another

*Specified excerpt from *Carl R. Rogers on Encounter Groups* by Carl R. Rogers. Copyright © 1970 by Carl R. Rogers. Reprinted by permission of Harper & Row, Publishers, Inc.

aspect of this nondirectivity with regard to experience lies in the fact that in client-centered therapy there is no preliminary strategy nor planning for therapy. Rather, therapy is considered to be an adventure from moment to moment, in which it is not necessary that the therapist understand in advance the heart of the client's problem (Rogers et al., 1967, p. 509). As a matter of fact, we rely on the assumption that what is really important to the client will come up in therapy. The only instruction we give ourselves is to follow as receptively as possible the experiential flow of our client. Neither the therapist nor the client knows in advance where this will lead. Thus we have not "mapped out" anything, nor have we decided in advance that certain contents must be explored.

With this difference between content and form in mind, it seems sensible to have a closer look at the research of Truax (1966a) and Murray (1956). Their findings are sometimes quoted in support of the thesis—which is not qualified sufficiently—that Rogers "conditions verbally" (see also Lieberman, 1969a, 1969b; Truax, 1969; Wachtel, 1979). Both authors examine whether certain modes of behavior of the client are reinforced more than others, and whether the more frequently reinforced behaviors increase as therapy progresses. Truax (1966a), in a case study of 85 sessions, viewed empathy, acceptance, and nondirectivity as social reinforcers[3] and examined whether the level at which Rogers offers these attitudes correlates with nine dimensions of client behavior. Positive correlations were obtained between the therapeutic attitudes and five dimensions, and four of the dimensions showed higher levels in the later therapy sessions. These four dimensions include differentiation of feelings, the development of understanding, problem-orientedness, and the degree of similarity in style of expression between the client and the therapist. These results indicate that Rogers reinforces client experience, but they do not support any conclusions with regard to content selectivity, because the dimensions refer to formal qualities of the process of exploration. This is less clear with regard to the dimension "similarity in style of expression." Truax did not define what he really meant by this dimension. Elsewhere in his article he described the "stylistic characteristics of the therapist" as the therapist expressing himself in a personal, concretely simple, and tentative way (Truax, 1966a, p. 4). These are characteristics that can, through modeling if you will, direct the client in a vivid and receptive manner toward his own experience. Furthermore, it was also found that the two most content-oriented dimensions of client behavior are not differentially responded to by the therapist. These dimensions are the degree of anxiety of the client and the extent to which she expresses negative as opposed to positive feelings.

In contrast, the research of Murray (1956) indicates that Rogers reinforces some experiential contents more than others. In a case study of eight sessions, Murray examined the effect of subtle approvals and disapprovals on the verbal behavior of the client and found that Rogers approves of desires, plans, and ways of behavior in the direction of independence and self-assurance (for instance: "And that makes you feel pretty good, I presume"; "That sounds like quite a step"), whereas he responds slightly disapprovingly to intellectual defense (for instance: "Can you really consider your own reactions, not an intellectualized abstracted picture of them?") and to a number of aspects of the client's sexual problems. Murray also found that the approved categories increased and the disapproved categories decreased as therapy progressed. Do these data confirm more than a formal experience-orientedness—that is, that Rogers accepts some experiences more than others? I would tentatively answer that it is not always possible to separate form and content in the concrete therapeutic process: trying to deepen the process of experience of the client sometimes means that the therapist looks for openings to shift the conversation to other layers of experience (and content). This is the case with sexuality in Murray's case study. Whereas in the beginning phase of the therapy the client believed that his problems were mainly of a sexual nature, Rogers sensed that his sexual problems were in fact an expression of a more fundamental problem of self-respect and maturity. That is why he tried to push through to what he believed to be a deeper level. Moreover, supporting and encouraging the growth to more independence is probably co-determined by Rogers's view of optimal functioning: he sees self-determination and self-responsibility as the offshoots of an experiential way of living. The slight disapprovals with regard to certain experiential contents (for instance, fear of independence) do not signify that Rogers fails to accept and understand these feelings, and certainly not that he rejects his client as a person. The fact is that he does not support these experiences or assent to them as a positive end point, but on the contrary seeks to differentiate them further in the hope that they will evolve in a constructive way.

From all this it may appear that even client-centered therapy cannot be anything else than a directive process. We are formally directed toward keeping in touch with and expanding the experiential field of the client, and we also have an ideal of optimal functioning that may direct our interventions as well. Throughout the therapeutic process, however, it remains important that we remain open to what the client experiences at every moment, whatever the content may be. This is of course an ideal that is never fully realized.[4] Our own personalities and blind spots prevent us from noticing certain experiential contents of our clients or require that we leave them untouched and dare not really deal with them. Also our training within a certain therapeutic orientation can sharpen or blunt the sensitivity for certain experiential contents. We can only hope that training and experience help to restrict such non–task-oriented forms of selectivity to a minimum, in order to keep our influence on the process of change of the client as clean as possible. Rogers evidently does not object to influencing; in recent years he has revealed himself as a "quiet revolutionary" (Rogers, 1977). What he does object to is control and manipulation, external pressure, and the use of power (Rogers & Skinner, 1956). A central idea of client-centered therapy is that in the end the client himself leads the show. As "process experts" we contribute to it; but the client decides whether he responds to it or not, how fast and how far he goes, to what extent our interventions bring new life to his experience, and so on. Such a process is consequently not a blind conditioning in the orthodox sense, but a personally desired process of influencing that takes place as consciously as possible, and in which the client gets the last word.

CONFRONTATION AND UNCONDITIONALITY

Against the background of the above statements I want to formulate some reflections with regard to confrontation in client-centered therapy. Client-centered therapy is known as a "soft" therapy. It can be asked to what extent a client-centered therapist confronts his client and whether such confrontation is compatible with an attitude of unconditional acceptance.

1. First and foremost I believe that client-centered therapists aim toward a high degree of *self*-confrontation within the client. Rogers's basic idea has always been that the main task of the therapist consists of creating a safe climate in which the client can focus on his or her inner experience. This reduced interpersonal fear and increased inner concentration (Rice, 1974, p. 302) allows the client to go deeper into his

own experience. A "self-propelling process" is started through which the client integrates the parts of his experience that he had previously denied to awareness and evolves further from it. The acceptance of the therapist becomes an important support for the client in this often painful process of self-confrontation. At the same time, an attitude of acceptance assures that the therapist will not stand in the way of this unfolding experiential process or sidetrack it.

2. Although this central idea retains its importance, the contribution of the therapist has been gradually reformulated in more active terms. Whereas, in the initial period, theory postulated what the therapist should not do (the so-called "don't rules"), more recently his contribution has been described in a more positive way—namely to maximize the experiential process of the client (Gendlin, 1970). In this perspective, the therapist's receptive attitude remains important, but this does not exclude the therapist from taking initiative at certain moments in order to stimulate the client's experiential process. It is in the framework of this evolution that confrontal interventions have increasingly obtained a place within client-centered therapy. Without going into great detail I would like to illustrate this more concretely. First, with regard to empathy, it is clearly indicated in the more recent formulations that the therapist reflects deeper lying meanings.[5] Rogers speaks of feelings the client is hardly aware of. Gendlin talks about implicitly felt meanings. Rice contrasts maintenance reflection to *evocative reflection*, by which she means that the therapist tries to open up the experience of the client through evoking experiential elements that are not yet integrated into his cognitive construct of self. Thus a confrontal aspect of empathy is now explicitly acknowledged. On a more concrete level this has been illustrated in an article written by Troemel-Ploetz (1980), in which the author reveals the restructuring, interpretive, and even paradoxical aspects of three empathic interventions.

Furthermore, client-centered therapists have come to attach more importance to bringing in their own here-and-now experiences. The impressions I form about my client and the feelings he stirs in me can be important material for the client; it can be useful as a stimulus to explore further himself and his relational patterns. This does, however, involve a loosening of the client-centered principles of continuously staying in the experiential field of my client (Rogers, 1959a, p. 190): when giving feedback, I indeed confront the client from my own frame of reference with something that does not explicitly, and sometimes not even implicitly, occupy him or her.

As a matter of fact, client-centered therapy is in the process of evolving toward a more broadly conceived experiential psychotherapy (Gendlin, 1974). Thus the former nondirective rules can be transcended in an experiential way by using clinical concepts, giving "homework," bringing in auxiliary techniques—all of these can be done in a client-centered manner, in which the experience of the client remains the continuous touchstone with regard to anything brought in by the therapist.

3. Are such confrontal interventions at odds with an attitude of unconditional acceptance? According to the meaning I have given to unconditional acceptance, I believe they are not. For confrontation does not in any way mean that I reject my client as a person or that I stop trying to understand his experience.[6] First of all, not every confrontation stems from feelings of irritation. For instance, I might confront my client with his strengths and possibilities, or with facets of his experience that are hardly conscious, or even with positive feelings on my part. In addition, there are confrontations that have to do with our relationship. Such moments of confrontation stand the best chance of having a constructive effect when I can experience and communicate a deep feeling of engagement.

In the context of confrontation, I would like to finish this chapter by briefly giving some "confrontation rules" that appear in the client-centered literature and that I also find important (see, among others, Boukydis, 1979; Carkhuff & Berenson, 1977; Gendlin, 1968, pp. 220–225, and 1981a, pp. 127–144; Rogers, 1970b, pp. 53–57).

First of all, there is the importance of timing. In a first session I cannot yet say what I can easily say later on. The relationship should first have acquired sufficient safety and momentum. Moreover, I believe that my impressions and feelings in the first sessions are still too superficial and insufficiently shaped to bring them in.

It is also important that I clearly communicate my feedback and reactions as something of my own; that is, as a self-revelation without imposition. This gives a more personal touch to the interaction, sustains its nonjudgmental character, and implies that I am willing to face my own part in the difficulty. When setting limits, for instance, it is important that I clearly formulate them as coming from myself. When I do so, my client is indeed confronted with *my* reality, but the chance that she will feel rejected is reduced.

I should also try to communicate clearly that my reactions are connected to her concrete behavior and not to her as a person. Therefore, it is important that I provide feedback with as much concrete detail as possible, touching on how this experience has grown in me, and what in her way of interacting has given rise to it. At the same time I ought to have a keen eye for the needs that underly her behavior. For instance, if I draw a person's attention to the fact that she always smooths the edges, or if I point out to spouses that they are communicating in an indirect way, then it is important that I also focus on the meaning of this behavior. The distinction I am trying to make between person and behavior is, however, not always felt by my client. Sometimes she feels rejected as a person even if this is not the case in my experience.

This leads me to the last "rule," which includes the basic attitude that inspires all my interventions as a client-centered therapist: being continuously in touch with the way in which my client experiences the confrontation and responding to that.

NOTES

1. Translated from G. Lietaer, "Onvoorwaardelijke Aanvaarding: Een Omstreden Grondhouding in Client-Centered Therapie." In: *Gedrag, Dynamische Relatie en Betekeniswereld. Liber Amicorum Prof. J.R. Nuttin.* Leuvense Universitaire Pers, 1980, 145–159 (a). Reprinted by permission.

2. In a revised definition of unconditionality Barrett-Lennard (1978, p. 5) also stresses that this attitude is directed at the person of the other and not at concrete behaviors:

> ... variation in regard toward another is conditional to the extent that (a) it is contingent on varying or alternative behaviors, attitudes, feelings or ways of being of the other *and* (b) is experienced in the form of a response to the person or self of the other.... In the event that differentially positive or negative reactions to particular behaviors carried no message of approval/disapproval, liking/disliking, etc., for the self or personhood of the receiving individual then they would not imply conditionality.

For a contrary view, see Schmitt, 1980.

3. Together with Gurman (1977, p. 536) I believe that it is simplistic to understand the Rogerian basic attitudes as mere reinforcers. Certain clients can experience these attitudes as "aversive stimuli" because of their personal learning history. This can, for instance, be the case for nondirectivity with dependent clients and for warm acceptance with suspicious clients.

4. Rogers himself emphasizes this very strongly (1957, p., 98). This attitude also appears in the reactions of a number of psychoanalytically

oriented and existential therapists to fragments from three client-centered therapies. Truax and Carkhuff (1967b, p. 503) summarize their comments as follows:

> Particularly striking were the observations by almost all the theorists that the client-centered process of therapy somehow avoids the expected and usual patient expressions of negative, hostile, or aggressive feelings. The clear implication is that the client-centered therapist for some reason seems less open to receiving negative, hostile, or aggressive feelings. Is it that the therapists have little respect for, or understanding of their own negative, hostile, or aggressive feelings, and are thus unable to receive those feelings from the patient? Do they simply "not believe" in the importance of the negative feelings?

5.   Some quotations will serve as illustrations. Rogers (1975a, p. 1833): "At its best, such understanding is expressed by comments that reflect not only what the client is fully aware of but the hazy areas at the edge of awareness." Gendlin (1967, p. 399):"[My response] lets the patient experience not only what he already knows he feels, but also what he almost but not quite feels (so that he feels it clearly, after it is spoken of)." Rice (1974, p. 298): "[The therapist] tries to sense as accurately as possible 'this is what it was like to *be* the client at that moment.' It is his flavor of the total experience that he tries to give back to the client as concretely and vividly as possible. Hopefully, the client can then use this reflection to deepen and enrich his own awareness of the total experience and thus to broaden his construction of it."

6.   In this sense Gendlin writes (1970, p. 549):

> But unconditional regard really meant appreciating the client as a person regardless of not liking what he is up against in himself (responding to him in his always positive struggle against whatever he is trapped in). It includes our expressions of dismay and even anger, but always in the context of both of us knowing we are seeking to meet each other warmly and honestly as people, exactly at the point at which we each are and feel.

4 Beyond Reflection: Emergent Modes of Empathy

Jerold D. Bozarth

> It is one of the most delicate and powerful ways we have of using ourselves. In spite of all that has been said and written on this topic, it is a way of being that is rarely seen in full bloom in a relationship.
>
> (Rogers, 1980, p. 137)

With this comment, Rogers refers to the concept of empathy. A short version of Rogers's (1957a) definition of empathy is that of perceiving "the internal frame of reference of another with accuracy and with the emotional components and meanings which pertain thereto as if one were the other person, but without ever losing the 'as if' condition" (p. 210). This chapter is about the concept of empathy as developed in psychotherapy. As such, empathy is examined as a conceptualization that has often been equated with the technique of reflection.

The equating of empathy with the particular technique of reflection has resulted in: (1) conceptual confusion between empathy and reflection; (2) a focus on operational methods for acting empathic; and (3) a limitation of the empathic response modes of therapists. The chapter includes a review of the role of empathy in client-centered therapy and an examination of Rogers's personal style in therapy sessions. The influence of Rogers's (1957a) statement concerning the necessary and sufficient conditions of constructive personality change and the subsequent alteration of the definition of empathy are considered. In addition, empathy is viewed as a way of being for the therapist rather than a particular technique. As such, therapist responses may be idiosyncratic to the therapist, to the client, and to their experiencing of each other.

THE CONCEPT OF EMPATHY

Early in his career as a psychotherapist Rogers discovered that carefully listening to clients in an attentive way was helpful. A suggestion from a social worker who had Rankian training helped him learn to "listen" for feelings through discerning the patterns of the clients' words. Rogers (1980) states that this suggestion greatly improved his work as a therapist at that time.

The use of tape-recorded therapy sessions permitted Rogers, along with his students and colleagues, to recall and analyze therapist responses. They were able to identify responses that encouraged or inhibited client expression.

Rogers (1980) suggests that the emphasis upon therapist *responses* instead of the empathic *attitudes* of the therapist led to "appalling consequences" and "complete distortions" of client-centered therapy (p. 139).

It is noteworthy that, in his early work, Rogers (1951) emphasized that the counselor's function was that of assuming

> in so far as he is able, the internal frame of reference of the client, to perceive the world as the client sees it, to perceive the client himself as he is seen by himself, to lay aside all perceptions from the external frame of reference while doing so, and to communicate something of this empathic understanding to the client. (p. 29)

Rogers (1951) expresses concern that the counselor's role has been misunderstood. It is not just that of clarifying and objectifying the client's feeling. He refers to a paper he presented in 1940, which states, "As material is given by the client, it is the therapist's function to help him recognize and clarify the emotions which he feels" (p. 27). His comment about this statement is quite significant:

> It [the statement] is, however, too intellectualistic, and if taken too literally, may focus on the process in the counselor. It can mean that only the counselor knows what the feelings are, and if it acquires this meaning it becomes a subtle lack of respect for the client. (p. 27)

This admonition by Rogers has, for the most part, been forgotten. Therapeutic training has increasingly focused upon specific counseling skills and techniques while missing the essence of the person-centered approach: that the individual is the source of his or her own resources and expertise when empathically understood and unconditionally accepted by a congruent person.

Part of the reason for equating reflection and empathy was the influence of analyses of Rogers's own responses in his therapy sessions. Therapists eager to learn how to be empathic and teachers eager to learn how to teach empathy have often fulfilled Rogers's fear by focusing too narrowly on response techniques rather than on empathy as an attitude or way of being. An early example of the prevalence of the reflection response in Rogers's own work is found in the session between Rogers and Miss Mun (Rogers & Segal, 1955). The section that he identifies as the crux of the interview is laden with examples of reflection:

MISS MUN: I read an article about this and it's really very hard to diagnose, so I don't hold that against him at all. But he feels he has to be sure.... I'm frightened because I think they're having to be sure it isn't cancer and that really frightens me terribly and, ah, I think it's when I let that thought come to me...that maybe it is what it is, that's when I feel so dreadfully alone.

ROGERS: You feel as though if it's really something like that, then you just feel so alone.

MISS MUN: It's really a frightening kind of loneliness because I don't know who could be with you in this moment.

ROGERS: Is this what you're saying? Could anyone be with you in fear or in a loneliness like that?

MISS MUN: [Cries.]

ROGERS: It just really cuts so deep.

MISS MUN: I don't know what it would feel like, I mean if there were somebody around that I could feel sort of as though I did have someone to lean on in a sense. I don't know if that would make me feel better or not. I'm sort of thinking that this is, well, something that you just have to grow within, inside yourself, something you just have to stand, just tolerate. It will take two weeks before they know. Would it help to have somebody else around or is it something you just have to really be intensely alone in, that the, well, I just really felt that way this week. Just so dreadfully, dreadfully all by myself.

ROGERS: Just a feeling you're so terribly alone in the universe almost and whether, whether anyone could help, whether it would help if you did have someone to lean on or not. You don't know.

> MISS MUN: I guess part of it, basically, there'd be a part you'd have to do alone. You just couldn't take somebody else along on some of the feelings, and yet it would be sort of a comfort, I guess, not to be alone.
>
> ROGERS: It surely would be nice if you could take someone with you a good deal of the way, under your feelings of aloneness and fear.
>
> MISS MUN: I guess I just have.
>
> ROGERS: Maybe that's what you're feeling right at this minute.
>
> MISS MUN: And I think it's a comfort.
>
> (Quoted by permission of Pennsylvania State University. Author's transcription.)

Analysis of this section might lead to the conclusion that reflection is empathy (and, possibly, to the reductionistic and not very logical conclusion that empathy is reflection). That Rogers himself is more concerned with the attitudinal than the technical aspects of the interview is revealed by his following comments on this session:

> I think that in some sense what goes on in therapy is that you feel enough caring for this person to really let him or her possess his own feelings and live his own life and that you also recognize that the most that can be given to another person, not the least, but the most that can be given to another person is to be willing to go with them in their own separate feelings as a separate person, and I feel that there was a good deal of that in this interview.... I think one could put that in more general terms and say that what the individual experiences in therapy is the experience of being loved. (Quoted by permission of Pennsylvania State University. Author's transcription.)

As analyses of transcripts of interviews suggest, Rogers often demonstrates his "willingness to go with a client" by reflecting the feelings (and thoughts and comments) of the other person. The analyses do not, however, communicate his "willingness to go with the client" with long moments of silence or the "emotional involvement" that he experiences with Miss Mun. In other words, Rogers's empathy involves much more than just reflection in this therapy session of the 1950s. The tendency at that time, however, was to teach client-centered therapy by emphasizing the response pattern of reflection.

In the early 1960s, there appeared to be some changes in Rogers's response patterns in therapy. In the classic film interview with Gloria, Rogers (1965) expresses his feelings for his client in a touching and important therapeutic moment:

GLORIA: ...I like that whole feeling. It's real precious to me.

ROGERS: I expect none of us get it as often as we'd like, but I really do understand it. [Pause] M-hm. That (referring to her tears) really does touch you, doesn't it?

GLORIA: Yea, and you know what else, though, I was just thinking I feel it's a dumb thing that, umh, all of a sudden when I'm talking, gee, how nice I can talk to you, and I want you to approve of me, and I respect you, but I miss that my father couldn't talk to me like you are. I mean I'd like to say, gee, I'd like you for my father....

ROGERS: You look to me like a pretty nice daughter....

GLORIA: ...I keep, sort of maybe, underneath feeling like we're close, you know, and it's sort of like a substitute father.

ROGERS: I don't feel that's pretending.

GLORIA: But you're not really my father.

ROGERS: No, I meant about the real close feeling.

GLORIA: Well, see, I sort of feel that's pretending too because I can't expect you to feel very close to me. You don't even know me.

ROGERS: All I can do is what I am feeling and that is that I feel close to you in this moment.

(Quoted by permission of Psychological Films, Inc. Author's transcription.)

Although Rogers departs from reflection in some instances, he persists in walking in Gloria's world and staying with her momentary experiences by using a reflective mode. The verbal responses that demonstrate his empathy remain predominantly reflective and readily lend themselves to be modeled. But despite his continuing reliance on reflection, Rogers's focus is on the attitudinal or experiential aspects of therapy, as revealed by his comments in the film about the interaction with Gloria:

I very quickly become oblivious to the outside situation.... I find myself bringing out of my own inner experience statements which seem to have no connection with what is going on but usually prove to have a significant relationship to what the client is experiencing. And, as is characteristic of me, there are not more than one or two statements or incidents which I recall from the interview. I simply know I was very much present in the relationship, that I lived it in the moment of its occurrence, and I realize that after a time I may remember it, too. But, at the present time, I really have a very non-specific memory of the whole interview. (Quoted by permission of Psychological Films, Inc. Author's transcription.)

While Rogers has continued to use reflection as a major empathic mode, he has become more self-expressive and has, at times, used other means of communicating his empathic understanding. His comments in the demonstration film with Kathy (Rogers, 1975c) include references to the empathic way of being:

> I want to meet this client as a person, for the encounter to be that of two persons. I don't require any advanced information about her. I'll work with whatever she wishes to reveal about herself. I hope that I can first of all be myself, be real in the relationship. I often find it easy to feel a caring for the client, but I can't predict in advance whether I will feel that. I like to let myself enter into her inner world of feelings and perceptions as accurately and sensitively as I can. In order to experience that kind of empathy, I'll need to lay aside, as far as possible, my own biases and perceptions. The extent to which I can do that will to a considerable degree determine the progress she is able to make in the time we have together. I feel I am a responsible therapist. I am responsible for doing my best to create a facilitative climate in which she can explore her feelings in the way that she desires and move toward the goals that she wishes to achieve. It's in this deep sense that my approach to therapy is centered in the client, aiming to implore him or her to search out and experience the areas of conflict or pain, to perceive self in new ways, to choose to follow new options in behavior. If in my own self I find feelings other than those of caring or understanding, I'll feel free to express those, but as my own feelings, not as any judgment of or guide for the client. (Quoted by permission of Psychological Films, Inc. Author's transcription.)

Clearly, the empathy Rogers strives for is much more than that which reflective modes might communicate. However, an example from the film reveals that his verbal responses (those that can be readily modeled) are still primarily reflective:

KATHY: I have to give equal time to all my dimensions. We just had, you know, I just felt in touch with my vulnerability, but now I'm feeling angry. Like it's none of your business what I'm feeling.

ROGERS: Getting very close to the vulnerable part of you, damn it, stay away.

KATHY: That's right, that's right. What do you want to do that for? You got other things to do.

ROGERS: So you're putting up all kinds of guards against me and striking out. What the hell are you doing so close to the vulnerable part of me? Why don't you do something else? Hum.

KATHY: It's the part that keeps me lonely.

ROGERS: Uh hum. Uh hum. Umnh. So that pushing apart, that angry pushing away part is what keeps you very lonely.

KATHY: It's like I don't really trust that I can trust you to know that I can tell you this and that you may feel a little something about it but what you know, I mean, you know.... A nice story or so, big deal.

ROGERS: What I'm hearing there is that I feel that I don't really care; it's just a story or something.

KATHY: Right.

ROGERS: But what if I do care? What if I do care?
(Quoted by permission of Psychological Films, Inc. Author's transcription.)

In numerous statements during his career Rogers has tried to convey the idea that empathy is a qualitative and holistic experience of the therapist. There is, moreover, as Hackney (1978) notes, a difference between experiencing and communicating that experience. Hackney's suggestion to the counselor is to "experience the feeling, first, comprehend it as best as you can, then react to it" (1978, p. 37). The response Rogers (1980) suggests is to communicate "your sensings of the person's world" (p. 142). His way of communicating these sensings is often through the use of explicit verbal reflections. The verbal reflective mode of Rogers, which is predominant in his sessions, has often been interpreted by others as the sole way to be empathic, while other modes that he uses, including intuitive responses and self-expressions, have been virtually ignored as alternative expressions of empathy.

REFLECTION AND EMPATHY

A landmark statement by Rogers (1957a) helps to resolve the conceptual confusion between the technique of reflection and the process of empathy. In this statement, he identified six necessary and sufficient conditions for positive personality change to occur. One of these conditions was empathy. Empathy was defined as perceiving "the internal frame of reference of another with accuracy, and with the emotional components and meanings which pertain thereto, as if one were the other person, and without ever losing the 'as if' condition" (Rogers, 1959b, p. 210).

This statement was a landmark because Rogers's hypotheses concerning the core conditions for successful therapy transcended theoretical orientation. An implication of this statement was that a therapist was not necessarily expected to reflect to be empathic. The therapist could find his or her own way of entering the internal frame of reference of the other person, did not have to follow the reflective response patterns ascribed to client-centered therapy, and could even have other theoretical orientations. The therapist could be his or her empathic self without being concerned about how to appear empathic. By extrapolation, this statement releases the empathic therapist to do many things and be more spontaneous.

Barrett-Lennard (1962) operationalized the concept of empathy in a way that stimulated much productive research by examining how clients perceive their therapists. But this operationalization of the concept of empathy tended to narrow its meaning. For better or for worse, the quantification of the quality of the therapeutic relationship had begun.

A study of psychotherapy with schizophrenics at the University of Wisconsin (Rogers, Gendlin, Kiesler, & Truax, 1967) was perhaps the next major occurrence in the process of the objectification of empathy. The development of research scales offered the opportunity to refine the quantifiable definition posed by Truax (1961). Truax incorporated another factor in the definition of empathy by adding the observable behavior of the therapist. Empathy was, according to Truax and Carkhuff (1967a):

> more than just the ability of the therapist or counselor to sense the client's or patient's private world as if it were his own. It also involved more than just his ability to know what the patient means. Accurate empathy involves both the therapist's *sensitivity to current feelings* and his *verbal facility to communicate this understanding* in a language attuned to the client's current feelings. (pp. 45–46)

Thus there was an emphasis upon therapist responses. Truax, as noted by Hackney (1978), modified Rogers's definition in a way that stressed observable phenomena that could be measured, rather than the *experience* of empathy by therapist and client.

Later, Carkhuff (1971) further altered the definition of empathy by placing even more emphasis upon behavioral and verbal manifestations. Although this operational definition of empathy was originally intended for research, it was also applied to the training of therapists. Thus the therapist's reflective communication of empathy became a standard index of effectiveness. Reflection became a focus in therapist training because it provided readily identifiable therapist messages which could be observed and improved.

In short, the development of empathy in therapists was replaced with communication skills training. Such training models reduce the intersubjective experiences of empathy, unconditional positive regard, and genuineness to issues of response technique. Although developed from the concepts articulated by Rogers (1957a), these narrow operationalized definitions of interpersonal dimensions as skills have altered and restricted the original meaning of the constructs. Nevertheless, the operational definition of empathy has been quite prominent because of its applicability to research and training. Corcoran (1981) summarizes the restrictive effects of this development:

> All the operational definitions provided by Truax, Carkhuff and their associates are different from the concept which Rogers hypothesized as a necessary ingredient of effective therapy. The necessary condition of sensing the feeling of the client has been replaced with perception and reflection of affect, the meaning and content of the client's message. Thus, accurate empathy by definition is a communication process, which may not reflect the empathic experience. (p. 31)

Plum (1981) identifies the essence of the concern when he asserts that

> skill approaches to communication training mistakenly place skillfulness, rather than meaning, at the heart of personal communication. The focus on behavior as the essential element in communication lead to serious, and often inadvertent, distortion of our views of human nature and interaction. (p. 3)

Hackney (1978) points out in his review of the evolution of empathy that "the construct has undergone an evolutionary process that has altered its meaning and moved its locus from an internal state to an external process" (p. 37).

This shift in focus from an internal to an external process also renewed the authority of the counselor. In other words, the therapist rather than the client becomes the expert on the client's feelings.

Martin's (1983) definition of empathy reflects this distortion. Empathy is "communicated understanding of the other person's intended message" (p. 3). This is a far cry from walking in the world of the other person "as if" you were the other person. Moreover, Martin's conceptualization of the therapist's goal exemplifies this shift from attending to the client as expert to the assertion of the therapist as expert. Empathy (even by reflection) is no longer being "able to adopt his (client's) frame of reference, to perceive with him, yet to perceive with acceptance and respect" (Rogers, 1951, p. 41). It is, rather, the goal of the therapist "to get as far ahead of the client as you can but have the client recognize what you say as part of what he or she meant" (p. 256). In contrast, the critical point of the person-centered approach is that the individual is the source of his or her own resources and expertise when empathically understood and unconditionally accepted by a congruent person.

The misunderstanding of, and the misdirected movement away from, the primary assumptions of the person-centered approach appear to be the major reasons that reflection and empathy are so often equated. As Hackney (1978) chides, "Both the researchers and trainers should remind themselves that empathy is not a communication process. It is not words and statements" (p. 37).

The term "reflection" was adopted by Rogers (1980) from Rankian practitioners with the intent to "reflect these feelings back to the client" (p. 138). The way the therapist utilizes this technique, according to Rogers (1951), "is to reconstruct the perceptual field of the individual at the moment of expression, and to communicate this understanding with skill and sensitivity" (p. 289). This is, in essence, a technique to help the therapist to be empathic and to check whether or not the therapist is understanding the client. Several points are worth emphasizing:

1. Reflection is a way for the therapist to become empathic, to check whether or not he or she understands the client, and to communicate this understanding to the client.

2. Reflection is primarily for the therapist and not for the client. Reflection is one way for the therapist to enter the world of the client. It is the walk in the world of the client that assists the client toward growth.

3. Reflection is not empathy. It is a way to help the therapist become more empathic.

4. Empathy is not reflection. Empathy is a process of the therapist entering the world of the client "as if" the therapist were the client. Reflection is a technique that may aid the process.

5. Other modes of empathy have not been considered. Other modes are usually not as easily observed and analyzed as are the

verbal formats of reflective statements. The dedication of Rogers to quantitative, scientific inquiry influenced the nature of what would be examined by others, although his major thrust of inquiry has been a qualitative, heuristic examination of the nature of things.

Reflection, then, is a method that the therapist may use to be empathic but one that may also create nonempathic therapist ventures. It behooves us to consider what other modes might permit a more complete immersion into the world of the client.

EMERGENT MODES OF EMPATHY

How can the therapist experience the world of the client? The answer being proposed is that the therapist develop idiosyncratic empathy modes predicated upon the therapist as a person, the client as a person, and the therapist-client interactions.

Several authors have questioned the purpose of reflective responses. Judge (1979), for example, suggests in an article on reflection that the therapist's task is "not to reveal to the client the presence of existing emotions or feelings but to help in the creation of emotional attitudes" (p. 22).

Rice (1974) approaches the idea of idiosyncratic empathy responses in her formulation of evocative reflection. Evocative reflection allows the therapist to respond with metaphor, personal reaction, or initiative action. It seeks "to open up the experience and provide the client with a process whereby he can form successively more accurate constructions of his own experience" (p. 290).

Idiosyncratic empathy emphasizes: (1) the transparency of the therapist in relationship to the other person; (2) the person-to-person encounter in the relationship; and (3) the intuition of the therapist. The basic premise is that the role of the person-centered therapist is that of being transparent enough to perceive the world nonjudgmentally, as if the therapist were the other person, in order to accelerate the formative tendency of the other person toward becoming all that he or she can become.

As a way to explore emergent modes of idiosyncratic empathy more concretely, consider this multiple choice question:

Which of the following statements is most indicative of an empathic response?

1. I'm having strong sexual feelings toward you.
2. When I took my Volkswagen engine out, the car rolled down the hill, hit the rabbit pen, etc., etc.
3. You feel as though you lost contact with the physical world.

The third response is the one that would typically be designated as the empathic response. The other responses are extreme statements that would be considered absurd by many therapy supervisors. I believe that either of these ostensibly absurd responses might be the most empathic response in a particular interaction. The following examples attempt to clarify these statements.

Response 1 (I'm having strong sexual feelings toward you.)

As the supervisor of a student therapist listened to the student's taped session with a client, he had strong, consistent sexual feelings toward her. They had worked together as student and teacher for two years in a relationship that had never involved sexual connotations. The supervisor turned the tape off and said, "I'm having strong sexual feelings toward you." As they explored this experience of the supervisor, the student revealed that she had been having strong sexual feelings toward her client. She was disturbed and was quite embarrassed by having such feelings. The supervisor's expression of his feelings had captured the very essence of her strong sexual desire toward her client.

It seemed that the supervisor's feelings represented an empathic understanding of the student's inner world rather than any separate feelings of the supervisor toward the student. This was more apparent when the supervisor's feeling disappeared after the student began to explore her dilemma.

Response 2 (When I took my Volkswagen engine out, the car rolled down the hill, hit the rabbit pen, etc., etc.)

A client had struggled with great intensity to tell her therapist "something" she "had to tell" him. She could not reach this point after a prolonged, intense, and painful struggle during one session. Several days later, she returned for another session and immediately asked the therapist, "What have you been doing?" The therapist intuitively responded to her question with a long story about his efforts to repair his automobile. Although he gave her frequent opportunities to change the topic, most of the session involved his descriptions; for example,

"When I took my Volkswagen engine out, the car rolled down the hill, hit the rabbit pen, etc., etc." Later, she indicated that she appreciated that the therapist shared those experiences and did not try to force her to return to the struggle. She needed a respite from the struggle. She identified this action as highly consistent with her "state of being" at the time and later reported that it enabled her to identify the core of her struggle.

The therapist's comments were understood by the client as giving her respite from the struggle and communicating that the therapist was in touch with her inner state.

These incidents are examples of following Hackney's (1978) suggestion to "experience the feeling, first, comprehend it as best as you can, then react to it" (p. 37).

These examples may offer some idea of empathy developed through idiosyncratic therapist-client interactions. A more extensive review of a therapist-client interaction is described next.

IDIOSYNCRATIC EMPATHY—
A THERAPIST-CLIENT VIGNETTE

Pamela was a 30-year-old woman who had been seen for 40 therapy sessions over 13 months. She had exhibited "deviant" behavior in several graduate courses. As she put it, "I often refuse to talk and sometimes get out of my chair and walk around." She explained further, "Sometimes they [instructors] try to use behavior modification techniques with me and sometimes I let them think they are successful." The instructors confirmed her descriptions. She offered minimal responses in most classes and appeared to be able to assess the degree of deviance her instructors would allow. The therapist met her in an unstructured group that met for 24 hours. She exhibited similar behavior in that group. She refused to talk. At times she sat far off curled in a corner. At other times she walked around the circle of 20 group members. She quite competently rebutted confrontations by group members through the use of nonverbal behaviors such as hiding behind a chair and refusing to look at them.

After visiting the therapist several times "just to talk," Pamela asked if the therapist would be willing to see her in therapy to "just be with me [because] no one is willing to just let me beee [making buzzing sounds like a bee]."

After therapy had been discontinued, she had an appointment to meet with the therapist for the purpose of developing a videotape that might be used for teaching purposes. It was immediately obvious that she was distraught. As she entered the office, the therapist asked: "What's going on?" She sat sullenly with her hair covering most of her face. The next one and a half hours were spent in silence.

The therapist thought to himself, "I have complete faith in your resiliency to resolve your struggle."

She walked the rather large room. The therapist thought, "I feel so hurt and rejected. Did Harold reject you? It could have been several people or something else, but I think you feel Harold rejected you. But I know you don't want to talk about it."

She stood in the corner. The therapist thought, "What a bad girl am I!"

She went behind a table and lay face down on the floor by the therapist's desk. Fifteen minutes later, the therapist turned on a table lamp, turned off the overhead lights, turned on a tape recorder which plays soft music, and sat in his chair next to Pamela. After 20 additional minutes of silence, Pamela said, "I have to go now."

The therapist followed her to the door and said, "Will you call me?"

She shook her head "no" with a very pained look on her face.

The therapist sat for nearly five minutes alone in a meditative state of mind until interrupted by a knock on the door. It was Pamela, who said, "I couldn't leave you like that."

Pamela then talked about being rejected by Harold. The therapist thought, "I hate everyone, including myself."

She talked of "thinking of killing" herself.

The therapist asked, "Why?" and thought, "You don't seem to me to feel that self-destructive."

She responded, "Because I don't want to live any more."

The therapist thought, "That is a very good reason and accurate for you, too. That is how you feel right now. Now is important."

"Oh, yeah," responded the therapist.

Pamela looked out of the window to see people walking below. "I wish I had a BB gun so I could shoot all of them," she said. "I wish it were a rifle," she continued, "so I could kill them all. Except the one there in a white blouse—I'd use an ax on her."

The therapist responded, "I don't get the ax for her."

"So it could be bloodier," said Pamela.

Pamela continued expanding this homicidal scenario. She would go from floor to floor, line up victims, and find gory ways of destroying them. The therapist joined with this fantasy several times: "Maybe a shotgun would be better.... You could lay them on the floor.... I'll remember not to wear a white shirt."

The session ended in this vein. The next day the therapist received a letter from Pamela that included the following excerpts:

> Today is Saturday morning and I think "silly me" I really would like to be calm and sane where Harold is concerned—what the hell makes him so important to me?...
>
> Sometimes like yesterday I am surprised that I can seriously contemplate suicide as a "viable" option. Annette, a friend of mine, I told her about being in your office with you and talking of shooting people and hatcheting them to death, and she said she's surprised you didn't Baker's-Law me [commit me to an institution for the insane] and that I should be careful around whom I verbalize my derangements.
>
> I'm so aware of there being much more to life and by damn I want it.
>
> I'm so glad you didn't make those "appropriate" responses which are so often so inappropriate. You really did understand me.

The therapist did not attempt to communicate understanding of Pamela's intended message through reflection. He did, however, enter her world as if he were her. At one point, the therapist went through the homicidal imagery with her to the extent that he extended the imagery with vivid visualizations. Reflective responses would have been "'appropriate' responses which are so often so inappropriate," as Pamela so eloquently put it.

Pamela worked successfully as a counselor-supervisor in a preschool hospital ward for nearly a year. At last contact, she owned and operated a kindergarten. She views herself at this time as being able to cope with many disappointments and able to respond in acceptable ways to others.

SUMMARY

It is my contention that reflection has been equated with empathy so often that other empathic modes have been virtually ignored. These other modes are not standardized responses but idiosyncratic to the persons and interactions between the persons in therapy sessions. Such modes are learned by therapists as they are allowed to affirm their own personal power as therapists. The assumption by Rogers (1980) of the self-actualizing tendency is as basic a premise for the development of therapists as for the facilitation of clients. It is the "empathic understanding by another [which] enables a person to become a more effective growth enhancer, a more effective therapist for himself or herself" (p. 159).

Although reflection may be empathic, this verbal communicative mode can also lend itself to violation of the basic premise of person-centered therapy: that the individual is the source of his or her own resources and expertise when empathically understood and unconditionally accepted by a congruent person. The person-centered approach is the application of the assumption

> that the human being is basically a trustworthy organism, capable of evaluating the outer and inner situation, understanding herself in its context, making constructive choices as to the next steps in life, and acting on these choices. (Rogers, 1977, p. 15)

The technique of reflection, especially in its application within human relations training models, may violate this assumption by placing the locus of control and authority in the therapist rather than in the client.

I also contend that the equating of reflection with empathy has restricted the potency of therapists. The focus on empathy as a verbal clarification technique limits the intuitive functions of therapists. It counters the type of experience that Rogers (1980) more recently describes in himself:

> I find that when I am closest to my inner, intuitive self, when I am somehow in touch with the unknown in me, when perhaps I am in a slightly altered state of consciousness, then whatever I do seems to be full of healing.... There is nothing I can do to force this experience, but when I can relax and be close to the transcendental core of me, then I may behave in strange and impulsive ways in the relationship, ways which I cannot justify rationally, which have nothing to do with my thought processes. But these strange behaviors turn out to be *right*, in some odd way: it seems that my inner spirit has reached out and touched the inner spirit of the other. (p. 129)

Of the three ingredients of successful therapy originally postulated by Rogers (1957a), empathy has been most consistently taught in the education of therapists. Empathy lends itself to verbal explication and analysis more readily than do the concepts of unconditional positive regard and congruency. As such, reflection is a logical medium for being empathic. Empathy is not necessarily communicated by the "reflection of feeling." It may often be communicated through the intuitive, idiosyncratic attending of the therapist. Moreover, idiosyncratic modes of interaction are more likely to enable the therapist to "walk in the world of the other."

5   The Client's Client: The Edge of Awareness

Eugene T. Gendlin

Theory and experiential specificity can seem far apart. Not so! The most basic theory and the most specific experiential detail thrive on each other. In this chapter, I will first present some new experiential specifics, and then I will use them in a brief theoretical statement.

In the last decade we have learned much about the client's side of the therapeutic process. With this new information, we developed a very specific knowledge and practice called *focusing*, about which there have been some new developments in the last three years.

NEW EXPERIENTIAL FINDINGS

What is that from which the change-steps come?   The client's side of the change process has usually been discussed in relation to the question "Exactly to what, in the client, should the therapist respond?" The usual answer was "the feeling," but that term can be confusing.

No, it is not exactly "the feeling," although responding to that is a step in the right direction. We want to respond to that in the client from which change-steps come. Let me therefore ask instead "What is *that*, in the client, from which change-steps come?" It is not exactly "feeling," certainly not the familiar and identifiable feelings. Change-steps come rather from an *unclear* "edge," a "sense" of more than one says and knows.

We now call such an unclear edge a *felt sense*. Since it is felt, how does it differ from the usual clear and recognizable feelings?

76

Two differences between feelings and felt sense: the felt sense is unclear and less intense. For example, a client may feel angry and say why. In an effective therapy process that would "open up" and further steps would arise. But suppose the client says: "I'm angry, I told you why, and that's all. Nothing further comes." Let us say the therapist has responded to the anger and its reasons. What exactly is not happening?

When therapy works, certain *steps* of process would occur here. Do they come from the feeling of anger, exactly? Many therapists think so. They lead their patients to feel such anger more and more intensely. They assume that process-steps come from feelings and that, if process-steps do not occur, the anger must not have been felt sufficiently. But people often have the same feelings over and over, quite intensely, without change-steps occurring.

Conversely, change-steps might occur thus:

CLIENT: (silence)...(breath)...feels sort of heavy...like it *wants* to stay angry....

THERAPIST: Something there *wants* to stay angry.

CLIENT: Mhm...(silence)....Oh...(breath)...yah...if I stop being angry I won't do anything about it...Yes...I'd love to just say it's OK and not have to cope with the situation. I've done that so often.

These steps did not come exactly from the feeling of anger. Rather, the "heavy" quality is what opens into these steps. That heavy quality is the felt sense. More intensity *of anger* would not bring it up. The heavy quality is not as strong as the anger, for the felt sense is less intense than ordinary feelings. Without quiet concentration one may lose hold of it. *From* a felt sense very intense feelings can come, but the felt sense itself is less intense.

People change through feelings they have not consciously felt and expressed before. More intensity of familiar feelings does not bring change. People often feel and strongly express repetitious feelings, yet process-steps do not occur.

The steps of change and process do not arise directly from the recognizable feelings as such. They come, rather, from an *unclear*, fuzzy, murky "something there," an odd sort of direct datum of awareness. But most often there is no such datum at first, when people turn their attention inward. Typically one finds the familiar feelings and no indefinable sense.

One person describes it this way:

For a long time I could not find that unclear "sense." I would pay attention to emotions, but they seemed to be just what they were, clear and obvious, and felt in my body. The breakthrough about this came when I began to notice that the emotions had more to them. An analogy: if the emotion were a triangle with smooth edges and fixed angles, the felt sense appears when I look more closely and find that a cloudy shape sticks out from behind the triangle.

Once they have it, people say the unclear sense *was* there all along, unnoticed. Before, however, it simply was not there. Its first coming is a striking event in its own right.

The difference between the usual bodily sensations and a felt sense of something in one's life.   While people think of a problem, or have troublesome feelings, they are usually uncomfortable in their bodies. But, although the feelings may be experienced physically, they are not bodily discomfort as such.

If during a strong feeling someone is asked to attend to the stomach and chest, to "see if you are comfortable there," the unease that he senses is quite different from the feeling.

This bodily unease turns out to be less intense and not as rough on the person as the strong feeling.

There is typically also an odd sort of gratitude that comes from this bodily discomfort, as if *it* were thankful for one's attention.

Many people (about a third to a half) have difficulty attending directly to the comfort or discomfort in the middle of their bodies. They do not sense the middle of the body from inside. That seems strange to those who have always done it. People have to discover this simple human capacity before they can find the felt sense. We have developed specific little steps to remedy this difficulty; for example: "Put your attention in your right toe...now in your knee....Can you find your knee without moving it?...Now your groin....Come up into your stomach; how is it in there? Warm and fuzzy, or how?"

Once people can sense the stomach and chest from inside, there is a further distinction; the really important one.

Ordinarily bodily sensations are, for example, a belt that is too tight, or a pain, a stomach ache, sexual arousal, the heart pounding. But these sensations are only physical. The uneasy sense *of* a situation or problem is also there, in the middle of the body. (It may be positive: the opening-out sensation in the chest is the sense *of* some freeing event.)

The difference is that the ordinary bodily sensation does not contain an *of*. The sense of your belt being too tight does not contain in itself the complexities and reasons why you tightened it: it is just the belt's pressure. However, a very similar bodily sensation of tightness may come in your stomach as your sense *of* a whole situation. *That* equally physical *tightness* is the felt sense *of* that situation. Implicit in it are more of the complexities of the situation than you know or could think.

Most current bodywork methods miss the felt sense because they work just with physical sensations, usually of the peripheral muscles.

Emotions make bodily sensations—one's heart pounds and one coughs, spits, pants—yet *the physical sense of the implicit complexity* is not *in* those bodily sensations, nor in the emotion. The felt sense differs from both.

Another exact specification: in Gestalt therapy spontaneous images and emotions come from bodily attention without a felt sense. The person does not have a sense of the source from which they come. That source does not itself come as a datum. For example, imagery and words pop in while one attends to tense shoulders, but there is no felt sense in the shoulders. Either before or after such spontaneous material comes, the person could (but in Gestalt therapy usually does not) attend to the middle of the body, where a felt sense of the shoulder-tension and of the imagery could come.

The felt sense comes in the middle of the body: throat, chest, stomach, or abdomen.

The difference between denied experience *and what comes from a felt sense.* The body sense *of* a situation (the felt sense) is always new, fresh, the way the body *now* has the problem. Some content from the past may come also, but the felt sense is always more, the new whole of the now.

This is very often misunderstood. Some therapists want the content to be about the present, the so-called "here and now." But past experience is always implicit in any present. Other therapists think nothing can come in a person except a reliving of some repressed past. But the experienc*ing* is always present. Reliving a past event is the present experiencing of it—fresh, now—and has the quality of the present interaction.

Therapeutic steps are not a re-emergence of denied experience. What matters most for change-steps is precisely the *new* implicit complexity of bodily living. Of course the past is in it. But the felt sense of *now* is much more than the contents from the past, which may stand out.

Change-steps can arise from the felt sense of reliving the past, but they may not, if the past content alone is emphasized and the quality of the whole does not form as a datum.

Change-steps have amazing wisdom and creative novelty. They are nothing like mere emergences of the past. It may have seemed so, because past events are often dramatically part of a present therapy process. Also, in traditional theory all experience had to come from the outside. For example, imagination could only be some (perhaps scrambled) version of what was once seen or heard externally. Today we recognize the vast creativity of imagination, far beyond what could be assembled from external experiences. And the change-steps involve much more than imagination alone.

The change-steps on which therapy depends take account of more simultaneous requirements than one could ever coalesce merely by thinking, let alone by thinking simultaneously. The felt sense is that new whole from which such steps come.

Therefore, we must emphasize the difference between denied past experiences and the whole bodily sense of now. But *that* is often not there to be sensed. A person may have to be quiet and deliberately let that holistic sense come as a datum.

The difference between feelings inside a problem and the felt sense of the whole. Whether one attends to a whole situation or to some tiny aspect of it, the bodily felt sense of that will be a whole. This sounds contradictory, I know. But the bodily sensing of the smallest aspect of anything is an implicitly complex whole, not really smaller than the sensing of some large topic. It is always the whole bodily living of....

This wholeness is a characteristic of the felt sense.

The usual feelings and emotions are only parts of a situation. With those feelings, we feel *inside* a problem, surrounded by it, part of it. But if we become distant and "objective," we don't feel the problem at all. In ordinary experience there is no way to feel a problem as a whole we confront.

The sensation may arise only in the left side of a nose, but when the body's living of that sensation becomes a datum, it is sensed as "that whole thing."

Process-steps are changes of that whole. The entire map changes. The step cannot be located on the previous map.

The difference between very deep relaxation and the felt sense. Hypnosis and very deep relaxation have been found and discarded by Freud and many others since then. We must work with more than *consciousness*, but not by narrowing or circumventing the conscious client.

The felt sense that I also call *the edge of awareness* is the center of the personality. It comes between the conscious person and the deep, universal reaches of human nature where we are no longer ourselves. It is open to what comes from those universals, but it feels like "really me." The felt sense and each small step comes already "integrated" and not as so-called "unconscious material."

The felt sense is always a freshly made, unique living. Its inward *coming* is sensed as more truly *me* than the familiar feelings.

Against vivisection. The reader may now check how well I have communicated up to now. Can you follow this specification?

The most common sort of unhelpful inward activity today is not mere intellectualization or rationalization, nor even experiencing and analyzing the same feelings over and over. Today the most common ineffective attempt to help oneself inside is what we now call *vivisection*. One is very active "upstairs" in one's mind, drawing maps and attempting to understand one's trouble, thinking this, and thinking that, but instead of merely intellectualizing, one feels in one's gut every move one makes upstairs! Just about all these moves *hurt*.

Attending to these hurts and gut feelings generated by one's own cutting is not focusing and is not to be recommended!! In the days when people were largely out of contact with their feelings, the map-making upstairs was mere intellectualizing. Now it is worse! That is your gut you are now cutting up, this way or that, as directed *from* your head.

The inward process we are specifying involves keeping quiet and sensing the unease in the body directly, wholly, as it comes, without putting one's maps, cuts, and distinctions on it. If you let your attention go *directly* to the bodily unease, you feel a little bit better.

Then let *that unease* make the map, let *that* sort itself into whatever parts or pieces it falls into on its own. But begin always with "that whole business" and not with anything you cut out of your living inside.

However well you think you have defined a problem, consider it as also undefined. Use what you have been calling it merely as a pointer and call it "all that," whatever it may be and whatever may go with it, without first cutting it up and feeling the effects of this cutting.

Teaching the client role. We began "teaching" the client how to find such a felt sense many years ago, when repeated research studies (Gendlin, Beebe, Cassens, Klein, & Oberlander, 1968; see also Klein, Mathieu, Kiesler, & Gendlin, 1969) had shown that those who did not approach therapy in this way became failure cases. Today what we call *focusing* can be shown to anyone.

Then and now we teach listening (the therapist role) as well as focusing to the public. I am going to use some examples from the beginnings of such teaching in order to pursue our question, "What is *that*, from which change-steps come?"

For example, a client (or a person to whom we were listening) is asked to check an empathic response. "Please don't just agree out of politeness. *Is* what was said back to you quite right?" But the person in the client role might check only the words: "Yes, that's what I said."

What exactly is wrong with that, as a reaction to a listening response?

When therapy is effective, the client does something more with a listening response than just checking the words. What more?

What do we assume the client will do with a listening response?

We hope and assume that clients will *check* the response, not against what they said or thought, but against some inner being, place, datum... "the felt sense"; we have no ordinary word for *that*.

An effect might then be felt, a bit of inward loosening, a resonance. What seemed to be there was expressed and heard. It need not be said again. For some moments there is an easing inside. (In theoretical terms the interpersonal response has carried that forward.) Soon something further comes. What *was* there turns out to have more to it.

We hope the clients will *check* not only what we say, but also what they say, against *that inward one*. Thereby a distinction arises within the person: the usual self is checked against the felt sense.

Those research clients who are later successful differ from failure cases in exactly this respect. It can be heard on the tape. After saying something, they often stop to check. For example: "I feel helpless...

uhm...is that right?..." After a silence they might then say: "No... that's not right.... uhm...I can sense it, right there, but I don't know what it is. (silence)...Oh, (breath)...whew, yes, it's...." as a large shift occurs. Or they might say: "...oh...one thing about it is...." as some new facet appears.

It turns out that the deliberately speaking client to whom we relate is *not* the one to whom our responses are chiefly addressed! Rather we hope the speaking one will take our responses down to consult that other one, the felt sense. We hope the client will let that one speak, will wait for what comes from it, will work to find words that "resonate" with it, rather than interrupting, lecturing, or interpreting it.

Here we discover a fascinating analogy: that of the client's client.

The client's client. In specifying the client's side of the therapy process we discover a distinction within the person. This distinction is a strong corroboration of client-centered therapy.

The felt sense is the client inside us. Our usual conscious self is the therapist, often a crudely directive one who gets in the way of our inward client all the time. That therapist frequently attacks in a hostile way or at least wants to use all the old information, claims to be smarter than the client, talks all the time, interrupts, takes up time with distant inferences and interpretations, and hardly notices that "the client" is prevented from speaking. That "directive therapist" hardly knows the client is there. That "therapist" starts without the client, as the old joke had it, and goes on indefinitely without the client.

Research shows that those clients succeed who are client-centered with their felt sense.

Of course the felt sense is not a person within a person, but a certain kind of self-response process.

But it would be imprecise to call it being client-centered "with oneself." Rather, one needs the distinction within the person between the usual self and the felt sense. The latter is exactly that part to which client-centered responses are directed.

From Plato to Freud people have distinguished different parts of the psyche. Here now arises a distinction that is best delineated in client-centered terms.

The felt sense is the client's client. The client's attitudes and responses toward the felt sense need to be those of a client-centered therapist! And that is *focusing.* I can therefore specify focusing further, if you will consider some client-centered principles in this new way.

Here are some client-centered maxims that acquire a new meaning when applied internally, within one person.

Usually the felt sense does not even form and come unless the inner "therapist" first gives attention and silent waiting time. The client's inner "therapist" (his conscious self) must shelve much knowledge and surmise, must refrain from many interesting interpretations, and prefer instead to wait silently while for some time nothing much comes.

We find it hard to put aside all we know about ourselves and about the specific problem so that we can hear what comes from the felt sense.

At first, our "directive therapist" often interrupts. Interpretations and inferences continue in our heads. We must "shelve" these again and again so that we can listen to the felt sense.

Our felt sense may at first seem less sophisticated than our reasoning. If we receive and resonate that initial contact, however, soon what comes is more intricate and more correct than anything we could *think*.

We learn that what comes from the felt sense has its own logic and its own good reasons, even if these are not immediately apparent.

We do not impose our values to give direction to the ensuing steps. On the contrary, we often learn through experiencing with the client that some ways of living and feeling can be good, although our values seem opposed. Now they don't conflict, and yet we didn't discard our values. The initial values play a role *and* are also altered in such steps.

We try to receive whatever comes from a felt sense. We let it be, at least for a while. We try not to edit it, change it, or immediately push it further.

Neither do we agree with what first comes from a felt sense. We know there will be further steps. We develop an attitude of welcoming whatever comes, even if it seems negative or unrealistic. We know that further steps can change it. Such steps can come only if we first receive and welcome what is now here.

Sometimes we have an idea, but we don't decide if it is right. We keep it tentative and consult the felt sense. If there is an easing, a resonance in response to what we propose, we attend to that till more comes from it.

New specificity. Here I do not want to repeat the focusing instructions and the troubleshooting specifics that were presented in a very detailed way in *Focusing* (Gendlin, 1981a). I would like to present the most recent work. Therefore, what I can say here is not sufficient to enable people to find focusing for themselves.

We divided the focusing instructions into six "movements." We now find it essential to teach these parts *separately*, giving time and *individual attention* to each person with each part.

I will summarize these six and offer one or two new specifics on each.

1.   Just as we would not tell clients at the start of an hour what to work on, so also we don't let the internal directive therapist quickly set the topic. The client might spend a minute or two scanning inwardly, sensing the various things that are there, only then choosing what to work on.

The first focusing movement, "making a space," was once a simple preliminary. Before actually focusing, one took a kind of inventory of what was in the way of feeling good in the middle of one's body. To do this, one attends *there* and senses what, just now, is in the way of feeling good there.

For example, one might find: "Oh...sure, my sadness about my breaking up with ----.... Yes, of course, that's there...(breath) and...oh, I have to call the dentist,...and...gee, I'm tired!" Three or four things, usually of very unequal importance, might happen to be what one finds. Each of these is greeted kindly and "placed" somewhere in a space in front of oneself, one by one. In the center of one's body one feels some physical relief with each placing, even though these problems have not been focused on, only shelved. In this freed space one begins to focus on one of these or on something else.

From this humble preliminary movement a method of working psychotherapeutically with cancer patients has developed (Gendlin, Grinder, & McGuire, 1984; Kanter, 1982). It began because cancer patients were reputed to be characteristically poor at sensing their bodies from inside. It seemed a good, clear research prediction that they would be unable to do the first movement of focusing. Instead, they could all make a space and find the good bodily energy that then arises.

A new, more elaborate version of the first movement opens a vast space that has more kinds of significance that I can discuss here.

2.   In a very directive therapy the patients are often inwardly silenced. What would come in them, step by step, cannot arise, because these therapists do not intend what they say to be inwardly checked and

corrected by the patient. Describing their therapy hour, such patients usually report "what my therapist says.... "

Client-centered therapists (perhaps all effective therapists) intend what they say to be corrected by the client. Often what is *not* right in a response lets what *is* right suddenly arise more sharply in the client.

Inside ourselves, too, something can come distinctly to correct what we try to tell ourselves. For example, some little thing went wrong today. We tell ourselves "It's all right.... It doesn't matter.... Soon I will have forgotten it.... Mature people don't get all upset about such trivia.... It's OK.... It's OK.... Look at it this way..." and so on. Each of these responses is contradicted by the discomfort that "talks back" and vividly corrects our attempts to think it away.

When a discomfort is already there, one can turn and attend to it. But often there are only the familiar feelings.

To let the felt sense come is the most difficult part of focusing. One specific technique is based on the effect I just described. There is an irony in making use of this effect. Although knowing that there is a problem that is not "OK," one deliberately says, inwardly, "It's OK, the whole thing is all right. I'm quite comfortable about all that." Putting one's attention in the middle of the body, one usually senses, suddenly and vividly, *the body talking back*, giving one a much more distinct body sense of that particular problem or situation. What an interesting effect this is!

A bodily sensation can come and talk back so as to correct wrong statements. The body can understand the words and knows the situation too. It can disagree with our words. (In the theoretical section we will reformulate this in better terms.)

A medium level of relaxation is needed for this bodily talking-back. Because most people spend the day with their bodies at maximum tension, they sense few variations in it. On the other hand, too much relaxation prevents this bodily talking-back. In hypnosis, for example, the body actually gets comfortable when you tell it to do so. No felt sense will come to correct the words.

3. Therapists can paraphrase most of what a client says, but are wise to keep crucially charged words the same. We might paraphrase a long story as merely "what they did." But if the client uses the word "apprehensive," we would not change it to "scared" or "worried" because then the client might lose hold of the connotation that word right now holds. Such a word can be a "handle" that helps us hold onto a whole suitcase.

In focusing, when a felt sense arises, one concentrates on its *quality*, and tries to find a *handle-word* for that quality. Just trying for a word helps one stay with a felt sense as a bodily sensation, rather than going into the familiar feelings and thoughts of the problem. Is it "jumpy" or more like "heavy"? Is it "flat" or perhaps "crowded" or "pushed back" or how? Might an image fit that quality? The most important function of doing this is to help stay with the felt sense. If nothing fits, call it *that quality*.

4.   When a quality-word seems right, we *resonate* it, as in a client-centered response. We ask, "Does this word (or image) really fit?" The felt sense must answer.

The body's knowledge of words is surprisingly fine and demanding. A given quality-word resonates. Other words that seem equivalent are rejected by the body. If the felt sense remains static, if the word doesn't do anything, the word does not resonate. Try another. When a word or phrase or image fits, a slight but grateful physical effect comes *each time* you think the word (or freshly repicture the image).

With this physical effect the whole problem is loosened in the body. Now we advise doing it several times, not just once.

5.   How often as therapists are we happy that we resisted making an interpretation that seemed so very right?... A few moments later the client's directly sensed unclarity opens and totally alters what the problem seemed to be. Often our interpretation was not even on the right topic.

That phenomenon also happens inside. One knows a lot about oneself, after all. And yet *this* holistic, unclear felt sense "knows" more. When a step comes from it, one's whole map of some trouble changes.

Of course the felt sense cannot answer if it is not there, just now. Remembering it from a few moments ago is not good enough. Now, "Is the felt sense still there?... Ah... there it is again." (If it does not come, try saying the problem is all solved....)

I have written about the felt shift as a flood of physical relief. But even a slight bit of "give" subtly changes the whole: it feels good to shift ever so slightly when a problem has been stuck for a long time. When normally tense and mobilized, one might miss it. Monitor for bits of slight relief in the felt sense.

Pursue thoughts, images, or anything else that brings such a bit of relief.

6.   We do not argue with what comes in the client or call it unrealistic, selfish, or bad. We *receive* anything the client offers. We

give it time. We don't instantly ask "And why is that?" or "What's the next step?"

The steps of change can come only from this, so we must let it be for a little while.

Recently we have begun to alert people to notice how the inner "directive therapist" can rebut and obliterate what comes with a felt shift. This can happen so swiftly, one might not notice. No sooner does something come with that characteristic shift or "give" inside, than it is gone again! What happened? Someone inside quickly said: "That's unrealistic, foolish. I can't afford it. That would be quitting. That can't be right."

This sixth movement, *receiving*, needs separate teaching. With practice one learns to move old voices aside before they crowd out the physical sense of the shift. Instead, one can *repeat whatever words came with the shift, sensing if they make that shift again*. In this way the shift is there for a stretch of time. Let the old voices stand aside and wait. This is only a little step. I am making no decisions yet. This little step came only just now. Let me keep it for a little bit and see more what it is.

In a minute there can be another round of focusing. But right now, let me see if I can sense this shift, over and over.

About instructions. The scheme presented in these six guidelines is very helpful, but we must not rigidify it. Humans are vastly more complex and surprising than any scheme, let alone a simple one of six parts.

We give *split-level instructions*: "Try to apply our instructions as exactly as you can, but the moment they seem to do some violence in you, stop, don't run away; instead, see directly what you have there." On one level, "please follow," and on another level, "please don't follow" the instructions.

After all, we are specifying and teaching the individual's own *inwardly arising* process. The split-level instruction is to find the individual's process with our diagram or to find where the diagram fails.

When they are just beginning to learn focusing, most people come to a point when they *laugh* and say: "Oh,... that was the trouble.... I was trying to 'do it right,' and that got in my way." After this laugh, they know.

For example, a felt shift comes on our diagram at the fifth movement. In fact it can come any time. Of course the therapist would receive what came.

Many therapists have found it very effective to teach focusing directly to their clients. Such didactics need to be clearly marked off from the regular therapeutic interaction.

Focusing during therapy. All these instructions can be used during psychotherapy, but in a certain way. This brings me to a wider principle.

There are many theories and many other useful avenues of therapy. All of them can be used on *a client-centered baseline*. By this I mean: *whatever I say or do in therapy is instantly checked against the client's inward response.* That is, I rarely say or do two things consecutively without a client's expression between. Then I respond in a listening way to whatever the client expresses and again to what further comes. I always give *priority to the client's own step*. Whatever else I can do must wait.

That approach transforms the character of interpretations, and any other useful avenue of therapy.

I must *swiftly discard* whatever I tried if it did not help, so that it does not get in the way of the client's own process.

At first clients think they must explain why what I said was wrong. I often interrupt: "Oh, I can see I was wrong. Sense again how it is for you." Clients who work with me soon recognize that what I say is no statement about them but an invitation to them to sense inwardly. I often verbalize this at first: "But is that right...or how should that be said?"

Once people know that this is my intent, what I say wrongly is much less disturbing and can be swiftly discarded.

Even when helpful, other things must not replace listening too often. (That certainly includes focusing instructions.) Too many helpful interruptions block the client's own inwardly arising process, or worse, never allow it to arise. *There must be long periods when I purely listen and reflect.*

How focusing transforms talking. Most people live in their talking as they talk. Especially in client-centered therapy, clients are accustomed to "lay out" their problems and concerns. The attention is on what is being said. Focusing changes this. Whatever the client wants to do is still welcomed, including this kind of talking. But now the expectation is not that the laying out of the issue will do the job. Rather, the change-steps will come through inwardly sensing the edge. When *that* opens, the process moves.

This requires that client-centered responses point precisely. Not enough is gained if the response is more or less right. A good response points and makes contact with *that* from which the client spoke, rather than restating what was said.

When the client did not express an unclear edge, we can point to *that*. To do so leads to a number of specific response modes:

1. Just saying a deeply felt spot over a few times quietly and slowly can help a person discover the broader bodily sense from which steps come.

2. At times the therapist can say, "Let's be quiet for a moment, so you can sense all that." Or, if true, the therapist can say "Wait...I'm still feeling what you just said...uhm...." These are ways of slowing the talking down so more can happen.

If the client then goes right on talking, we would respond as usual and not stick to some suggestion of ours.

3. We can sometimes add to the content something like: "...and *that* is not yet clear," or "...and you don't know yet what *that* is," or "...and there is this sense there, that it could become different, but it's not clear yet how." People are socially accustomed to stop talking when they come to an unresolved edge. It often helps to refer to that edge as such.

4. Even when no edge seems to be there, the client might find one if the therapist refers to one as if it *were* there, as a concretely sensed version of what was said.

For example, the client says: "I must not want to do this (get a job, meet new people, write an assignment) since when the time comes, I don't do it." A regular client-centered response might be: "You think you must not want to, since somehow you don't do it." A focusing-inviting response might be: "*Something in you* doesn't want to..." or "There's some *sense of* not wanting to..." or "When the time comes, *something* stops you."

Here is another example. The client might say, "I really think that's why I stay with him; it's because I need the security." A focusing type of response might be: "You're pretty sure it's for security, *that sense there, of holding onto him.*"

Almost anything can be reflected with an implicit invitation to sense "it" as *that*, right there. If you tell me that you like this chapter, I could reflect that you have *a liking* of my chapter there. You might then more directly find that datum, that sense, that place in you where you like it, that spot, *that*.

What I described here may seem only a grammatical form, and an awkward one at that. Better grammar can probably be devised. But there is a great *difference between talking about and pointing.* Many clients talk about. Some of them can turn inward and attend directly, as soon as a therapist points.

5. Focusing can be taught with occasional small-scale instructions. Explicit didactic focusing-teaching is much swifter, but it ought to happen in a time set aside for it, not in the midst of an ongoing therapy process. But, as single bits, the instructions can fit into, and aid, the client's ongoing process.

All the instructions and specifics I have offered here lend themselves to being used singly at points when the client might use them. All focusing instructions and specifics can be used this way. The client can ignore such single instructions. They do not disrupt one's regular way of responding. Whatever the client does or says can be responded to acceptingly.

We can explicitly invite the client to see if it is possible to find such a sense inwardly, by adding, "Can you sense *that* now?" or "Can you feel that not-wanting, now?" Or, "If you stay quiet inside for a minute, can you sense this not-wanting you think must be there?"

Here are more examples: "If you thought right now of going to the newspaper to look for a job opening...what kind of feeling-quality would come in your body?" Or even: "Stop for a minute. I'd like to ask you something. Can you put your attention in the middle of your body? How is it in there right now?" (The client says it is fine in there.) "Now think of this whole thing about looking for this job.... What comes in there?..." (facial expression) "...OK, stay with that for a minute, gently."

It is often important to help people discover the bodily aspect of the unclear edge. Many people have never attended inwardly in the body in that way and need a little while to discover it.

Another example.

CLIENT: I'm just so angry.
THERAPIST: Your anger is right there.
CLIENT: Oh, it's always there. I'm sick of that anger.
THERAPIST: Let's try something. Take that *whole* situation, all of it, more than you know, everything that goes with it, and kind of step back from it as if you were going to look at *all* of it, like a big picture that takes up a whole wall in a large building.... What comes in your body when you do that?

In this way the therapist can occasionally insert any of the focusing instructions and specifics at points when a client who knows focusing would probably let an unclear felt sense arise.

But, whereas the pointing reflections can be made frequently, instructions must remain occasional if they are not to disrupt the client's ownership and inner impetus of the process. The therapist must not constantly make good things happen with instructions. There must be empty spaces and time for the client's inwardly impelled process to arise.

If the interaction becomes troubled, or if the client has feelings about being instructed, this must instantly take precedence. Focusing-teaching can be tried again later.

THERAPIST: Can you get that painful sense now, if you put your attention to your body and, very gently, just stay next to it?

CLIENT: I don't like it when you tell me what to do inside myself.

THERAPIST: You don't like me directing inside you, and you want me out of there. Of course. I'll stop doing it.

CLIENT: But...uhm...I *do* want what you know about.

THERAPIST: Oh, sure, I'll show you that method some time soon.... You want me out of your space, but you don't want me to get away.... Right?

THEORY: WHAT IS THE SOURCE OF PROCESS-STEPS?

The following is a very brief theoretical statement. More is presented in a long work that is still unpublished (Gendlin, 1981b) and in my philosophical works (Gendlin, 1962, 1973, 1978–79).

The question. Our question is the same as in the first section, but now we ask it as a theoretical question, although I will continually refer back to the specifics we have discussed.

We observe that process-steps have an intricacy and a power to change us far superior to our concepts. What comes in process-steps surprises us. A much more sophisticated "territory" shows itself than we are capable of formulating or inventing. And a step is not only itself but leads to further steps.

What is this superior knowing? Are such steps just unrelated to concepts? How do they differ from the more familiar form of cognition? What is the source of this intricacy and its steps?

We have to rethink our basic concepts about the body, feeling, action, language, and cognition to answer this question.

Implicit concepts. We have seen that process-steps move beyond the explicit concepts we deliberately apply. But many more concepts are always already *implicit* in any human experience.

The many concepts and structures that are implicit in this wider order do not function as explicit concepts would. A welter of old theories, mutually exclusive patterns, and systems are always implicit in our experience, far more of them than we can think. Explicitly, the many contradictory concepts would cancel out. Implicitly, not only do they function together, but they are always only a small part of the implicit order.

Concepts (the kind that seem separable from particular contexts) are a late and immensely important human product, enabling people to build the world further and further. And because humans have already done much of that kind of building, old concepts are always implicit in any situation and experience.

But nature is vastly *more* organized than this late and important development can account for. Even the purest logical thinking involves this greater order to support it. There is always a whole implicit context of intricately ordered understandings without which the explicit concepts do not work. These understandings don't consist only of concepts.

But is there another way to theorize other than by conceptual forms? Even if there were not, it is wrong to equate order with concepts. Of course, if there were no other way to theorize, we would have to stop with this mere denial. We could not think further.

The problems of theorizing in another way have been treated in my philosophical writings.

Any concept can always be used as its conceptual form or as the wider implicit order that we instance at the time we use that concept. The wider order cannot be said or conceptualized. But with a concept we can always move either logically or in process-steps from this wider order.

Language. Language is a larger system, different in kind from abstractable concepts. Some decades ago, linguistic analysts showed that words are not used in accord with the abstractable patterns we call concepts. They tried to explicate rules for how words are used in various contexts to have certain effects in situations. But even this attempt failed. The same word is used in an odd assortment of situations in which it works differently. The meaning of a word is not a concept, nor can the contexts of its use be stated.

If you speak more than one language, you know that. There is often no single translation for a word. In the foreign language a word's cluster of contexts is not that which comes with any one word of ours. From the contexts we get *one* feel for how that one word works.

Language in use is very finely "ordered," well beyond the abstractable conceptual type of order. Abstract concepts are certainly always implicit in the use of words, but even the whole mutually contradictory welter of them does not come close to the kind of order that governs the use of words.

Theoretical proposition 1:   The use of words (and also the use of concepts) is implicitly ordered. This order is different from, and greater than, the kind of order concepts make. A welter of old concepts is always implicit in any human situation but cannot determine what we say or do next.   Linguistic analysts have concluded that a native speaker knows the language as one "knows" how to ride a bicycle without being able to say how. The misuse of a word gives one a "sour feeling," as one of them said. They did not ask how knowledge more intricate than one can define can be in a feeling. But we want to ask this question.

Feelings and interpersonal situations.   Feelings are usually thought of as internal things, entities, little objects. Indeed they are a sort of datum inwardly "there," but how do such thinglike data and inner space come about?

The traditional notion of *affects* assumes that they are already thinglike. Other little things are memories, desires, values, needs, perceptions, information, and so on. To make these assumptions neglects to explain how these feelings form.

Of course when we use these words they do work, but *that* with which they work is far from being such a clear-cut entity. If we begin with *that* in the case of the word *feelings*, we soon discover that they are not just affect-things but have a wealth of complexity in them. How can we think about why that is?

An emotion is part of events, or as I want to put it: emotions come in stories. They occur in a certain spot structured by the story. Traditional living was usually a repeatable story, with the recognizable emotions in the right places. There seemed to be a fixed "keyboard" of them. In modern urban society the stock routines are failing. We can manage few situations just as we are supposed to do. Our stories are more varied and complicated. Therefore, the major pure emotions occur in us more rarely.

Feelings (if you follow my use of these words) often have no name. We have to tell the situational story in detail to convey the feeling. From this we see that an emotion or a feeling *is* our living in that story.

Theoretical proposition 2: Feelings and interpersonal situations form one system. The situational complexity is lived in the feelings; felt and lived complexity constitutes situations and is not something added to them. We do not separately experience a situation as if it were merely external and then "react" to it with one of a set of feelings, as the usual theory asserts. Situations are not external, so that feelings would be internal additions to them. On the contrary, so-called external facts are always made with implicit assumptions and livings.

Affects are not additions to facts. Facts are and mean what was and will be lived and felt by someone.

The single mesh of feelings and situations is always already inherent in any "external" fact. That mesh is more highly ordered than abstractable concepts, although it always includes an implicit welter of those. Nor can feelings and situations *be* put into words, although the system is partly patterned by language. A nexus of words is always implicit in feelings and situations. But living is not determined in advance to remain within extant language forms. The reverse is true: when we live and speak oddly we also change that implicit nexus of language. New uses of words are then implicit.

The body. Feelings and emotions must *come* or we don't have them. We can remember them and believe they ought to be there. But for us to have them they must *come*. And this is always a bodily coming.

The coming of feelings in the body is also the coming of the situational detail, some of which is always linguistically patterned. Our interpersonal actions are, or include, speech-acts. Therefore, words, too, have this character.

Words, too, must *come*. If they don't, we are stuck. There is no inner dictionary in which to find them. We are quite dependent on their coming.

Abstract concepts also *come*, and when the body is tense they might not!

Theoretical proposition 3: We live our situations with our bodies. Feelings and actions, the use of words, and also thinking are bodily processes. Actions, words, and thoughts are implicit in the body. We can now understand how the body knows and responds so precisely to words, as I described in the first section. Of course. Language is situational structure. Feelings and situations come in the body. It follows that the body knows language. But now we need to change the usual concepts of the body, to think clearly how concepts, language, and situations are *implicit* in it.

Two puzzles in particular need clarification:

1. A present bodily event implies *further steps* of action and words.
2. An internal bodily event implies *external* objects and situations.

Time, change, and datum.   Process-steps give us a new time-and-space model, called *carrying forward.* (This concept was discussed in Gendlin, 1964, but has been elaborated since then.) Our change-steps do not occur on a linear time continuum. In therapy we change not into something else, but into more truly ourselves. Therapeutic change transforms the individual into what he or she really *was* all along. But this sentence makes sense only if the word *was* does not refer to the familiar temporal positions behind us. Rather, it is a second past, read back retroactively from now. It is a new *was* made from now. Let us use this new concept of time instead of reimposing the old one.

Each small process-step contains this new *was*. For example: "Oh...now I can feel the anger that bored feeling really *was*...." The anger *now* seems to have been there before. But it is a step of carrying forward. We have two pasts now: we have the anger that *was*, but we also recall the fuzzy boredom that *was* actually on the linear time line behind us.

Only retroactively can we get to this *was*. Only from now *was* it there before. Time seems retroactive when we examine the process-step relation in linear time. Actually the new time relation is more complex. Linear time can be defined as a simpler model within it.

It is not just false to say that this now is what *was*. We cannot express that relation in the old concepts. *That* change and time relation is made in process-steps.

There are many different variants of this *was*-relation in therapy, thinking, poetry, action, and other processes. The varieties of this *was* are also the various senses of *implicitness* and *carrying forward*.

Situations, too, have this carrying-forward pattern. We don't speak of a situation unless it is difficult to meet. Otherwise we have already acted and events flow on. But when there is a situation to be met, we don't immediately know the "right" action. That action is in one way indicated by the situation (the action must fit and meet it) and in another way not indicated since we are puzzled. The situation may be new and unusual, yet it implies the action needed to meet it. Later events reveal what the situation *was*. Therefore, with hindsight we see what the right action *was*. This *was* characterizes the carrying-forward relation.

The situation does not contain the right action as a problem in geometry contains its answer, logically following from the givens (though even in geometry one must often draw an additional line and create further to find that sort of implicit answer). The way a situation implies an action to meet it is very finely ordered and demanding, yet the action will also change the situation and not merely follow from how the situation is already formed.

We can say that *an action* is *a change in a situation*. But it is not just any change. The *implicit* action is the one that will change the situation as the situation demands to be met. And *a situation* is *the demand for some action*. The two are reciprocal: the situation *is* the implication of a change in situation. A situation is an implication of a change in itself.

Now we can formulate the carrying-forward relation forward and not only backward (as a new *was*). A situation *is* the implication of its own change. Put more generally:

Theoretical proposition 4: Any event is the implication of subsequent events. An event implies its own change. Subsequent events carry forward, if they change this event into what it was *the implication of.* The implied next event is *not* already formed and determined; only the present event is.

Other changes, in addition to carrying forward, often happen. The implied next event might not occur at all. It does not exist as formed if it does not occur.

Carrying forward leads us to conceptualize an event (anything) in a radically unusual way. An event not only *is* in some way now, but any event also *is* the implication of its change.

One need not insist that anything is like that conceptualization or that this new model is always superior. But the process-steps in therapy and focusing are better thought about in this way. Many other aspects of human behavior become more clearly thinkable with this model (at least as one of several we might use).

The *was* of carrying forward as a characteristic of bodily life. Hunger, for example, *is* more truly an eating that hasn't come yet than a state that eventually leads to death (which of course it also is). Which way would you define *hunger?* Would you bring eating into the definition, or would you only say how hunger *is* while it is still hunger?

Physiology studies the body very successfully with a conceptual model of atoms positioned at linear space and time points, but we will never grasp the unity of body and psyche in that model. The psychological cannot be related to such a body. But this is not because what is physical and biological differs from the behavioral and psychological, but because the conceptual model currently used in biology and physics is inadequate. Even physics needs the model of process-steps: our model alters just those assumptions that currently account for the major anomalies in physics (Gendlin & Lemke, 1983).

In our new model, biological events *are* in two ways: they are now just so, *and also* they are the implication of subsequent events. Let us not separate some vitalistic entity—drive, need, push, motivation, desire—as an unseen motor by which each discrete event is connected to the next. Indeed, let us not assume discrete events that are present only at some time "point." Such discrete events require an external "observer" to connect them, as physics now assumes. But we are such observers, and we study such observers! We live our own progression, and the formal continuity of points is only one oversimplified derivative.

Any bit of process is the implication of a next step. From that step, backwards, the implicit seems to have been what now forms. Actually the implicit *is* for any subsequent event that would have one of these retroactive relations.

The environment is part of what is implied next. If future body processes are implicit, so are the external circumstances that are involved in them. The hungry body implies not only feeding, but of course also food.

Any living process is always both environment and organism. The body is itself a piece of environment. We think of a living body as separate from everything around it, but the body is also made out of that. It is also itself an "internal environment." For example, the bloodstream is the environment of the cells. Each internal tissue has its environment. The body *is* both environment and living process. Every cell is both, and again every part of a cell. Body and environment are one system, one thing, one event, one process.

Just as feeding *and* food are implicit in a body process, so also are the next action *and* the people and things that would be involved in the action. In this way we understand more clearly how a bodily event (feelings, too) is implicitly an external complexity in the environment, for we bodily feel the actions that our situations implicitly are.

Many of these actions are or involve words, of course, and we feel those also in the body. Especially when the implicit actions can *not* happen do we sense acutely in the body that they are implicit now.

The implied action—for instance eating—might not happen because there is no food. An implied action cannot happen if the people and things it involves are missing.

What is an object? What is an inner datum and its inner space? Earlier I said that we cannot start by assuming already split-apart inner entities or objects like feelings, memories, perceptions, and so on. We need to ask how such inward *data* come about. Are they just given? I said no; external facts, too, are made with our feeling and living. We can now understand this more clearly.

In the traditional view the outer *objects* are simply given and we react. For example, when we are hungry, eating is *our reaction to* food. In that way of thinking, food is an object by itself. Eating is a reaction to it. I want to turn that around. Let us say instead that eating isn't just a *reaction to* food. Rather, food becomes an *object* only with the organism's digestive process, which runs through stages of hunger, food search, feeding, satiation, defecating, and, after a while, hunger again. At the feeding part of this cycle *the body implies* food and cannot go on without it. At the defecation part of the cycle *the body implies* the ground in which feces can be buried.

To put it this way allows me to say that food is *not* first an object to be reacted to with feeding. Food is an object *because* it carries the digestive process forward.

In this way we theoretically derive the concept of an ordinary *object* from the concept of *carrying forward*. Now the two concepts imply each other.

Theoretical proposition 5: Bodily process always involves the environment. By implying the next bits of process, the body implies its next environment. Carrying forward happens when the implied future environment comes into being. The part of the implied environment that might or might not occur is called an object. *An object is what carries a process forward.* Food changes hunger into satiation. An object (an environment that carries the implied forward) changes that implication. Hunger implies its own change, which occurs if food does.

Food and all its characteristics are implicit in hunger. But hunger could also be carried forward by something new. The implicit is never only formed. Intravenous feeding can carry digestion forward and so can odd foods. The concept of implication contains both the fine detail of the familiar object or event and also the carrying forward of the process that the object or event implies.

The organism's interaction with the object is a process that takes time, although I prefer to say the process *makes* time. The process makes time by carrying forward. From the time it makes, one can derive the simple linear time in which simple things seem just to be.

The different avenues of therapy are different objects that carry forward. There are different kinds of *objects* and kinds of carrying forward. As food carries bodily process forward, so also do our physical motions, interpersonal actions, words, conceptual steps, dreams and our work with them, as well as other people's words and their actions toward us. These carry the same single system forward, but in different ways. They cannot replace each other.

The different avenues of therapy can be recognized in these kinds of carrying forward. Everyone can learn to focus, but everyone also dreams, feels, thinks, speaks, acts, interacts, moves, imagines, and sometimes spontaneously acts out. None of these avenues of therapy should be strange to us. Why make exclusive *methods* of therapy, each using only one of these, when every client has them all? It happens because we find it hard to learn how to respond along all of them.

Methods using different avenues of carrying forward can all be used on a client-centered baseline, and to seek process-steps. This changes them. Their conflicting rationales and styles drop away and they fit together, because as avenues of human process they were never separate.

For example, interpersonal responses are one important kind of carrying forward. An empathic response might add nothing to the content, but it is an interpersonal *object* that carries the body forward in an utterly different way than the same content would if felt or said alone.

We find focusing very powerful when done alone, but easier to do deeply when another person silently keeps us company (and receives anything we do or say). Here is a pure instance of interpersonal carrying forward! In silence only the receptive attention of another person is added. That alone is an irreplacable kind of carrying forward.

An inner object *or datum is also a carrying forward*. We have seen how the outer objects derive from process. The *inner objects* (and their time) are also created by the organismic process that they carry forward.

In ordinary action we see and feel the objects in the situation. When the "feeling" becomes an object, we say it *was* there all along. Actually this datum object is a new carrying forward made from the previous one.

"Unfelt feeling" is not a good concept. There was feeling in action. Then symbolic carrying forward made *a feeling datum*. That was not there before.

We can now clarify the fact that we change by feeling a feeling that was there but not felt. "Unfelt feeling" is contradictory, and "feeling one's feeling" is redundant. But these expressions do refer to common events we can now clarify: Why would a person change merely by becoming aware?

Feelings are not things like stones that can be buried and still exist in the same shape. The coming of a feeling datum is a carrying forward, a further and different living. People say, "Now that I know I feel this way, what can I do about it?" Usually they don't know. Neither does the therapist. It is very fortunate that the whole system is already changed in the new carrying forward that makes a *feeling* an object.

Theoretical proposition 6: The seeming thing we call an internal datum is a carrying-forward process. Its coming changes the body and its implicit further actions. Food is not simply a given. It is made into that *object* by the continuous bodily process it carries forward. So also, the seeming thingness of a feeling is its lasting through the process it carries forward.

After a new feeling, new actions may be implicit. A feeling is a change in what is further implied, which will make more change.

Sometimes what a feeling implies cannot occur. The implication is not carried forward and does not change further. Then the feeling is remade freshly, over and over, whenever the person lives in that situation physically or symbolically.

Then it seems no longer true that "feeling the feeling" is a change. Actually it is, but the feeling is an implication of further change that does not happen. The feeling is therefore formed again and again.

Feeling vs. felt sense. Feelings and emotions are *parts in* a situation. For example, anger comes in a certain slot in a story and carries it forward in a partial way. We are taught to count to 10 when angry, because the anger is *not* a sense of the *whole* situation. If we do what the anger implies, we may later be sorry. That is because the anger does not carry forward the whole situation. Therefore, the further actions the anger implies do not meet it all.

Ordinary feelings and the actions they imply carry forward only part of the situational whole. We see that easily in new situations. None of the usual feelings and their implied actions quite fit. New actions are needed. Such novel actions do not come from the recognizable emotions and feelings, since these *objects* are made in carrying the usual story forward in a familiar way.

Is there a way to have a *datum* of the *whole* implicit complexity? The felt sense (previously described) is that datum. We can see the difference when people move from a feeling to the felt sense. The feeling is made from (and understandable from) the known, formed story detail. But in the felt sense the implicit situation is a much larger whole.

The implicit situation as a felt sense is a single mesh from which endless detail can be differentiated: what happened to us, what someone did, why that troubled us or made us glad, what was just then also going on and made this especially good or bad, what we now need to do about it and with whom, why that is difficult, what usually happened in the past with others, how we feel about that and how we feel about feeling that way about it, what we sense others are thinking, why it's wrong and why it's right, and on and on.

Yet the felt sense from which all this can come is single, sensed as *that* bodily quality, there. The bodily felt sense is a new type of object or datum. The whole process of implication itself becomes a datum, a sensed *that*. The whole is changed by being carried forward by this new type of *object*.

To let the bodily sense of the whole implied context become a datum is a new type of carrying forward. Some people in all ages could do this, but it is new to most people.

Novel steps are also implicit. Because we have often observed certain bodily processes like digestion, we know the implicit next step. When we have often seen certain traditions and cultural routines, we know in advance what action a situation implies. Later we say it *was* implicit.

But something new could also carry forward and be what *was* implicit. With current concepts one cannot think clearly about novelty in bodily life and physics, but obviously the universe and evolutionary forms could not have developed if novelty had been impossible. The difficulty in thinking about novelty lies not in nature but in *the type of concept* that reduces everything to fixed units that can only be rearranged or reorganized to explain anything new. Genuine novelty is a puzzle for that kind of concept. The difficulty belongs to the kind of concept, not to physics or bodies.

Especially in modern urban society we often live ourselves into a new and odd situation. Such a situation *is* implicit actions that have never as yet been formed by anyone.

We know when routine actions will not suffice. How do we sense and appreciate the subtle oddity of a new situation? We could not, if we could only feel and think the familiar. But this is not so. When we feel "stuck," this stuckness is a sense of more, which corrects our attempts to say or do something usual. The stuckness *is* our sense of the puzzling situation, the implicit words and actions we have been unable to devise. The stuckness is a finely organized sense of why usual ways won't do, and of what would. The stuckness is an implication of . . . new next steps never as yet formed.

If the situation is new and odd, the implicit action has never existed. Yet it is implicit!

Theoretical proposition 7: An event that has never occurred before can be implicit. This often happens in creative thinking, in art, and in the process-steps of psychotherapy and focusing. The steps are new, but neverthe-

less they were *implicit in the physically experienced felt sense of the situation or problem.* The whole complexity of situation-feeling is implicit in bodily process. This includes whatever makes the situation difficult, and has made easy routine actions inappropriate. The body's implication (and, if a datum forms, the body's "feeling" of the situation) includes more organized complexity than we can as yet think, say, or act upon. There is no certainty that a process-step will come. But if one does, it will have a greater intricacy than we could have thought, said, or done before that step.

Theoretical proposition 8: The datum or object we call a felt sense exceeds in intricacy what we could previously think, say, or act upon. The old forms are implicit, but more organization is already involved that makes them inappropriate in very exact ways. The very coming of a felt sense as a datum is a carrying forward of this greater order. From the felt sense (in subsequent steps) one can form new and more finely tuned explicit words and actions that could not have been devised before.

"Direction." Let me show how this theoretical proposition leads "further." Living tissue is some way now, but it also *is* implicitly its subsequent events. We define and name it from knowing what it usually implies, as we define hunger by feeding. But actually the implicit is some event that carries forward. Any bodily process could be carried forward in a different way than before. The implicit is never *only* already formed. Like a situation that must be met, the implied action is not a fixed form.

Countless situational aspects and their linguistic and conceptual differentiations are implicit in the body. The familiar routines are a carrying forward of a vast complexity. They are further developments from earlier routines, which are even now still implicit in our bodies along with the later ones.

When we live oddly, the routinely formed actions and words are implicit, but now they do not carry the whole implicit bodily complexity forward. Our "stuck" body-sense is usually thought of as a feeling without words, or as "preverbal," but that is not correct. The felt sense does contain the language and the situational contexts of words. It is not *preverbal!* And it implies the new next steps of speech and action that have never as yet formed. The coming of the felt sense has already elaborated and further developed the implicit linguistic and situational system.

Now we understand theoretically how the body-sense can be so finicky about words used in focusing. We understand how new action and speech is more intricately implied by the body than we can define.

In therapy people without great verbal resources become raw poets, refashioning words to speak from process-steps. What comes freshly is often more intricate than ready phrases.

Theoretical proposition 9: A felt sense is not preverbal. Its forming and coming as a datum is a new living forward of the implicit complexity of situation and language. When we live oddly, the implicit acts and speech are silently altered. Language is always part of situational structure. The body "knows" (the felt sense is) the implicit complexity with its language. When we live, act, or speak oddly, further poetic novelty is already implicit. Therefore, a missing next step is not indeterminate, or unorganized, as so many people want to say. An implicit, missing next step is *more* finely organized than the routines, and that is why we cannot easily find or devise words or actions. Please note: In such a case the routines are still implicit, and can be done and said. But whatever was the implicit next step is still the implicit next step, even after we do or imagine the routines. That is how we know that they have not carried this implication forward.

An odd situation's implication is *more* organized than the usual routines and contains them. The novel implicit is not unrelated to familiar concepts, phrases, and actions. It includes these *and* the exact reasons that they will not suffice.

We arrive here at a new concept. Traditional thinking has only fixed form or open possibility; if a next step is implied, it is thought of as already formed. Or, if the next step is open, this is thought to be *indeterminate* and *less* ordered. We find instead that novel living is *more ordered* and includes old forms in a more demanding organization that makes them insufficient.

A new concept arises if we keep these two together, as we find them together: a more orderly, demanding implication *and* novelty. Indeed it is the greater orderliness of this implication that requires the novelty.

The body's implication of a next step is very familiar to everyone: inhaling implies exhaling; hunger implies feeding; cramped sitting implies stretching. Notice how the word *implies* is used in these phrases. From them you can also follow what the word does. Thus in odd situations the body implies phrases and actions that have never been formed. Then words can work as they never did before.

When this greater organization is carried forward, its further implication is also changed. New steps are implied and ensue. The process of steps is not determined within old forms. The process *directs itself*.

I will use the word *"direction"* in quotations to say this. Any body process has "direction": what will carry forward is very finely organized *and* just this organization is an implication of new steps. In many situations only new steps can carry the body forward.

Theoretical proposition 10: *Bodily implication of concepts, words, feelings, and actions has its own "direction": the next steps are not as yet formed, hence the "direction" is not definable. Nevertheless, it is a more demanding organization, inclusive of more order, than familiar steps can carry forward. The coming of a felt sense is itself this wider carrying forward, and the further steps show that.* A person's inner "client" is not a formed content but a process of self-responding. We cannot aid the development of this process by making impacts on the person that circumvent this self-responding and its steps.

A living event *is* not only what appears; "it" also *is* an implicit carrying forward.

"It" is like an unfinished poem that very finely and exactly requires its next line, which has never as yet existed. One can feel the next line implied from reading the lines up to this point. What is written already requires its further steps. But the written part will also change somewhat when the next lines come. The poem written so far implies its own change. There might be more than one way, but finding even one is not easy.

I cannot know what I did or said *to this person* if I don't see the person's inward reception of it, *and the further steps that might come from that.* Conversely, when I speak for myself to others I need them to wait and come with me along the steps that emerge. I need them to listen and follow my steps, and not to react to the first thing I say. They cannot know from one static bit what I mean, nor can I know without the process of steps. If I move in self-responding alone, the steps will not be those that can come with this person.

The listening and focusing process is of crucial *political* significance (Gendlin, 1984).

Once people are accustomed to being listened to, and know the inward checking of focusing, they are quite "spoiled" for the usual type of authority. They often express shock at the unhappy fact that most teachers, gurus, and leaders cannot listen. "How *could* ——— have told me this about me without asking me?!... He didn't even stop to find out what I was speaking from...."

What authorities say cannot get inside them in the old way, because "inside them" is a self-responding process of the sort I describe. Rather, the attempt at the old kind of authority is experienced as stupid. But also inside the individual, the representatives of external authority and merely imposed cognitive form must wait, listen, and dialogue with what comes in these more intricate steps. The inner authoritarian is no mere analogy but an actual representative of the form-imposing ways of "reality."

People who are accustomed to listening *can* be cowed by power, and do *not* necessarily develop political insights even about what is happening to them. There are many other dimensions to the political problem today. But listening and focusing are one vital dimension. A kind of human organization is coming, which would not again be the imposition of power by some over others.

Thomas Gordon's PET network has taught listening to half a million people and continues. Our network teaches focusing and listening to the general public. When these processes are regularly taught in the schools and are part of the social fabric, much can change that at present cannot. People will be able to be together in ways they now don't know of. Politics is human organization and not mere ideas or forms.

It is hard not to overstate or understate the importance of focusing. It makes process-steps very frequent and lets them be sought at any point. Without it therapy brings change haphazardly and rather rarely. Focusing makes specific what every mode of therapy intends but does not specify. The source of steps, the edge of awareness becomes *itself* a datum. The very coming of that datum is a crucial carrying forward. From that datum come entirely new and subtler steps of speech, thought, feeling, and action. It is a new development of the human individual.

But the other modes of carrying forward are of course equally human and irreplaceable.

6   Self-Concept and Identity: Overlapping Portions of a Cognitive Structure of Self

Desmond S. Cartwright
Mary Jane Graham

INTRODUCTION

Common sense tells us that there has to be much in common between self and identity, between Rogers's (1959b) construct of *self-concept* and Erikson's (1963) construct of *identity*, despite their being embedded in quite different theories. But what exactly *do* these two constructs have in common? And can we spell out in more detail just how they differ?

In this chapter, we will examine these questions and try to suggest some answers by translating both self-concept and identity into a common language based on cognitive theory.

After defining the major theoretical terms, we will propose that self-concept and identity are overlapping portions of a person's cognitive structure of self. Some categories in that structure belong both to the self-concept and to identity. The structure as a whole is hierarchical, with the self-concept partly occupying higher regions in the hierarchy.

In the second part of the chapter, we will report two empirical studies, the results of which tend to be consistent with the hypothesis of hierarchical structure. In the third part of the chapter, we will examine the sense of identity more closely, introducing a new construct—the *perceived social image*—and exploring theoretically the role it plays in relating identity to the self-concept.

Self-Concept, Identity, and Cognitive Structure

Self-Concept. Carl Rogers defines self-concept as follows:

> The organized, consistent, conceptual gestalt composed of perceptions of the characteristics of the "I" or "me" and the perceptions of the relationships of the "I" or "me" to others and to various aspects of life, together with the values attached to these perceptions . . . available to awareness . . . fluid and changing . . . a process, but at any given moment it is a specific entity which is at least partially definable in operational terms by means of Q-sort. (Rogers, 1959b, p. 200)

Identity. Erik Erikson has described a person's "sense of identity" in the following way:

> The sense of ego identity . . . is the accrued confidence that the inner sameness and continuity prepared in the past are matched by the sameness and continuity of one's meaning for others. . . .[Ego identity is] more than the sum of the childhood identifications. It is the accrued experience of the ego's ability to integrate all identifications with the vicissitudes of the libido, with the aptitudes developed out of endowment, and with the opportunities offered in social roles. (Erikson, 1963, p. 261)

Cognitive Structure. The cognitive theories underlying the present analysis chiefly concern the formation and function of categories. Three main types of theory have been formulated, as discussed by Carver and Scheier (1981) in their work on self-regulation. There are *instance* theories, in which the category is a simple collection of instances; *prototype* theories, in which the category is represented either by a best real instance, as in Rosch's theory (1973, 1978), or by a point in multidimensional space best representing the category (e.g., Posner, 1969); and *frequency-distribution* theories, in which a category is defined by frequency distributions of attributes (e.g., Bourne, 1981a).

Category constructs have recently been used by several theorists in the study of person-perception (see Bruner, 1957; Krull & Wyer,

1980; Ostrom, Lingle, Pryor, & Geva, 1980). From this point of view, person categories or trait categories are as applicable to perception of the self as they are to perception of other people.

Cognitive Interpretation of Self-Concept. The self-concept may be considered as a structure of cognitions about the self. In particular, it can be seen as a structure of categories about the self.

A category is assumed not merely to be a collection of instances but also to have a label referring to relevant attributes abstracted from instances or examples of the category. There may be best instances or prototypes. For example, a person might say: "I am resilient under stress." When asked to describe this quality in more detail, she replies: "Well, I have picked up my life again after a shattering divorce. That's the best evidence for resilience I know."

Notice that the example uses self-descriptive statements like those in the Butler-Haigh Q-sort (1954). The items in this Q-sort have been widely used, notably by Rogers in case studies (1954) to operationalize the self-concept. The Butler-Haigh Q-sort items were taken from statements made by clients in therapy at various stages of treatment. Typical statements include "I am different from others," "I am worthless," or "I usually like people." These are *characteristics* of the "I" or "me." More precisely, they are statements describing perceptions of such characteristics.

Rogers's use of the term *perceptions* seems to imply *conceptions* rather than sensory-perceptual representations. Rogers speaks of a "conceptual gestalt of perceptions of the characteristics of the 'I' or the 'me....'" Now, *characteristics* are not instances but relatively stable and distinctive features of a person that are likely to be manifested in particular instances. They are dispositions, like "strong-willed and venturesome." Clearly the person is not actually displaying a strong will all the time, but only on certain occasions. For example, a person cannot be strong-willed when asleep. And when awake the person may often be pliable and not venturesome at all. But her strong will may be definitely manifested in occasional instances, such as one weekend going it alone to the top of Long's Peak on the north face in a snowstorm.

A disposition refers to a tendency to behave in a certain way. But a conception of a disposition (or a "perception of a characteristic") is a cognition or representation that seems best described as a category. A category like "venturesome" sums up salient features of several remembered instances of venturesomeness. A subsequent similar event can be stored as another instance of that category.

Self-concept, then, can be seen as a collection of self-descriptive categories. It is a "conceptual gestalt" overall, but the elements of the gestalt consist of categories.

Levels of Generality. Notice that Q-sort items such as "I am different from others" refer to very general characteristics. Some less general statements also appear in the Q-sort, however, such as "I just cannot make up my mind," or "I am stubborn." During a therapy hour, a client would no doubt also mention particular instances of such characteristics. For example, a client might say "My mother wanted me to get rid of that sick dog, but I just wouldn't." This could be an instance of "stubbornness."

For such a person's self-concept, then, there is a hierarchy of categories. At the highest level of generality is "I am different from others." At a lower level are categories of "cannot make up my mind" and "stubborn." Quite possibly indecision and stubbornness are examples of the ways in which this person differs from others. He might say: "You see, on most things, I can't make up my mind. And yet I am so stubborn once an idea does get into my head. That's what makes me so different from other people."

These considerations suggest a slight but significant change in our understanding of the self-concept as a hierarchy of more and less general cognitive categories referring to characteristics of the self.

Categories and Instances. Rogers's theory of the self-concept seems to refer to categories at some level of generality. The person's life and memory, however, are comprised of actual events or instances. These are presumably stored as quasi–sensory-perceptual representations (memories, images) of events connected by some feature with a given category or characteristic.

Suppose a person says "I am not bold." This is a less general characteristic. It is also a class of representations (or a category of instances) that share an evidential feature: "In school I did not stand up to that bully that awful day"; "At parties I do not go up and speak to someone who attracts me"; "I could not go out in the dark and find out what was making that weird noise last night"; "I could not imagine myself going up to the president of the bank and telling him what I think."

Although Rogers's definition of the self-concept does not include the level of instances, this does not mean that he ignores instances. How could he, when his therapeutic intent is to understand fully the flavor of the client's experiences? But Rogers (1959b) explicitly distinguishes between experiences and self-concept. Experiences may or may not be symbolized accurately and incorporated into the self-concept. In present terms, this means that an instance may or may not be classified correctly into a relevant category.

Figure 6.1 offers a graphic illustration of the ideas expressed so far. Within dashed lines is the self-concept. Within dotted lines is identity, to which we turn next.

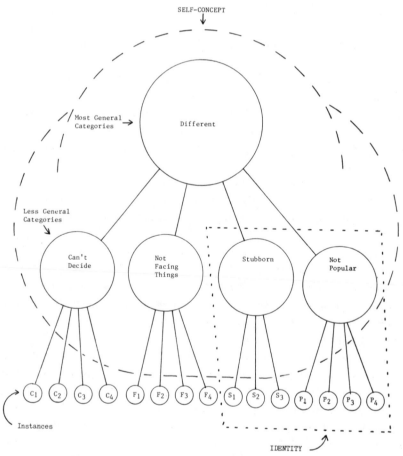

FIGURE 6.1. Representation of a cognitive structural model of the self-concept and identity.

Identity and Self-Concept in Cognitive Terms. How might we see the relationship between Erikson's construct of identity and Rogers's construct of the self-concept in Figure 6.1? Identity has previously been interpreted as a structure of actual and possible images of the self in various situations, roles, behaviors, identifications, and so on (Cartwright, 1979). It therefore consists, in part at least, of actual instances as represented in memory (memory images), and also categories at the lowest level of generality.

In Figure 6.1, identity is represented as a portion of the individual's total cognitive structure that overlaps with the self-concept. The overlapping portions are in the lower levels of generality. Identity and self-concept differ in that identity includes instances, and self-concept includes the most general categories.

Figure 6.1 suggests that some lower categories in the self-concept are not included in the sense of identity. This feature will be discussed in more detail below. Briefly, we suggest that characteristics such as "I feel I am not facing things" or "I can't make up my mind" are less likely to be included in identity than items like "stubborn," "not bold," or "I am a dominant person."

STUDIES OF THE COGNITIVE MODEL

Study One: Self-Described Categories and Imaged Instances

Instruments. Recent work with Erikson's theory has shown it possible to measure the sense of identity through imagery techniques. Specifically, the person is asked to let a verbal item evoke an image and then to rate the vividness of the evoked image on a seven-point scale. A typical item might be: "In a group discussion, stating and defending your beliefs on some political issue." Such an item reflects the identity element of faith or principled convictions that is the adult form of earlier childhood trust. A child's sense of trust comes with favorable resolution of nuclear conflicts in the first stage of psychosocial development, "trust versus mistrust." In Erikson's theory each such stage contributes an element to identity formation during adolescence. Briefly stated these elements are beliefs, service, aspirations, and occupational participation in society.

Through imagery techniques it has been possible to assess identity and several other major constructs in Erikson's theory, namely the

Freudian constructs of ego, superego, and id (Jenkins & Cartwright, 1982; Cartwright, Jenkins, Chavez, & Peckar, 1983). The assessment of self-concept has typically been carried out using self-descriptions either in questionnaire or Q-sort format. For the present study self-descriptive items were taken mainly from Butler's (1972, p. 152ff) account of follow-up factors in clients' Q-sorts. Fourteen very general items were included in a scale of high self-esteem (HSE). Several categories were assessed through less general items, some of which were adapted from the original Q-sort items. These categories were designed to cover the major constructs in Erikson's version of psychodynamic theory: namely, ego (EGO), superego (SUP), id derivatives (IDD), and identity (ITY). The complete self-descriptive instrument is shown in Table 6.1.

A different instrument was used to assess instances, namely the Study of Imagery (see Cartwright et al., 1983). Instances of all four less general categories were represented in items calling for images and ratings of their vividness, as described earlier.

For *ego*, a typical item might be "Successfully planning a party"; for *superego* it could be "Berating yourself for having done something wrong"; for *id derivatives*, it might be "Longing to hold someone in a romantic embrace"; for *identity*, it might be "Feeling good about a piece of work you have completed."

Subjects. The instruments were administered to 215 students in a sophomore class as part of their classwork. The modal age was 19; roughly 60 percent were female.

Results. Results are shown in Table 6.2. They will be examined in the context of four hypotheses.

1. *An instance i of a category A belongs to its own category A more clearly than it does to any other category K.* This notion is similar to Rosch's (1978) proposal that an instance belongs to its own category and is distinguishable from other categories. The idea of *belonging* may be interpreted as (1) *grouping* (in the sense of Gestalt psychology's unit formation in perception); as (2) *distance* in multidimensional scaling; or as (3) *correlation* between appropriate measures. The third meaning is used here.

It seems appropriate to compare categories at the same level of generality. Therefore, in Part B of Table 6.2, we compare an instance item's correlation with its own category scale, and its average correlation with the other three less general scales. For example, imagery instance item EGO 1 correlates $r = .105$ with the self-descriptive EGO category scale. Its average correlation with scales SUP, IDD, and ITY is $\bar{r} = .012$. For item EGO 2, the two values are $r = .155$ and $\bar{r} = .024$. Instance item S'EGO 1 should belong to the self-descriptive SUP category scale, since $r = .272$ and $\bar{r} = .004$.

There are 20 comparisons of an r- value with an $\bar{r}$- value. In each case the r- value exceeds the $\bar{r}$- value. If these comparisons could be considered statistically independent, a sign test would be significant with $p < .01$.

2. *A category belongs more to itself than it does to other categories at the same level of generality.* This hypothesis refers to the distinctiveness of a category or the goodness of its unit formation (again in Gestalt psychology terms). In psychometrics, it means that a measure of a category should have higher self-correlation (homogeneity-type reliability) than correlation with other categories.

In Table 6.2, Part A, this hypothesis receives support. Each of four alpha coefficients is substantially higher than the average correlation between a given category scale and the other scales at the same level of generality. Assuming four independent binary tests, $p < .062$ (the minimum) for this hypothesis.

3. *A category at a higher level of generality belongs more to itself than it does to categories at a lower level.* In Table 6.2, Part A, it may be seen that the mean absolute coefficient or correlation between HSE and four scales of lower generality is $\bar{r}_{abs} = .52$. The 99 percent confidence interval about this mean extends from .33 to .71. But for HSE, $\alpha = .83$, outside of the confidence interval. Assuming independence, this result is consistent with hypothesis 3.

4. *A category A belongs more to itself than to instances A_i of A.* In the psychometric form, this hypothesis means that the average of item-total correlations for items composing the category will be greater than the average of correlations between instance items A_i and the scale measure of category A.

In Table 6.2, Part B, the five instance items EGO 1–EGO 5 correlate with category scale EGO $\bar{r}_{AiA} = .200$. By contrast the average item-total correlation with scale EGO is $\bar{r}_{it} = .395$.

For SUP, the comparable values are .452 and .585; for IDD, .207

TABLE 6.1. Self-Descriptions

This survey gives 36 words or phrases with which a person might describe herself or himself. People differ on these things and there are no right and wrong answers.

Please simply indicate *how much each word or phrase describes you as you see yourself today*. Use the separate red answer sheet with the letters A–E having these meanings:

A. Least like me
B. Somewhat unlike me
C. In between
D. Somewhat like me
E. Most like me

1. Like people [a]
2. Determined person [b]
3. Do not contribute enough in life [c]
4. Criticize myself a lot [d]
5. Hopeless [a-]
6. Unemotional [e-]
7. No problems of self-control
8. Not sure of what my talents are [c]
9. Low self-esteem [a-]
10. Impatient [e]
11. Trust my spontaneous reactions to things [a]
12. Am easy on myself [d-]
13. Have a positive attitude toward myself [a]
14. Passionate
15. Feel depressed often

19. Have to drive myself to get things done [a-]
20. Often blame myself for things [d]
21. Am accomplishing quite a bit in life [c]
22. Calm [e-]
23. Despise myself [a-]
24. Unsure about my beliefs (political, religious, etc.) [c]
25. Poorly adjusted [a-]
26. Give up easily [b-]
27. Trust my emotions and feelings [a]
28. Forgiving toward myself [d-]
29. Afraid of what people think of me [a-]
30. Restless [e]
31. Emotionally mature [a]
32. Know who I am [c]
33. Easily make up my mind [b]

16. Know where I am going [c]
17. Tolerant [a]
18. Assertive [b]

Please pick one of the items above that is *most like you*. Would you briefly describe *two* recent experiences which show how that item applies to you.

(1) _____

_____

_____

(2) _____

_____

_____

SCORING:

The minus sign indicates item was reverse scored.

    a. Items for self-esteem.
    b. Items for ego.
    c. Items for identity.
    d. Items for superego.
    e. Items for id derivatives.

34. Responsible
35. Insecure inside myself [a-]
36. Am a failure [a-]

117

TABLE 6.2. Results of Preliminary Study, College Student Sample ($N = 215$)

A. Alpha coefficients,[a] intercorrelations, means, and standard deviations of five category scales.

| | Less General Category Scales | | | | More |
	EGO	SUP	IDD	ITY	HSE
EGO	.614	-.238	-.118	.585	.616
SUP		.775	.279	-.274	-.569
IDD			.525	-.268	-.315
ITY				.742	.570
HSE					.833
Means	15.14	11.80	12.95	21.43	55.82
S.D.s	2.62	3.44	2.80	4.36	7.20

B. Correlations between imagery instances and category scales.

| Imagery Instance | Self-Descriptive Category Scales | | | | $\bar{r}^{b}$ |
	EGO	SUP	IDD	ITY	
EGO 1	.105	-.100	-.028	.163	.012
EGO 2	.155	-.057	.028	.100	.024

EGO 3	.111	-.057	-.101	.130	-.009
EGO 4	.385	-.081	-.057	.303	.055
EGO 5	.246	-.036	-.046	.202	.040
S'EGO 1	-.098	.272	.219	-.110	.004
S'EGO 2	-.047	.580	.154	-.075	.011
S'EGO 3	-.104	.491	.173	-.173	-.035
S'EGO 4	.162	.336	-.003	.123	.094
S'EGO 5	-.118	.580	.144	-.163	-.046
ID 1	-.065	.157	.275	-.018	.025
ID 2	.099	-.028	.096	.140	.070
ID 3	.069	.082	.075	.036	.062
ID 4	-.296	.281	.293	-.306	-.107
ID 5	-.129	.325	.295	-.158	.013
IDENT 1	.115	.094	-.026	.120	.061
IDENT 2	.162	-.024	-.067	.173	.024
IDENT 3	.283	-.035	-.191	.364	.019
IDENT 4	.313	-.115	-.049	.323	.050
IDENT 5	.173	-.006	-.023	.274	.047

[a] Alpha coefficients in main diagonal of correlation matrix

[b] The values of F are average correlations between an instance item and the three self-descriptive scales which are not in that item's category.

and .320; for ITY, .251 and .485. All differences are in the expected direction, and a sign test of significance, assuming independence, yields $p = .062$.

Conclusion from Study One. The data obtained appear to be consistent with the overall hypothesis of a hierarchical structure of categories in self-concept and of categories and instances pertaining to the construct of identity. How do we know that the "hierarchical structure" contains categories at different levels of generality? Study Two addresses this question.

Study Two: Judgments of Generality

Aims of the Study. The notion of *generality* is unclear. It could mean simply the author's opinion. To examine the intersubjective validity of such a term, a large sample of respondents were asked to make paired-comparison judgments of generality.

Subjects. Students in a single class responded to items presented on an overhead projector and spoken by the instructor.

Instructions. In order to ensure common understanding of the word *general* the judges were first instructed as follows: "According to the Oxford American Dictionary, the word *general* means of or affecting all or nearly all; not partial or particular."

Next, instructions specific to the judgment task were given as follows: "You will be shown eight pairs of statements, an A and a B statement in each pair. Your task is to judge which statement of the pair is more general,

$$A \underline{\hspace{2cm}} or$$
$$B \underline{\hspace{2cm}} ."$$

Materials. The eight pairs of statements were all taken from the Butler-Haigh Q-sort. The point of using these materials was to see whether that Q-sort contains variations in category generality.

Results. The judgments were tabulated according to the proportion of judges choosing a statement as the more general one of its pair. These results are shown in Table 6.3.

TABLE 6.3. Paired-Comparison Judgments of Which Statement of a Pair is More General as a Description of Self (N=309)

Statement		Proportion Saying Statement is More General
1A.	I am not assertive.	.75
1B.	All you have to do is insist with me, and I give in.	.25
2A.	I am responsible for my troubles.	.11
2B.	I am a responsible person.	.89
3A.	My personality is attractive to the opposite sex.	.07
3B.	I have an attractive personality.	.93
4A.	I despise myself.	.35
4B.	I am worthless.	.65
5A.	I put on a false front.	.53
5B.	I am no one. Nothing seems to be me.	.47
6A.	Self-control is no problem for me.	.78
6B.	It is not difficult to control my aggression.	.22
7A.	I am likable.	.79
7B.	I am liked by most people who know me.	.21
8A.	I have to protect myself with excuses, with rationalizing.	.19
8B.	I have the feeling that I am just not facing things.	.81

In all pairs except 4 and 5, the proportion judging one statement more general is significant at $p < .01$.

Conclusion. Paired-comparison judgments made by a large sample of judges show that there are different levels of generality in self-descriptive categories as reflected in statements used in the Butler-Haigh Q-sort.

Discussion of the Studies

The studies above, as well as several others conducted, tend to support a cognitive structural model of the self-concept. Logical, psychometric, and judgment approaches all suggest that "characteristics of the 'I' and the 'me'" vary in generality.

The item "Know where I am going" was earlier judged to reflect a sense of identity and was part of a scale to measure that sense (see Table 6.1). The centrality of this item reflects the importance of identity as a portion of the self-concept. Yet the role of identity in the total cognitive structure goes beyond the self-concept, especially in imaged instances. Moreover, the sense of identity also involves constructs of quite a different kind than straightforward "perceptions of characteristics of the 'I' and the 'me.'" This topic will be addressed in the next section of the chapter.

THE SENSE OF IDENTITY

Sameness and Continuity in Self-Concept

Erikson's description or definition of the sense of identity, as quoted at the beginning of this chapter, has many parts. For the present we shall concentrate on the first part only, the confidence that inner sameness is matched by the sameness of one's meaning for others. Even this one part of the definition is complicated enough, so we will break it down and examine first the notion of sameness and continuity, both as sensed by the individual and as seen by other people. Then we will ask how it is that the person senses a match (or mismatch!) between her inner sameness and the sameness of the meaning she has for others.

A Sense of Sameness and Continuity. My sense of sameness means the confidence I have that I am the same person who went to sleep last night in this room, the same person who had a twenty-eighth birthday three weeks ago, the same one who was earlier planning a ski trip to Vail during the break and who now gets the gear ready for that trip today.

My sense of continuity may stretch back to earliest childhood, to memories of people and places where I spent happy days at play. I remember how I felt when I was temporarily lost in a big city and how on occasion I get the same kind of abandoned, scared feeling if I lose my way in the mountains while cross-country skiing.

Memory and Sameness. The sense of continuity and sameness resides in memories, items of a person's history. There is a flow from past to present. Sally is presently employed in the bank partly because she applied for that job last year. She qualified because of her grades in college or high school. If Tom is District Attorney today, it is partly because Tom passed the bar exam five years ago and entered law school three years before that.

Sally and Tom both recall their work in school—taking exams, filling out application forms, and so on. They remember doing those things and know that the person they now call "I" is the same person who did all the things that led up to the present position.

Sameness and Self-Concept. Your sense of inner sameness and continuity is an important feature of your self-concept. The statement "I am an assertive person" means "I have been, am now, and expect to continue being a person who is assertive." It implies continuity in that characteristic. When Rogers says that the self-concept consists of perceptions of the characteristics of the "I" or the "me," he means that the characteristics are pretty much continuous.

An important part of our sense of inner sameness, then, is given by the particulars about ourselves that do remain the same. My name, body shape, agility, sharpness of vision, and so on, remain the same over fairly long periods of time. These and other characteristics represented in my self-concept provide the content and evidence for sameness.

Our Sameness and Continuity for Others

Other People Have Memories Too. The sameness that we know through our own memory is not available to other people. How do they identify us?

Erikson emphasizes the importance of sameness and continuity in our meaning to others. Other people have their own memories about us. They recognize us as the same person from day to day by our appearance.

Acquaintances may say such things as: "Hi, Manuel. How's it going?" When they get the name right it means they remember correctly what your name is and that they have seen you before. They also imply an interest in the continuity of your life, because here they are asking about the most recent period in your life: "How's it going?"

Friends often treat us with more detailed evidence of recognition. If one says, "You seem low today," it means she knows my usual level of mood and notices a difference today: it is lower than usual. In providing this rapid acknowledgement of my usual state and today's temporary difference, a friend confirms that I am the same person whose usual mood she well remembers.

Plans Together.   Friends and business acquaintances may also confirm the continuity of their plans together.

"Hi! You ready for the big game? Did you find out if Joe can make it? Did you pick up the tickets yet?"

Such remarks tell me I am the same person who started these plans with my friends. They tell me that my friends are expecting me to do my part, carry out in fact the things I had agreed to do in order to complete the group plan. They remember that I am the one who made these plans with them.

Abilities and Interests.   Erikson says that ego identity puts what a person can do with what he or she is interested in doing together with what opportunities exist in society to do those things. Abilities and interests are characteristics of a person, and opportunities arise in part when other people see these abilities and interests.

An ability is a potential to learn a skill and accomplish certain goals or complete a particular kind of task. One child may be very good with hands and feet in team sports. Another may be good at writing. Another creates designs in paints and clay and colored paper. Together they organize a group to promote and support the school soccer team, with brochures and posters for advertisements. Each one in such a working group has particular abilities that can help the group achieve its goal.

Of course a child may have the ability but not want to do that kind of thing. He or she just may not be interested. Or sometimes people lose interest in something. If you are very good at pool but do not wish to play any more, you have lost interest.

Other people often know what a person can do (ability) and also what a person wants to do (interest). Sometimes they are surprised when they find out that a person has lost interest. But they know it is the same continuous individual who still has the ability but now has changed interests.

Social Image.   What other people know about your abilities and interests is part of your social image. A social image of Raoul exists in the minds of the people who know him.

When a school class wants to do a project, teachers and children think about who would be good at doing particular jobs. They need someone to build the scenery for a play, perhaps, someone with carpentry skills. Then someone is needed to design costumes. Someone else is needed to make the costumes. Someone has to play the leading role; others are needed for different parts. They try to pick the most suitable person in each case.

Often, when planning such a project, people actually ask a question such as: "Now, who could we get to do the scenery? Who is good at carpentry?" Each member of the group scans his or her memory for the social image of a person who is suitable for the particular requirements, carpentry in this case. That social image must contain at least a name (such as Raoul) and the knowledge that that person has carpentry skills and interests.

A social image contains the characteristics of a person as perceived by others. As William James said of the "social self" (James, 1890, p. 294), there are as many social images of an individual as there are other people who recognize him. If only 20 people recognize me, then there are only 20 social images of me. If 50 people recognize me, then there are 50 social images of me.

Each social image will contain perceptions of various characteristics such as appearance, abilities, and interests.

Sameness and Continuity of Our Meaning for Others. When Erikson stresses the importance of continuity in our meaning for others, he seems to be talking about what we have called the "social image." Is there a corresponding construct in Rogers's theory?

Rogers has written that one portion of the self-concept includes "perceptions of the relationships of the 'I' or 'me' to others…" (Rogers, 1959b, p. 200). These relationships presumably have recognizable continuity and sameness over time. The notion of the "I" and the "me" is a reference to George Herbert Mead's famous distinction between these two aspects of self. Mead discussed in detail the difference between the "I," which is aware of social "me," and the "me" itself. The "me" is the object of the "I's" awareness. It is very much a part of society, a physical body functioning with various characteristic abilities and tendencies in the person's social milieu (Mead, 1967, p. 173ff).

In Rogers's formulation, we are told quite explicitly that it is the person's own conceptions (perceptions) that are important. He does not refer to the social image directly; rather he says that a portion of the self-concept consists of perceptions of the characteristics of the "me" and of the relationships of the "I" and the "me" to others. So we might conclude that Rogers considers a person's self-concept to include perceptions of social characteristics.

Rogers therefore alludes to the social image, but, as it were, from the vantage point of the self. By contrast, Erikson is explicitly concerned with social opportunities and with the social image of a person.

Matching Inner Sameness with Sameness in Our Meaning for Others

According to Erikson, our sense of identity is the accrued confidence that our sameness is matched by the sameness of our meaning for others. How can a person develop such confidence? It is not enough that other people have an accurate social image of a person, one that matches that person's self-concept. Such an image would be fine in itself, but it does not specify whether the person knows what social image others have of him.

We seem to lack yet one important link in the chain: the individual's perception of the social image that others have of him. The individual must have some knowledge of it, some conception of what others think about her.

Perceived Social Image. One way to find the missing link is to propose that the person not only has a self-concept but also a concept of her social image. That is, the person perceives or has a conception of the way others see her. We will call this the *perceived social image.*

The Sense of Identity as Confidence in a Match between Self-Concept and Perceived Social Image. The confidence that one's inner sameness is matched by the sameness of meaning for others can now be expressed as a feeling of certainty that one's self-concept is matched in relevant matters by one's perceived social image. That is, I am confident of a match if what I think about myself coincides with what I understand you to think about me.

Figure 6.2 displays relationships among several constructs. The person represented in this figure works at a steel mill, is married, and is an expert fisherman. Three of the people who recognize him are represented in the figure: his wife, the mill foreman, and his fishing

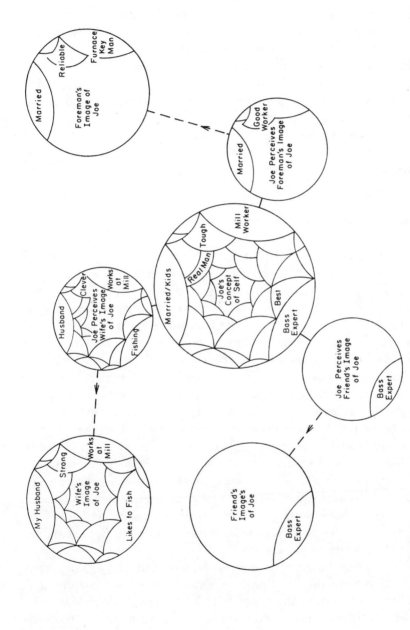

FIGURE 6.2. Representation of one person's self-concept, three social images of the person, and the related perceived social images.

friend. Each has a social image of Joe, but each image is different. The friend knows Joe only as a fishing companion. The foreman knows Joe only as a steel worker, and also as a married man. Joe's wife knows Joe in a good deal more detail, though sometimes her image is hazy. For instance, she does not differentiate the kind of fisherman he is, but she does have more detail on the meaning of his work.

In each case Joe's perceived social image is pretty accurate. The crucial concern, however, is the similarity between what he perceives as the social image and how he sees himself, his self-concept. In each case the perceived social image and the relevant portion of the self-concept appear to match quite well. As far as the figure shows, then, Joe apparently must be confident of the match between his inner sense of sameness and the sameness and continuity of his meaning for others. In other words he has a strong sense of identity.

The Self-Concept and Identity

A Cognitive Structure Model. Earlier in the chapter we advanced the position that the self-concept consists of a structure of concepts, categories, and instance classes. The levels of generality range from the most general concept (such as self-esteem) to the least general class of particular instances (such as the class of instances in which Joe plays and catches a crafty bass). It was suggested then that identity consists of one set of such categories and classes of instances. Now we must expand these notions to include the role of perceived social images.

As suggested in Figure 6.2, it seems useful to suppose that the perceived social image consists of concepts, categories, and instance classes pertaining to what other people think. Possibly there is one structure for each perceived social image; but perhaps some measure of assimilation occurs between structures: that is, the person develops a generalized concept of how he or she appears to others. Such a concept would have the same three-dimensional structure as the self-concept: the perceived image would be scanned for similarity with relevant portions of the self-concept, and those relevant portions would mainly consist of the identity portion.

We may now imagine two circles of the kind that Rogers has often used in depicting the relationship between the self-structure and experience (see Rogers, 1951, pp. 526, 527). One circle contains the categories (self-descriptive statements) of characteristics in the self-concept that are also tagged as relevant to identity. Another circle contains the categories of characteristics in the perceived social image. The sense of identity is stronger if the two circles overlap more closely.

An Implication of the Model. If we have a representation of the categories of characteristics in the self-concept, and if there really are some that overlap with identity, it seems likely that they would be distinguishable. Moreover, we might expect that they would be distinguishable by the readiness with which they can enter into other people's social images and hence be reflected back in some way to form the perceived social image. Can we find such a distinguishable subset?

Toward a Test of One Implication. After preliminary work it was decided to use the set of 100 items that Rogers and others had used in several researches (Rogers & Dymond, 1954).

There appeared to be a distinguishable subset of items that referred to characteristics that might be more obvious to other people. Within this subset were included the following: "I am a competitive person," "I am shy," "I am assertive," "I am a hostile person," "All you have to do is insist with me and I give in."

By contrast there appeared to be a subset that would likely not be obvious. These included: "I usually feel driven," "I don't trust my emotions," "It's pretty tough to be me," "I have the feeling that I am just not facing things," and "I try not to think about my problems."

In a brief study of 30 judges (all college seniors in a class on personality), all five "obvious" items mentioned above were judged to be obvious by 80 percent or more of the judges. The five "not obvious" items were so judged by 83 percent or more of the 30 judges.

Hypotheses about Obvious and Nonobvious Characteristics. If a majority of judges agree upon distinguishable sets of more and less obvious characteristics, then it further seems likely that these characteristics would also show up more easily in an individual's perceived social image. This could be tested by comparing the time taken to throw a Q-sort using such items to represent a particular social image with the time taken to throw a Q-sort consisting of items that are judged not obvious. Alternatively, the accuracy of a perceived social image should be greater when it and the social image are described in terms of the set of obvious items.

Testing the Overall Model of Identity. Once suitable sets of items are secured, it should be possible to design studies that compare the degree of match between self-concept and perceived social image with other indices of strength in the sense of identity. These might include the interview designed by Marcia (1966), the questionnaire described by Constantinople (1969), or the imagery vividness scale of identity (Cartwright et al., 1983).

CONCLUSION

We have compared Rogers's construct of self-concept with Erikson's construct of identity by formulating both as portions of a hierarchically organized structure. The structure consists of categories differing in levels of generality. Lower levels categorize discrete perceptions, while higher levels refer to more abstract characteristics of the individual. The self-concept encompasses all levels of categories, but excludes representation of specific experiences. Identity is made up of "obvious" lower-level categories and imaged examples.

Erikson's definition of identity includes the idea that a person's "inner sameness and continuity" are "matched by" the "sameness and continuity of one's meaning for others." We have suggested that categories common to self-concept and identity provide "inner sameness" and are matched (or not matched) by categories in another cognitive structure, namely the individual's understanding of how he or she is viewed by others. We refer to this view as a *social image* and to the individual's conceptualization of that view as the *perceived social image.*

It is critical that the perceived social image be included in attempts to understand the difference between identity and the self-concept. The self-concept is a superordinate construct including many aspects of identity, while identity also involves the perceived social image.

7   The Fully Functioning Person: Theory and Research

Julius Seeman

A remarkable aspect of the personality theory evolved by Carl Rogers has been his insistent emphasis upon the higher reaches of human potentiality. Theorists from the clinical tradition derive their data from their close and intimate observation of troubled and conflicted persons. Thus many clinical theorists hesitate to venture too far into the realm of optimal functioning. Harry Stack Sullivan, for example, lamented wistfully that he could not say much about human maturity because his patients left him just as they were approaching that stage. Freud suggested that the goal of psychoanalysis was to transform neurotic misery into plain everyday unhappiness. Rogers, on the other hand, has insisted on looking within the troubled musings of his clients and comprehending the durable capacities forming there. In the end he could see these capacities in action. From this he has given us his perceptions and visions of what is possible in human development.

The Rogerian concept of the fully functioning person serves as the starting point of a wider exploration in this chapter. What I shall present here is some sampling of the broad canvas of theory and inquiry concerning optimal functioning, including the work of Rogers. Such a review will reveal the confluence of concepts that have been advanced and the confirmations afforded by empirical study. We shall see, then, how the work of Rogers and of others touch similar dimensions of human experience and accent the central themes that characterize personal integration.

As to the sequence of topics in this chapter, I shall begin with a summary of the two major statements concerning optimal functioning made by Rogers, then present the other conceptualizations, and finally review some empirical studies that shed light on the characteristics of personality integration. If we confront the theories of optimal functioning with the experimental evidence, we shall be closer to knowing what is so about the nature of human potentialities.

A Preliminary Note on Terminology

The domain of the fully functioning person has not yet fully found itself; it is a domain as yet so unsettled as to have produced several sets of terms to describe virtually the same phenomenon. And so this review will include a number of constructs that encompass essentially the same meaning, as, for example, the self-actualizing person (Goldstein, 1939; Maslow, 1954), personal soundness (Barron, 1954), positive mental health (Jahoda, 1958), personality integration (Seeman, 1959), the concept of competence (White, 1959), the fully functioning person (Rogers, 1963b), and the maturing person (Heath, 1965).

If there is diversity in all this terminology, there is no corresponding ambiguity in meaning. All the foregoing constructs reflect a common theme, namely, the description of persons at the upper end of the human effectiveness continuum. What is more, there is a remarkable degree of underlying consistency in the theory and research that support the use of these constructs. As this review will reveal, there are basic continuities in definition and in data that give substance to the meaning of these terms and give promise that a sturdy body of knowledge is in the process of development.

ROGERS'S VIEW OF THE FULLY FUNCTIONING PERSON

Carl Rogers, perhaps more than any other clinical theorist, has paid attention to the development of a theory of optimal human functioning. One of his early papers was entitled "The Concept of the Fully Functioning Person" (Rogers, 1963b). Oddly enough, though the paper was written in 1953, it was not published until a decade later. In my judgment, this paper is one of the most compelling descriptions of the optimally integrated person.

In the paper, Rogers emphasizes three broad attributes of fully functioning persons. Such persons are open to their experience, they live in an existential fashion, and they trust their direct organismic experience as a basis for choice and action. A passage from Rogers's near-poetic description of the fully functioning person will convey the flavor of his account:

> He is able to experience all of his feelings, and is afraid of none of his feelings. He is his own sifter of evidence, but is open to evidence from all sources; he is completely engaged in the process of being and becoming himself, and thus discovers that he is soundly and realistically social; he lives completely in this moment, but learns that this is the soundest living for all time. He is a fully functioning organism, and because of the awareness of himself which flows freely in and through his experiences, he is a fully functioning person. (Rogers, 1963b, p. 22)

There are two elements in the foregoing description that warrant special attention, because they foreshadow so clearly the findings of subsequent empirical study. One element concerns the pervasive organismic processes to which Rogers refers in describing the fully functioning person. In this respect Rogers has captured the conception of the comprehensive human system that has come to characterize descriptions of the highly integrated person.

The second element in Rogers's description is a corollary of the first, namely the free flow of information within the person. Rogers's description suggests that the optimally integrated person has developed the capacity to receive and process the data of immediate experience to the fullest extent and thus has the best possible basis for decision and action. The probability of effective behavior is thus maximized.

The next significant theoretical contribution that Rogers made to the literature of personality integration is derived from his study of the therapeutic process. In his chapter "A Process Conception of Psychotherapy," Rogers (1961) tracks the successive stages of effective functioning as observed in psychotherapy by noting the movement toward awareness of self and the progressively greater access to the data of immediate experience.

Rogers approached the task by studying the basic data of the therapeutic process as captured by recordings. Out of this study he was able to discern a sequence of seven stages that appeared to characterize movement in psychotherapy. The general direction of movement went from fixity to change, from rigid structure to fluidity. Thus the most primitive stage was marked by rigidity and remoteness of experiencing, a lack of communication with one's inner experience and feelings. The successive stages were all in the direction of movement toward communication of self, capacity for immediacy of experience, and full living in the present.

An illustrative descriptiton of the sixth stage may convey the essential components of this advanced position. Some characteristics that Rogers uses to describe this stage are as follows:

> A feeling flows to its full result
> A present feeling is directly experienced with immediacy and richness
> This immediacy of experiencing...[is] accepted (Rogers, 1961, p. 145)

It is evident from the foregoing account that Rogers is describing not only a sequence of stages in therapy but, more fundamentally, a portrait of increasingly effective functioning in general development. It is evident also that there are close connections between his process conception of psychotherapy and his description of the fully functioning person. They share the same emphases on fullness and freedom to experience, the quality of being in touch with self, and the consequent utilization of oneself as a source of information. Rogers maintains a theoretical consistency that integrates both theory and practice in his approach to personality and psychotherapy.

OTHER THEORIES OF OPTIMAL FUNCTIONING

Maslow

By any criteria, Maslow (1954) must be regarded as one of the foremost modern theorists in the area of self-actualization. His study of self-actualizing persons represented one of the early efforts to derive an empirical analysis of the attributes of psychological health in persons. And though his study was more an observational description than a controlled study, the characteristics he observed hold up remarkably well in the light of later studies.

In Maslow's list of attributes, the first captures a central facet of the integrative process, one that was destined to be validated again and again by subsequent researchers. This attribute was "more efficient perception of reality and more comfortable relations with it." Maslow not only emphasized here the central role of reality perception but specified *efficient* perception, a feature that turns out to be particularly descriptive of high-functioning persons.

Maslow's second criterion—"acceptance (self, others, nature)"—turns out to be equally accurate in the light of subsequent discovery. This criterion is one of the most frequently observed indices of positive functioning. In particular, a positive view of self stands out as a hallmark of self-actualizing persons, as I shall indicate more fully later in this chapter.

Many of Maslow's further listings divide naturally into two larger categories—those concerned with the quality of interpersonal relationships and those concerned with aspects of individual personality characteristics. Illustrations of this latter category include a sense of autonomy, spontaneity, enjoyment of solitude and detachment, freshness of appreciation, and a principled ethical sense. With respect to interpersonal relationships, Maslow suggests that there is a well-developed sense of empathy for other persons in general and a capacity for intimacy in specific relationships.

Maslow took care in describing self-actualizing persons not to make them unreal paragons of virtue. He recognized that such persons were not free of conflict, guilt, hostility, or other emotions of less than noble status. What did distinguish the high-functioning persons, however, was their resilience, flexibility, and capacity to cope with circumstances. The capacity to deal with adversity was in fact one of the distinguishing marks of the self-actualizing person.

Psychoanalytic Ego Psychology

One of the major developments in psychoanalytic theory has been the emergent emphasis on ego psychology. The early period of psychoanalytic theory had emphasized the power of the instinctual or drive-related aspect of human functioning and set severe limits on the power of reason and choice. Ego psychology evolved in growing recognition that human personality had a more reality-oriented and adaptive side, and that persons had resources to cope, to thrive, to grow. Ego psychology postulated a higher ceiling for human development, with more room to consider the integrative possibilities in human nature. In this connection I shall consider here the work of Hartmann, Erikson, and Loevinger.

Hartmann. One of the earliest and most productive ego psychology theorists was Heinz Hartmann (1939, 1958). Perhaps the most notable contributions advanced by Hartmann were built upon his postulation of a conflict-free ego sphere. The significance of this position rested in the fact that it challenged a core element of psychoanalytic theory, and so its effects radiated pervasively to many other concepts in psychoanalysis.

It will be recalled that Freud (1923) had pictured an ego that was a weak derivative of the id, an ego whose sole energy was borrowed from the id. Such a formulation necessarily placed the person's reality resources in a position secondary to the more primitive life of the impulses. Hartmann's formulation constituted a fundamental revision of Freud's concept. The suggestion that aspects of the ego had an autonomous status meant that a person's potential for development was not anchored to impulse nor limited by it, but rested more centrally in intellective, reality-based resources available to the person.

In reasoning thus, Hartmann did not ignore the power of irrational forces in the individual's personality, nor did his theory in any way imply absence of human conflict. What he did argue was that an effectively functioning, integrated person had the capacity to endure conflict and even to grow in the process. As he put it, "the rational must incorporate the irrational as an element in its design" (1939, p. 314). The profound meaning of this statement must be recognized for what it is—a theoretical *tour de force* that inverted the classical Freudian formulation of the id-ego relationship and made possible a theoretical base for an ego psychology that could hospitably envision the higher reaches of human functioning.

According to Hartmann, two of the central functions of a mature ego were adaptation and synthesis. These functions were complementary in nature, encompassing as they did the outer and inner dimensions of a person's relationship to self and others. Concretely, adaptation was the process of relating to the outer world in competent and harmonious ways, while synthesis consisted of the inner organizing and integrating activity of the ego. In his treatment of adaptation Hartmann expanded the earlier psychoanalytic emphasis on intrapsychic dynamics and brought out the importance of the environmental context in considering adaptive processes. He asserted that adaptation could be defined only with reference to specific environmental settings. Through this emphasis, he foreshadowed more recent formulations of personality in terms of interactions between person and environment.

Hartmann put forth the phenomenon of synthesis as a basic activity of the ego, the organizing function that blended disparate demands and led to integration of thought and action. Hartmann's contributions were important, not only in their own right, but also through their impact upon the emergent field of ego psychology. In particular, his emphasis upon the positive aspects of human potentiality is evident to this day.

Erikson. Erik Erikson, in his volume *Insight and Responsibility* (1964), has a chapter entitled "Human Strength and the Cycle of Generations." It is a chapter in the emerging tradition of the newer psychology, one that flows directly from the kind of affirmative emphasis set by Hartmann. Erikson was able to integrate the psychoanalytic domains of structure and development with explicit emphasis on developmental processes.

The result is a deepened portrayal of the human potentialities to which developmental process may lead. Here too, as with Hartmann, one finds an expanded perspective. Erikson employed a set of constructs not limited to constraints of classical psychosexual theory, but extending rather to broad reaches of human conduct. I will not sketch the entire developmental scheme, but focus mostly on the developmental expression of mature persons as Erikson describes them, calling upon the earlier qualities only as needed. It is to be understood, however, that Erikson saw the developmental sequence as a set of contingencies with the mature stages dependent upon adequate mastery of the earlier ones.

The characterological attributes assigned by Erikson to the mature person include love, care, wisdom, and generativity. These qualities have an interwoven and sequential character that may not be immediately evident. For Erikson, love is "the mutuality of mates and partners in a shared identity" (1964, p. 128). Moreover, it is a "mutuality of devotion forever subduing the antagonisms inherent in divided function" (1964, p. 129). Erikson's reference to antagonisms embodies his view that in the phenomena of love the sexes are bipolar in function and hence more separable than in some of the ego functions such as competence. Mature love, then, transcends the bipolarity and is characterized by reciprocal giving. It is here that love and care meet, for care is "the widening concern for what has been generated by love" (1964, p. 131). It is both a cogenerational and an intergenerational phenomenon, linked in the latter case to the continuity of the species itself.

It is at this point that generativity comes most clearly into play, for it is the impulse to creativity, the need to bring into the world ideas, works, and persons. Inherent in this characteristic is humankind's deepest social essence, the need for connection to other persons and the need to be needed. Thus, at the mature level of development, the accent is on special qualities of interpersonal relationships that permit both intimacy and individuality and that provide the social nourishment requisite to human continuity.

Loevinger. Loevinger (1976) follows in the tradition of modern psychoanalytic ego psychology, and in doing so has made a unique contribution. She combines the classic psychoanalytic categories of structure and development in such a way as to derive a novel blend. Whereas classical psychoanalytic theory traced successive stages of development by focusing on psychosexual changes, Loevinger mapped successive states of ego development. A further contribution of significance in Loevinger's work was her combination of a conceptual and empirical approach to the charting of developmental sequences. She operationalized a scale of ego development by means of a sentence completion test (Loevinger & Wessler, 1970). A considerable body of research in ego development was thereby fostered. Since the emphasis of this essay is on optimal development, I shall describe only the latter stages of Loevinger's developmental scale.

For practical purposes, the Autonomous Stage (I-5) represents the optimal level attained except in rare cases. The autonomous person deals with life in much more differentiated ways than is the case in earlier developmental stages. Antonomous persons are able to perceive the multiplicity of roles through which persons live and to meet these demands through flexible behavior. They not only recognize their own need for selfhood, but also acknowledge the need for autonomy of others. Feelings are accepted and experienced, including pain and sorrow as well as joy. Such persons are socially aware and realistic.

The final stage, the Integrated Stage (I-6), is much less well delineated by Loevinger. She alludes to Maslow's description of the self-actualizing person, but views this stage as one rarely attained and difficult to describe. On this basis, the practical ceiling of development for most persons is represented by the Autonomous Stage.

Loevinger makes no claim that ego development is synonymous with positive mental health; indeed, she goes to some lengths to insist on distinctions between the two. For example, she suggests that positive mental health can characterize children, yet necessarily they would be at the earlier stages of ego development. But there is no gainsaying the relationships between the two broad concepts of ego development and positive mental health or personality integration. Our own studies (Seeman, 1983) show that attributes akin to Loevinger's advanced ego development stages distinguish high-functioning children from less fully functioning children even at early developmental levels. Ego development must then not be viewed as chronological absolutes— Loevinger asserts this fact also—but as developmental levels that help us understand the direction of human maturity.

General Conceptualizations

In this section I wish to present a sampling of the significant general analyses of optimal human functioning: those analyses that are not imbedded in a specific theory of personality. I have included in this group the work of Marie Jahoda (1958), Brewster Smith (1950, 1959, 1966, 1968, 1969, & 1978), and Robert White (1959).

Jahoda. The work of Jahoda (1958) represents perhaps the most comprehensive early analysis of the characteristics subsumed by the concept of positive mental health. She approached her task by surveying extensively the relevant literature that dealt conceptually or empirically with the topic of positive functioning. A perusal of the reference list makes it clear that very little empirical research on the topic had yet been done before 1958. There appear to be about five references to empirical research in a bibliography of 90 items. Yet it must be said that in the list Jahoda had available the most prominent and authoritative writers, as, for example, Gordon Allport, Ruth Benedict, Eric Erikson, Kurt Goldstein, Heinz Hartmann, Henry Murray, and many other well-known writers in the area. Thus it may be said that Jahoda was in a position to distill the contemporary understanding of positive mental health.

In her work, Jahoda synthesized the extant literature by setting forth six categories of concepts, as follows:

1. *Attitudes toward the self.* The effective person has high self-acceptance and self-esteem, a clear sense of identity, and accessibility of self-relevant data to awareness.

2. *Growth, development, and self-actualization.* This criterion speaks to the potentialities of the developmental process. It assumes

that there are individual differences in the extent to which persons grow psychologically and realize their potentialities. The optimally integrated person will, in Maslow's terms, reflect evidence of growth motivation as compared with deficiency motivation. Illustrative behaviors would include the ability to go beyond concern for self and care about others, the development of ethical values, and a flexible capacity for change.

3. *Integration.* This criterion refers to the harmonious relatedness of all aspects of a persons's behavior. It means the capacity to act in terms of a coherent and consistent "ground plan" (Erikson, 1964) for living.

4. *Autonomy.* According to Jahoda, this criterion together with the next two have in common an emphasis on reality orientation, the capacity to perceive and act upon elements of life as it is. With respect to the specific criterion of autonomy itself, what is meant is the development of internal standards and values such that autonomous persons may act upon their own signals rather than through social vigilance or social anxiety. Autonomy in no sense implies solipsism, but rather an inner regulation that includes awareness of external data.

5. *Perception of reality.* It is implicit in this concept that reality orientation refers to events concerning persons as well as things—that reality includes social as well as physical reality. In this sense, personally effective individuals display maximal perception in social awareness and sensitivity, free from need-distortion. The criterion implies the ability to perceive events as they are and to proceed through reality testing rather than through untested assumptions about the external world.

6. *Environmental mastery.* Effective persons not only perceive reality accurately but act upon their perceptions. The ability to come to terms with events, to meet and deal with them directly, is one criterion of personal effectiveness, at least in Western culture. This criterion thus deals with performance and success as well as with motivation. The Piagetian concepts of assimilaton and accommodation are relevant here: effective persons turn the environment to their own uses when possible and appropriate and adapt to circumstances when necessary.

What Jahoda offered was a multiple-criteria approach to the definition of positive mental health. This approach recognizes the complexity of the phenomenon and permits assessment in terms more sensitive than an all-or-none approach. Further, the multiple-criteria approach has turned out to be compatible with the framework of empirical studies as they have evolved since Jahoda's presentation. Reports discussed later in this chapter will illustrate the application of multiple-criteria approaches (e.g., Heath, 1965, 1977; Seeman, 1959, 1983; Smith, 1969).

Smith. Brewster Smith, one of the few psychologists to have made long-term contributions to the area of personal competence, has written steadily since 1950 (e.g., Smith, 1950, 1959, 1966, 1968, 1969, 1978). His 1950 paper was written some time before the domain had any claim to systematic inquiry. Thus he was left to make do with a combination of his own observations and the theory available at the time. In this context his first paper turned out to be a remarkably prescient synthesis of the field.

Smith advanced three criteria as touchstones of personal effectiveness: adjustment, integration, and cognition of reality. Adjustment refers to a homeostatic process in which the needs and capacities of the person are in a dynamic balance with environmental demands, and integration refers to a complex coordination of function that allows one's full energies to remain available for use, with the implication here that one had a consistent central core of self that could be brought to bear in the realization of life's central goals. By cognition of reality, Smith meant a reality-based perception of self and one's relationships to the social environment. The capacity to perceive reality accurately, free from distortion, was a necessary corollary to the other two characteristics.

Later work by Smith showed progression along several lines: further elaboration and clarification in conceptual analysis and forays into supporting empirical work (Smith, 1959, 1966). He further elaborated his view that the complexity of the phenomena relating to positive functioning required multiple parameters of description. To this view he added the advocacy of a systems approach as a way of achieving added synthesis and power in the analysis of effective functioning (Smith, 1959).

White. Robert White's paper on the concept of competence (1959) gained early prominence and still remains one of the more widely quoted papers in the domain of human effectiveness. His paper sets forth a dialectic approach to the exploration of human motivation, with special reference to the formulation of alternatives to drive theory emphasis as advanced by Freud and Hull. White cites the widespread indicators that primates seek out occasions for novelty, excitement, and stimulation. Included in these tendencies are the evident needs for environmental contact and exploration.

Out of these considerations, White postulates the importance of two related concepts, competence and effectance. Thus he speaks of *competence motivation*, which he defines as directed, selective, and systematic behaviors that satisfy a need to deal with the environment. While White considers such possible goals of this activity as self-assertion, control, and mastery, he returns again and again to the basic premise that the goals are simply the need to transact with the environment.

But White does not leave the issue at that. He proposes that the motivational aspect of competence is imbedded in a quality that he refers to as *effectance*. White explains effectance motivation by linking it to such activities as cognizance, construction, mastery, and achievement. The outcomes of these activities, when successfully accomplished, result in the subjective experience of efficacy, a state of satisfaction and fulfillment that represents its own reward.

A DESCRIPTION OF THREE MAJOR RESEARCH PROGRAMS

Heath's Research

Any report of research on human effectiveness must take account of Heath's major contributions to this domain (1965, 1977). Heath combined an approach that had a rich theoretical structure on the one hand and an extensive empirical range on the other. This combination resulted in fundamental contributions to our understanding of human potentialities. His first study (1965) was an in-depth study of Haverford College students, and his second work (1977) was a multicultural study utilizing an essentially similar design. I will review his first study here.

Heath utilized a conceptual structure centered on developmental theory. For him it seems to be a happy choice. The structure permitted him to formulate concepts referring to the maturing process, to specify attributes and behaviors that characterize this process, and to select or develop instruments that assessed it. In short, the theory served a central integrating function.

There were numerous consistent findings in the data that confirmed the theoretical propositions with respect to maturity. In the personal domain, affirmative self-image was positively related to findings of the structured and projective personality measures and to the assessment of the judges. What emerged was a coherent picture of maturity as seen from all these frames of reference.

A major thrust in the findings referred to the relationship between self-image and cognition performance. The high maturity group showed superior intellectual skills and academic performance as compared with the low group, even though the groups had been equated on the entrance examination scores. Furthermore, the high group showed greater capacity to withstand the effects both of distracting and personally disturbing information. All of these results point to a characteristic that I have referred to elsewhere (Seeman, 1983) as *intellectual efficiency*. The high groups simply functioned with greater intellectual efficiency.

The men in the high groups had high reciprocal interaction with others in their environment. They were seen by others as effective, judging by their frequent selection for leadership positions. Also, they chose active participation in extracurricular activities. In other words, the high-group men showed high environmental contact. Perceptions of family relationships were strikingly different for the high and low groups. There was a highly consistent report of positive family strength and positive relationships for the high group, in contrast to conflictual relationships reported by the low group.

There were differences in the records of the contrasting groups with respects to physical health. More men in the immature group were ill for every diagnostic category in the student health records. Heath reported that "the most noticeable differences were for more immature than mature men to report fatigue, headaches, localized pains and 'accidental' types of injuries such as finger, arm, and leg sprains" (1965, p. 155). In terms of visits to the infirmary, one third of the high-group members had three or fewer visits, while every immature group member had four or more visits in a two-year period.

Heath summarized his findings in a section entitled "Toward a Definition of Maturity" (1965, p. 334ff). The structure of his findings is in every way compatible with the concept of the fully functioning person and adds valuable, empirically confirmed specificity to our understanding of such persons.

The Berkeley Studies

Next to be reviewed here is a series of research programs that produced a variety of studies in effective behavior. The locale was the

University of California at Berkeley. Studies were conducted in several of their research instiues. The first study to be reported here was done at the Institute of Personality Assessment and Research (IPAR). One of the major studies was reported by Barron (1954), dealing with an investigation of personal soundness in graduate students. It was a wide-ranging study that looked at a broad array of variables relating to excellence of personal functioning. The variables included behavioral observations and assessment by a trained psychology staff, perception tests, self-description, the MMPI, and life history variables.

The research participants were 80 graduate men selected from a pool of 433 students who had been rated by their faculty on a measure of personal soundness. The 80 participants were brought to the Institute in groups of 10, each group spending a weekend in a "living-in" arrangement for assessment purposes.

A description of the high-ranking individuals in personal soundness may be derived by noting the adjectives most often endorsed by the department faculty and assessment staff. Among these descriptive terms were the following adjectives: adaptable, organized, alert, dependable, confident, efficient, foresighted, resourceful, realistic, and helpful. These descriptive terms imply flexibility, good reality contact, self-acceptance, and interpersonal effectiveness—characteristics that are congruent with much of the other research.

It was in the life history variables that some of the most telling results were observed. The information was obtained through a biographical data sheet and a series of four in-depth interviews with each respondent. The variable that most clearly distinguished the high-soundness group from the low-soundness group was that the high-soundness individuals established intimate and enduring heterosexual relationships. Other variables clearly associated with high soundness were positive relationships with siblings, stability of the home and family, a strong and positively valued father, early development of social facility, and an early health record free of serious illness.

Many of the foregoing characteristics link this study with other studies of personal effectiveness. The early development of effective interpersonal contact, the capacity for intimacy, and the clarity of the family structure all touch on factors observed in other studies. Barron's study therefore serves as a cross-validation of the characteristics thought to be associated with effective functioning.

A longitudinal study conducted at the Institute of Human Development will be reported here next. The principal author of the report was Jack Block (1971). The study was not designed *a priori* to identify highly integrated persons. The fact that Block's inductive analysis of the data resulted in the emergence of effectiveness factors is thus all the more compelling.

A factor analysis identified five personality types for males. Type A displayed a cluster of characteristics clearly indicative of high personality integration and effective functioning. They were characterized by high self-acceptance, a sense of well-being, independence, intellectual efficiency, and high socialization. Their family history showed stability, clarity of parental role structure, and nurturance without overprotection.

The factor analysis results for the female sample is rather more complex. The high-integration characteristics that have emerged from other research seem to be divided between two of the typologies in the Block study—that is, no single comprehensive high-integration portrait emerges for the women.

The two typologies that most closely match the high-integration characteristics of other studies were named by Block "Female Prototypes" and "Cognitive Copers." The first of these typologies were dependable, likable, cheerful, protective, overcontrolled, and feminine. Block saw them as well adjusted in the context of a conventional feminine role.

The second factor typology, the Cognitive Copers, showed high loadings in the characteristics of verbal fluency, ambition, dependability, introspection, and openness to experience. The most influential aspect of the family background appeared to be the strength of the mother, who emphasized the life values of an intellectual orientation and of rationality. The father had less impact and was less often available. Both parents were even-tempered and affectionate with each other.

Block's data call attention to the cultural matrix in which the data were obtained. In particular, the emergence of a female prototype factor calls attention to the milileu in which the females were brought up and to the values of our society at that time. It would be of great interest to conduct a comparable study at this time, when sex role stereotypes are being challenged and new definitions are being evolved.

Seeman's Research

I wish now to describe a program of research in which I have been involved for some 25 years, a program designed to enhance our understanding of the optimally functioning person. In presenting this material,

I shall first elucidate the conceptual framework that has given structure and direction to the research, and then present some of the empirical findings derived from application of the theory.

The research began with an attempt to devise criteria for assessing the outcomes of psychotherapy. In my capacity as coordinator of research at the University of Chicago Counseling Center, I was involved in the planning of a major research project on the outcomes of client-centered therapy. An early step in this task was an effort to conceptualize the characteristics of the post-therapy, or well-integrated, person. An initial statement in this connection was set forth as follows:

> We may accept as a premise that the body is governed not by anarchy but by a series of biologically given developmental laws or regularities....In our complex culture the chances for intrapsychic disturbance of these laws are manifold, and thus the need for therapy arises. In these terms we may think of therapy as the removal or assimilation of these intrapsychic disturbances and the return to organic order or integration. (Seeman, 1956, p. 99)

The key term here is *organic order or integration,* for that term is a first approximation to a definition of an effectively functioning person. A modification of the foregoing term was made later (Seeman, 1959), so that the phrase *organismic integration* served as the key organizing framework for the research. Here the term *organismic* is intended to suggest a pervasive phenomenon that includes all of a person's behavioral subsystems: biochemical, physiological, perceptual, cognitive, and interpersonal. The term *integration* indicates a transactional process that blends these subsystem behaviors in ways that are congruent, harmonious, and adaptive.

It is essential in understanding this framework to regard these subsystem behaviors in systems terms. Angyal (1941) defines a system as *unitas multiplex*—that is, a system with multiple components held together and unified by organization and intercommunication. System elements do not stand alone or act in isolation. They are parts of a whole. This was the essence of the framework that I had chosen to develop.

The foregoing concept has wide support in the literature of personality integration and represents a useful framework for understanding personality integration. Smith (1959) argues for a system concept. Jahoda (1958) refers to "the relatedness of all processes and attributes in an individual" (p. 36). Perhaps the most cogent systems explanation of integration is one made by Brody (1973) in his chapter on the systems view of humans. In the chapter, Brody defines a person as "a hierarchy of natural systems interconnected by various patterns of information flow in feed-back circuits" (p. 71). He then defines health as the harmonious interaction of hierarchical components, and disease as a state of disruption of the harmony of the hierarchical structure.

This system concept helps to identify what I mean by organismic integration. The highly effective person has well-integrated organismic behavior with minimal disruption or distortion, a high degree of coordinated information exchange, and an excellent capacity to receive and transmit data.

Empirical studies derived from this conceptual structure have sought to look at the ways in which the behavioral subsystems of highly integrated persons exhibit distinctive functions. A good illustration of the theory may be noted in a study by Behrends and Seeman (1982). We postulated that high-integration persons would display rapid biofeedback effects. In the biofeedback process, the cognitive subsystem and the physiological subsystem are jointly involved. In our study the participants were requested to modify their peripheral skin temperature. They were given information by an audible tone that signaled whether their temperature was rising or falling. They were thus expected to coordinate this cognitive input with their physiological state.

Organismic integration theory proposes that fully functioning persons would have a high capacity to perform the biofeedback task efficiently. This turned out to be the case. Our high-functioning group, in contrast to a normal control group, modified their skin temperature in the predicted way, whereas the control group showed no change in the biofeedback situation. The characteristic use of control groups within the normally functioning range of behavior has been a standard part of these studies, intended to permit a more finely tuned differentiation between typical normal functioning and high-level functioning (Seeman, 1983).

One study carried out with second- and third-grade children will illustrate typical design characteristics (Seeman, Barry, & Ellinwood, 1963). The purpose of the study was to investigate aspects of the cognitive and interpersonal behavior of high-functioning children in a play setting. The locale of the study was a university-affiliated laboratory school. Peer rating scales and teacher rating scales were used to select the highest-functioning children and an age and sex equivalent group from among the low-scoring children. Each child was then seen individually for 10 40-minute sessions in a play therapy room with a therapeutically trained adult. Trained observers made behavior ratings at five-minute intervals on a rating scale that assessed interpersonal behavior—e.g., time used in interaction with the adult, efforts to control the adult's behavior, response to limits, and the like. Ratings were also made along a cognitive dimension with a scale that assessed the play themes developed by the children. This latter scale spanned the range from sporadic nonthematic play through degrees of organization in play, with the extreme range representing repetitive, perseverative play.

On the relationship dimension, the high and low groups showed pronounced differences. The low group exhibited much controlling behavior by hostile dominating efforts or anxious dependency, and by negative responses to limit-setting; the high group's behavior was characterized by expressive peerlike behavior, with little effort to structure or control the adult's behavior and little need for limit-setting. The high-group children divided their time almost exactly evenly between the adult and the materials in the room, while the low-group children spent about three-fourths of the time with the adult.

On the cognitive dimension of theme development, the children in the low group exhibited perseverative behavior in 30 percent of their play, while the high group showed moderate theme development and complete absence of perseverative play.

The foregoing results suggested that children as young as seven or eight years of age could develop a relative degree of autonomy in relationships, characterized by horizontal, nonhierarchical, peerlike behavior with an adult. At the cognitive level, they could create organization in their world without any need to hold onto that organization. They felt free to leave what they had done, explore anew, and create new organization.

An illustrative study with young adults indicates ways in which the conceptual framework provides continuity of design and opportunity for cumulative knowledge. Some years after the completion of the foregoing study, Cooley and Seeman (1979) undertook a study designed to investigate the phenomenon of interpersonal distance as it related to personality integration. The procedure involved the placement of felt figure pairs on a cloth field. Each participant placed four pairs of figures, one pair at a time, on a cloth field with instruction to place the figures "where you think they belong." For each figure pair, one figure represented self and the other represented a parent or friend.

Our intention was to measure the distance between the figures as an index of the way in which the respondent perceived the relationship. During the pilot study, Cooley noticed that some respondents placed the figures not only in terms of horizontal distance but also in terms of a vertical relationship. Questions to the respondents as to the reason for the placement elicited statements referring to a hierarchical, status-related perception of the relationship. These explanations were remarkably reminiscent of the hierarchical relationships exhibited by the low-integration children in the play behavior study, and we incorporated the notations of vertical placement in our design.

Results of the data analysis indicated that 23 percent of the high-integration group used some instances of verticality—that is, 77 percent of the respondents used an exclusively horizontal plane in all four of their placements. By contrast, 53 percent of the non-high group used some instances of verticality in their placement. Moreover, every instance of verticality in the high group's placements involved self-parent pairs, whereas the non-high group used verticality with peers as well as parents.

The pair of studies just described reveal a phenomenon that was observed frequently in the results of studies with different age groups, namely, that there was a striking degree of developmental continuity in the behavioral characteristics of well-integrated children and adults. Clear indices of integrative processes are evident in children as young as six years of age.

Several further studies will be reported more briefly, as illustrations of findings that emphasized characteristics of high-functioning persons. A study by Duncan (1966) utilized a peer rating scale developed specifically to identify high-functioning persons. He then identified a number of characteristics that personality integration theory specified as indicators of effective functioning: a positive self-concept, an internal locus of control, an internal locus of evaluation, a high degree of environmental contact, creativity, and intellectual efficiency. All analyses were significant except for the creativity variable.

A study by Lewis (1959) sought to devise a peer rating scale that could be used to describe the behavior of high-functioning children. His criteria consisted of independent ratings by parents and a measure of intellectual efficiency. For the latter measure, Lewis held intelligence constant and predicted that high-functioning children would nevertheless show superior achievement in reading and arithmetic. Results confirmed this prediction. It was also the case that parent ratings and peer ratings were highly congruent, indicating that high-functioning children were readily identifiable.

Finally, another study (Seeman, 1963) was designed to elicit teacher judgments of high and low functioning among public school children. A 20-item rating scale was used. The results indicated that all 20 items differentiated clearly between the high-functioning and low-functioning groups. Interestingly enough, the item that best differentiated the two groups was one that dealt with personal awareness and environmental contact. The specific wording of the item was as follows:

Easily distracted by events	Aware of things going on around him (or her). Lively interest in environment	Little interest in events around him (or her). Unaware of environment
1	2	3	4	5

One of the major insights emerging from this research program concerns the high degree of developmental continuity evident in the behavior of high-integration individuals of all ages. The clear implication of these findings is that effective behavior evolves very early in life and continues to be evident in chronologically older persons.

A SYNTHESIS

It is time to try for some perspective on what this chapter has said about the fully functioning person. In doing so, I want to recall the original intention of the paper, which was to see how "Rogers's work and the work of others touch similar dimensions of human experience and accent the central themes that characterize personal integration."

I believe that the review in this chapter affirms the congruence between Rogers's original formulation and the subsequent empirical inquiry. The congruence is all the more striking because Rogers's earliest description of the fully functioning person was written before there was a significant body of experimental literature on which to draw. One sees here the power of the clinical process in the work of deriving insights and generating hypotheses. It is only later that the task of validation is carried on by experimental measures—that is, by the kinds of controlled observation not afforded through the clinical process.

How, then, do Rogers's early formulations about the fully functioning person and the subsequent empirical literature dovetail with each other? A useful way to conceptualize this relationship is to consider the interaction of process and content. The description by Rogers was a process description. In it he tried to capture the essence of the fully functioning person's mode of experiencing, the quality of the person's livingness. The subsequent empirical studies provided more detailed data on the consequent behavioral repertoire available to the fully functioning person—that is, the content of the person's behavior. Together, the process and content descriptions begin to offer a comprehensive and coherent understanding of the fully functioning person.

It may be useful now to juxtapose these process and content descriptions. The analysis by Rogers is in essence quite simple. He emphasized the person's mode of *functioning*, calling attention to the free flow of awareness within the person, the sense of the person's in-touchness with both internal and external signals. In providing this analysis, Rogers also called attention to the total human-system pervasiveness of the process.

The empirical literature amplifies this analysis by detailing the many behavioral sequelae of the person's free-flowing awareness. At the basic organismic level high-functioning persons are healthier, in terms both of longitudinal health history and daily functioning. They are more in touch with their physiological organisms, as evidenced by responsiveness to biofeedback data (Behrends & Seeman, 1982). At a more global level, their efficient perception of reality has many ramifications for effective functioning. High-functioning persons generate more information, and more differentiated information, than their less well-integrated peers. High-functioning persons have higher environmental contact and consequent environmental mastery. At a cognitive level, such persons function with intellectual efficiency, making maximal use of their resources.

One of the correlates of effective functioning is the secure sense of self exhibited by high-functioning persons.

In my own reflections about the empirical evidence, I have concluded that the most striking single finding is the often-repeated conclusion that high-integration persons have a *positive self-concept*. These persons display a high degree of self-esteem, confidence, and trust in themselves. This conclusion is quite in accord with the conclusion reached by Heath (1977) in his studies. In his summary of his own work, he said that "the four most powerful predictors of the maturity of men in three different cultures were measures of self-concept" (p. 183).

In system terms this conclusion about the centrality of the self-concept makes sense. The definition of self is a central organizing dynamic that filters the perception and construction of reality, that channels decisions and actions, and that defines the person's sense of place in the world. The concept of self is the fulcrum of the personal system.

Evidence concerning the organizing power of the self-concept comes from a growing body of research in the sphere of information storage and retrieval. Studies of incidental memory point to the role of the self-concept in organizing and producing information. For example, L. Rogers (in Cantor & Kihlstrom, 1981) conducted a study in which he presented two dimensions of information processing, a semantic dimension and a self-reference dimension. In the semantic dimension the respondents were asked to deal with the meaning of adjectives, while in the self-reference dimension the respondents were asked to deal with the relevance of the adjective to self. It was under the self-reference conditions that subsequent memory for these adjectives was highest. Results of this kind have been observed frequently enough to result in the conclusion that "the self-concept is the richest schema in memory." Taken all in all, then, we may point to the phenomenon of the self-concept as a key element in personal effectiveness.

The trust in self and the consequent willingness to use one's own immediate data of experience provides a personal climate that enhances many other aspects of effective personal functioning.

High-functioning persons display a sense of autonomy that not only enables them to function independently but also releases energy for positive interpersonal relationships. The research repeatedly alludes to positive family relationships. Outside of the family, fully functioning persons display a minimum of status-oriented relationships and an accent on horizontal, peerlike relationships. They have resources to go beyond self and, in Erikson's terms, to display caring and generative relationships with attendant capacity for empathy.

Where, then, do we stand in our efforts to comprehend the fully functioning person? It seems amply clear that the process conception put forth by Rogers has captured an essence that has withstood the test of time and evidence. Beyond that, the subsequent empirical inquiries have amplified in content terms the component elements of competent behavior. By now we have every reason to assert that we have successfully embarked upon a course designed to permit an understanding of the fully functioning person.

8   A Countertheory of Transference

John M. Shlien

INTRODUCTION TO THE PROBLEM

"Transference" is a fiction, invented and maintained by the therapist to protect himself from the consequences of his own behavior. To many, this assertion will seem an exaggeration, an outrage, an indictment. It is presented here as a serious hypothesis, charging a highly invested profession with the task of re-examining a fundamental concept in practice.

Mine is not an official position in client-centered therapy. There is none. Carl Rogers has dealt with the subject succinctly, in about 20 pages (1951, pp. 198–217), a relatively brief treatment of a matter that has taken up volumes of the literature in the field.[1] "In client-centered therapy, this involved and persistent dependency relationship does not tend to develop" (p. 201), though such transference attitudes are evident in a considerable proportion of cases handled by client-centered therapists. Transference is not fostered by this present-time–oriented framework in which intensive exploration of early childhood is not required. While Rogers knows of the position taken here and has, I believe, been influenced by it since its first presentation in 1963, he has never treated the transference topic as an issue of dispute. This is partly so because of his lack of inclination for combat on controversial issues; he prefers to do his own constructive work and let evidence accumulate with new experience.

Why then should client-centered therapy take a position on an issue of so little moment in its own development? For one reason, the concept of transference is ubiquitous. It has a powerful grip on the

153

minds of professionals and the public. While client-centered practice has the popular image of a relatively self-effacing therapist, it holds to a standard of self-discipline and responsibility for the conditions and processes it fosters, and it could not fail to encounter those emotional and relational strains so often classed as transference.

There are many separate questions asked in the assertion at the start of the chapter. *What* behavior of the therapist? Leading to *which* consequences? *Why* invent[2] such a concept? *How* does it protect? In re-examining the concept of "transference" how do we, to use Freud's words, "inquire into its source"? And if this inquiry comes to a controversial conclusion, what evidence and motive will lead to the next level of opinion?

Throughout, we will consider only the male therapist–female patient data. Such was the critical situation when the term was invented. The first five case histories in the 1895 landmark *Studies on Hysteria* (Breuer & Freud, 1957) are Anna O., Emmy von N., Lucy R., Katharina, and Elisabeth. Of course this was natural, the "wandering womb" being thought a property of females. It set up the image of the most sensitive relationship (older man, younger woman) most suspect in the minds of the public (whether skeptic or enthusiast) and the combination most common for many decades.[3] Indeed it is possible that without the sexually charged atmosphere thus engendered, the concept of transference might not have developed as it has, if at all! We will never know whether that would have been more gainful in the development of responsible and effective therapies. We do know that it would have caused the loss of a mass of intriguing and convoluted literature in the field, and certainly we would not have psychoanalysis as presently defined.

For psychoanalysis, transference is *the essential concept:* "sine qua non," "an inevitable necessity," "the object of treatment," "the most important thing we [Freud and Breuer] have to make known to the world," without which "the physician and his arguments would never be listened to." In addition, it contains and subsumes all the elaborate support structures: the primary significance of sexual instincts, psychic determinism, the unconscious, psychogenetic theory, the power of past experience. Crucial in theory! In practice, it comforts, protects, and explains.

Transference is also supposed to distinguish psychoanalysis from other forms of therapy. Perhaps it is meant to do so, but this becomes moot through contradictions in the literature, which variously asserts that transference is peculiar to psychoanalysis, but also common in everyday life. Whether unique or universal, it is in widespread use throughout most psychodynamic systems. One distinction it does serve: that between professional and paraprofessional, or sophisticate and literalist, and in general between those in and out of power. If transference is no longer the singular hallmark of psychoanalysis, it at least marks those "in the know," whether novices or not. Once thought a most dubious notion, it was in Freud's mind "a new fact which we are thus unwillingly compelled to recognize" (1935, p. 385). Currently, "unwilling" more aptly describes the attitude of psychologists toward re-examination, even abandonment, of the idea. But re-examination is necessary if we are to re-evaluate the usefulness of the concept.

It seems most appropriate to begin this re-evaluation with the early history of the concept. The case of Anna O. provides the cornerstone on which the theory of transference is generally thought to be based. More than a dramatic and moving affair, it is of momentous importance to the field, and its effects still influence theory and practice. Though psychoanalysis and/or other forms of psychotherapy would somehow have developed, all present forms owe much to the observations based on this seminal case. To properly honor those pioneers whose struggles began at this human point of origin, it is necessary to study their thoughts and experiences not as a scholarly exercise but as a means of evaluating the promise and limitations of resulting methods.

The accounts begin in the *Studies on Hysteria* (Breuer & Freud, 1957) first published in 1895. Details of treatment were reported cautiously, out of respect for the still living patient, and for other reasons. Anna O. was, by all accounts, remarkable, and, for that time, so was her treatment. In her twenty-first year, she was described by Breuer and others as a person of great beauty, charm, and powerful intellect, with a quick grasp and surplus energy. Living in a comfortable but monotonous environment at home, she was hungry for intellectual stimulation. She was poetic and imaginative, fluent in German, English, Italian, and French. Much of her waking time was spent in daydreaming, her "private theatre." She was also sharp and critical, and therefore, Breuer tells us, "completely unsuggestable" (though he routinely used hypnosis), needing to be convinced by argument on every point. She was tenacious and obstinate, but also known for immensely sympathetic kindness, a quality that marked most of her life's work. She had never been in love. In short, she was young, attractive, intelligent, lonely; it was she who named psychotherapy "the talking-cure," and she was a near-perfect companion for the also remarkable physician-pioneer in this form of treatment. (He was 38 at the time, admired, loved, respected, and of high professional and social status). Both deserve all the tributes given, and more.

Through the experience of Anna O. with Breuer, the material used as the basis for the theory of "transference-love" (as it was then called) was gathered, but it was Freud alone who later invented that theory to interpret that material to Breuer and the world. In the meantime, Freud's invention had been fostered by experience of his own with at least one other female patient.

The case is described by Breuer in 1895 (Breuer & Freud, 1957, pp. 21–47), who wrote that he had "suppressed a large number of quite interesting details" (true), and that she had left Vienna to travel for a while, free of her previous disturbances (not quite so true, for she was taken to a sanatorium where she "inflamed the heart of the psychiatrist in charge" [Jones, 1953, p. 225], and was temporarily addicted to morphine). By the time Breuer reported the *Studies* a decade later, he could write that "it was a considerable time before she regained her mental balance entirely" (p. 41). Even so, he had confided sorrowfully to Freud in an earlier discussion that he sometimes thought she were better off dead, to end her suffering. The "suppressed details" may in part be related to his sudden termination of the treatment and the patient's shocking emergency regarding her "pregnancy" and his "responsibility." James Strachey, editor of the 1957 translation of *Studies on Hysteria*, says Freud told him of the end of Anna O.'s treatment: "the patient suddenly made manifest to Breuer the presence of a strong unanalysed positive transference of an unmistakeably sexual nature" (Breuer & Freud, 1957, p. 41, fn.). This is a retroactive interpretation, of course, since at the time of its occurrence neither Breuer—nor perhaps even Freud—yet had any idea of "transference." That idea builds, and more complete information is released, as Freud describes the case in both oblique and direct references in lectures and other writings from 1905 to his autobiography in 1925. Still more explicit communications are released in Ernest Jones's biography of Freud (1953). In 1972, Freeman, a well-known popular writer, published a "novelized" biography and report of Anna O. and her treatment. (None of these is exact, verbatim, or anything like "original data.")

Even so, the somewhat guarded report by Breuer gives us a privileged view of his work. The editor of *Studies* tells us that Breuer had little need of hypnosis because Anna O. so readily "produced streams of material from her unconscious, and *all Breuer had to do was to sit by and listen to them without interrupting her*" (Breuer & Freud, 1957, p. xvii, emphasis added). That is *all?* As you will see later, I argue that this is no small thing. It may not seem much to the editor, perhaps not much to the renowned physician, but to the lonely, grieving, and desperate woman, it must have seemed a treasure. At that period, young ladies were given placebos, referred from one doctor to another, generally treated with patronizing attention or benign neglect. Breuer and Freud were precious rarities in that they listened, took seriously. Would that Breuer had done more of that, and had done it steadfastly *through to the end.* Listening is behavior of great consequence. The pity is that he cut it short at the critical last moment.

Meanwhile, there were many other behaviors. We can only estimate their consequences. He fed her. She was emaciated, and he alone was able to feed her. He could give her water when she otherwise would not drink. No doubt there were other nourishing figures in her life, but he was clearly one himself. He paid daily visits. She held his hands in order to identify him at times when she could not see. When she was exhausted, he put her to sleep, with narcotics or suggestion. He restored mobility to paralyzed limbs. He hypnotized her, sometimes twice in a day, taught her self-hypnosis, and then "would relieve her of the whole stock of imaginative products she had accumulated since [his] last visit" (1957, p. 36). He took her for rides in his carriage with his daughter (named Berthe, which was Anna O.'s real name). He read her diary—a notably tricky business either with or without her permission. He forced her to remember unpleasant experiences.

For this much alone, would you think that Anna O. (or anyone), regardless of previous experience with others, had reason (real, not imaginary) for feelings such as gratitude? hope? affection? trust? annoyance? intimacy? resentment? fear of separation?

Finally, there was the ending. Breuer had been preoccupied with his patient, and his wife had become jealous and morose. There had been improvement, indeed. But also, according to Jones's 1953 account, Breuer confided to Freud that he decided to terminate because he divined the meaning of his wife's state of mind. "It provoked a violent reaction in him, perhaps compounded of love and guilt, and he decided to bring the treatment to an end" (Jones, 1953, p. 225).

Exactly how he announced this decision we do not know, except that he conveyed the message that she was well and did not need him. That evening he was called back by the mother and found his patient "in a greatly excited state, apparently as ill as ever." She was "in the throes of an hysterical childbirth" (Jones, 1953, p. 224).

Certainly that is an interpretation of her "cramps" and utterances that might commonly occur. We have no first-hand information as to what the patient thought or meant. Every report is second- or third-hand, through Freud about Breuer, and that usually through Jones, who wrote, "Freud has related to me a fuller account than he described in his writings"; some of that account is quoted as follows:

> The patient, who according to him [Breuer] had appeared as an asexual being and had never made any allusion to such a forbidden topic throughout the treatment, was now in the throes of an hysterical childbirth (pseudocyesis), the logical termination of a phantom pregnancy that had been visibly developing in response to Breuer's ministrations. Though profoundly shocked, he managed to calm her down by hypnotizing her, and then fled the house in a cold sweat. The next day he and his wife left for Venice to spend a second honeymoon....[4] (1953, p. 224)

> Some ten years later, at a time when Breuer and Freud were studying cases together, Breuer called him into consultation over a hysterical patient. Before seeing her, he described her symptoms, whereupon Freud pointed out that they were typical products of a phantom pregnancy. The recurrence of the old situation was too much for Breuer. Without saying a word, he took up his hat and stick and hurriedly left the house. (1953, pp. 224–226)

A somewhat more explicit (but still far from detailed or verbatim) report is cited in Freeman (1972, p. 200). Freud writes to Stefan Zweig (a relative of Anna O. by marriage):

> What really happened with Breuer I was able to guess later on, long after the break in our relations, when I suddenly remembered something Breuer had told me in another context before we had begun to collaborate and which he never repeated [emphasis added]. On the evening of the day when all her symptoms had been disposed of, he was summoned to the patient again, found her confused and writhing in abdominal cramps. Asked what was wrong with her, she replied: "Now Dr. B's child is coming!"[5]

Freud added, "At this moment he held in his hand the key," but "seized by conventional horror he took flight and abandoned his patient to a colleague" (Freeman, 1972, p. 200).

Here is one final quotation from Breuer himself in his own report. "The element of sexuality was astonishingly undeveloped in her. The patient, whose life became known to me to an extend to which one person's life is seldom known to another, had never been in love" (Breuer & Freud, 1957, pp. 21–22).

What then, "really happened"? We will never know. Two exceptional (in my opinion, magnificent) people of great intelligence and noble spirit came close to understanding. He knew her well. Probably she knew him better than he thought. The knowing appears to have been precious to both. Understanding failed at a critical point. They dropped the key.[6] It is tragic; it is to weep. Thankfully, we know that both carried on vital and constructive lives for many years.

If you are a woman, reading this will probably bring different reactions than those of the typical man. Perhaps you feel more sympathetic to the patient. If you put yourself in the therapist's place, supposing this could be your case, you know at least that you could think to yourself, and possibly say to Anna O., "Unlikely that it is my child in the physical sense, since I am a woman like yourself, but perhaps you mean that I am somehow parent to your pain, your growth, your condition whatever." (If you think that a woman therapist would never face such a situation, consider the implications of that for transference theory.)

More difficult if you are a man, putting yourself in this imaginary situation. You might say, "I am one of that ascetic sect who submitted to voluntary sterilization in order to make my life less anxious or vows of chastity more organic, as it were, so it is unlikely, etc." as above. Not only an absurdity with which few readers would identify, but in this case useless, since Anna knows Breuer has recently fathered a child. (There is another source of security, transference theory, but it has not quite yet been invented.)

Meanwhile, return to the fact that it is Dr. Breuer who is directly and immediately involved, and return to Anna O. What might they be thinking, meaning, saying to each other in this perilous moment, at best and at worst? God knows what words she uttered in which of four languages (for she was known to speak a "gibberish" of mixed tongues when ill). We do not know what he heard, nor what he said, nor what he told Freud was said. Nor what Freud told Jones; nor how accurate Jones's translation (not always, we know). But let us take it that Freud's letter to Zweig is the most authentic; in it, Anna says, "Now Dr. B's child is coming" (Freeman, 1972, p. 200), or "Now Dr. Breuer's baby is coming. It is coming!'' (p. 56). (Do these little differences matter? Yes, they show us how too thin is the ice upon which we skate our conjecture.)

Anna might have thought, felt, or said, for example:

Dr. B—a baby. I feel like a baby!

Would you abort my child? Then don't abort my treatment.

You know me so well, but you thought I was sexually under-developed, had never been in love, had no romantic feelings— although you knew, for instance, that I loved to dance. Well, I've grown. Thanks to you in good part. Now Dr. Breuer's child has become a woman. I'm ready at last for that sexual release. It is coming!

When you were late for our appointment one morning, you apolo-gized and told me [as he did] that it had to be so because your wife was having a new baby and you had to stay up all night. If that is what is more important to you, look, I'm having one too.

Why did you tell me so suddenly that you could not continue to see me? Your reasons sounded false. I know so well your voice, your eyes. What is the real reason? If you must lie to me to leave me, I must lie to you to keep you.

Only hear me out. I mean you no harm as you leave. We have touched. You massaged me, fed me, gave me life, comfort, discipline; made me tell things I would not tell anyone else. I felt loved, and I must tell you in the ultimate way, I love you too. You are handsome, kind, distinguished. If all of this does not justify my excitement and love, what does? Life together is impossible, I know that. Sex is really not that important to me either. But love is. A child would be. I want *someone* to love. I am in great pain over it.

None of these possibilities begins to describe conversations to which they might have led. Meanwhile Dr. Breuer, on his part, might have thought, felt, or said something like:

What did I do to deserve this?

My God, you are really out of your mind (again).

You cannot think that I...(or can you?)

We've never even discussed such a thing [which they hadn't].

It never entered my mind [if indeed it hadn't].

Is this more of your "private theatre"? Not amusing.

You are punishing me.

Damned embarrassing. I already have problems at home.

Here is the ruination of my reputation/family/livelihood/method/ hope/everything.[7]

In a more benign mood—

You don't want me to leave you.

Perhaps I have been both too caring and careless, left you unfairly.

What are you growing, laboring to deliver?

What part did I play?

I am touched and honored that you choose me.

Have I led you to expect more than I can give?

Have we time to talk before you go to the hospital?

[Or, best of all] You are in pain. Let's try to understand. I will postpone my trip and work with you.

Freud, as we already know, discussed this case with Breuer more than once. There is some evidence that Breuer felt not only uncertainty about it, but guilt and shame as well. In the late 1880s, years after *Studies on Hysteria* was written, Freud tried to persuade Breuer to write more about it. Breuer had declared the treatment of hysterics an ordeal he could not face again. Freud then described one experience so well known now through his autobiography (1948, p. 48) in which he too had faced "untoward events." As Jones described it:

> So Freud told him of his own experience with a female patient suddenly flinging her arms around his neck in a transport of affection, and he explained his reasons for regarding such "untoward occurrences" as part of the transference phenomena characteristic of certain types of hysteria.[8] This seems to have had a calming effect on Breuer, who evidently had taken his own experience of the kind more personally and perhaps even reproached himself for indiscretion in the handling of his patient. (Jones, 1953, p. 250)

Momentarily this comforted, explained, and protected Breuer, but only momentarily. At first, Breuer agreed to join in the publication and promotion of the idea of transference. As Freud writes many times, "'I believe,' he told me, 'that this is the most important thing we two have to give the world'" (Breuer & Freud, 1957, p. xxviii). Then Breuer withdrew his support for the theory and the complete primacy of sexual etiology of neuroses—support Freud needed and urgently sought. "He [Breuer] might have crushed me... by pointing to his own first patient [Anna O.] in whose case sexual factors had ostensibly played no part whatever" (Freud, 1948, p. 6). That Breuer was ambivalent, that he neither crushed nor supported, Freud put down to Breuer's suppressed secret of the case. Breuer may have had serious and sincere doubts on other scores. They agreed to disagree, citing "the natural and justifiable differences between the opinions of two observers who are agreed upon the facts and their basic reading of them, but who are not invariably at one in their interpretations and conjectures" (J. Breuer/S. Freud, April 1895, quoted in Breuer & Freud, 1957, p. xxx). Breuer, quite possibly intimidated by the nature of his suppressed material and his loyalty to colleague Freud and patient Anna O. did not press his arguments, whatever they might have been; Freud did, and swept the field.

Now we have transference.

DEFINITIONS AND DEFINERS

A few definitions are in order. There are dozens. They change over time and between authors. The main theme is constant enough that the proponent of any form of "depth psychology" can sagely nod assent, though Orr writes, "From about 1930 onward, there are too many variations of the concept of transference for systematic summary" (1954, p. 625).

Circa 1905

What are transferences? They are new editions or fascimiles of the tendencies and phantasies which are aroused and made conscious during the progress of the analysis; but they have this peculiarity, which is characteristic for their species, that they replace some earlier person by the person of the physician. To put it another way: a whole series of psychological experiences are revived, not as belonging to the past, but as applying to the person of the physician at the present moment. Some of these transferences have a content which differs from that of their model in no respect whatever except for the substitution. These, then—to keep the same metaphor—are merely new impressions or reprints. Others are more ingeniously constructed; their content has been subjected to a moderating influence—to *sublimation*, as I call it—and they may even become conscious, by cleverly taking advantage of some real peculiarity in the physician's person or circumstances and attaching them to that.[9] These, then, will no longer be new impressions, but revised editions. (Freud, 1959, p. 139)

The new fact which we are thus unwillingly compelled to recognize we call "transference." By this we mean a transference of feelings on to the person of the physician, because we do not believe that the situation in the treatment can account for the origin of such feelings. (Freud, 1935, p. 385)

By transference is meant a striking peculiarity of neurotics. They develop toward their physician emotional reactions both of an affectionate and hostile character, which are not based upon the actual situation but are derived from their relations to their parents. (Freud, 1935, p. 391)

There can be no doubt that the hostile feelings against the analyst deserve the name of "transference" for the situation in the treatment gives no adequate occasion for them. (Freud, 1935, p. 385)

Why should anyone feel hostility toward him? "Actually I have never done a mean thing," wrote Freud to Putnam (Jones, 1957, p.

247). Not many can make this disclaimer, and not all believe it borne out by Freud's record (Roustang, 1976). Still, if he only *thinks* this of himself it is more fitting that hostile feelings toward him would be seen as unjustified by his behavior. What matters here is the analyst's proclamation of innocence—a stance that permeates transference theory throughout. While an *ad hominem* argument is of limited use, there is a principle to which readers in this field must surely subscribe. It is that *every honest theory* (and related practice) *of personality and psychotherapy must reflect the personality and experience of its author.* How could it be otherwise?

Freud continues this definition thus: "The necessity for regarding the negative transference in this light is a confirmation of our previous similar view of the positive or affectionate variety" (Freud, 1935, p. 385). This "necessity" is part of that strange logic in which the second assertion proves the first! Is transference useful? Yes, it overcomes resistance, enables interpretation; it is your chief tactical ally. "The father-transference is only the battlefield where we conquer and take the libido prisoner" (Freud, 1935, p. 396).

In sum, the patient's feelings *"do not originate in the present* situation, and *they are not deserved by the personality of the physician,* but they repeat what has happened to him once before in his life" (Freud, 1927, p. 129, emphasis added). The "once before" is experience "in childhood, and usually in connection with one of his parents." As put most simply in *The Problem of Lay Analysis* (Freud, 1927), "The attitude is, to put it bluntly, a kind of falling in love" (p. 129). We must not forget, "This affection is not accounted for by the physician's behavior nor the relationship nor situation" (1935, p. 383).

So, the analyst is not responsible, the situation is not responsible, even though there may be some "real peculiarities" visible in the physician or circumstances. Transference is a neurotic peculiarity. Whether it is a normal (common) trait is also unclear, but the transference neurosis is a feature of analysis—that is certain.

There are some updatings. They will not make a basic difference, but it is worth noting that Fenichel tried to alter the absolute exemption when he wrote in 1941:

> Not everything is transference that is experienced by a patient in the form of affects and impulses during the course of the analytic treatment. If the analysis appears to make no progress, the patient has, in my opinion, the right to be angry, and his anger need not be a

transference from childhood—or rather, we will not succeed in demonstrating the transference component in it. (Fenichel, 1941, p. 95)

Later positions (Macalpine, 1950; Menninger, 1958) suggest that the analytic situation itself is regressive and thus somewhat influential if not responsible, and Waelder (1956) says, "Hence transference is a regressive process. Transference develops in *consequence* of the conditions of the analytic situation and the analytic technique" (p. 367, emphasis added).

The qualifications make concessions and corrections, but no one anywhere questions the basic concept, per se. Oddly, they only serve to strengthen, never to cast doubt. The situation *is* regressive because it turns all the patient's attention inward and backward toward earliest experience, and the therapist is made to seem bland, neutral, indistinct, even invisible. It is like a form of sensory deprivation—yet that term is a misnomer, for what is lost in sensory deprivation experiments in *ordinary* stimulation. Other forms are elevated into unusual prominence. So it is with the presence and with the pronouncements of the therapist in this regressive situation.

Or, if transference is considered as a matter of "projection," the question arises, "*What is the screen?*" The answer was implied, though it seemed not to be recognized in the first deep crack in transference theory—"countertransference." The instant that concept was developed, it should have become clear that the analyst's presence was more than a blank. Presumably countertransference was to be kept at a minimum. Until recently, definitions of and attention to it have been relatively minimal (except for one sector where it seems most nearly innocent, appropriate, and "natural": that is, work with children).

As Freud began to give attention to countertransference, he viewed it as responsive or reflexive rather than as an originating characteristic of the analyst. "We have become aware of the 'counter-transference' which arises in [the physician] as a result of *the patient's influence*[10] on his unconscious feeling" (Freud, 1910, p. 122, emphasis added). This is a far cry from the notion of one of my students, who thinks that transference lies in wait with the therapist and his wishes or expectations, while the countertransference is on the part of the patient! The psychoanalytic positions on countertransference range from treating it as a hindrance to be overcome[11] to welcoming it as a sensory asset ("third ear") (Epstein & Feiner, 1974, p. 1). In any event, one can hardly claim "no responsibility" on a "nobody home" basis if it is admitted that *somebody*, with *some* palpable characteristics, is there. The question now becomes, "What is the nature of these characteristics?"

The therapist is in truth a person of some distinctiveness, some identity, no matter how discreetly hidden. He has some self-concept—an image of what he is and wants to be. Perhaps the more truly modest and humble, the more he will be surprised by intense idealizations of himself by others. If plain (he thinks), how much more inappropriate for the patient to think him handsome.

But perhaps he is not really modest or humble. That may be only a professional attitude. When Freud wrote to his wife Martha, telling her of Anna O.'s strenuous affection for Dr. Breuer and of the consternation on the part of Breuer's wife, Martha replied that she hoped that would not happen to her (a common concern of the therapist's spouse). Freud "reproved her for her vanity in supposing that other women would fall in love with *her* husband: 'for that to happen one has to be a Breuer.'" (Jones, 1953, p. 225). It was not really *her* vanity at issue, it would seem, but her concern over *his* exposure. He did not quite give the assurance that she wanted,[12] and of course, it *did* happen to her husband. As the theory predicted that it would. Perhaps it already had. At some point, reported in his autobiography, Freud had discontinued hypnosis after an "untoward event" of his own. The patient, being aroused from a trance, threw her arms about him "in a transport of affection." At any rate, Freud dropped the method of hypnosis (was "freed of it") shortly after and took a position behind the couch. Embarrassment may again have been a factor (he did not like to be "stared at" for several hours a day). Some aspect of self-image certainly was a factor: hypnosis was compared to the work of a "hod carrier" or "cosmetician," while analysis was "science," "surgery." Perhaps it was more dignity at stake than modesty.

Though modesty was a thread often pulled. He wrote to Martha: "to talk with Breuer was like sitting in the sun; he radiates light and warmth. He is such a sunny person, and I don't know what he sees in me to be so kind."

To Martha herself, "Can there be anything crazier, I said to myself. You have won the dearest girl in the world quite without any merit of your own"[13] (Jones, 1953, p. 110). Granted that this is the romantic hyperbole of courtship. Granted too that there are fluctuations in mood and tone as times and situations change, so that we hear this humility from the same powerful genius who called his real nature that of the *conquistadore.* Still, the license we give to "without merit" is like that we give to the supposedly indistinguishable therapist who receives what *he* does not deserve in the service of carrying out the conditions for transference. "Can there be anything crazier, I said to myself." Yes, a few things. One is institutionalizing false modesty such as that, by denying the characteristics in the situation and the personality of the analyst—denying so completely that a neurosis is cultivated by and for both parties while it is the very object of treatment. And all in the name of sanity, clarity, and honest scrutiny.

INTERIM THOUGHTS

On the way to proposing a countertheory, it is reasonable that I describe some experiences that, over the years, led me to departures from the common beliefs in psychoanalytic theory that I once held.

1.   For 15 years I was on the staff at the University of Chicago Counseling Center, and I replaced Carl Rogers as executive secretary when he departed. Eventually, one develops the reputation of a "therapist's therapist." My clientele consisted largely of junior professionals. Three were interns on a psychiatric rotation from the university hospital. They were taught by their medical faculty a good deal about transference. They discussed their experiences as psychiatrists-in-training. One, a shy, diffident young man, was especially articulate about the onset of transference as he perceived it in a slightly older woman patient. He felt a rising excitement. "This is it." He also felt that he was being handed a power about which he was both pleased and embarrassed, and of course embarrassed by his pleasure and his embarrassment. Not only was transference theory an "armor in his ordeal," but a source of *downright satisfaction.* He felt "as if I were wearing a mask. I smiled behind it. I could have taken it off. I thought of that, but I was too confused about what I'd have to uncover. Behind it, I could be detached, amused, be more thoughtful and responsive." It was a revealing bit of information on the inner experience of transference in a young adherent of the theory. In addition to our discussion, I suggested he talk to his clinical supervisor about it. I wondered how many therapists acknowledge their pleasure so honestly. Weeks later, I took a neighbor and his four-year-old son to the emergency room. My client was on duty. I helped hold and soothe the little boy while Dr. G. sewed stitches in his head wounds. We

worked in a kind of harmonic unison over this child of French-Iranian extraction, who knew little English and was pained and frightened. We did it well. In our next session, Dr. G. told me that he had felt as if it were "our child." Did he mean his feminine qualities and my masculine ones (or the reverse)? No. If it must be put in familial terms, we were brothers, he thought. So did I (though neither of us actually had brothers). One might easily see in this an expression of transference and/or countertransference. I found neither. We had an experience that made us feel like brothers.

2.   I attended a discussion of religion between Bruno Bettleheim and Paul Tillich. Bettleheim took the general position outlined in Freud's *Future of an Illusion* to the effect that the urge toward religious belief was a "projection" of the longing for a father. That seemed most plausible to me. Tillich answered, "But what is the screen?" Not a weighty reply, to my way of thinking at the time, but increasingly I realized that "it" cannot be nothing.

3.   One evening I overheard a client in the next office. She wept and shouted, "No one has ever treated me this way before. I love it, I can't believe it, but I'm afraid every time I come." I thought she was banging on the desk to emphasize her points. At the end of the evening I went to that counselor's office. "For God's sake, Russ, what were you doing?" He explained, and I heard fragments of a primitive audio-disc recording. The banging was the steam pipes. The client was saying, "No one has ever understood me this way before. No one. I can't believe it. I love the feeling of 'at last, someone knows, someone cares.' But when I come back next week, with the rest of my garbage, will you still understand? I couldn't bear it if you didn't."

I did not know the content of what was understood, but was most struck by what understanding meant to her and thought about it for a long time.

4.   I once taught a course with the prominent Adlerian Dr. Rudolph Dreikurs—a hearty, gruff bear of a man. In one class he seemed especially heavy-handed. Students were angry and critical. During the intermission, he said, "Do you notice the hostility? There is a lot of negative transference here." I told him my observations, and he was perplexed, crestfallen. He had taught hundreds, even thousands, and no one had complained. They usually loved him.

5.   In 1971, during the period of the "revolution in mental health" (community organization, demystification, "radical therapy" and politics

to fit, etc.), a consulting psychiatrist and practicing analyst told me, "It is amazing. Some of these paraprofessionals I'm supervising can do anything we can do—except the handling of the transference." I wondered—what would he say if there *is* no "transference"?

6. Over many years, I have been perceived in many different ways. Humble and proud, kind and cruel, loyal and unreliable, ugly and handsome, cowardly and brave, to name a few wide-ranging contradictions. Someone must be mistaken? No, they are all true. This sense of my self, sometimes selfish, sometimes generous, makes me hesitate before characterizing someone's perception as a distortion. One client dreamed of me as a little boy, one she held on her lap—and I a white-haired father of three grown children, as she knew. But she too was correct (and she had her own reasons for the caretaking dream). There is that side of me. I could cast it off, but keep it for my enjoyment. I have been seen as a lion, rabbit. True, I can be hard and soft. Is that unusual? Though happy to have been married for 40 years, I could, when young, have fallen in love frequently—with ease, passion, tenderness. Seriously? Sometimes seriously enough to last another lifetime, probably, but not so seriously that I think I am the only man for this only woman for me.[14] While I do not respect the philanderer because of the damage he is likely to do, reading Jones's judgment that "Freud was not only monogamous in a very unusual degree but for a time seemed to be well on the way to becoming uxurious" (1953, p. 139) struck me as curious and doubtful. It is, however, a condition that would more readily incline one toward transference theory—at least as a supporting illusion. But if that is not my condition or my personality (and I am not certain it was his), should his theory be my theory?

Then, about my granddaughter. I dearly love this child. From what previous experience do I transfer this affection? Yes, I dearly loved my two daughters and my son when they were three-year-olds, too. But whence came *that*? Sooner or later, it has to be *de novo*, original. We know from work in comparative psychology that most women and many men show signs (such as pupillary change) of great attraction to the typical "configuration of infant"—large head and small body. In short, it is an instinct, and it *produces its natural consequences each time for the same instinctive reasons, as if each time were the first.* This child knows me, trusts, loves me too. Is *her* experience transference? Transfer of what? From where? Is mine transference and hers countertransference? Neither one. That is the answer.

The real question is, "What conditions bring about the original experience, the first of its kind without precedents?" Then "What if those conditions again prevail?" Put another way, "If every perception depends on the past, what if there is no past?" (And for a still different outlook, "What if the future is more important than the past?" That is, if what people want and hope to have happen determines their perception of the present as they try to shape it for their imagined future!)

THE NEXT STEP

History of its origins aside, transference is a shorthand term for qualities and characteristics of human interaction. Any shorthand will fail to represent the particulars of a unique relationship. Rather, the shorthand will obscure (in a sometimes comforting way, to be sure) the realities of the relationship. The concept of "father-figure," for instance, needs to be unravelled; what characteristics is it supposed to represent? What do such concepts as "parent" or "infantalizing" mean? In the remaining pages, an alternative view is presented, hopefully to clarify the realities that the shorthand forms fail to represent.

A COUNTERTHEORY

If transference is a fiction to protect the therapist from the consequences of his own behavior, it is time to examine some behaviors—and their normal consequences. This does not start with any implication of villainy. It is simply that since "transference-love" is the consequence most fraught with concern, and was the original instance in development of transference theory from which all its extensions come, we should examine the behaviors responsible for the development of affectionate and erotic feelings.

First, there is the situation, its true conditions. Dependency is a built-in feature for the petitioner at the beginning, and the treatment itself often promotes further dependency. The patient (or client) is typically anxious, distressed, in need of help, often lonely. The therapist, presumably, is not. Instead, he holds a professional role (especially if a physician) that ranks at or near the top in continuing sociological surveys of romantic attractiveness to women seeking husbands (ahead of astronauts and other celebrities).[15] The situation is set for intimacy, privacy, trust, frequent contact, revelation of precious secrets.

Second, it is also the case that there is an ongoing search, on the part of most adolescents and adults, for sexual companionship. With some ebb and flow, the law of propinquity operates in every state. It requires only the opportunity for intimacy. One does not need to look into therapy for arcane and mysterious sources of erotic feelings. They are commonplace, everywhere, carried about from place to place. Psychotherapy will encounter sexual attraction as surely as it encounters nature. The simple combination of urge and situation is a formula for instant, if casual, romantic fantasy.

Third, there is in action and fact a supremely important special factor in a behavior to which all therapists subscribe and try to produce. It is *understanding*. As Freud bluntly put it (of transference): "It is a kind of falling in love." Let me put this bluntly too: *understanding is a form of love-making*. It may not be so intended, but that is one of its effects. The professional Don Juan knows and uses it to deliberate advantage. That alone may make it an embarrassment to the therapist who does not wish to take advavntage and is hard pressed to deal in an accepting but nonpossessive way with ordinary feelings that conventionally call either for some response in kind—or rejection. Such difficulty does not relieve him of the responsibility. Intentionally he has been understanding, and this alone will, over time, activate in the patient some object-seeking components of trust, gratitude, and possibly sexual desire.

In this same context, misunderstanding is a form of hate-making. It works equally well since being misunderstood in a generally understanding relation is a shock, betrayal, frustration, disillusionment.[16]

Understanding and misunderstanding and their ambivalent interplay are the primary factors in this thesis about "positive and negative transference," but there are numerous supplementary behaviors. To supplement misunderstanding, for example: waiting, asking for the key to the bathroom, paying (possibly for missed appointments), cigar smoke, various subordinating and infantalizing conditions.

The most convincing evidence for this simply but profoundly effective thesis probably lies in one's own experience. It was, however, called to my attention by a combination of events, such as that overheard client in the next office, and another fortuitous circumstance. A Jesuit priest took a year of sabbatical study at the University of Chicago, and I was able to see some of the basic data on which he based his study of how it feels to be "really understood" (Van Kaam, 1959). A simple-seeming question, but of great significance. By chance, the first question naire respondent I read was that of an adolescent girl, a 17-year-old student in a parochial school. This Midwestern bobby-sox type is hardly a match for the sophisticated European Anna O., but they are equally real, and, I suspect, would have understood each other. As to how she feels, in substance and spirit, when she experiences under standing, she wrote:

> I felt as if he, my boyfriend, had reached into my heart and had really seen my fears and understood how much my religion meant to me. My whole being wanted to cry out how much I loved him for that understanding. My body felt so alive and I wanted to tell everyone how happy and exuberant I was. I wanted everyone to be happy with me. I wanted to hang on to that understanding and pray it would never be lost to me.
>
> Whenever I am understood by anyone, I feel a fresh onset of love for anyone or anything. I can't sleep right away because I don't want that understanding to fade, and somehow it seems to me that it will probably be lost in the morning.
>
> My body seems to have a terrific pounding sensation and I want to cry out something which I don't know how to express in words. I feel more sure of myself. I want to give. I want to give everything I have to make this person who understands happier. I want to live the full minute of every day. Life seems so much richer when you know someone understands, because to me, one who understands is the one who cares and loves me and I feel love and security and peace. (A. Van Kaam, personal communication, 1961)

I submit that this is not an atypical reaction, but simply one heightened, if not refined, by the enthusiastic vigor of an adolescent girl. She tells us how being understood affects a human being psychologically or physiologically. Why should such effects be labeled "transference"? They do in fact *originate* in the situation and through the performance of psychotherapy (when that is indeed benevolent). The reaction might better be called "originalence." It is not transferred, not inappropriate. It is the normal and appropriate reaction. It might come about in someone who had never been so understood before. It might come from no past experience, but from a wish that the past had been different, or from the hopes and dreams of the future!

For example, there is the filmed interview between Carl Rogers and Gloria (Rogers, 1965), of which a portion is reproduced below. Near the final section, she feels deeply understood in a way that brings tears and a feeling she calls "precious." She wishes her father had been so understanding—but that had *not* been the case. The typical audience witnessing this becomes tense and alert. There is uneasy laughter. They have been taught what to think of this, and the moods range from scornful to sympathetic, for there is a general feeling that transference has reared its head (and the anticipation that Rogers might be caught in a dangerous "Freudian" situation). It can be read that way. It can equally be read as her response to understanding *such as she never had* from her father, her wish that she could have a father like that, not like her own. Is that transference?

Rogers, on display and well aware of this issue, makes certain that he does not deny or reject, and while his response may not be the perfect model, it acknowledges the admiring wistfulness, his appreciation in kind of her, and continues in an understanding mode.

ROGERS: I sense that, in those utopian moments, you really feel kind of whole. You really feel all in one piece.

GLORIA: Yes. (Rogers: M-hm.) Yeah. It gives me a choked up feeling when you say that, because I don't get that as often as I like. (Rogers: M-hm.) I like that whole feeling. It's real precious to me.

ROGERS: I suspect none of us gets it as often as we'd like, but I really do understand. (pause) M-hm, that (referring to her tears) really does touch you, doesn't it?

GLORIA: Yeah, and you know what else, though, I was just thinking... I feel it's a dumb thing that, uhm, all of a sudden when I'm talking, gee, how nice I can talk to you, and I want you to approve of me, and I respect you, but I miss that my father couldn't talk to me like you are. I mean I'd like to say, gee, I'd like you for my father. (Rogers: M-hm.) (pause) (Rogers: You...) I don't even know why that came to me.[17]

ROGERS: You look to me like a pretty nice daughter. (a long, long pause) But you really do miss the fact that you couldn't be open with your own dad.

GLORIA: Yeah, I couldn't be open, but I...I want to blame it on him. I think I'm more open than he'd allow me. I mean he would never listen to me talk like you are. And ah, not disapprove, and not lower me down.

(Rogers, 1965. Quoted by permission of Psychological Films, Inc. Author's transcription.)

"ORIGINALENCE" VERSUS A FORM OF "REPETITION-COMPULSION" IN PSYCHOLOGICAL THOUGHT

One of the errors in transference theory is the illogical assumption that any response that duplicates a prior similar response is necessarily replicating it. Similar responses are not always repetitions. They appear to us to be repetitions because, in our effort to comprehend, we look for patterns, try to generalize. There is breathing as a general respiratory pattern, but my most recent breath is not taken because of the previous one: rather for the same reason the previous breath was taken.

In the first instance, the original love of the child for the parent is not transferred. There was no earlier instance. What then? This original love developed for the same sorts of reasons or conditions that will again produce it in later life. Provide those conditions again and they will produce (not reproduce) it again and again, each time on its own. The produced experience is mingled with memories and associations, but those are not the conditions. Memories may seem to reproduce. If so, they reproduce the *conditions* (for fear or passion, for example), and it is again the *conditions*, not the memory, that account for the response.

How did any particular affect come into being in the first place? If love developed through the parents' understanding (of what the child needs in the way of care, in the development of its whole mental life from language to thought) further understanding should elicit love too; but consider, *every second instance might as well have been the first.* Warmth feels good to the body, not only and perhaps not at all because it felt good when one was an infant, but because it *always* feels good. The need is "wired in" as an innate physiological requirement. When one tastes a lemon at age 30, it tastes sour not because it tasted that way at age three. It *always* tastes sour, the first time at any age, whether or not ever tasted before, and all following times for the same reason each time.

This experiential evidence explicitly affirms that any therapist has an active and response-arousing set of roles and behaviors. He is loved for what makes him lovable, hated for what makes him hateful, and all shades in between. *This should be the first hypothesis.* Whatever it does not account for may be described as another phenomenon, but understanding and misunderstanding will, I believe, account for the major affects of love and hate. This does not begin to analyze the complex interactions beyond understanding and misunderstanding. Whatever they are in any given case, there too therapists play their part. The first principle is for the therapist to eschew the pretense of innocent invisibility and to reflect upon what, in the situation and his (or her) behaviors, does in fact account for those "untoward events" that brought transference theory into being. Adoption of this principle may engender a sense of vulnerability and remove not only the shield but some of the most ornamental of therapeutic trappings as well. This is not the most inviting prospect for the contemporary psychotherapist. It is easier to have an exotic treatment for an intriguing dis-ease, and for the patient there may be some allure as well.

Is there no transference, whatever, at any time? Of course there is, if you wish it. The material is there at the outset. It can be cultivated, and it can be forced. Emotional attitudes *will* be expressed, through indirect channels if open expression is discouraged. Like seeds, emotions and perceptions will grow straight and true in nourishing soil or crookedly through cracks in the sidewalk. One can encourage distortions, and then analyze them. It is a matter of choice. As with any fiction, "transference" can be turned into a scenario to be acted out, creating a desired reality.

At the beginning, there is always prejudice. Upon first meeting, stereotyped judgments and appraisals based on prior experience will be applied to the perception of the new unknown. In a state of ignorance, what else can one do to make meaning?—unless it is the rare instance of those who are able and willing to approach new experience with suspended judgment, and a fresh, open view. Except in the latter cases, prejudgment applies. Then if the reality of the new experience is concealed, attention turns inward. If the reality is available to be known as needed, prejudice fades; judgments and appraisals appropriate to that reality will develop. For example, if red suspenders (and it could be blue eyes, swastikas, peace symbols, skin color, size, shape, combinations of signals) are worn by a person you meet, and if you have been mistreated by someone wearing red suspenders, you will be wary of the new person. If you are permitted to know more, and wish to do so, the effect of red suspenders will be cancelled or supported or become trivial, depending upon your whole knowledge of the new reality. But if the new reality is concealed, attention searches for focus and meaning and, from a relationship standpoint, projections reign. Transference, or what passes for transference, can then be cultivated. Yet it is neither inevitable nor necessary. It is an obstruction. That some derive benefit from its analysis may come from the concentrated self-examination and the presence of attentive intelligence on the part of therapist—both of which are possible in at least equally pure form *without* the transference neurosis.

Will there be any change in basic transference theory? Is it possible to bring balance through corrective criticism? Not likely. Such "balance" is only a temporary concession. The theory itself does not allow for balance. It is too heavily weighted (nearly all-or-none) because its logic cannot bear disturbance. As for the basic position, it is as entrenched as ever. For the public it is high fashion and popular culture: diverting, entertaining. For the professional it is a tradition, a convenience, a shield, stock-in-trade, a revealed truth, and a habit of thought.

How strong a habit of thought is illustrated by an instance described in the study by a sophisticated and sympathetic journalist, J. Malcolm, under the title "Trouble in the Archives" (1983). It reports a "striking example of Eissler's[18] remarkable freedom from self-justification" (p. 132) in a case history. "He treated a wealthy older woman during the years before her death, and was so helpful that, in gratitude, she changed her will and left him a huge amount of money." He could not accept it for himself and ordered it returned to beneficiaries or donated to charities. However,

> the husband of a relative of the deceased whose legacy had been diminished because of the change in the will, formally objected to the probation of the will. He happened to be an analyst, and his argument was that Eissler had exercised "undue influence" on the patient through "the unconscious utilization of the transference." (p. 132)

Malcolm writes, "The case history ends with a wonderful twist." Since the matter had caused painful embarrassment, what had been seen as a "loving gesture" was re-interpreted by Eissler as "an expression of her hatred of him—an expression of the negative transference that had never been allowed to emerge during treatment" (p. 137).

It can be interpreted in other ways as well. The ex-patient may indeed have wished him well, may even have expected that if he could not use the money for himself he could choose to support charitable interests of importance to him. On the other hand, she may have enjoyed the amusement afforded by anticipation of cleverly hurting both her analyst and her relatives with one stroke. Two other observations remain. First, she was treated, even after her death, like a psychiatric patient and therefore a minor or incompetent. She could not exercise her choice about what was, after all, her money, because (1) her judgment was forever suspect, (2) it dispensed something of considerable value to others, and (3) it did not suit those who survived her and who could either call upon, or were called upon by, transference theory. Second, everything suffers (not entirely without compensation) *except* the concept of transference. One might think that since it was born of embarrassment, it might now die of embarrassment. But no, that is its charm. It merely changes color, never questioned, only reconfirmed.

CONCLUSION

I have offered a brief for a countertheory, not in the sense of a complement or counterpart, as in "transference and countertransference" but in the sense that *counter* means opposite. If transference is a theory, this is the counter: personality and situation aside for the moment, *the therapist is responsible for two fundamental behaviors— understanding and misunderstanding—which account for love, or for hate,* and their associated affects. These, as well as other behaviors and the situation and personality of the therapist, may account—should first be held accountable—for the whole of what passes for transference.

The power of understanding has been featured to account for the phenomenon called "transference." That use should not hide the point that it is this very power of understanding (not the transference, transference-love, or love itself) that heals. Understanding makes for healing and growth; misunderstanding makes for injury and destruction.

The proposition that "understanding heals" does not make understanding the exclusive property of client-centered therapy. Far from it. Client-centered therapy has a constant theme in its focus on understanding: early, in its method of seeking confirmation from the client; later, in its stress on empathy (as a form of understanding and even a "way of being") and how such understanding is best achieved. That stress is evident throughout this book. That is its emphasis, not its proprietary claim.

The emphasis on understanding is stressed at this final point to indicate that, while love is a blessing, love is not enough. Ultimately we are trying to account not only for transference love, or for love in general, but for *healing*. Even romantic love ("falling in," or choosing to be in) gives promise of, and is given in the hopes of receiving, understanding (which may or may not be delivered). Being "in love" often assumes understanding to exist even where it does not. When love *is* present, it is either the environment for or the consequence of *understanding*. Though the two are strongly associated, love does not heal. Understanding heals. It also makes one feel loved, or sustains love already felt, but the healing power is in the understanding.

Knowing that does not make the conduct of therapy easier in the slightest. It may, however, help us to separate therapy from the rest of life. It seems that we can quite well love, and take love from, those to whom we do not devote the considerable or sometimes near-consuming effort to fully understand. *That* is the difference between real life in ordinary relations and equally real life in therapy. If and to such extent as they could be brought together, so much the better; if not, all the good in either case.

To conclude that it is not love that heals may be a disappointment to many. The role of the healer is appealing. So is that of the benefactor who dispenses love. Therapists and others find these roles all too gratifying. But no, the "healer" takes credit for a process inherent in the organism, if released, and love is only therapeutic or enduringly beneficial if expressed through understanding. The act of understanding may be the most difficult of any task we set ourselves—a seemingly mundane "service role" requiring kinds of intelligence and sensitivity so demanding that some people are truly seen as gifted. Even that is not the final cause. It still remains for the client to *feel* understood.

To realize that it is the *understanding* that promotes the healing will direct us to the remaining problem for psychotherapy and psychology: we do not know the mechanisms by which understanding promotes healing or even the mechanisms of understanding itself. That knowledge cannot come from a theory such as transference, which has been a roadblock and a pointer in the wrong direction for almost a century. That knowledge may not come from *any* present version of psychotherapy, but rather from more neutral realms of cognitive, social, and developmental psychology, to the ultimate benefit of a new theory and practice.

NOTES

1. *Transference* does not appear in the index of his earlier *Counseling and Psychotherapy* (1942b).

2.   Inventions are man-made: thus *invent* is used to offset Freud's use of the word *discovered*, which implies a fact found or truth revealed.

3.   Social and economic conditions that create anxiety neuroses in women and enable men to become physicians have changed enough to bring about some evening of opportunity. Fortunately, women can more easily find female therapists. There are also more cross-sex, same-sex, bi-sex, and other permutations. We know relatively little of these many parallels of the transference model, but may be sure that the concept is now so well established that it will appear as a "demand characteristic" in its own right. It has become part of the pseudosophisticated belief system of informed clients.

4.   I do not include Jones's additional comment that this trip resulted in the conception of a daughter "who was later to commit suicide in New York"; it now appears to be an inaccurate report.

5.   One point must be stressed. There is only, but *only* Freud's reconstruction in this momentous history. No other source whatever. How much Freud wanted this data, how much and how often he pressed Breuer for it, we do not know. In his autobiography (1948, first published in 1925), he wrote: "When I was back in Vienna I turned once more to Breuer's observation and made him tell me more about it" (p. 34). In 1925 he still speaks of "a veil of obscurity which Breuer never raised for me" (p. 36). This prodding, though, eventually cost them their friendship. How much Breuer's support meant to Freud we do know. How highly motivated to get this information, which he sometimes says Breuer would never repeat for him, we also know. Yet it is all Freud's reconstruction; and in 1932, when he wrote the cited letter to Stefan Zweig, he still seems wanting of confirmation. "I was so convinced of this reconstruction of mine that I published it somewhere. Breuer's youngest daughter read my account and asked her father about it shortly before his death. He confirmed my version, and she informed me about it later" (Freeman, 1972, p. 200). To what "reconstruction" does this refer, that he published because he was so convinced yet unconfirmed? Hot pursuit, without a doubt, but the facts are still reported with slight discrepancies, and never by anyone but Freud.

6.   To what? Not necessarily the arcane lock Freud had in mind. Perhaps the door to a more literal and still more courageous exploration.

7.   I have personally known psychologists and psychiatrists who far exceeded Breuer's relatively innocent transgressions, i.e., theirs were "sins" by the informal definition, "included exchange of bodily fluids." Results included divorce, marriage to the patient, suicide, murderous thoughts and a probable attempt, career changes, and the development of new theories. The late O.H. Mowrer's therapy based on real guilt and compensation (1967) is an example of the latter, as he often announced to professional colleagues.

8.   This is either the instance that is sometimes described as the patient being just aroused from a hypnotic trance, and with a maid-servant unexpectedly knocking or entering, or it is a separate but prototypic scene.

9.   Women are especially good at this, he writes. They "have a genius for it" (Freud, 1935, p. 384).

10.   This too is the patient's doing? Does this material not reside in the being of the physician? Or, of an interactive quality, does the transference arise in the patient as a result of the physician's influence?

11.   In a letter dated 1939 about a case now becoming infamous, Freud wrote to Jung, "After receiving your wire I wrote Fraulein Sp. a letter in which I affected ignorance...." (McGuire, 1974, p. 230) and says of Jung's mishap,

> I myself have never been taken in quite so badly, but I have come very close to it a number of times and had a "*narrow escape*" [in English]. I believe that only grim necessities weighing on my work and the fact that I was ten years older when I came to psychoanalysis saved me from similar experiences. But no lasting harm is done. They help us to develop the thick skin we need and to dominate "counter-transference" which is after all a permanent problem for us. (McGuire, 1974, p. 231)

12.   "Later he assured her that the anatomy of the brain was the only rival she had or was likely to have" (Jones, 1953, p. 211).

13.   "But a week later he asks why he should not for once get more than he deserved. Never has he imagined such happiness" (Jones, 1953, p. 110).

14.   My wife, with good taste and judgment, advises ("after all, this is not your biography") omitting this entire section. I would like to but a main point of the chapter is that theory is in part biographical, stemming from thought, observation, self-concept, and an idea of how to look at the future.

15.   A current social psychology suggests that love, especially sexual love, is the result of status and power factors. "A love relationship is one in which at least one actor gives (or is prepared to give) extremely high status to the other" (Kemper, 1978, p. 285).

16.   This should not be overlooked: the therapist wants, and sometimes demands, to be understood by the patient or client. Whether dealing in reflections, interpretations, or hypnotic suggestion, he wants these understood. Feels good about it if they are, inadequate and "resisted" if they are not. Indeed, the therapist may have the same response to understanding as does the patient! Tempered of course by wisdom, maturity, self-awareness, and other not-always-present virtues.

17.   Popular wisdom says that young women may seek "father figures." A less popular and somewhat masked understanding is that men may seek "daughter figures" in a reciprocal fashion not so readily fit to transference theory. Whatever motives for either party—whether benign caring, dependency, exploitation, fulfilling of various hopes and desires—the seeking moves in both directions. So neither party may be justly accused of entirely uninvited or unrewarded responsibility. This is not necessarily to explain the particular

case, but to add a statement of general interest in the re-analysis of transference theory.

18.   Kurt Eissler, a towering figure in the psychoanalytic movement, of whom one of his colleagues says, "Eissler is not loveable, and he knows it" (Malcolm, 1983, p. 152). Yet his patient may have found him so, and rightly, for the very reason of his understanding behavior—when, if, and inasmuch.

9   Client Tasks in Client-Centered Therapy

Laura N. Rice

The special quality of the relationship in client-centered therapy has been widely recognized and has had a profound impact on the whole field of psychotherapy and counseling. Less clearly recognized, even by client-centered therapists, is the potential power of the *working* relationship to enable the client to accomplish crucial therapeutic tasks. I have recently proposed a distinction between primary relationship factors and task-relevant relationship factors in client-centered therapy (Rice, 1983). The primary relationship factors are those aspects of the relationship that can lead *directly* to new interpersonal learning for the client. For instance, it is from the experience of feeling unconditionally valued by the therapist that clients begin to learn to value and respect themselves. Also the therapist's evident trust of clients' inner experience enables many clients to begin to view their inner awareness as a valuable resource for guiding their lives. These primary relationship factors are important for all clients and absolutely crucial for some.

The task-relevant relationship factors, on the other hand, exert their effects more indirectly, in the sense that they help to establish the working conditions that are optimal for facilitating particular kinds of self-exploration. Clients bring into therapy experiences from current life situations and from the recent or more distant past and attempt to explore and to reprocess them in ways that can lead to new data about themselves in relation to their world. Different kinds of *cognitive-affective reprocessing tasks* can best be facilitated by different kinds of task-relevant relationship factors. Even in a given class of tasks different steps require somewhat different kinds of therapist focus. These two relationship factors are important in varying degrees for different clients, but the primary relationship variables take precedence over the task elements for many clients.

The central theme of the present chapter is that a successful client-centered therapy involves the resolution of a series of cognitive-affective reprocessing tasks, and that therapists can become much more effective facilitators of these reprocessing functions if they can recognize and understand some of the different classes of tasks that clients undertake in productive psychotherapy. Client-centered therapists have been somewhat reluctant to entertain the idea of choosing different ways of responding to different clients or to the same client at different times. They have felt that in this kind of selective responding they might lose the very spontaneity and humanness that is the core of the primary relationship conditions. In my experience, however, the selective use of different therapist responses to facilitate particular reprocessing tasks need not be inconsistent with the primary relationship conditions. The client will still be the expert on his or her own experience while the therapist will still be the expert on process. In other words, the therapist will be somewhat process-directive, but the "track" that is being followed will be the client's own. Another hesitation has stemmed from the idea that such differentiated ways of responding presume a kind of diagnostic labeling. As I will discuss later, the approach does not involve labeling or classifying individuals, but a moment-to-moment *process diagnosis*, in which the therapist recognizes how best to facilitate the kind of reprocessing that is of concern to the client at that particular moment. The important challenge for the next few years is to identify and explicate some of these process variables and to learn how to maximize these special qualities selectively and expertly and thus to make client-centered therapy more effective for different people.

The basic client-centered mode is ideally suited to the tasks of cognitive-affective reprocessing. I will describe more specific kinds of therapist facilitation later, but at this point I would like to indicate three basic aspects of the client-centered working relationship that distinguish it from working relationships in other therapeutic orientations. First, the therapist is always tuned to the client's internal frame of reference, the client's experience of being in the world. We try to look through the client's eyes, hear through her ears, get a kinesthetic sense of what it is like to *be* the client at any given moment. We want to get a real sense of the idiosyncratic ways in which the client is construing his or her own world. We are not comparing this construal with how it "really" is, but, for example, we are sensing that the client isn't just seeing snow but is seeing "ruthless, engulfing snow" or a "soft, insulating blanket of snow."

A second important aspect of the working relationship is that the therapist's responses almost always point inward. Certainly at times the focus is on the relationship in a very interpersonal sense. At other times the therapist is self-disclosing. But the therapist is not someone to be coped with, argued with, or looked to for agreement or approval. Most of the time the therapist fosters an active kind of inner tracking on the part of the client. There is an intense inward deployment of attentional energy directed toward discovery and exploration of new inner experience.

The third important aspect of the working relationship is its moment-to-moment quality. The therapist does not begin with an assessment of core conflicts, faulty cognitions, or any other diagnostic assessment. The therapist does not have a treatment plan. But the experienced therapist does have a moment-to-moment awareness of what needs to be heard that is free-floating but not purposeless. Rather than being constrained by our own hypotheses, we are free to hear *process markers* that signal our clients' *need* to reprocess some experience that is troubling or unfinished and their present *motivation* to explore and understand it. We don't feel the need of a treatment plan because of our underlying assumption that anything that is live and/or troubling for our clients is a possible entry point for a productive journey of exploration. With suitable facilitation from the therapist, clients can follow their *own* trails. Thus we can rely on the moment-to-moment process diagnoses or markers that tell us that there is something here that the client needs and wants to explore.

It is illuminating to place client-centered therapy on a continuum of therapeutic approaches. At one end would be cognitive-behavioral approaches in which cognitive structures are examined directly and compared with "reality." Even when the targets of change are cognitive structures involving affective components, the approach in cognitive therapy is that of a "learning lab" (Mahoney, 1979), in which present cognitive structures are challenged and new ones are explicitly taught and encouraged. The focus of such therapy is on directly changing the cognitive structures rather than on the attempt to discover new and compelling experiential data that will lead to reorganization of one's own construal systems. At the other end of the continuum would be approaches such as primal therapy, some of the body therapies, and some Gestalt approaches, in which the focus is on stimulating the client to get in touch with strong affect and impulses and to intensify them by encouraging direct expression or acting out. Dramatic new experiential material emerges, but there is often little emphasis on re-examining and reprocessing these new self-discoveries.

Good client-centered therapy seems to me to be in the middle of the continuum. The client is engaged on a journey of exploration, closely accompanied by the therapist. Past episodes can be re-experienced at a high level of arousal, and the client can become newly and poignantly aware of feelings and reactions. Yet there is always an exploratory stance. The client feels safe enough to look for and examine new experience and to find the search energizing and fascinating even when it seems to have negative implications. Neither the therapist nor the client knows in advance what the crucial new data will be, and neither will try to impose hypotheses on the data. The new data will be idiosyncratic and not predictable in advance, but the exploration will have a self-directed, purposive quality. When it is concluded, the client will have a sense of resolution, involving not only the relief of having expressed previously unexpressed feelings, but also a new understanding of self-in-the-world. It is this combination of discovery of irrefutable new experience with purposive re-examination and search for new understanding that can provide the ideal working conditions for resolving the cognitive-affective reprocessing tasks of therapy.

THE STRUCTURE OF COGNITIVE-AFFECTIVE REPROCESSING TASKS

I have suggested above that successful client-centered therapy involves the resolution of a series of cognitive-affective reprocessing tasks. Different tasks are important for different people and for the same person at different times. In general, it is not useful to attempt to predict the precise nature of these tasks in advance, but rather to attend to client's process markers as they arise during therapy. For each class of task there is a marker that can signal to the therapist that the client is ready and motivated to explore and reprocess some self-relevant area of experience. These markers consist of clients' statements together with their manner of expression. For instance, the marker for one class of task, which I call *problematic reactions* (this will be analyzed in detail later), appears when clients recount a particular incident in which they reacted in a way that they themselves felt to be inappropriate, exaggerated, or otherwise problematic in that they did not understand their own reactions.

I am further suggesting that the successful resolution of tasks of a given class will involve certain essential client steps. The content of the task will, of course, be different for each one, but there will be certain recognizable structural similarities. The primary focus in this approach is on first isolating and understanding the *client* steps that are necessary for resolving a given class of task. Then if the therapist is aware of these essential steps as a process road map, she can respond in different ways that are designed to be optimally facilitative at different points. This does not involve a "treatment plan" in the usual sense of specifying particular content or issues to be worked on, but rather a more precise form of the process awareness that guides all client-centered therapists. Experienced therapists are aware of cues that signal the presence of something that must be "heard." These cues may be found in the client's tone of voice, choice of words, stance toward what is being expressed, and so forth. These cues can be recognized as signaling a potential task, whether it be to move to the next higher level of experiencing (Mathieu-Coughlan & Klein, 1984), to be able to accept in oneself some previously unrevealed attitude or action, or to explore and reprocess some poignant but unassimilated past experience. Furthermore, these cues suggest something about the optimal form and focus of the therapist's responses. The experienced therapist has implicit and sometimes explicit knowledge of what is likely to facilitate such tasks. The more the therapist can recognize explicitly what happens and *how* it happens, the greater the likelihood of its happening more often and with more complete resolution.

The strategy I am proposing here for improving client-centered therapy is to tap into this pool of implicit clinical wisdom, isolate a number of seemingly powerful cognitive-affective tasks, and make intensive analyses of them. Rice and Greenberg (1984) have proposed a new research paradigm for understanding the internal structure of the interactions in different therapeutic orientations by means of "rational and empirical task analysis." This research strategy involves a focus on patterns of client process during change-producing episodes, a study of the client process in the context in which it occurs, and the use of fine-grained *descriptive* process measures. The product of this approach is a model of the series of client processes that seem to be necessary for successful resolution. Once we can isolate and understand these essential client steps, we are in a position to evaluate the efficacy of different therapist responses for facilitating the different client process steps. This is quite unlike the approach that has been used in most therapy process research—that of identifying certain therapist behavior as "good," and summing across samples of interviews to evaluate the therapist's performance.

CONCEPTUALIZING THERAPEUTIC CHANGE IN TERMS OF COGNITIVE THEORY

I have found it productive to use the concepts and language of cognitive information-processing theory to describe and attempt to understand some of the important tasks in client-centered therapy. This seems to be the most relevant body of psychological theory and research for attempting to describe and explicate the internal client operations that are essential mechanisms of change. Furthermore it provides a somewhat orientation-neutral common language for thinking about change mechanisms across orientations. A common language is badly needed if we are ever to understand the commonalities and uniquenesses in different orientations and learn to make optimal use of the contributions of each.

I want to stress here that in advocating the use of cognitive information-processing theory as a conceptual structure for understanding therapeutic change, I am not talking about the *methods* used in cognitive and cognitive-behavioral therapy to effect change. It seems to me that a primary target for change in most therapeutic approaches could be conceptualized as the relatively enduring cognitive structures (schemas) that function to assimilate input and organize output. The basic differences between orientations lie in the *methods* used to effect the schematic changes, and these differences can also be clarified by analyzing them in terms of cognitive theory and research. Goldfried and Robins (1983) have recently made a similar point from the perspective of the cognitive-behavioral therapist.

Perceptual-cognitive theory seems like an especially good fit for client-centered therapy. Indeed, Rogers in his early theoretical statements seems to have anticipated many of the ways in which current cognitive theorists view the person (Rogers, 1951). One of Rogers's crucial assumptions was that our perceptions of the world and ourselves will have a decisive influence on what we do and that, if our perceptions change in the course of therapy, then many behaviors will change without ever being worked on directly. The person's perceptual-conceptual system was specified as the target of therapy, and at the core of the system was the self-concept. Even his assumption concerning the individual nature of each person's perceptual-conceptual system is consistent with the view of many cognitive theorists that perception is a constructive process in which perceivers are active in creating their own psychological reality (Neisser, 1976).

One might question the match between cognitive information-processing theory and client-centered theory on the ground that most cognitive theorists have been concerned with the perception of people and objects in the external environment while client-centered theory has been more concerned with the self-concept and self-perception. I think that the two directions can be profitably combined. Client-centered therapists have focused primarily on the self-concept and have been insufficiently concerned with schemas relevant to individual perceptions of and transactions with the world. The implications of this point for the actual conduct of therapy will be explored later. Coming from the other direction, social-cognitive psychologists have become increasingly interested in studying the role of self-schemas in the storage and retrieval of information about self and others and their role in our interpersonal encounters (Cohen, 1981; Markus, 1977; Markus & Smith, 1981; Swann & Read, 1981; Taylor & Crocker, 1981). Several conclusions emerging from this research will sound very familiar to client-centered therapists. The research suggests that as people form self-schemas on the basis of experience in a particular domain they tend to become increasingly resistant to information that does not fit into these particular self-schemas. This parallels the Rogerian view that experience that is inconsistent with the self-structure cannot be symbolized accurately in awareness (Rogers, 1959b). Second, social-cognitive psychologists stress the dominant role of the more "extensive" self-schemas in relation to the schemas that concern other people and objects. In other words, self-schemas that define what one is like, what one needs, or what one should do, often play a dominant role in differentially activating the schemas involved in construing one's world.

One further point that needs to be made concerning the applicability of cognitive theory for understanding therapy is its relative neglect of affect. The view that the arousal of affect follows and is dependent on a cognitive appraisal of the stimulus has until recently been the dominant one in cognitive theory. It is also a core assumption underlying the therapeutic strategies of such cognitive therapists as Ellis and Meichenbaum. This view has always seemed contrary to the intuitions of client-centered therapists concerning the human ability to track and differentiate new facets of feelings. Perhaps the greatest impetus for re-examination of the cognitive position has come from Zajonc's proposal that affect and cognition are processed differently, involving somewhat separate systems, and that affect often preceeds cognition (1980). Other theorists have considered perceptual processing to be a complex sequence involving affect as an early and influential part of the sequence (Blumenthal, 1977; Fiske, 1981; Leventhal, 1979). This complex issue is currently generating excitement and research among both cognitive therapists and cognitive theorists (Greenberg & Safran, in press). The relevant point here is that using a cognitive framework for attempting to understand the reprocessing tasks of client-centered therapy need not neglect the role of affect either in the original experience or in the reprocessing of it.

EVOKING AND REPROCESSING PROBLEMATIC REACTIONS

In this section I will focus primarily on the resolution of one class of cognitive-affective reprocessing tasks that has been intensively analyzed, the *problematic reactions*. The steps of the rational and empirical task analysis of this class of tasks is reported elsewhere (Rice & Saperia, 1984). In this chapter, I will present a fine-grained description of the client steps that lead to the resolution of this class of event as an illustration of the kind of clinical understanding that can emerge from such a task focus.

In my own clinical experience I have observed that clients often describe incidents in which they reacted in a way that they considered to be strange, inappropriate, or exaggerated. The crucial element in these recountings seems to be that clients feel their *own* reactions to be problematic in some way. Sometimes these incidents are directly connected to themes emerging in therapy. At other times there is no apparent connection, but it is somehow very much on the client's mind and is recounted in a rather lively fashion. The fact that the clients' own reactions appeared puzzling to them seemed to me to be a strong indication of a real readiness at that moment for self-exploration.

I have also found that many clients move very quickly into a discussion of the strangeness of a given reaction and disapproval for its maladaptiveness. Such discussions are usually only mildly productive, and they seem to deflect us from grasping the flavor of the actual incident, even to the extent of sealing off the incident. On the other hand, when I am able to ignore the discussion of their "reaction to the reaction," even though those feelings might be uppermost in their attention, and focus clients vividly on the incident itself, new self-discoveries seem to emerge. Clients become aware of the differentiated quality of their own affective reactions. And what is even more interesting, they often seem to become compellingly aware of the perceived aspects of the situation that apparently triggered their reaction. They seem to be able to discover in an immediate, irrefutable manner some of the idiosyncratic ways in which they were construing the stimulus situation and the role of these construals in triggering the problematic reaction. The result of these two new kinds of awareness in relation to each other is a feeling of relief, a sense of understanding that their own reactions, however odd or maladaptive, make a kind of "organismic" sense. It also seems to lead to some positive changes in later interactions in similar kinds of situations and in some cases to a broader self-understanding.

These clinical observations suggest that the recounting of a problematic reaction can be seen as a marker for one kind of potentially productive therapeutic task, a class of tasks that would be worth studying in detail. The aspect of the therapist's participation that seems to be crucial to the unfolding and resolution of this kind of client task is the vivid evocation of the *particular* incident, with its particular sights and sounds and feelings (Rice, 1974). It is this act of recreating and staying with a particular problematic incident that seems to be the cornerstone of the approach to this task and the aspect of therapist participation that differs most from the usual client-centered approach. Furthermore it has become increasingly clear that a cognitive-affective reprocessing model would be a useful one for attempting a detailed understanding of the different processes and internal operations in which a client needs to engage in order to reach successful resolution. It was this growing awareness that led me to perform an intensive analysis of this class of tasks using the approach proposed by Rice and Greenberg (1984).

I will outline here the necessary steps on the path to resolution, keeping the focus on what the client needs to *do* to reach successful resolution, and, wherever possible, will speculate about the kinds of cognitive-affective client operations that may underlie the observable behavior. Once we can recognize these essential client steps, we can identify much more clearly the kinds of therapist reflections and reflective questions that are likely to be maximally facilitative. The sequence of client steps that leads to resolution of a problematic reaction is shown in Figure 9.1. For the sake of clarity, the discussion of these steps will consist of four general phases, although transitions are not usually as clear-cut as the model would suggest. For instance, phase III often overlaps with phase II.

Phase I—Positioning for Exploration

The client describes an experience that contains the three elements that constitute the marker for a problematic reaction: (1) the client is able to recount a particular instance in a particular situation; (2) the client is pointing to some internal or behavioral reaction of his or her *own*; and (3) the client gives some indication that this reaction is seen as problematic. By *problematic* we mean that the reaction is felt to be peculiar, unreasonable, exaggerated, or inappropriate—that it does not seem understandable to the client. For example, one client said, "I was driving on route six and I got so bothered by the cars behind me that I turned my rear-view mirror up. I even left it up for the next three weeks!" Here the tone of surprise and disapproval in the client's voice made it amply clear that this reaction was felt to be problematic. If the statement of a problematic reaction is expressed in a generalized form such as, "I sometimes get panicked when the tutorial leader calls on me," the therapist typically asks the client if he or she can think of a specific incident when this happened. When no specific incident is forthcoming at the time, it is not possible to proceed with it, but the client is encouraged to watch for such an incident in the future. This, incidentally, has proved to be a very productive kind of "homework" for some clients. After the client has stated the problematic reaction, the therapist tries to reflect it in a way that recognizes the "reaction to the reaction" so that the client will feel heard but leaves the focus of the reflection on the problematic reaction itself. For instance, one client said, "I got jealous and angry the other night at a party. It just didn't make any sense. The whole thing was stupid and childish and my girlfriend was thoroughly irked at me." The therapist responded, "It seems irrational to you now, but at the time you just felt awful!" The focus of the reflection was not on the reaction to the reaction even though it clearly involved strong feelings.

The therapist then tries to get a real feel for the situation that forms

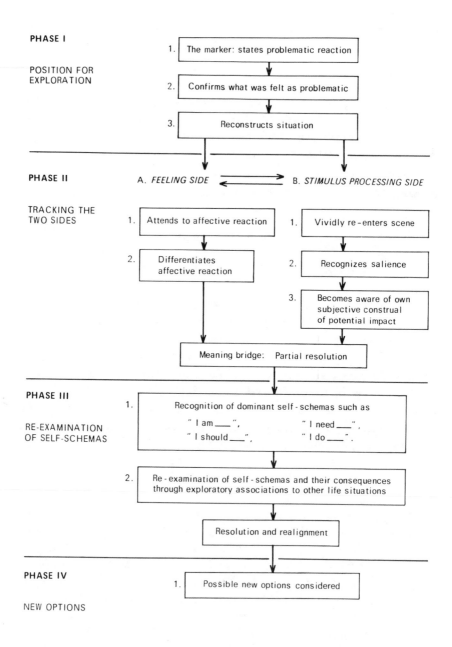

PHASE I

POSITION FOR
EXPLORATION

1. The marker: states problematic reaction

2. Confirms what was felt as problematic

3. Reconstructs situation

PHASE II

TRACKING THE
TWO SIDES

A. *FEELING SIDE*   ⇄   B. *STIMULUS PROCESSING SIDE*

1. Attends to affective reaction

2. Differentiates affective reaction

1. Vividly re-enters scene

2. Recognizes salience

3. Becomes aware of own subjective construal of potential impact

Meaning bridge: Partial resolution

PHASE III

RE-EXAMINATION
OF SELF-SCHEMAS

1. Recognition of dominant self-schemas such as

" I am ___ ",   " I need ___ ",
" I should ___ ",   " I do ___ ".

2. Re-examination of self-schemas and their consequences through exploratory associations to other life situations

Resolution and realignment

PHASE IV

NEW OPTIONS

1. Possible new options considered

FIGURE 9.1. Phases in the resolution of problematic reactions.

192

the context for the problematic reaction and stimulates the client to recall and to some extent re-experience the stimulus situation. In the case of the jealous boyfriend, for instance, after the client had confirmed his feelings at the time, the therapist said, "So you and your girlfriend were at a party—at somebody's house I guess? And something happened—something that really got to you?" This reflection also helped to pinpoint the moment at which the reaction was triggered. The client replied, "Yes, we were standing around talking, and she and the guy next to her smiled right at each other—and I just erupted inside."

If the first phase is successful and the particular experience in its unique context has begun to come alive, the client is now in a position to begin the second phase.

Phase II—Exploring the Two Sides: Inner Reaction and Perceptual Processing

Phase II involves the discovery of a *meaning bridge* between the quality of one's affective reaction and the idiosyncratic, subjective nature of one's construal of salient elements of the stimulus situation; that is, one's reaction is seen to fit the stimulus situation as construed. Phase II is a complex one, involving two different kinds of exploratory focus. Client and therapist will probably move back and forth between the two sides several times during the exploration. But the *open edge* of the therapist's reactions and reflective questions should always be on one side or the other. Each edge of the experience needs a separate and distinct kind of attentional energy. Attending to both sides at the same time seems to lead to abstraction rather than new exploration. At the latter part of the phase the two sides may merge, but the exploration seems to be maximally facilitated in the earlier part by keeping the exploratory energy focused on one side or the other. In a real sense both kinds of exploratory focus are experiential. Although perceptual processing (construal) is usually considered to be a cognitive function, the act of becoming compellingly aware of the nature and subjectivity of one's own construal of the situation involves an inner experiential focus.

Whether the therapist will first attend to side A or side B will depend on a complex judgment. The correctness of this decision does not seem to be crucial, however, since it is possible to switch back and forth later.

Side A. **Exploring the Differentiated Quality of One's Affective Reaction.** When the reaction experienced by the client as problematic is an affective one (as opposed to behavioral or analytical) and when this feeling seems to be re-aroused as the incident is recounted, the therapist should probably focus immediately on the differentiated qualities of the affective reaction.

Most client-centered therapists are quite comfortable with the kinds of reflections appropriate to side A. They try to reflect in a way that pick up the differentiated quality of the feeling. The therapist may sense and reflect "a kind of cold, knotted anger," for instance. Or a new facet of the feeling may come out: "I was angry but I was a little bit afraid too." The only difference here is that the therapist tries to stay with the feeling in the *particular* situation rather than joining the client in exploring other incidents of this kind.

In the party example above, the therapist reflected feelings vividly, trying to get a differentiated sense of the client's feeling at that particular moment. The client began to realize that what he was feeling was more anger than jealousy, and he got in touch with a sense of feeling "put down." The focus moved over to the perceptual-processing side several times while phase II was unfolding and then moved back to the "feeling side." The feeling became more differentiated and the client developed an increasing awareness of the stimulus-connected quality of the feeling. He recognized that he wanted to "squash" the other guy, but felt helpless to do so.

If, as the feeling is explored and differentiated, it becomes less vivid, and the impetus to explore it further dissipates, the therapist does not push for further differentiation of feeling, but switches the focus to side B. Often the client spontaneously switches the focus to the processing side and the therapist follows. Whenever the search is on the feeling side, the therapist may use vivid fragments of the stimulus situation to maintain a high level of arousal, but the open edge of the reflection is on the feeling side.

Side B. **Exploring One's Idiosyncratic, Subjective Construal of the Stimulus.** For other clients, especially those who are primarily aware of their behavioral reaction as problematic, the therapist should probably start with side B, although here again some switching back and forth will occur. For some clients the search is not easily made through affective differentiation. For these clients, asking about feelings seems to be somewhat unproductive and frustrating. The more productive approach seems to be to help them to re-enter the scene at a high level of vividness and arousal so that there is a kind of re-experiencing of the incident and its impact. But at the same time the therapist tries to help the client keep a part of his or her attentional energy in a deliberately exploratory stance.

The therapist's reflections and reflective questions used in side B are less typical for client-centered therapists and will therefore be discussed in some detail. When the explorations of this side are success-ful, the client discovers the nature of his or her idiosyncratic, subjective construal of the potential impact of the stimulus situation, together with an awareness of the subjectivity of this construal. It is not a question of correctness of construal, but an awareness of the meaning the situation has for the client rather than an automatic attribution of meaning to the stimulus.

The client is engaged in somewhat different kinds of processes in the three substages of side B, and somewhat different kinds of therapist responses are appropriate at each substage.

Substage 1. The first step is for a client and therapist to recreate the stimulus context of the problematic reaction. This was done to some extent in the first phase, but is done much more vividly and completely here. It is very much a joint effort. The client's description reverberates in the therapist who then tries to reflect it vividly, even trying out aspects in a tentative way to stimulate the client to check against his or her own experience and correct or elaborate. This process seems to cue the memory by drawing from the context in which it was originally formed. When one recounts an experience, one's memory of it may be very condensed and may not contain the elements that were most crucial at the time of the event itself. This is not in most cases a defensive process, but a difference in the kind of processing that takes place under different circumstances. The crucial aspects are potentially available but not easily accessible except in the context of the newly evoked experience. Often when the therapist tries out details, the client will unhesitatingly correct them. The therapist's reflections and reflective questions serve to cue material from episodic memory that might otherwise be unavailable. There is considerable evidence in the cognitive literature that memories can be more readily retrieved if the context of the encoding is similar to the context for retrieval (Craik & Tulving, 1975; Tulving, 1974).

In the party example, the following interchange took place:

THERAPIST: I wonder if we could go back to the situation so that I could get the flavor of it. You were all standing around—kind of in a circle—all talking together?

CLIENT: No. The music was so loud I could only hear the person next to me. She was across the circle, talking with this guy.

THERAPIST: I see. So the music was blaring and all you could do was look across and see their lips moving, but you couldn't hear what they said.

CLIENT: Yeah, and he said something to her and then they smiled at each other, and then he looked right over at me.

Substage 2. Once the scene has begun to come alive in this internal way, the client may become aware of the aspect or aspects of the situation that were salient for him or her. The therapist can help in this by searching tentatively for salience.

For instance, the above dialogue continued as follows:

THERAPIST: And there was just something about his look—I don't know—something that got to you?

CLIENT: Yeah. Sort of a smug twist of the lips, kind of self-satisfied. You know?

Searching for salience may be done a number of times during the exploration, each time in an attempt to identify the focal point for the client at that moment. Sometimes this stimulates the client to search and explore. Often clients can recognize instantly and with sureness what had felt salient for them in the scene.

It is this sense of salience that is the nucleus of the client's subjective construal. Vivid experiential recognition of it provides the entry point for clients to begin to explore their own subjective construal of the situation.

It is possible to speculate in cognitive terms about the mechanism whereby recognition of salience becomes a crucial entry point (see Taylor & Fiske, 1978). Some features of this particular stimulus situation are momentarily salient for the client, probably because of past experience and a link with certain self-schemas. Certain dominant schemas are automatically activated and the client engages in a kind of *automatic* perceptual activity rather than a slower and more complete series of perceptual cycles (Greenberg & Safran, 1980; Toukmanian, in press). Thus a stimulus situation that would ordinarily be processed more completely and accurately, thus leading to more usual reactions, is processed in an automatic fashion, thereby triggering a problematic reaction. In therapy, the original stimulus situation is vividly evoked: the same features are salient as in the original experience, and they can be recognized by the client. This, in turn, points to the special focus of the client's immediate, subjective construal of the situation. Salience is a useful entry point because the original sequence is reactivated, but, in contrast to the original situation, part of the client's attentional energy is used for exploratory self-observation.

Substage 3. The client's awareness of her idiosyncratic subjective construal is the final element in the side B process. This third substage has a complex focus. On the one hand, it is important for the client to develop a kind of "double vision," to become aware of the self rather than another as agent in one's own construals. But we don't want to stimulate an "as if" or role-playing stance. This feeling must be both genuine and subjective. There are many ways to stimulate this approach to exploration. For instance, the therapist might say, "I'd like to get the flavor that had for you"; the client, by trying to convey this "flavor" to the therapist, gets more and more in touch with it. It is here that I find metaphors especially helpful. What the client is describing comes for the therapist in the sense of an image—visual, auditory, kinesthetic—of how the scene was experienced, what it seemed like to the client. The therapist tries out his or her own metaphorical image here and if it matches that client's experience it will not only be accurate in the sense of capturing the essence, but it will also have the quality of exaggeration, of extreme subjectivity. For instance, in response to the client who felt intense pressure from cars behind him, the therapist said, "I get an image of someone behind you—not exactly with a knife—but saying 'get going!—move it!—do what I want!' "

Once the client gets in touch with her subjective construal of the potential impact of the stimulus situation, the awareness will usually have an affective quality, and the client may get further in touch with her feelings. For instance, in the example of the jealous party-goer, the client mentioned the smug, self-satisfied twist of the lips. Then the following dialogue took place:

THERAPIST: Almost as if he was saying, "Look, little boy; look at clever me."

CLIENT: (Laugh) Well, not quite that bad, but I guess it did seem kind of like he was patronizing me—sort of like, "you're the outsider."

THERAPIST: Oh, I see. Kind of, "*We* are having an intimate, witty conversation. *You* are just a spectator."

CLIENT: Yes, that's it. And I felt sort of helpless, even shrunk a little. Like, "that's the way it is."

Once the client gets in touch with the subjectivity of his construal of the stimulus situation, together with the differentiated "about" quality of his inner reaction, a sense of understanding, of a meaning bridge, arises between the two. The differentiated reaction, however peculiar or self-defeating, is felt to be understandable and natural and there is a sense of relief. As one client put it, "It seems to make sense now. Like before it was just kind of—just very frustrating because it did seem so senseless. But in this context it's like it's more sensible. In terms of my own feelings and reactions to things instead of just kind of—like—weird."

The above description may sound like a planned strategy, but actually it is more a matter of the therapist's feeling that the process isn't moving, that the memory is losing its lifelike quality, and then switching to the other side, always using the vividness of the stimulus as an entry point. There are blind alleys along the way; what seems to be an evocative image will fade out and become intellectualized. A number of times the therapist may have to draw the client's attention back to the scene, exploring for salience and getting into new aspects of stimulus construal. This process involves a kind of detective work, but the therapist does not begin the search with a preconception of what is important. In this kind of detecting, both client and therapist are listening for newness and the therapist is following the client's trail. The therapist is process-directive but not content-directive.

Some clients seem to work much better on one side than the other. Although some work on each side seems necessary, some clients primarily take the feeling route while others seem to achieve their breakthrough primarily from the stimulus-processing side. My observations suggest that clients who are not very much in touch with their own feelings and are somewhat detached from their inner awareness are much more productive when the focus is on the construal side.

The client-centered preoccupation with response to feelings has led us to neglect the focus on the client's perception of the potential impact and possibilities of the human and physical environment with which we are constantly interacting. Therapists often devalue clients' accounts of maladaptive or unsatisfying transactions in their day-to-day lives, viewing these episodes as "recounting" or "story-telling." And yet, the discovery of one's subjective construals can be just as experiential and just as productive as the discovery of feelings.

Although task resolution is only partial at the end of phase II, the combination of self-discovery of some of one's own construal systems, with a vivid sense of the consequences of these construals, seems to set the stage for phase III. The client is highly motivated to explore his or her own relevant self-schemas.

Phase III—Recognition and Exploration of Self-Schemas

In phase III, clients move into an explicit attempt to understand and re-evaluate some of the relevant self-schemas, and the therapist facilitates the process simply by hearing and responding sensitively to these explorations. For example, one client had glimpsed in phase II an intense need to "get through" to people she cared about and also recognized her construal of the situation as one in which it was impossible to get through. In phase III she focused more directly on this intense sense of "I need," owning it as a basic aspect of herself, but also recognizing the intense sense of vulnerability that stemmed from her attempts to meet this need. Another client recognized her tendency to organize her life into "slots" that *must* be filled before she went on to the next part of her life, and the impossible pressure that this put on her. Later in phase III she explored how incredibly different she felt, even in the same situation, when she construed it as belonging in a different slot.

It is important to note that the exploration of phase III is not just an intellectual analysis of the self in the sense of seeking and comparing patterns. Clients are able to make exploratory associations to other life situations, using their inner experience aroused in the problematic situation as the internal referent for the exploration. Some other, seemingly different, situation might be found to evoke the same inner reactions, while two seemingly similar situations might be found to evoke quite different reactions. This process seems to be most productive when it is spontaneously engaged in by the client and, indeed, starting even in phase II, this broadening-out process seems to be a natural part of the exploration. The therapist does not instigate this process, but once it starts she tries to hear statements that identify new relevant self-schemas and reflect them as owned by the client. It seems to be this process of new recognition of self-schemas and their decisive effect on one's construal of the situation that enables clients to re-examine them and thus to begin to loosen, reorganize, or in some cases, own, as truly part of their own value system, these relevant self-schemas. For instance, the man at the party began to explore his feelings of comfort and expansiveness in social situations in which other people seemed to view him as "an expert in his field." He compared these feelings with those he had in other social situations in which he didn't feel "on top of it." He also began to explore the idea of "just being with people" and how satisfying it might be.

One future point should be mentioned here. When a client brings in a problematic reaction that is clearly perceived as related to the problems and issues he is currently struggling with, then this re-examination and loosening stage usually stays centered more or less around the original situation. When the incident is something that seems to have no apparent connection with current issues, as in the case of the client who was made extremely anxious by the cars behind him, the trail may legitimately lead away from the original situation into a related but more central situation that is now felt to be related.

In both these kinds of situations, the client comes to a realization of some significant aspects of her own self-in-the-world concept, and the ways in which these complicate or even distort her interpersonal (and other) transactions with the world. Sometimes the most important new realization is awareness of a far-reaching "I should" that permeates one's construal of an unexpected variety of situations, unnecessarily curtailing options. For another person it may be a realization of a strongly felt personal need that has not been fully owned before. For someone else it may be two self-schemas such as the "caring mother" and the "university student" that have seemed to be in an inevitable conflict, but that can now both be owned and a satisfying merger planned.

Developing a new awareness of these self-schemas and re-evaluating others that were taken for granted leads to a fuller resolution than that achieved at the meaning-bridge stage and thus leads into the final phase. This phase involves the exploration of possible new options. These may be fairly concrete solutions to circumscribed problems, or a broader sense of freedom to rethink a number of situations. In some cases the whole experience seems to tap into a much broader problem, like a family situation; no new options are immediately seen, but at least the client has a new vantage point from which to tackle the problem.

Phase IV—Awareness of New Options

The final phase is the exploration of new options, viewed in the light of loosened and reorganized self-schemas. Often these emerge spontaneously as an awareness that apparently limited possibilities are not, and that negotiations are possible. Or the client may become aware that some aspect of her habitual style is unsatisfying or even self-defeating and make plans to experiment with a different style. I've also found that when new options are not spontaneously mentioned it can be productive to ask if there seem to be any new possibilities now, either for the initial situation or in a more general sense. This seems to serve as a stimulus to think about change and even to plan new things with which to experiment in the coming week. If none are readily forthcoming, it may mean that the client must resolve additional, related tasks before implementing new options. But here again the therapist does not attempt to predict or plan what task needs to be undertaken next. It is the client's own track that is being followed, and further markers will emerge to signal readiness for the next reprocessing task.

FUTURE DIRECTIONS

The intensive analysis of this one general class of tasks, the evocative unfolding of problematic reactions, has proven to be a productive experience for the research team, as clinicians and as investigators. We are continually fascinated by the way in which the cognitive-affective reprocessing of a single troubling episode can lead into a widening series of self-discoveries. Although as therapists we might have had some hunches about the direction that resolution would take, the actual resolution, when it emerged, was richer, more individual, and much more satisfying than could have been predicted in advance.

We have begun to study a number of other classes of tasks with recognizable process markers, attempting to identify some of the client steps that are essential for successful resolution of these tasks. This kind of intensive analysis is especially appealing to graduate students who are oriented toward both clinical practice and therapy research. The excitement of clinical experience is often lacking in the research process, and, in contrast to so much of the clinical research literature, the findings can have immediate implications for the conduct of therapy.

Ever since Rogers's early process formulations, process research has been a central concern among client-centered therapists. There has always been a focus on trying to gain an understanding of a complex, powerful, and very personal process. I hope that a number of client-centered therapist-researchers will engage in the kind of research reported here, identifying and intensively analyzing new classes of tasks, and thereby making explicit some of the available store of implicit clinical wisdom.

10   Person-Centered Gestalt: Toward a Holistic Synthesis

Maureen Miller O'Hara

A glance at the range of approaches available to the student of psychotherapy will show that human science has yet to develop a unified system of thought. Unlike other sciences, which despite temporary disagreement generally tend toward integration, psychology, especially psychotherapy, still tends toward the proliferation of new approaches.

Client-centered therapists have generally kept themselves apart from other humanistic therapists. New developments in the client-centered tradition have not been integrated into more comprehensive schemata. Instead distinctly new therapeutic approaches have emerged, such as *focusing, parent-effectiveness training,* or *dialoguing.* In a similar spirit Gestalt therapy attempts to maintain its separate identity as a distinct system. A recent directory of Gestalt training programs includes no listing for programs offering Gestalt in combination with other approaches.

If, however, we look through the several hundred self-descriptions listed in the counseling and therapy section of the Association for Humanistic Psychology Resource Directory (1980), it appears that the day-to-day practice of psychotherapy is a different matter. In describing what they actually do with their clients, the great majority of therapists list more than one "brand name" therapy. Despite the fact that individual practicing psychotherapists (humanistic ones, at least) appear to view their own work as a synthesis of more than one identifiable approach, serious attempts at theoretical integration are rare.

Within the camp of humanistic psychotherapies, client-centered therapy and Gestalt therapy would seem to be very different. Rogers himself has on occasion used Gestalt therapy as an example of a highly manipulative, therapist-directed process that stands in contradiction to the nondirective stance of the client-centered therapist. Rogers (1977) wrote:

> The expert is at times definitely the authority (as in the Gestalt therapist dealing with the person in the "hot seat"), but there is also recognition of the right of the individual to be responsible for himself. There has been no attempt to rationalize these contradictions. These therapists take a paternalistic stance, or follow the medical model, believing that at times control is best vested in the therapist, at other times (to be decided by the therapist) control and responsibility are best placed in the client's or patient's hands. (Rogers, 1977, p. 18)

Cochrane and Holloway (1974) and Stanley and Cooker (1976) have attempted theoretical integrations of client-centered therapy with Gestalt, but both papers represent mergers rather than a real synthesis. They leave the contradiction identified by Rogers untouched. Both works emphasize the ways that the methods or techniques of each can be used sequentially during a psychotherapy session. Cochrane and Holloway attempt to show how the more active therapist-initiated techniques of Gestalt therapy can be employed in the process of client-centered therapy, in which the direction of the therapeutic process is under the control of the client. Stanley and Cooker describe how the basic core conditions of client-centered therapy can enhance Gestalt techniques.

In this I wish to be somewhat bolder. I propose to take a look at both client-centered and Gestalt theory and practice in the light of certain more recent ways of thinking. In particular, I will explore the idea that the contradictions are in large part artifacts of a way of thinking that abstracts individual persons from their contexts, and that holistic thinking offers a way to reconcile such contradictions.

In discussing client-centered therapy and Gestalt therapy from a holistic perspective, I hope to show that this way of thinking offers psychologists a useful model with which to examine persons in relationship—in particular, the relationship between client and therapist in the process of psychotherapy.

Clients seen by psychologists in the West, especially in the United States, have a clear, lived sense of "I," which they refer to as "myself," and which is the same "I" throughout life and distinguishable from other selves. Changes can occur in this lived sense, but in the West we prefer them to be gradual enough to be integrated within the continuity of an "I-ness" that comes out of the past, is experienced in the present, and will persist into the future. Radical transformations or discontinuities of this sense of identity are generally experienced as terrifying. Not to know who you are, to lose the sense of continuity and futurity of experience, is felt as a loss of self and is equated with madness. A clear sense of autonomy, individuality, and identity are prized along with recognition and respect of that identity by others.

Not in all cultures, however, does the concept of *personhood* imply a strong sense of a distinct and stable self. In some aboriginal cultures there are elaborate adolescent initiation rites that involve inducing states of consciousness in which a sense of discontinuity between childhood and adulthood is deliberately exaggerated. This is accomplished through the use of psychoactive drugs, changes in manner of dress, changes in living arrangements and social expectations, name changes, abandonment by parents, and even physical change such as tattoos and other body alterations. All this is aimed at interrupting any sense of permanent identity separate from the group. A mature member of the group is one who has "died" and has been "reborn" into the collective in some new form (Jung, 1964). In Buddhist tradition maturity is equated with a loss of self. A permanent sense of "I-ness" is considered to be an artifact of limited awareness.

It is important to note that these differences in the experience of *self* are not just different ways to conceptualize universal perceptions. They are real differences in the ways the self and the world are perceived and given meaning. Shweder and Bourne (1982) convincingly demonstrate, on the basis of cross-cultural studies, that the concepts of *personhood* and *individuality*, and the perceptual consequences of those concepts, vary substantially from culture to culture. In comparing North Americans and Indians, for example, they showed Americans to consider persons as autonomous, distinctive, separate, and abstract, existing free of society yet in society. Indians, on the other hand, have a concept of "man in society," but do not view this person as an autonomous individual. The person is seen as regulated by strict and complex rules of relation and interdependence that are "context-specific and pluralistic." A person is judged in terms of social roles and situations. Americans, when asked to describe someone, give abstract descriptions, such as "She is a principled person" or "He is insecure." Indians, on the other hand, give contextual descriptions, such as "She remained strong in adverse circumstances," or "He remembers his mother on holidays." For Indians, a person may achieve autonomy only by *leaving* society. The holy person renounces the world, but this is not done as a means of finding one's *self*, but as a way to lose *self* as a separate soul and to merge with the "ground of all things, God." Shweder and Bourne (1982) term the Western world view "ego-centric/contractual" and the Indian view (which is, they point out, the view most widespread amongst world cultures) "holistic" or "socio-centric/organic."

Evidence from my own clinical work and workshop experiences persuades me that even within larger cultural groups such as "Westerners," there exist subgroups that also differ from each other in this regard. Carol Gilligan's research (1982) into conceptions of self and morality suggest that North American men are more egocentric/contractual while women are more sociocentric/organic in their respective world views. Class and ethnicity also seem to have an effect. Furthermore, it is appropriate to describe contemporary Western society as one in transition, wherein the egocentric world view is no longer consistent with what we now understand to be an interdependent planet. One reflection of this change in perspective is the considerable interest in indigenous and Oriental cultural beliefs, which are seen by many as a possible remedy for the excesses of the Western egocentric view.

HOLISTIC THINKING: AN ALTERNATIVE TO REDUCTIONISM

Toward a Holistic Science of the Person

I do not believe there is much to be gained from an attempt by Westerners to become like Indians. I find no grounds for enthusiasm in the current rash of gurus and ashrams as a solution to problems of Western cultural and psychological life, particularly since much of the profoundly wise teaching of Oriental masters becomes transposed into egocentric thinking almost automatically by Western disciples.

Nor do I believe the human potential movement, to which both Rogers and Perls have made important contributions, can be held responsible for the emphasis on individualism in our society (Lasch,

1979). It is more reasonable, I think, to see egocentricity as both cause and effect of forms of language, religion, government, law, and economic arrangements that emphasize autonomy, individual responsibility, and ambition.[1] In this respect, I believe Rogers and Perls (especially in Perls's collaboration with Paul Goodman) helped to lay the groundwork in the Western psychological community for the establishment of a more sociocentric/organic world view, but they did not go far enough. Both emphasized the organic, open-ended nature of life, but embedded as they are in a Western world view, both men attempted to account for sociocentricity in egocentric terms.

A conceptual framework is now emerging in many areas of thought that offers an alternative to reductionistic visions of a world (from atoms to people) composed of discrete, bounded objects that can be known in an abstract, "objective" way. This is the concept of *holism*.

Holistic thinking asserts that it is not possible to know an entity in isolation or in the abstract. The *parts* of a *whole* are necessarily altered by their participation in the larger whole. Holism seeks to elaborate the *relations* within and between part-whole unities.

In biology, for example, it is no longer meaningful to consider the DNA molecule to be self-replicating. In order to understand how a copy of a DNA molecule is made, we must recognize the participation of the whole cell—for example, the concentration gradients of nutrients, the function of enzymes and organelles, and the state of the cell membrane. We must also include external factors such as culture medium and temperature. What holistic thought attempts to do is recognize this complex interrelation of factors and at the same time provide a means of delineating levels of organization that can help researchers select the appropriate level of study. Such a recognition of interrelation permits us to define the level of analysis to include those factors that are likely to be of importance in determining events and to exclude those likely to be irrelevant. Therefore, under ordinary circumstances, it is possible to study the replication of DNA without including a host of contextual but irrelevant information.

Holistic thinking tries to establish an antireductionistic model, an understanding of nature as the hierarchical arrangement of inter-dependent levels, each level forming an entity that is distinct and coherent in itself and influenced in relational ways at the boundaries of adjacent levels. Higher levels may not necessarily be understood in terms of their lower-level components, and the *whole* may not be derived simply by extrapolation of the parts.

Entities have been given the name *holons* by Koestler (1978), which he defines in terms of both intrinsic factors and relational factors. The behavior of a holon is understandable in its existence as a distinct whole, its *particularity*, and by its participation in a more inclusive or "higher order holon." Entity behaviors associated with participation, Koestler calls *integrative.* Wholeness and partness are dual aspects of all levels of reality from the subatomic to the galactic.

Rules and Strategies

Another basic tenet of holism is that each level of organization is governed by *fixed rules* that lay down what is possible but leave options of *variable strategies* within those fixed rules. The rules determine how the game can be played, but flexible strategy will determine how the game will actually be played.

The person is also governed by fixed rules of individual functioning, such as the limits of physical strength and personality. This means that, at any particular moment, capacities are finite. These capacities can and do expand (more later about this), but even within these finite limits the individual has a multitude of strategies available. The available strategies will be governed by the individual's limits, but what the appropriate strategy will be is determined by the demands of the situation. The individual is free to choose how to participate in a larger holon up to the limits of the lower-order rules.

The rules governing the possible behaviors at any one level are characteristic of that level. The rules governing subatomic particles are clearly different from the rules of even the next higher level—the atom. Electrons may behave as either waves or particles; atoms may not. Atoms may behave as elements or compounds governed by the rules of chemical combination. The higher-order rules may not break the lower-order rules, but they may limit their expression.

On the human level the rules governing the behavior of individuals are different from those that govern groups, and again, higher-order group behavior may not break lower-order rules. They may, and in fact do, determine which of the strategies available to the individual seeking to express his basic nature will be appropriate to the demands of the situation.

This means, for example, that a man may express himself differently to his family than he would to his co-workers. He might be sexually provocative with his wife, but not be so with his boss. To understand his sexual approach to one attractive woman and his avoidance of another, we must understand the rules at the higher order. The outward expression of his sexuality is limited by the different demands of the two situations, and watching him act in one is a very poor guide to predicting his behavior in the other. This is not to say that his actual expression is determined by (and predictable on) the basis of the demands of the higher-order holon. It is only to say that, if we wish to *understand* the differences in his behavior in the two situations, we must include an understanding of the higher-order (group) rules.

Lest we fall into the trap of determinism, we must recognize that, as we move up the levels of organization, and the holons become more complex, the degree to which behavior is limited by rules and the degree of flexibility in strategy change. Chemicals have strict rules of behavior and few options. People, at a highly complex level of organization, have a great deal of flexibility in their options. More importantly, one of the *rules* at the human level is that the person learns; another is that the person has the capacity to become conscious of *automatic behavior rules* and turn them into flexible strategies. This rule-changing rule expands both rules, as learning becomes habit and as habits become conscious strategies. The person is, potentially at least, recreated by each new situation: *who* he or she is—i.e., the *rules*—can be changed by participation in the workings of the larger social level. And because human groups are composed of participating persons, the rules of the whole will be influenced by changes in individuals within it. This has enormous implications for the practice of psychotherapy, an activity conducted in a relationship of at least two persons.

PERSON-CENTERED GESTALT: TOWARD A SYNTHESIS

Person as Holon

In trying to elaborate a person-centered, Gestalt concept of *person* that is consistent with holistic thought, I have followed Koestler's vocabulary (1978).[2] Koestler calls that aspect of the two-faced holon, in which it is whole unto itself, its *particularity* or identity. The characteristics of an entity that give it wholeness are said to be *self-assertive* qualities or behaviors. As the entity participates in a larger configuration or higher-order holon it is no longer best understood in self-assertive or individualistic terms, but in *integrative* or self-transcendent terms.

The *person* as holon is understood either in particular terms as a *whole* (as an individual with an identity, having self-assertive qualities) or in integrative terms (in terms of *partness*, participation, and self-transcendence). *Wholeness* and *partness* can be seen as fundamental aspects of all holons, including persons and their groups.

Consciousness as an Activity of the Person

Consciousness is a *relational* activity implying both a *knower* and a *known*. It is also characteristically *human*: it includes sensing, recognizing, and making meaning of experience. Consciousness implies *selectivity*.

Human beings select elements of their experience relevant to some purpose. Elements of interest are included in a perceptual configuration, and those that are irrelevant are ignored. A basic tenet of Gestalt therapy considers this an active inclusion and exclusion process under the control of the individual. Perls rejected the idea that perception (and its selectivity) was a passive phenomenon under the control of unconscious urgings. Instead, he asserted that the construction of *gestalten* was an activity occurring in the present situation, and that through increased awareness of the situation, a person could discover personal participation in the activity, thereby opening the possibility for new configurations to be recognized.

Depending on the scope of what is included in the formation of a figure, we can say that consciousness can be *focused* or it can be *expanded*. It may include less than the "whole person." We may be conscious of a pain to the exclusion of everything else. In midrun a sharp hamstring pain will be attended to above all other activities that until a moment before had been included in the runner's consciousness: the race, breathing, fatigue, the wish to win. On an intellectual plane, we might focus on nothing else until the correct word for a poem is found. Consciousness may be expanded to a state of full *self*-awareness wherein persons are fully awake, integrated within themselves, accepting and sensible of all aspects of autonomous identity. This is the state of consciousness valued in the recent writings of Rogers (1980) and of therapists who follow his person-centered approach (Raskin, 1980). Consciousness also may be expanded further, embracing and including even larger configurations such as *relationship*, *group*, *society*, *world*, or even *universe*. At this level of expanded awareness people understand one another in terms of both wholeness and participation.

The *person* may be seen as a locus of consciousness, varying in degree of focus or concentration. Because consciousness is relational, how concentrated and exclusive, or how inclusive and expanded, it will be is simultaneously a function of lower-level *intrapersonal* conditions, interactional boundary relations, and the processes of higher-order phenomena.

Psychological functioning can now be examined in terms of *functional appropriateness*: the degree of inclusiveness or exclusiveness of consciousness. Healthy functioning implies that a person's awareness will include all dimensions of concern at a given moment and exclude those that are irrelevant to present purposes.

Exclusive consciousness is not *per se* better or worse than inclusive consciousness. There are times that are appropriate for limiting consciousness to a subwhole, as with our runner. The famous Gestalt "empty chair" dialogue between unintegrated *parts* of an intrapsychic conflict is another situation in which exclusive consciousness is more appropriate. Most psychotherapists have probably encountered a person able to give wondrously rich accounts of dream-life, body sensations, and images, who can express emotion with great intensity, while being incapable of maintaining relationships or keeping a job.

Consciousness of *self* as an autonomous whole, distinct from the group, is appropriate to situations requiring self-assertive, creative, initiating actions or choices. It is this ability to sense one's *integrity* and to express it, sometimes in conscientious opposition to the group, which protects the group from becoming a crowd or herd, at the same time protecting the individual from becoming enslaved by the mass, by ideologies, or by outdated cultural practices. Difficulties may occur, however, on the relationship level, or in situations that require sensitivity of influences beyond one's own skin. When relationships are seen from this egocentric viewpoint they must, as Shweder and Bourne (1982) point out, be reduced to a series of contractual agreements. Everything that happens must be accounted for in individualistic terms: if I feel bad, then the source of the difficulty resides either within myself or some other. Credit and blame are laid at the door of the individual, resulting in an inability to solve relational problems that have origins in higher-order dynamics.

There are situations in which it is appropriate for consciousness to expand beyond individual boundaries, transcending *self* to include the larger configuration in which one is but a part. Relationships, teams, collectives, organizations, systems of thought, and cultures are higher-order holons of human experience that exhibit directions, purposes, patterns, and problems affecting their *parts*. Conscious participation in collective endeavors, whether teamwork, psychotherapy, scientific research, political movements, or family, necessitates expansion of consciousness to include the whole and the parts.

A systematic examination of common patterns of psychological distress in terms of inappropriate focus or expansion of consciousness must await further work, though much of the theoretical formulation of Gestalt therapy, laid out in the work of Perls, Hefferline, and Goodman (1951), can readily be viewed from within this framework. The advantage of a concept of relevant or appropriate consciousness (as elaborated here) over Gestalt theory is in providing a way to include intrapsychic, individual, interpersonal, cultural, and environmental levels of human experience within one theoretical framework.

Appropriate Consciousness

The idea of appropriate and inappropriate consciousness introduces the obvious question: "How is *appropriate* defined and by whom?" As stated in the beginning, the question of authority has been a prominent feature of client-centered theory. The difference between client-centered attitudes and what is perceived as the authoritarian attitude of Gestalt therapy is often cited as an irreconcilable difference of the two approaches. Reconciliation is possible if we evaluate appropriateness in terms of purpose. We need to know the purpose of an action before we can address the question of whether consciousness is appropriately expanded or focused. In other words, the project at hand determines what is relevant to its accomplishment. If we wish to make a trip to Los Angeles, a list of the medicinal plants of New England, no matter how beautiful, is not relevant. A map and the ability to read and drive are much more to the point.

Implications for Psychotherapy

Rogers (1977) insists that it is the client who determines the purposes of the therapeutic enterprise. Correspondingly, a fundamental aspect of Gestalt therapy is the notion that the focus of therapy is on the way the emergent situation organizes and coordinates action toward completion of unfinished situations.

Psychotherapy is a joint project of at least two participants. In holistic terms it is a multileveled situation. There are *whole* individuals and there are participants in *relationships, dyads,* or *groups.* These levels are also parts of larger configurations such as professions, families, classes, cultures, and genders.

A client's difficulty may be on any or all of these levels. The attention of the psychotherapist should be addressed to the increase of awareness and to the development of consciousness of the components of experience that are relevant to the present predicament of the client.

Components of inner experience may be relevant but missing, as when a person chronically prevents a particular feeling from coming into awareness and being consciously recognized. When a person can neither understand nor change continual hostile reactions from an intimate, it is sometimes the case that the person is not aware of the hostile quality of his own expression. Directing attention inward permits the person to concentrate attention, "making out" or recognizing a previously ignored experience. The object of Gendlin's (1981a) focusing techniques is precisely this experiencing of previously unclear aspects of on-going existence. Dreamwork, fantasy exploration, free association, psychoanalytic method, and cognitive analysis may all be of profound importance in restoring the capacity to be conscious of relevant *internal* processes.

It must be emphasized, however, that the contrary may also be true. Not all situations are best understood on the intrapsychic level; inclusion of too much intrapsychic detail in a higher-order process (such as a relationship) may be very inappropriate.

The fact that persons are at one and the same time individuals and parts of relationships means that in order to facilitate change the therapist must be able to know the client on different levels and in many aspects within a level. On the level of wholeness, any dimension of individual functioning may affect the whole person. Physiological state, posture, and body flexibility participate in the formation of the ground of relevant experience. Mental states, learning, language, memories, and the ability to concentrate or empty the mind are interrelated with emotional state. A holistic view of the person asserts that there is no aspect of the individual that necessarily has more significance than any other. Feelings, for example, are not necessarily more important than either the processes or contents of thought. Foci of attention may move many times in a therapy session. At one moment, the therapist-client pair may explore a body sensation of the client, the next moment an emotion, thought, dream, or memory, depending on what is of concern at the moment.

It may also be appropriate to move outward from the individual into the relational world, where integration and its impediments become more relevant. A here-and-now exploration of the on-going process of the therapeutic relationship, or attention to the client's life as a person in society, may be the correct level of attention.

A holistic view of people, and of psychotherapy, implies that any level of organization, from physiology to politics, each with its characteristic rules and strategies, may conceivably be relevant. This is wide territory indeed. Since we have removed pre-established *rules* for determining the appropriate level of attention in psychotherapy, and have also removed from the therapist easy recourse to the security of professional authority, we must ask what remains as a suitable guide for where to work within the psychotherapy session.

I have already discussed the client-centered proposition that the client's purposes direct the overall therapeutic enterprise. We take it as a given that when a client seeks out a psychotherapist, it is because he or she has a purpose, or agenda, in doing so. The client-centered therapist differs from most other therapists in adopting the client's agenda rather than imposing his own values and purposes on the therapy. The therapeutic attitude is thus one of *service,* wherein the self-assertiveness and autonomy of the therapist as a *whole* is subordinated to the purposes of the therapeutic dyad, which is determined by the purposes of the client.

Rogers (1951) describes with great elegance this attitude, which he considers necessary to the therapeutic enterprise. The therapist must accept unconditionally that the other is of value and that the on-going expression of the client is a reflection of the inherent tendency toward growth and actualization. The client-centered therapist risks aligning himself or herself with the purposes of the client based on a faith that these purposes are not random or arbitrary, but related to the basic tendency toward healing and evolution.

Empathy Reconsidered

If the client's purposes are the best guide to the appropriate focus of attention, it follows that the therapist needs to be able to discern, from moment to moment, and overall, what the client is reaching for in his or her process. In client-centered therapy the way the therapist gains access to these tacit dimensions of the client's experience is through empathic listening (Rogers, 1951).

In descriptions of client-centered therapy it is the client who is expressive and the therapist who listens empathically. In person-centered Gestalt terms, we would say the therapist is in a self-transcendent (or expanded) state of consciousness and that the client is in a self-assertive (or exclusive) state. Listening, watching, and wanting to understand another's view are all self-transcendent activities.

Much of the writing on empathy gives the impression that it is a very special *skill*, and that it is the therapist who *has* it. I believe this stems from an attempt to explain integrative, inclusive consciousness in self-assertive, individualistic language. This contradiction is apparent in Rogers's discussion of the qualities of therapeutic relationships as related to movement in therapy. He cites Barrett-Lennard's research with his Relationship Inventory (Rogers, 1961). In all the items of the inventory, the "other" is seen quite distinctly: "He cares about me" and "He tries to understand me." This is not the language of connection Shweder and Bourne (1982) describe, but is egocentric/contractual language. Even if the client *feels* connected, there is no way to express this feeling through the items of the inventory. The words *we* or *relationship* appear nowhere in the list of items cited by Rogers (1961).

I believe we can better understand the activity of empathic listening in terms of relevant consciousness and whole-to-part relations within the holon of *therapeutic relationship*. Empathy loses its status as the activity of one autonomous individual with respect to another and becomes understandable as an expansion of one person's consciousness to include the relationship with another of which he or she is a part. Once a person has expanded consciousness in this way, the skills required to know the other are ordinary relational skills common to all participants of a shared human life. There *is* specialness in moments of empathic contact, but I believe the specialness resides in the willingness to surrender an individualistic world view in order to "belong" to a relationship and be attuned to its purposes.

This is a particularly *special* event when it involves a professional psychologist in a relationship with someone who is confused, afraid, and contradictory, as are many of the people who are clients of psychotherapists. At the beginning of therapy it may be the therapist alone who is willing to expand consciousness in this way, the client remaining defended, isolated, and even at times apparently subversive of her own overall purposes. As therapy progresses, the client may also come to align herself as an individual with the purposes of the therapeutic dyad, thereby opening up the possibilities of change resulting from participation in a higher-order entity.

It is almost a cliché to say that the whole is greater than the sum of its parts. In human groups, even those of only two people, the potential knowledge and wisdom of the whole group can be greater than the wisdom of any of the individuals separately. A group is, at times, capable of complex and refined action that, while based on its members' capacities, may surpass each person individually. Individual participants can gain access to group-level possibilities if they are able to expand their individual consciousness into the larger dimension. In self-transcendent consciousness we can know the group as an entity, sensing its rules, its purposes, and its strategies in the same way that in egocentric consciousness we sense our own.

The foregoing line of thought gives us a way to understand how we can *empathize* with or know other minds. In a relationship or group we can be conscious of ourselves as autonomous, self-assertive individuals. We can also be conscious of our partness in self-transcendent terms, noticing how we are influenced by our participation in the higher-order holon. Similarly, we can know other participants in either autonomous or integrative ways. When we hear what others express, see them, follow what they say, and have a sense of them as individuals, we know them in terms of their wholeness. But, beyond this, we can also know them through their participation in the same group to which we ourselves belong. In the therapeutic dyad the relationship itself can be known. By becoming conscious of the on-going process of the dyad the therapist can know the client and his purposes through the subtle but nonetheless recognizable effect he has within the whole.

This line of argument may account for some of the seemingly magical and even *paranormal* events in therapy, as when the therapist and client simultaneously share the same image, glimpsing the future (knowing what is to come), or when the therapist makes a seemingly "out of the blue" statement that proves to be profoundly appropriate. In such moments it appears that the therapist knows more intimately the client's deeper purposes than the client himself is presently aware of. The therapist is not "inside the skin" of the client (a frequent description of empathy), but inside the skin of the dyad, of which he is a part. It is this capacity to know the other, termed empathic understanding in Rogerian therapy, which gives us a way of sensing on a deep level what the client is trying to accomplish, thereby sensing the level of consciousness appropriate to the purposes at hand.

And, of course, the same possibility exists for the client as well. There is the greatest potential for individual growth in psychotherapy when the client can also expand consciousness to include the whole therapeutic dyad or group. Client *empathy* is at least as important as therapist *empathy*.

Contact as the Currency of Change

In holistic thinking, organic growth and evolution are seen as a tendency toward organizing living matter into increasingly complex and inclusive wholes. A holistic view of psychological growth and evolution similarly recognizes the tendency of consciousness to expand toward the integration of subwholes into increasingly complex and inclusive wholes.

Contact is the activity permitting transcendence of previous consciousness boundaries, whether at the intrapsychic subwhole level of experience or at more inclusive levels. As long as entities are kept separate, with intact boundaries, they resist integration into a larger system. This is true of isolated cells, languages, cultures, and gene pools, for example. Only if contact is made at the boundaries does integration become possible.

Much attention is given in Gestalt theory to the activity of contact and its importance to the process of change in both human growth and psychotherapy. Many different possible boundaries for contact may be identified. These include body boundaries, familiarity boundaries, and ego boundaries, among others (Polster & Polster, 1973). The concept of a boundary of consciousness as elaborated here may include any or all of these Gestalt theory constructs.

In what form the boundary of consciousness is experienced will depend upon the specific concerns at hand, as will its appropriate level of exclusiveness or inclusiveness. Consciousness can expand and shift toward integration whereby growth occurs when contact is made between elements previously kept separate.

On a conceptual level, this contact may come about when previously ignored facts are acknowledged, thereby permitting a more comprehensive theory to be developed. On emotional levels, contact may occur when conflicting feelings can be simultaneously experienced as belonging together, permitting more richness and subtlety in emotional life.

Much work, at the level of the individual in psychotherapy, is aimed at the identification of such unintegrated parts of experience. Once identified, they can be seen from the point of view of their participations in the larger whole—the person. Gestalt "experiments" (such as dialogues) serve to delineate or to identify conflicting "introjections." The dialogue is a means of making contact with previously alienated aspects of experience, permitting a shift toward creative integration (Perls et al., 1951).

On the interpersonal level, transcendence of autonomy is also achieved through contact. Whenever there is true meeting at the autonomous boundary of consciousness, the *I*, there is an inevitable shift from autonomy to belongingness. There is a loss in the sense of separate identity and a gain in sense of participation. This is not to be understood as a loss of identity to the group but as an integration of identity with the group, in which "one *is* engaged and carried along, not in spite of oneself but beyond oneself" (Perls et al., 1951).

Self-Assertion—Integration as a Unity

Although it is possible to speak of autonomy and integration as distinguishable aspects of consciousness, they are, in fact, not separable. Wholeness and partness are seen as merely different aspects of *one system* (Koestler, 1978). As one aspect becomes exaggerated, there is a limit beyond which further exaggeration necessarily brings the other aspect to the fore. A commonly used Gestalt experiment is the exaggeration of one aspect of a *polarity* in order to approach the other, more difficult aspect. Closeness may be achieved through exaggerating distance, or decisiveness achieved by exaggerating muddle-headedness. Zinker (1977) describes many instances of this process, which he terms "going around the world."

An example from a large, person-centered encounter group might also illustrate this. John, a black North American, although wishing to cooperate in a group task, was having difficulty accepting the views of a co-participant, a white South African. John eventually exploded into spontaneous and whole-hearted expression of his rage and anguish at apartheid. It was a moment of total self-assertion, experienced, however, by everyone else present as a moment of integration. For the first time, John experienced himself and was experienced by the others as *part of* the group. Everyone participated in the act, passive but integrated as a group. When Nigel, the South African, responded in an equally autonomous and self-assertive manner, expressing the depths of his individual frustration at being a lawyer who had defended blacks challenging pass-laws (thereby incurring the suspicion of blacks and whites alike), a sudden shift occurred. Separateness melted as mutual comprehension took the place of antagonism. Both John and Nigel found an ally where they had seen an enemy. They experienced a oneness of purpose, not through trying to understand or integrate themselves, but through vigorous assertion of their separateness in each other's company.

In individual therapy, similar events occur. It is often at moments when client, or therapist, or both express themselves most individually and whole-heartedly that a sense of integration, unity, and oneness is most keenly felt. I must emphasize, however, that on an interpersonal level this is only the case when some commonly held purpose is moving the participants. In an interpersonal situation, if the participants are at cross-purposes, such self-assertion may simply exaggerate the conflicts, resulting in disintegration into more limited levels of organization.

A PERSON-CENTERED GESTALT SYNTHESIS: GROUNDS AND GAINS

If we look at films of Rogers and compare them with films of Perls we see a striking difference. What is obvious about Rogers, in the Gloria films for example, is that he *listens*: he really tries to understand Gloria and accept her without conditions. What is most obvious in Rogers is the self-transcendent quality of his empathic attitude. It almost seems that *he* disappears. He himself has said that it is difficult for him to describe afterwards what happened in a therapy session (DeRyck, 1982). In contrast, Perls confronts, challenges, expresses his opinions, and so on. What strikes us about Perls, in his session with Gloria, is the autonomous, self-assertive quality of his participation.

Rogers's approach is described as nondirective, while Perls's style is seen as actively directive. But such descriptions are based on a way of thinking that abstracts people and behaviors from their relational contexts. When we look at the relationships as wholes, we can see that Rogers's behavior has tremendous impact on Gloria, and quite deliberately so, as does Perls's.

A holistic view permits us to examine these sessions not only in terms of the styles of intervention (of the two therapists), but also in terms of the natures of the two relationships. A detailed examination of these two sessions is beyond the scope of this chapter, but it may be useful to point out a few obvious features.

Both relationships focus on Gloria's purposes. Unmistakably, it is the goal Gloria has set for herself that orients the two sessions. Both therapists faithfully follow this orientation, even at moments when Gloria herself does not. Gloria wants to be more "real" with herself and others, something that is difficult for her. Both relationships are markedly honest, and truthfulness is both valued and supported. Deviation from truthfulness draws the attention of all three individuals at different times. In both sessions, the therapists' perceptions are brought to the task of restoring to Gloria authenticity of experience and expression. The relationships are similar in their support of authenticity.

There are other similarities in the two relationships. Both exhibit qualities of good will, respect, caring, curiosity, support, and experimentation. Both relationships are male-female, with a distinctly father-daughter quality. Both sessions take place within the framework of psychotherapy, and the roles are correspondingly well defined. So is the time frame and the fact that these sessions are part of a filmed series. Furthermore, they exist within the same cultural framework of a common language, norms, and ideologies.

As we move from an egocentric view, treating Gloria, Perls, and Rogers only as separate individuals, and begin to look at higher-order entities, such as relationships and even larger contextual configurations, we can see more and more relevant similarities between the two sessions. It is my thesis that such a widening of perspective is not only relevant but is indispensable to a deeper understanding of effective elements in individual psychotherapy.

Obvious differences between client-centered therapy and Gestalt therapy, such as directiveness versus nondirectiveness, unconditional acceptance versus confrontation, and environmentalism versus free will, which may appear as contradictions when viewed from the level of individual behavior, can be reconciled by such a "widening of the frame" of analysis. The focus of this chapter has been to work toward a reconciliation of the seeming contradictions between client-centered and Gestalt therapies, in the hope of arriving at a coherent, person-centered Gestalt theory. The potential gains to be derived from using the conceptual tool of holism may go far beyond this, however, by permitting an examination of the whole enterprise of psychotherapy in search of a unified science of persons in the process of change.

NOTES

1. This admittedly paradoxical phrase clearly begs the questions of first causes. It is used here in the same way as saying that gravity is both cause and effect of the movement of bodies in space.

2. Another possible vocabulary is that of Andras Angyal who refers to autonomy and homonomy (Angyal, 1973).

11 The World of Family Relationships: A Person-Centered Systems View[1]

Godfrey T. Barrett-Lennard

It is almost a truism to say that the family is rapidly changing in most human cultures. Factors in this change include altering lifestyles and values; radical shifts in the linkages between sexual activity, conception and marriage; innovations in health and communication sciences; and a host of other transformations. Yet, in their evolving forms, family relationships still resiliently hold center stage in the interpersonal worlds of most of us, through much or all of our life cycle. These relationships remain especially critical in the formative interpersonal experience of nearly all children.

My central thesis in this chapter is that the membership structure of a family has direct and profound bearing on the relationships that are possible and likely to be experienced and, therefore, on the learning-developmental potentialities for each member. Particularly, family size and features linked to this central dimension are of great importance when focused through a lens that is jointly sensitive to interactive systems *and* inner experience. Much of human life is transactional and *transindividual* in its very nature. In the conception that follows, the experiencing person is not displaced but seen in fuller view; living not only as an *I* both with separate others and distinct you-and-I *wes*, but also through and among a diversity of *wes* in relationships with single and multiple *yous* and *thems*. Within each person's family, these relationships may be few or many, in number and in nature.

The perspective set forth here does not draw directly on pre-existing literature, although family resemblances, especially in respect to the client-centered tradition and open systems thinking, will be apparent. The most direct antecedent in my own work appears in a theoretical article in the small-group field (Barrett-Lennard, 1979b). During final revision of this chapter, intersecting work by two other authors came to view. In a short, important article titled "Balance Theory: Possible Consequences of Number of Family Members," Lindsay (1976) spells out the number of relationships at dyadic, triadic, and larger subsystem levels that are possible in families of varying size, as well as the range of combinations for a given family member.[2] Within its more selective and elaborated focus, Toman's classic work on family constellations high-lights effects on sibling position and sex composition, linked in turn to family size (Toman, 1976). It will shortly be more evident why I single out these contributors, although the pathway of each of us is separate in origin and quite distinct in substance.[3]

My viewing lens potentially adds much more than can be directly mapped in this paper and, partly for reasons of space, I shall focus directly on nuclear families consisting of two parents and from one to four children. It will be evident, however, that the analysis advanced could be adapted to single-parent families, families in which one of the parents has changed, families that include children of two previously married partners, instances in which a grandparent or other close relative lives with the nuclear family, and many other variations. It is obvious, too, that nonfamily relationships can become vitally important in childhood. Strong attachment bonds may develop with a nonfamily caregiver, with a teacher or peer, or with persons in other familiar roles; and for families in chronic difficulty or in crisis, an external relationship may be a lifeline for a young family member or for the family as a whole. These possibilities are quite consistent with, although not directly examined in, the approach presented.

Although often more complex in their totality, the kinds of family relationships and systems I will discuss involve, generally, person(s) A in relational interaction with person(s) B. In this A-B structure either A or B, or both, may be a single person, a twosome or a multi-person system or group. For convenience, A (on the left) will represent *I* or *we* (or *me, us,* or the equivalent) and B will stand for the *you, him, her, they,* or *them* side of the relationship. In the view advanced, the A-B interaction or relationship exists functionally only when experienced on some level by one or more of the participant persons. If not experienced, a possible A-B form would be considered inactive or latent as a relational system. Besides twosome *I-you* and *we* relationships, the most frequent single form (but far from the only other main one) in the family compositions examined is a triad in which, for example, a twosome *we* interacts with a single *you* or an *I* responds to a dyadic *you*.

ON PARENT TWOSOMES

The families considered begin as a couple, the parents-to-be. Any substantially connected twosome contains three experienced entities: the *I*, *you*, and *we* (or *us*). In the case of a parent couple, from the "outside" position of the child, there's Dad, Mom, and Dad-and-Mom as a dyadic *you* or *they* or *my parents*, etc. One of the changes now going on in families (if on a modest scale) is that of fathers fully sharing with mothers in direct caregiving to their chilren and also in a wide range of domestic homemaking activity. More often, a sharp division of labor and of role still applies, and fathers have little part in direct caregiving and housekeeping-homemaking activity.

Partly for the reasons just mentioned, children's perceptions of their parents' relation differ over a vast range and their experience of this relation is a main axis of their lived world. In one-child families, it is the only relationship *between two others* in the family that the child experiences. Further, this relationship does not encompass all aspects of the parental couple. Such a twosome develops a repertoire of behaviors, attitude, and style, a character—one might say, a bi-personality—of its own, distinct from that of either member taken singly. Such features of couplehood are usually sensed or seen to exist by the participants.

The specific features of a couple's *we* system often include a characteristic style and quality of communication and distinctive landscape of topical content. Typically there is a climate of feeling and attitude within which particular elements vary more or less predictably, spheres of understanding and of mis- (or non-) understanding, eggshell regions and pathways with firm stepping stones, and many other features that form the moving figure-ground matrix unique to that dyadic *we*. A parental *we* dyad can be an open system or a very closed one. It may work such that the partners move cautiously in step or in swing from harmony to counterpoint—moving easily from expression of acknowledged difference to convergent agreement. Mutual empathy, trusting openness, and strong and nonjudgmental caring stand out in the interplay of some *wes*, and, by contrast, others exist in which the partners implicitly conspire to tear each other down, perhaps jointly feeling that victory or victimization are the only alternatives. There is of course a myriad of ways that a twosome can be, in feeling, outlook, purpose and action.

Thus parental twosomes are not merely abstractions but living entities—in harmony or in painful internal conflict—with the dyadic equivalent of character and personality. And, while the resulting entity is vitally contributed to by each member of the twosome, that which emerges is of a different nature and has its own properties, distinct from either member considered singly. It also differs from any other dyad containing one of the same persons. Such dyadic wholes or systems populate our world more densely than do individuals.[4] In families, besides being of basic importance in their own right, dyads are fundamental building blocks in larger systems, beginning with triad forms, which also are in the foreground of this chapter in each family context.

THE ONE-CHILD, THREE-PERSON FAMILY

The whole family first in view is a triad. As implied, my focus on the various relational avenues and systems involved will be from the position of the child. (In larger families, in the interests of direct comparison and manageability, my analysis and portrayal is based on the position of the first-born child.)

To start with, there is the relationship with each parent, involving one same-sex and one opposite-sex intergenerational dyad. These primary relationships—shown schematically in Figure 11.1a—exhaust the family twosomes in which the child is a member.

In addition, there is one threesome that, from the child's position, takes three distinct, likely forms.

The Parental *You*

A main form, mentioned earlier, is the child's relation to the parents' own relationship, the many-sided process that is viewed as central to the parents' "couplehood" (with its own chemistry, founded in the parents' separate constitutions but not a simple composite or extension of them). In particular, qualities of the parents' intercommunication, of feeling between them, and of their ways of being a pair with others, will all bear on the child's experience and expectations of them as a (twosome) *you* with (a single) *me*.[5] In Figure 11.1a the parental

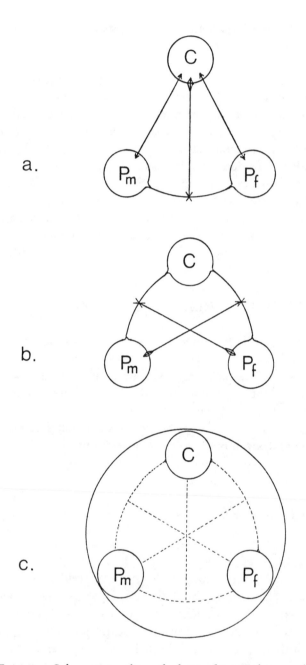

FIGURE 11.1. Schematic outline of relationships in the one-child family.

couple system is represented by the connecting *curved* line (as are *we* and *you* systems in later illustrations), and the child's relationship to this system is shown by the vertical straight line with an arrowhead cross, or stitch-like connection, at each end. (P_m and P_f refer to the male parent and female parent, respectively.) This relationship is necessarily intergenerational in structure.

The *We* Dyad Plus One

The child can also feel engaged within or as part of a *we* twosome with one parent, relating or interacting with the other, and this is the next form of triad in the three-person family. The first such experience is very likely to be with the child's mother as the other member of the *we* dyad, interacting with the father as the third person, *you* (or *he* or *him*). Later, it is highly probable that there will be episodes when the child is actively in a *we space* with the father, interacting with the mother from within this twosome. Either context is cross-generational, and there are no other avenues within the family for *we-you* interchanges and relationships. These two relationships are illustrated in Figure 11.1b.

In quality these relational interactions vary, of course, over a huge range. They encompass, for example, protective alliances with one parent in frightening conflict with the other; situations of felt connection with one parent and then the other in which the child is a human bridge between two adults whose own dyadic relation has atrophied, or is fracturing under stress; and experiences of a loving, sharing connection with the mother (say) in a joyful reunion, or other very positively experienced activity, with the father.

The *We* Triad

The third form of triadic relation occurs when the child experiences her family threesome as a single *we* or *us*—not arising solely in opposition or contrast to some outside *they*. A strong mode of this triad involves felt connection with each of the others, a sense of *their* interconnection and a clear feeling of unity or identity as a threesome. This is represented by the dotted lines as well as the solid circle, shown in Figure 11.1c. This form of triad may be positive or negative to an observer, in social valence or outside relation, but as felt from within there is a between-member bondedness and *we* sense that leaves no one out.

In summary, the child member of the three-person family experiences a one-to-one relationship with each adult parent; a relation with one adult twosome *you*; *we-you* (2–1) interchanges in which the *we* is always cross-generational and the *you* is always the other parent; and (rare-to-frequent) experiences of a whole-family threesome *we*. There is moderate structural complexity and great qualitative variety in these relational avenues and alternatives. Nevertheless, the total context of interpersonal relationship differs radically from that which would apply with the advent of a further child.

THE TWO-CHILD, FOUR-PERSON FAMILY

In a family of two children and two parents, a whole new world opens up for the first-born child, C_1, on whom my analysis is focused. In terms of *additional* relationships, let us see how different this world is.

A New Kind of Twosome

The child now experiences a third dyadic relationship of a basically new order, that is, with his sibling (C_2 in Figure 11.2a). It is a same-sex (SS) or opposite-sex (OS) relationship; and the age difference may be small enough that the two children inhabit much the same world together, or large enough that C_1 may be an important secondary caregiver, protector, or hero to C_2, and a bridge for the younger sibling to the world of older children in general, or to that of young adults. The SS and the OS alternatives have differing potential advantages and implications as avenues for interpersonal development. In Toman's (1976) view, compatibility in marriage—and the atmosphere created for children—is significantly influenced by the sibling relationships and position of each partner in their families of origin. The optimal combination in this respect occurs when backgrounds are complementary. A male parent who has younger sisters and a female parent with older brothers are an instance of a highly complementary pair. It is evident that one necessary condition for distinctly favorable (strongly complementary) combinations is that at least one partner has experienced an OS sibling relationship (see Toman, 1976, Chapter 10).

Triadic Relationships

The child's relationship with his sibling will sometimes take a *we* form (experientially and behaviorally), in which C_1 and C_2 are relating

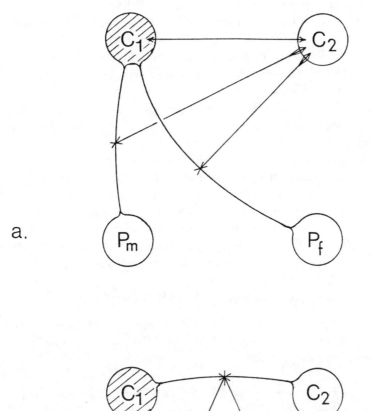

a.

b.

FIGURE 11.2. The new dyadic and *we-you* triadic relationships in a two-child family.

as a pair to one parent. One likely variant of this *we-you* triad is a partnership of common cause in conflict with the parent. A contrasting, positive case would be a much enjoyed play-partner experience with C_2, to which the mother or father responds in kind, without displacing either child or their on-going connection. (Figure 11.2b illustrates this general form.) Also open now is the avenue of being part of a parent-child *we* union, in relation to the younger child as the *you*. Instances of this kind—widely varying in possible quality—would be almost certain to happen with one parent and are likely to surface with the other as well. (See Figure 11.2a.)

A third new alternative channel in the triad sphere is that of experiencing oneself singly (*I* or *me*) in relation to one's sibling and a parent, perceived as a mutually engaged or allied twosome *you* or *they*. This seems most likely to arise first in relating to the younger child-and-mother pair and at a later stage to occur at times in relation to the father and sibling (P_mC_2), especially if C_2 is male and C_1 is female. The form of this relationship is illustrated within Figure 11.3a.

Four-Person Relationships—For the First Time

Foursome, or *quadral* (Barrett-Lennard, 1979b) interchanges and relationships now appear and develop. They also can occur in several different forms.

1.   Perhaps the most distinctly different new avenue is the experience of being one of a twosome *we* (for example, C_1C_2) in relation to another pair (P_mP_f, as *you* or *they*). Being by oneself in relation to the two adult parents (over the whole repertoire of their interplay and feelings with and toward C_1), as against having a sibling to be in off-and-on alliance with in relation to the parent pair, are extremely different situations with a wide new spectrum of learning possibilities. Aside from the allies-in-opposition mode, the pair-pair interaction may also involve situations, for instance, of expressively enjoyed play by C_1C_2, jointly responded to with lively, affectionate, and prideful pleasure by the parent couple. In Figure 11.3b this A-B interaction involves the upper pair versus the lower pair, as illustrated.

In a second kind of double-pair experience, each of A and B is a cross-generational, parent-child twosome. The specific combinations possible are C_1P_m–C_2P_f and C_1P_f–C_2P_m; that is, the two lateral pairs and the diagonal pairs, as arranged in Figure 11.3b. If the children are a boy and a girl, one of these combinations would be a father-son pair in

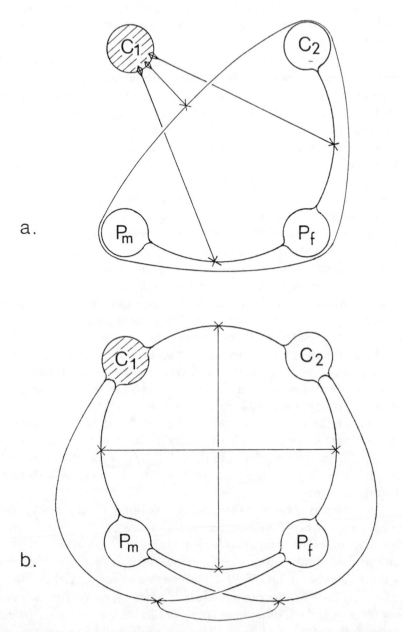

FIGURE 11.3. *I-you* (1–2 & 1–3) and double-pair (2–2) relationships in a two-child family.

relational interaction with a mother-daughter pair, and in the other possible combinations each parent-child pair would be of opposite sex. In the case of same-sex children, the pair arrangements would both be SS-OS.

The first of these cases (OS children) seems rich in potential for development of clear sex identity and the capacity to be at home in relating to persons of opposite sex, within and across generations. For SS children, who cannot directly experience and learn about the opposite sex from their own relationship, the parental model would be particularly critical in this sphere. Presuming there are no further children, either of the SS siblings is likely to be most at home in peer parternships or teams of the same sex and in fighting, playing, or working with members of their own sex. I would expect double *we* parternships with parents to occur sooner or more prominently in the case of OS children than with SS siblings. Viewed from a broadly psychoanalytic frame of reference, the described pattern would be especially prone to surface at the oedipal stage for children in OS parent-child combinations.

2. A further type of four-person interaction or system comes into play when the child experiences the rest of the family as a mutually involved group or threesome (with some joint attitude and/or sense of their own connection with one another) interacting with C_1 as a single. Looking at the same system a little differently, C_1 may at times be very conscious of her individuality and separateness, and simultaneously perceive the others as allied (openly or subtly) in their response. This system is thought more likely to occur when C_1 tends to feel rather isolated or the odd person out in the family, although it may also happen, for example, when the older child is experiencing a joint welcome from the rest of the family or feeling that the others are joined in responsive appreciation toward her. This $1(me)-3(you)$ pattern is illustrated within Figure 11.3a.

3. Inverting the last-mentioned possibility, C_1 is very likely also to have experiences of being one of a *we* threesome in relation to the fourth member of the family—both in visible interaction and in fantasy. An expected combination after C_2 arrives, especially if C_1 is at least two or three years older, is $C_1 P_m P_f - C_2$ interactions. However, the positions of C_1 and C_2 are so easily reversible in this configuration (in such a way that C_2 does feel the odd person out) that holding onto *we* experiences in the mother–father–older child system could well be a preoccupation for C_1. Specifically, if or when the parents readily shift their attention to

mutually delight in or together cope with the new child, C_1 may easily feel distanced or apart from the rest of his family. If there were one or two *more* siblings, this experience would be far less likely.

The potential *we* triads (including C_1) are most easily seen in light of the remaining member's position. For example, the fourth outsider or single person relating to the *we* may at times be the father, from his outside working/social world, or perhaps from a position of being the only male and breadwinner. Likewise, the mother may at times relate in a special way emotionally or in her caregiving role to $C_1C_2P_m$. If she is the only female family member the recurrence of this pattern may be increased. The possibilities mentioned here are illustrated in Figure 11.4.

4. Finally, there is the experience of being inside—jointly with three others—of a four-person *we*; "our family," as one quite unique membership group. Sometimes this *we* experience forms via sudden or gradual transition from one, or a fusion of more than one, of the main types of foursome pattern already described.

This completes my outline of the four-member family relationship systems, considered from the position of the older child. Compared to those that occur in three-person families, there is one quite new kind of dyadic relationship, three distinct new forms of triadic system, and four alternative kinds of foursome—at least one of these including two clear subtypes. Altogether—and without implying that a simple count is by itself a strong index of diversity (or complexity)—at least eight major kinds of relational associations and system, without counterpart in the one-child family, are now potentially included in C_1's interpersonal world. Four other kinds of experiential-relational system that apply in the one-child family are carried over as well. Only one system, the whole-family threesome, no longer applies. (In all, the four-member family yields at least 12 distinct kinds of relationship system, several of these with alternative specific membership—from the position of C_1.) Each of the dozen or so types carries unique potential in the sphere of interpersonal experience and learning.

Given that a second child makes a dramatic, typically profound difference, then a jump from two to four children can be expected to represent a further explosion of interpersonal avenues and systems, giving rise to a far more varied and often more roomy world within the family.

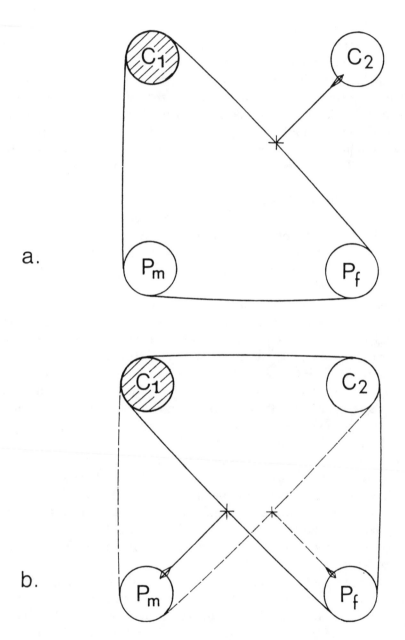

a.

b.

FIGURE 11.4. *We-you* (3–1) foursomes in a two-child family.

THE FOUR-CHILD, SIX-PERSON FAMILY

In this section, I shall again focus on the interpersonal avenues and systems *additional* to those delineated already for the one- and two-child families. However, a full illustrative listing of these avenues may become tedious to read straight through. Because of this consideraton, as well as space limitations, I can do no more than summarize the major differences experienced by C_1 when the family grows to this size.[6]

First, at the level of dyadic relationships, the main change is in terms of the appearance of diversity in sibling associations, including (three times out of four) *both* OS and SS relationships. There are now both 1–2 and 2–1 triad relationships in which all members are siblings. Foursome relations have mushroomed almost beyond recognition in potential variety and number. They now include double-pair, 1–3, and 3–1 forms composed entirely of siblings. Including the parents as well, a further range of distinct new subforms and a huge array of possible "cases" differing in specific member composition are encompassed. (Figure 11.5 suggests the scope of 2–2 relationships alone.) Quintet systems now appear, encompassing 1–4, 2–3, 3–2 and 4–1 I(*we*)-*you* forms, a variety of subforms, and a host of specific "choices" of member composition.

Relationship systems made up of the entire family include six basic forms, a variety of subforms (for example, within 3–3 triad-pair systems), and an array of individual cases bounded by the inclusion of all members. It is apparent that the full spectrum of main forms distinguished, at each level of system (from dyads to sextets), is very likely to be represented in C_1's experience. Some patterns would tend to be short lasting, readily giving way to others, in the family's process. Generally, the *we* or *you* groupings in multiperson interactions crop up in a range of contexts, including those in which they form whole relationship systems. Their specific quality depends on the context and vitally contributes to it.

Altogether, the six-member family adds several dozen major new forms and subtypes of relational avenue, including many larger systems compounded from smaller ones but not simply reducible to them. For a given person and family, no relationship system merely duplicates another system in all dimensions of process and experience. Each is a unique or distinctive vehicle for aspects of learning. Clearly, in larger families generally, relationships are of great range in separate kind and formidable complexity in total mosaic: their working entails a broad

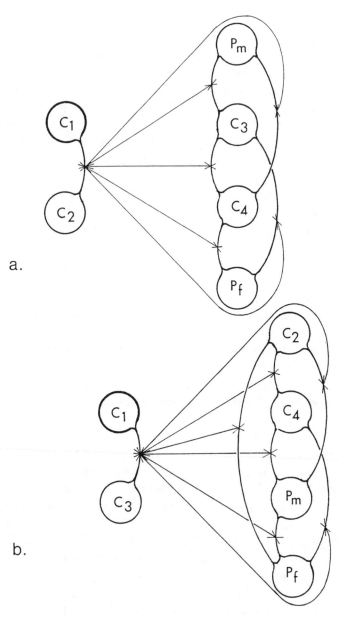

FIGURE 11.5. Illustrative *we-you* double-pair relationships in the four-child family (see note 6).

and subtle diversity of transitions from active engagement in one relationship to another and then a third—very often overlapping in membership; and the same compositional patterns come in a great variety of qualities. In particular, the six-person family potentially contains enormous riches for children (and adults), and the possibility also of tortuous relational systems and dysfunctional learnings. The territory of its potency is on quite a different scale from that of the smaller families.

CONCLUDING DISCUSSION

It is taken for granted in this chapter that parental attitudes are of very great importance in the experience and development of children. The view advanced opens another doorway to a further major source of influence. The vista sketched here implies that *without* basic variation in parental disposition and attitude, children in families that differ in size and linked feature of composition live in vastly different interpersonal-relational worlds. From this view another follows strongly, namely, that there is potential virtue in numbers—and other origins of variety—in families.

For the potential advantages of larger families to be realized, I would expect personal qualities of the parents and their relationship to have crucial, and greatest, bearing during the earlier life of the family. Actual effects of family size and composition would as well depend partly on the larger kinship system or any other community of belonging in which the family had its being. How long the family remains intact, or the members in active contact, whether there is loss and "substitution" (for example, of a parent), the experience of the children in settings outside the family, and whether other bonds they form effectively expand the family or contract it, are among many factors that will influence the development and quality of relationships within the framework and avenues elucidated. As children mature and relationships evolve within the family, cause and consequence are difficult to distinguish, and the same events can often be seen in either light. Indeed, simple linear views of causation can obscure more than they illuminate, as the interactive relationship systems within a family evolve, multiply, and develop their own dynamisms and character.

This chapter is to me the first stride in an inviting longer pathway. In a word, after the working-out of a charting method, I have described the inner world of families in terms of objectively possible relationship systems that have their effective existence in the experience of individuals. Structure-based system and individual experience are seen to be internal aspects of one whole in which outer-objective features and inner-subjective ones work in interwoven parternship, and where individuals partake of (conscious) systems and systems have individuality (living in consciousness). These views, in essence and full portrayal, necessarily have implications for working with couples, families, and communities in varied helping contexts, and experience in such contexts partly guided by this perspective should help to further refine it. The main ideas and approach would be useful in aspects of family life education and may contribute to features of social policy and of welfare practice in the family field. Not least, the system could be a stimulus to a variety of potentially useful lines of empirical work, some of which would help to refine it further. In earlier formulation, it has already provided the main basis for the following study by William Gomes.

Ten each of one- and two-child middle-class Latin American families (70 persons in all) provided the data for this exploratory work (Gomes, 1981). Respondents answered adaptations of the Relationship Inventory (Barrett-Lennard, 1978, in press) Form OS-S-42 (in Portugese) to describe (1) the dyadic relationships in the family from the position and experience of each family member; (2) the response of each pair of others from the standpoint of child members only[7]—mostly of high-school age; and (3) the whole-family we as experienced by each member of each family. The investigation is of most interest in respect to focus, original method, and features of the analysis, which it is not possible to detail here. Results were in accord with the view, for example, that youthful subjects often discriminated a single other responding with a different level of regard (or of empathy, etc.) than they experienced from a twosome including that other, and that they tended—with clear exceptions—to see the twosome responding at a level between that of each member described singly.

The way in which families were recruited, and the sampling data, imply that Gomes's one-child (1C) and two-child (2C) families were drawn from the same population, except in respect to size and any derivative or indirectly associated features. Not surprisingly, as between the two groups of families, corresponding relationships were much more alike than distinct in R.I.–assessed quality. One interesting divergence was that in 2C families mothers were generally seen by the children (C_1 and C_2) as responding more positively than were fathers on the relationship conditions. However, in one-child families—with children of similar age and sex distribution to C_2's in the two-child families—the fathers received slighty higher overall scores from child perceptions than did the mothers. (The mean age of the "only children" was 14.5 years.) If these results are replicated it would suggest that fathers are, or become, less "masculine" (or mothers less "feminine") in only-child families, perhaps that fathers share more fully in the nurturing of a single child, or that family equilibrium "requires" more equality of response from the parents.

Gomes looked at his data in several ways relative to the issue of within-family diversity and concordance of relationship, finding greater variety—aside from the forms of relationship system—in the 2C than in the 1C families (Gomes, 1981, Tables 21, 22, 23, and 26, and Figures 4 and 5). For example, among the various dyads in the four-person group, the experienced relationships were moderately different in average quality (P_fC_2 ranking first and P_mC_1 last), and within some dyads there was noticeable imbalance between the reported views by the two partners of the other's response. There was little diversity in these ways in and between the pairs in the three-person families. In Gomes's sample, however, mean whole-family *we* scores were higher in the larger families, especially from parental perceptions. Overall, the one-child families appeared both more cohesive and relationally homogeneous and less positively experienced as *whole* families than the two-child group. Some of the results may well be sample-specific, and there is a need for expansion and replication of the study.

Other particular and salient possibilities for research or application no doubt will occur to seriously interested readers. Broader questions and challenges that I presently see include the following:

1. Related to the general direction intiated by Gomes, how is the quality of significant forms of relationship in a family related to the quantity and variety of those relationships?

2. There is need to devise procedures that will systematically identify the particular relationship systems (especially the more complex systems in four-person and larger families) that in fact are active and/or eventfully recurrent in the lived world of children in their families.

3. How can knowledge be furthered with regard to the learning-developmental impact, generalizing beyond the family (or helping to potentiate experience and response in future situations), of widely differing family relationship systems and distinct qualities or episodes

within these systems? What detectable consequences of differing experience in 1–2, 1–3, 2–2, 4–1, and other systems, show themselves in future life relationships and social behavior? Can it be clearly demonstrated that *variety* of relational experience in families is beneficial, as I have strongly implied?

4. It would refine the perspective set forth to successfully study and track the development of relationships in families over time. The system offers a new angle of view in studying the life-cycle or psychosocial history of (nuclear) families. New longitudinal investigation influenced by this view would be very timely and could be extremely promising from theoretical and practical standpoints.

5. A challenging and potentially valuable focus of investigation is comparative study of larger families in which a small proportion of the possible relational alternatives are dominant, where much repetition and recycling of particular interactive processes occurs, and in which a much wider range of the potential relational systems is manifestly active (and much less simple repetition occurs).

6. Conducting couples and family therapy in a strongly person- and relationship-centered mode, and specifically with one's attention and awareness influenced by the thought and distinctions advanced, would involve new dimensions that should further anchor the system in the real world of family interaction and in all probability lead to useful elaborations of the thought. Connecting this context with research, the system would lend itself to study of the interior relational life of families before and after family therapy.

This is only a sampling of research-related questions and issues that spring from the system of thought presented. They are offered to suggest avenues, certainly not to limit them. I will end this chapter on a note reminiscent of its beginning, which again places my topic in the wider context that is part of its stimulus.

The family is a sociocultural inheritance from earliest antiquity, evidently rooted in our biological nature. It has been the basic social microcosm in which new human life generally begins and most formatively develops. Within another generation or two, altering lifestyles and the explosion of knowledge in biological and medical sciences could make it a matter of choice whether the family remains the primary social unit of our culture. The nature, qualities, and fate of the social microcosm of family connect integrally with the larger systems and society in which we interdependently live. Perhaps the family in any form so far known is literally already on trial for its existence. Coexisting with this possibility are others. One is that families are, or can become, a species of life raft crucial to the survival of our culture and civilization. Another is that they are, or will become, so unseaworthy that they contribute to the downfall of our civilization. Any of these possibilities imply that new perspectives, knowledge, and social-ecological consciousness regarding the potent and endangered species we call *family* is of profound importance and urgency.

NOTES

1. This metatheory of family relationships was first presented in colloquia at Kansas State University and Southern Illinois University in 1979–1980 and developed further for the First International Forum on the Person-Centered Approach held in Oaxtepac, Mexico, June-July, 1982. The present text is a further revision.

2. The main principles and the notation of balance theory (see Cartwright & Harary, 1956) have no visible counterparts in my analysis, although my sense is that a reader interested in both perspectives could draw and build on them together. In this regard, Taylor's (1970) work—which was a main bridge and point of departure for Lindsay (1976)—may also interest the reader (as it did me).

3. It may seem presumptuous of me to have largely bypassed other significant contributions to the understanding of family interaction and relationships. My reasons for this (relative) neglect combine strategy, happenstance, and prejudice—the last in its most generic meaning. Accounts that tend to view what happens in families as an interaction of roles (in literal or symbolic senses), even those that pay close attention to communicational interaction but without accompanying focal concern for subjective or intrapsychic processes, do not hold my interest. (My difficulty concerns the subjectively experiencing person getting lost or underemphasized, in terms of agency.) With respect to "happenstance," I entered the domain of this chapter by following a rich scent from other areas and not via a prior focus on research or practice in the family sphere. In regard to strategy, I *wanted* to formulate my own ideas before searching deeply for and into related work by others, especially work that excited my interest. Contributions in this category had started to come into view—for me—long before, with Watzlawick, Beavin, and Jackson's (1967) *Pragmatics of Human Communication,* and they lately include Kantor and Lehr's (1975) searching study, *Inside the Family.* Carl Rogers's

work is an ambient, fertile influence that, although not a direct stimulus to the structural systems features of my thought, has here and elsewhere helped me to tread my own path.

4.   As primary entities in social or collective existence, dyads not only give meaning to life but are themselves a basic form of life. And, typically, there are many more of them in any connected group or community (above three persons) than there are singles. Similarly, triadic combinations far outnumber singles in connected groups of five or more persons, and are critical in numerous life contexts. My paper "A New Model of Communicational-Relational Systems in Intensive Groups" (Barrett-Lennard, 1979b) complements the present chapter in reference to these and related issues.

5.   The child of course experiences each parent in a one-to-one relationship as well as relating to both at other moments in their twosome modality. At times, it must seem for the child as though three others are present—each parent as a single and the parental couple as a pair—perhaps all speaking or interacting with a different "voice" and attitude.

6.   Readers who would be interested in my total account and discussion of relationship systems in the six-person family (initially planned for inclusion in this chapter) are invited to write to me. The following passage has the particular aim of being useful, by its close illustration of method, to those who may themselves wish to generate the possible cases of a given relationship form in larger families. The illustration involves 2–2 foursomes in a six-person family. Suppose that C_1C_2 form the we twosome, as shown on the left of Figure 11.5a. Among the four remaining members there are five new possible dyads— illustrated on the right side of Figure 11.5a. The parental twosome is omitted here because C_1C_2-P_mP_f is not new to the four-child family. Correspondingly, if C_1P_m or C_1P_f (also "old-family" pairs) are an engaged we responding to another twosome, five new pairs are possible in each case. If C_1 and C_3 form the initial we, there are six dyads among the remaining members that could be involved in a double-pair transaction or recurring system. Because of the starting we, all combinations—visually presented in Figure 11.5b—are new. An exactly parallel state of affairs prevails if one starts with C_1C_4. By simple count, there are in all 27 specific possible cases, over and above the three that were illustrated in Figure 11.3b for the two-child family!

7.   Subjects were asked to describe the response of pairs of others (such as the two parents) "in the way that they generally respond to you when they are involved together as a pair. In this case, you need to think of the two people as one 'you' or 'they' in the way they respond to 'me' when they are also occupied with each other" (Gomes, 1981, p. 106).

12   From Person to System:
Two Perspectives

Ronald F. Levant

I have been teaching graduate-level courses on family systems theories on the one hand, and on personality theories on the other. A common concern in this field is how to connect—or better yet, integrate—these two domains of knowledge: the one that focuses on the person with the one that focuses on the system. In this chapter I will discuss two attempts to make the theoretical linkage from person to system. The first starts with psychoanalytic theory, and, using object relations theory as the bridge, derives a psychoanalytic view of the family. The second is a client-centered model that uses the notion of the family concept to develop a phenomenological framing of the family system. After considering each position from the perspective of how the connection is made between person and system, I will discuss each model of the person in the family from the perspectives of their epistemological foundations and their implications for therapy.

THE PSYCHODYNAMIC PERSPECTIVE[1]

Psychoanalytic Personality Theory

To provide a basis for understanding the psychodynamic view of the family, it will be necessary to discuss psychoanalytic personality theory because psychoanalysis is a complex body of theory that has evolved considerably over the years. The successive approaches to psychoanalysis have, through their departures from the original theory, created opportunities that were later utilized when the link from person to system was formulated. To set the stage thus for the psychodynamic perspective on the family, I will trace these departures, beginning with Freud's drive psychology, continuing with ego psychology, and concluding with the interpersonal and object relations schools.

Freud's Drive Psychology

Freud (1935) viewed personality development as a function of the struggle between the biologically based instincts of the id (sex and aggression) and societal constraints on their expression (as represented by the child's parents). The sexual instinct (libido) attaches to different body zones during the course of development. Psychosexual development thus progresses from the oral stage to the anal stage and then on to the phallic stage by the age of five. As the result of the conflict between the sexual instinct and parental restraint during the first five years of life, the infant acquires two personality structures: the superego, which represents an internalization of societal and parental values and prohibitions; and the ego, whose function it is to manage the acceptable expression of id impulses.

Freud's psychoanalysis is thus rooted in biology, specifically nineteenth-century biology. Nineteenth-century biology was heavily influenced by thermodynamics and the Newtonian-Gallilean world view on which it was based. This is a perspective, useful within its sphere of application, which seeks to distinguish cause from effect by isolating variables and examining their linear relationship. It is thus mechanistic and reductionistic, and models a closed system.

The Ego Psychologists

The ego psychologists took as their point of departure the least well-developed aspect of Freud's theory, the ego. (The ego in drive psychology is depicted as weak and embattled, housed between the overpowering id drives and the commanding superego.) Anna Freud (1966) extended the concept of defense mechanisms and elaborated the various ways in which the ego manages conflict. Heinz Hartmann (1939) made the distinction between defense and adaptation, and evolved the notion of a "conflict-free ego sphere," an area where the ego was not borne out of conflict and could function autonomously. This enabled psychoanalysis to account for certain day-to-day "neutral" or adaptive functions of the ego, such as memory, perception, cognition, and learning. As a result of this shift to a focus on the ego, more emphasis was placed on healthy adaptive behavior, as in Erikson's (1963) psychosocial theory and White's (1960) notion of competence motivation.

Interpersonal and Object Relations Theories

Interpersonal and object relations theorists (Sullivan, 1953; Klein, 1963; Fairbairn, 1954; Guntrip, 1971; Winnicott, 1965) helped separate psychoanalysis from biology by understanding the person in an interpersonal context. For the sake of space, I will focus on the object relations theory of Fairbairn to exemplify the general direction of this group of theories. Fairbairn's object relations theory portrayed the infant as starting out, not with an id teeming with primal instincts, but rather with a global ego. Libido is seen as the object-seeking, affiliative tendency of the ego and aggression as a defensive reaction of the ego to frustration or deprivation. Instead of the notion of three psychosexual zones (mouth, anus, genitals), the ego is seen as able to libidinize (or cathect) any part of the body it desires in the service of making a relationship (eyes, for instance). Libido is thus a term descriptive of the object-seeking nature of the human personality.

Object seeking is central to human existence. The process of personality development rests on the ego's relations with significant persons, initially and primarily in infancy, and thereafter with their internalized representations in the unconscious, which is the split-off and repressed part of the infantile ego.

Psychic wholeness is fundamental to mental health. In infancy, however, relations with nurturing objects can be sufficiently difficult so as to create "ego splits." As the infant experiences frustration of her needs, she internalizes the frustrating-nurturing object in order to have better control over the provision of gratification. The internalized frustrating-nurturing object, having bad and good parts, is split into a good object and a bad object. The good object is both retained as an ego ideal and projected onto the real external mother, who is thus idealized in order to make the relationship more comfortable. The bad object is split into an exciting object (the tempting mother who stimulates needs without satisfying them) and a rejecting object (the mother who actively denies need satisfaction), and these two bad objects are repressed by the ego.

Owing to the fact that the exciting and rejecting objects are both cathected by the original ego, these objects carry into repression with them parts of the ego by which they are cathected, leaving the central ego unrepressed, but acting as the agent of repression.

The resulting situation, depicted in Figure 12.1, is one in which the original ego is split into three egos. The central ego is the ego of daily living. It is attached to the ideal object (ego ideal) and is modeled after the idealized parents, with the disturbing (exciting and rejecting) elements split off and repressed. The libidinal ego, which continues to crave the nurturance from the exciting object to which it is attached, is the basis of compulsive overdependency in adulthood. Finally, the antilibidinal ego, attached to the rejecting object, adopts an uncompromisingly hostile attitude toward the libidinal ego, and thus has the effect of powerfully reinforcing its repression.

In this view, what Freud called the superego is a complex structure comprising the ideal object (ego ideal), the antilibidinal ego, and the rejecting object. Thus Fairbairn's object relations theory provides a psychology without an id at all and without a superego per se, but with an ego that is global at birth and synonymous with self, but gets split up as the result of difficulties in early object relations.

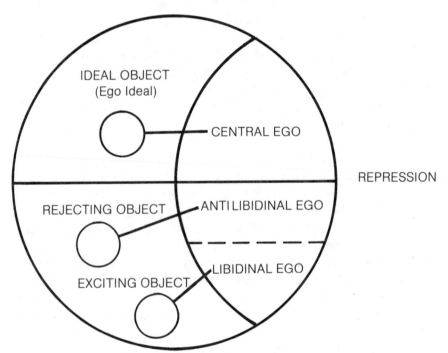

FIGURE 12.1. Fairbairn's object relational view of personality.

To the extent that early life experiences are traumatic, the splits are more intense and involve more of the personality, and the person is less complete or whole and depends to greater extent on the internal objects in adult life. The result is that external relationships get interpreted at an unconscious level in accordance with the internal objects (whether in terms of one's libidinal desires or one's rejected, split-off traits). Even more problematic, *"active, unconscious attempts are made to force and change close relationships into fitting the internal role models"* (Framo, 1970, p. 130).

Extension of Object Relations Theory into the Family Arena

It is now time to consider the ways in which the projection of the intrapsychic contents onto the interpersonal realm occurs, first with respect to marital interaction and then with regard to family interaction.

Marriage. H.V. Dicks developed a conceptual formulation of marital interaction based on object relations theory. He described how marital partners relate to each other in terms of their unconscious object-relational needs.

> This stressed the need for unconscious *complementariness*, a kind of division of function by which each partner supplied part of a set of qualities, the sum of which created a complete dyadic unit. This joint personality or integrate enabled each half to rediscover lost aspects of their primary object relations, which they had split off or repressed, and which they were, in their involvement with the spouse, re-experiencing by projective identification. The sense of belonging can be understood on the hypothesis that at deeper levels there are perceptions of the partner and consequent attitudes toward him or her *as if* the other was part of oneself. The partner is then treated according to how this aspect of oneself was valued: spoilt and cherished, or denigrated and persecuted. (Dicks, 1967, p. 69)

S. Lecker (1976) developed the beginnings of a typology of marriage. He started by simplifying object relations theory, describing intrapsychic life as consisting of two "aggregates of identity," the good and the bad internal objects. He then described four basic modes by which people deal with their internal objects. In the *paranoid mode*, the person identifies with the good object and projects the bad object onto the external world. In the *hysterical mode*, the person retains the bad object as an introject and projects the good object onto someone in his world. He idealizes others and is constantly burdened by somatic or psychic pain. The person using the *obsessional mode* retains both the good and the bad objects as introjects. He sides with the good object in a constant struggle to overcome the bad object. In the *phobic mode*, the person projects both the good and the bad objects. He seeks sanctuary with those on whom he has projected his good object, from those on whom he has projected his bad object.

Lecker then described some possible marital combinations of persons tending to use one or another of these modes as a predominant interpersonal style. He described the *paranoid-hysteric* marriage as possibly quite stable: "The hysteric wants to find strength—the paranoid can recognize only his good internal object. The paranoid seeks weakness in others—the hysteric is eager to confess to weakness" (Lecker, 1976, p. 197). However, with the birth of the first child the situation will change dramatically. There will be considerable conflict as one parent tends to derogate and the other idealize the child. This problem may be resolved when, with the arrival of a second child, one child is given the scapegoat role and the other the role of "angel." In contrast, the *paranoid-paranoid* marriage is explosive at the beginning: "Each partner seeks to rid himself of the bad object and find it in the other one who will become infuriated at such fault finding" (p. 197). However these marriages may be stabilized by the birth of a child who becomes the "repository for the bad objects of both members" (p. 197). This child is likely to be severely scapegoated.

The Family.   Framo widened the application of object relations theory beyond marital interaction to include multiple generations of a family. He described the process of *irrational role assignment* or *projective transference distortion* in which:

> The various children in the family come to represent valued or feared expectations of the parents, based on the parental introjects: sometimes the roles of the children are chosen for them even before they are born (e.g., the child who is conceived to "save the marriage").... In every family of multiple siblings there is "the spoiled one," "the conscience of the family," and "the wild one," the assigned roles are infinite. (Framo, 1965, p. 192)

The process of projective transference distortion is similar to the mechanism of *externalization* described by Brodey (1959, p. 385), in which "the inner world is transposed to the outside with little modification, and the part of the outer world attended to is selected *only* as it validates the projections, *other impinging realities being omitted*." The use of this mechanism leads to the formation of *narcissistic relationships*.

The same phenomenon has also been described by Zinner and Shapiro (1972) in terms of the defense mechanism of *projective identification* (Klein, 1946). The concept of projective identification underscores the notion that an individual cannot "get rid of" his projected objects without undermining the integrity or cohesiveness of his personality. A projection of one's introjects requires that one stay in contact with what is projected. Contact occurs through a process of identification with the person onto whom one has projected aspects of one's self. Zinner and Shapiro conceptualize this process of identification in terms of "the relationship between a subject and his projected part as he experiences it within the object" (1972, p. 525). The subject's behavior in this situation is governed by two principles. First, he will relate to the projected aspect of himself in the object as if it were an internal part of himself. Second, the object is induced or coerced to act in conformity with the way in which he is perceived. Zinner and Shapiro quote Laing to illustrate this latter process:

> We are denoting something other than the psychoanalytic term "projection." The one person does not wish merely to have the other as a hook on which to lay his projections. He strives to find in the other, or to induce the other to become, the very *embodiment* of that other whose cooperation is required as "complement" of the particular identity he feels impelled to sustain. (Laing, 1962, p. 101)

To summarize, we have the following theoretical model with which to understand the interaction of individuals within a family. The parents within the nuclear family have varying degrees of attachment to their introjected parental objects, depending on the severity of experiences of loss or deprivation during their childhoods. The parents have particular modes (e.g., paranoid, hysterical, etc.) of handling their introjects, and specific object-relational needs. Their relationship represents as close a fitting as possible of their "object-relational need-templates" (Boszormenyi-Nagy, 1965). This occurs through a process of bilateral projective identification. Those aspects of their object-relational needs that do not get resolved within the context of their marital relationship may get expressed in the assignment or induction, via projective identification, of irrational roles in their children.

Framo (1970) has shown how symptoms in children can be viewed as responses to the irrational role assignment—either as a form of compliance or as a method of resistance. For example, children who comply with the parental projection and take on the assigned role as the sole basis for their identity are candidates for a psychotic break. Other children may exaggerate the negative role attributes with a vengeance and develop behavioral problems and patterns of delinquency. Still others may struggle intrapsychically with their partial identifications and ambivalent feelings about their assigned roles. These children often develop neurotic symptoms such as obsessions, compulsions, phobias, and depression. A particularly troublesome but increasingly common-place role assignment is one in which the child is expected to be parent to his parents: *parentification*. This robs the child of the opportunity to be a child, forcing him into premature responsibility, and burdening him with guilt feelings attendant upon the crossing of generational lines.

Symptoms in one of the spouses is a little more complicated. It involves the interaction of the couple's personality weaknesses, formed in response to the projections of their parents, with the projective processes occurring in their marriage. Framo (1970, pp. 145–149) has described how symptoms in one spouse may in fact represent particular internal conflicts in the other, since the spouses "collusively carry psychic functions for each other." In the "dynamic economy of their relationship system," one partner will often be overadequate to balance the underfunctioning of the symptomatic spouse. Often, if the symptomatic spouse improves as the result of personal growth or psychotherapy, the other spouse may suddenly become symptomatic.

Thus the psychoanalytic perspective on the family is one in which persons are locked into overdetermined roles and behaviors to the detriment of their ability to function at their best level. Owing to this locked-in quality, attempts to change these families are thought to be extremely difficult. That is, family resistance is seen as much more formidable than other forms of resistance in that it is based on both the interlocking nature of individual family members' personalities and on mutual defensive patterns developed over the course of years of accommodation of family members to each other. Thus families will strongly resist change and seek to maintain the status quo, a phenomenon that family systems therapists have described in cybernetic terms, using concepts of negative (deviation-counteracting) feedback and homeostasis.

It is interesting to observe that, despite the efforts of ego psychology to expand psychoanalysis in order to make room for normality, and of the efforts of the object relations theorists to remove psychoanalysis from its connection with nineteenth-century biology, the mechanistic, closed-systems ideas that characterized Freud's psychoanalysis turn up in the psychodynamic view of the family: the homeostasis of the pleasure principle reappears as family homeostasis.

It is also interesting to note that the psychodynamic view of the family is fundamentally compatible with the views of most family systems theorists, who in this context can be seen as simply switching from a microscopic view of the interplay of the introjective and projective processes to a macroscopic view of the resultant interactional patterns and their underlying organizational structures. Bowen described this shift in focus as follows:

> When it was possible to attain a workable level of detachment, it was then possible to begin to defocus the individual and to focus on the entire family at once.... Once it was possible to focus on the family as a unit, it was like shifting a microscope from the oil immersion to the low power lens, or like moving from the playing field to the top of the stadium to watch a football game. Broad patterns of form and movement that had been obscured in the close-up view became clear. The close-up view could then become more meaningful once the distant view was also possible. (Bowen, 1960, p. 351)

The compatibility of these views, and the similarity of their position on resistance, is quite striking in view of the intense debates that have gone on between psychodynamic and family systems theorists (GAP, 1970; Zuk, 1971). In my view, aside from the micro/macro focus and terminology, the major issue that differentiates the psychodynamic family therapists from the family systems theorists (especially the structural and strategic) is their approach to dealing with family resistance.

Psychodynamic family therapists attempt to *work through* the resistance in what is seen as a very long and laborious treatment process. In this process, there is first the need to uncover the object-relational basis for, and meaning of, the symptom in order to defocus or detriangle the symptomatic person and achieve symptomatic relief. Second, all members of the family must go through a process of uncovering, working through, and ultimately resolving their attachments to their parental introjects.

Structural and strategic family therapists, on the other hand, attempt to *break through* the resistance by using directives of various kinds. The structuralists (Minuchin, 1974) tend to emphasize direct interventions or straight directives, in which the expectation is that the family will do what you tell them. These kinds of directives are termed *compliance-based*. The strategic therapists tend to emphasize paradoxical interventions, in which the expectation is that the family will oppose the therapist. These kinds of interventions are termed *defiance-based*. Among the strategic therapists there are some variations in how paradoxical interventions are used. Haley (1976), emphasizing the power or control dimension, uses paradoxical interventions as a form of therapeutic *aikido*, where the family's own momentum is utilized to unbalance their stuck patterns. The group at the Mental Research Institute (Watzlawick, Weakland, & Fisch, 1974) tends to emphasize the meaning dimension, attempting to "re-frame" the way in which the family conceptualizes its difficulties. Problems are seen as the result of the family's misdirected efforts to solve its own difficulties in living. And, finally, the Milan group (Palazzoli, Cecchin, Prata, & Boscolo, 1978) tends to emphasize the affective dimension, using interventions to change the valence with which family members' moves are regarded, using *positive connotation*.

THE CLIENT-CENTERED PERSPECTIVE[2]

An Alternative View

An alternative view of the family, one that is more optimistic about the family's possibility for self-directed change, provides the theoretical basis for a client-centered family therapy. This alternative conception of the family attempts to bridge, and possibly to resolve, the issue of focus that separates the psychodynamic and family systems camps: that is, whether the focus should be on the individual (oriented to the intrapsychic dynamic) or on the larger social unit (oriented to the multipersonal systems dynamics). This alternative view of the family involves a phenomenological, subjective framing of the concept of the family system.

The *individual orientation* attempts to explain family dynamics in terms of the intrapsychic dynamics of the individual members of the family. This is not likely to account for most of the variance of family interaction because family members understand each other's behavior, at least in part, in terms of the context of the family—its relationships, values, and traditions (van der Veen, 1969). The *family systems orientation* attempts to describe the dynamic interaction patterns and specify their underlying organizational structure. This perspective cannot account for most of the variance in individuals' responses to the same objective event simply because people experience identical events in very different ways.

The *phenomenological view* surmounts both difficulties. To paraphrase and adapt some of Rogers's propositions (Rogers, 1951): the person exists in a phenomenal world of which she is the center, and which includes internal and external realms of experience. The internal realm includes her experience of her intrapsychic dynamics; the external realm includes her experience of her family systems dynamics. The person behaves in a goal-directed fashion to maintain and enhance self in response to her perceived experience in both realms.

This is a view that takes into account both intrapsychic and family systems dynamics. Also, by placing the person in the center of the phenomenal field, we are in a good position to enlarge intrapsychic explanations of behavior by taking into account the social context of that behavior, and we can deepen family systems explanations of behavior by considering the subjective basis for idiosyncratic responses to the same objective stimuli. This view also assumes that individuals are motivated for maintenance *and* enhancement or growth (self-actualization), rather than primarily motivated to oppose change and growth. Finally, it allows the placing of responsibility for the conceptualization and actualization of family experience with the individual members of the family, who, by virtue of their position at the center of their phenomenal worlds, are best able to assume this responsibility.

The Family Concept

The notion of the *family concept* (a parallel of self-concept), developed by van der Veen, is central to the phenomenological view of the family. The family concept "denote[s] a person's awareness and conceptualization of his interpersonal family experiences.... [It] refer[s] to the person's experience plus the meaning he imparts to this experience" (van der Veen, 1969, p. 20).

> The family concept consists essentially of the feelings, attitudes, and expectations each of us has regarding his or her family life. The family concept encompasses a relatively stable and potent set of

psychological attributes. It is assumed to have several characteristics: It influences behavior; it can be referred to and talked about by the individual and it can change as a result of new experience and understanding. (Raskin & van der Veen, 1970, p. 389)

The family concept is analogous to the self-concept, in that it is an organized, cognitive-perceptual schema with associated affects that is based on experience (Rogers, 1951).

So far, this discussion of the phenomenological conceptualization of the family has focused on how the individual experiences the family. Let's turn now to a consideration of the family as a whole. The family as a whole consists of the *"shared consciousness by the parents and the children of their experience together"* (van der Veen, 1969, p. 7). The family concept provides the theoretical foundation for a phenomenological conception of the family as a whole.

Another way of viewing the importance of the family concept is to consider the role it plays in the members' definition and creation of their lives together as a family. The family is internally created by the members, both children and parents, and is not exclusively or even primarily a "given" of society, even though this may not be clearly apparent to the members themselves.... What, after all, would the family be without the ideas that the members themselves have of it? Our focus on the person's concept of the family seeks to bring the family out of the background of a universal given, into the foreground of an emergent and vital social grouping, a grouping that depends for its shape and substance on the efforts, purposes and ideas of each of its members. (van der Veen, 1969, p. 5)

R.D. Laing develops this argument further. He writes of "unification by coinherence.... We feel ourselves to be one in so far as each of us has inside himself a presence common to all [members of]...the family" (Laing, 1969, p. 5).

Each member incarnates a structure derived from relations between members. This family-in-common shared *group presence* exists *in so far as* each member has it inside himself.... Each member of the family may require the other members to keep the same "family" imago inside themselves. Each person's identity then rests on a shared "family" inside the others who, by that token, are themselves in the same family. *To be in the same family is to feel the same "family" inside.* (Laing, 1969, p. 13)

It can get considerably more complex of course:

> The family is united by the reciprocal internalization by each (whose token of membership is precisely this interiorized family) of each other's internalization. The unity of the family is in the interior of each synthesis and each synthesis is bound by reciprocal interiority with each other's internalization of each other's interiorization.... (Laing, 1969, p. 5)

To carry this observation further, the family concept is not simply "a member's view of the rest of the family in relation to herself. It also represents qualities concerning the entire family including oneself. It places more stress on 'we,' rather than 'they' versus 'me' " (van der Veen, 1969, p. 4). The family concept, then, is a concept of the multipersonal group, which leaves room for a systems conception. Or, using Laing's ideas, "*the family as a system*," "a space-time system," is what is interiorized in the family concept. "Relations and operations between elements and sets of elements are internalized, not elements in isolation" (Laing, 1969, p. 4).

Thus the family as a human system is not simply an objective thing existing in physical space and clock time. Rather, it is best understood as a lived space-time system that exists in the experience and action of each family member and in the stable patterns of interexperience and interaction of the family group. It is an intersubjective phenomenon, in contradiction to the objective (standing outside) view of the structural and strategic family theorists. In Laing's words:

> The "family" is no simple social object, shared by its members. The "family" to each of its members is no objective set of relations. It exists in each of the elements (i.e., persons) in it, *and nowhere else*. (Laing, 1969, p. 5)

Client-Centered Family Therapy

The application of client-centered principles to the family was quite a natural development. By 1970, client-centered principles had been applied to several therapeutic modalities, from action-oriented play therapy to interpersonally oriented group therapy, as well as to nontherapy activities such as teaching, administration, training of non-professionals, and prevention/enhancement programs (Rogers, 1951; Hart & Tomlinson, 1970). The reason for its wide application, and for its natural fit with family therapy, is that, fundamentally, client-centered theory addresses the processes of enhancing close interpersonal relationships (Rogers, 1961).

A client-centered approach to family therapy requires the same basic attitudes and activities of the therapist as do client-centered approaches to other forms of helping. The method begins with a deep trust in the ability of the family members to assume the responsibility for their own change and growth under certain facilitative conditions and a respect for their ability to make the decisions that are best for themselves about all aspects of the therapy, such as who will participate and to what extent; what the significant areas for discussion will be; what meaning will be derived from the experience; and what action(s), if any, will be taken. Related to this trust and respect, the therapist experiences a sense of nonpossessive caring and warmth for the family. She attempts to gain an appreciation of the internal frames of reference of the family members and to communicate her empathic understanding of family experiences. She tries to stay in contact with and follow the moment-to-moment changes in the family's experiential flow. She interacts with the family members on a genuine basis, being transparent about her own feelings and congruent with her own experience.

This is a therapy in which the therapist is not so much directive expert as coparticipant in, and facilitator of, the process of therapy. The role does not involve history-taking, diagnosis, treatment planning, or the use of therapeutic techniques to induce change (whether they be paradoxical maneuvers or interpretations). Rather, it involves facilitating the release and development of self-regenerative and self-enhancing powers within the family members. It also involves a direct encounter on a person-to-person basis with family members. It is a therapy based to a very large extent on the person of the therapist.

Current Issues

Not much has been written about a client-centered view of the family or family therapy. Aside from the work of the van der Veen group (1969, 1970) and my own (Levant, 1978b, 1982), I have been able to find only a few loosely related contributions. This remains an underdeveloped area in terms of theoretical and clinical writings. One of the questions that needs to be asked is, "Are any special modifications of theory or procedures of therapy required in order to take into account the special qualities of the family group?" I think that the answer is affirmative and lies with the further conceptual elaboration of the basic interpersonal qualities of the therapist: empathy, genuineness, and unconditional positive regard. As far as empathy is concerned, in family work the focus is not so much on the inner world of each family member (although that is useful at times), but rather on the felt meanings that individual family members experience in their relationships to other family members. But, whereas in individual therapy it is possible to keep the client figural and consider the persons with whom he has relationships as part of the phenomenal field, in family therapy all parties to a relationship (whether dyadic or triadic) must be kept figural (if not simultaneously, at least for a brief period of time). This is a difficult task that requires the therapist to balance multiple inner frames of reference in order to be empathic to all family members. The dimension of genuineness assumes increased importance in family work. In the work of Rogers, Gendlin, Kiesler, and Truax (1967) with nonverbal schizophrenic patients, it was necessary to be genuine in order to reach out and build a relationship; similarly, with families it is necessary to be genuine in order to be "let into" to the inner family system. Furthermore, the genuine emotional responses of the therapist to family pain or grief, appropriately expressed, can have a powerful impact on unfreezing stuck family relationships. Indeed, the dimension of genuineness has been shown in a recent review to be a key ingredient in family therapy from a wide range of theoretical perspectives (Kaslow, Cooper, & Linsenberg, 1979).

Finally, unconditional positive regard must be viewed within the epistemological context created by Bateson (1972) and others, and recently discussed by Dell (1982) and Keeney and Sprenkle (1982) in *Family Process*. Basically, they argue that much of contemporary family therapy is reductionistic and based on a misunderstanding of the principles of general system theory and cybernetics. Specifically, it is argued that much of family therapy is based on a first-order cybernetics of *observed* systems rather than a second-order cybernetics of *observing* systems (Steier, 1983). Maturana and Varela (1980) go even further to note that human systems are not only observing but self-creating or *autopoetic*. On the basis of such reasoning, Dell (1982) targets the notion of family homeostasis (the systems analog of resistance, discussed above) as the basic epistemological error that has resulted in the creation of an antagonistic dualism of therapist versus family. In its place he proposes the term *coherence* to reflect the self-creating or autopoetic qualities of living systems as described in the twentieth-century biology of Maturana and Varela (1980). To quote Dell:

Such epistemological error... is related in several ways to a system's *appearing* to resist change. First, if we expect a patient to act a certain way and cannot accept that she or he acts otherwise, then we have made an epistemological error and created "resistance." That error is far more common than therapists would like to admit. The so-called "resistant patient" is usually defined by his or her obnoxious unwillingness to cooperate with treatment. That patient, however, is not resistant; the patient is simply being who she or he is.... What we find obnoxious is the fact that the patient is not as we want him or her to be.

Another closely related way that therapists create "resistance" is to *expect* a patient's particular response to a therapeutic intervention. When the therapist's expectation is not borne out, the therapist has two choices. The therapist can either decide that his or her expectation was in error... or that the patient is resistant (i.e., the patient is obstinately defeating the treatment). A more subtle way to commit this same epistemological error is to decide that the patient is "not ready for treatment." Such a judgment, of course, is nonsense. It is not the treatment that determines how the patient will respond but the organization of the patient as a system. It would be more accurate (and more honest) to say that *the treatment is not ready for the patient*... [emphasis added].

In therapy, the organization of the system is the unalterable reality with which the therapist must contend. If that reality is denied, the system will be "resistant." Strategic therapists know that "resistant" patients can be changed by "going with the resistance." Nonsense. "Resistant" patients are "changed" by going with the reality—that is, by the therapist's accepting that the system is what it is and by behaving accordingly. *In short, there is no such thing as resistance*; there is only *misunderstanding of reality or refusal to accept reality* [emphasis added]. (Reprinted from Paul F. Dell, "Beyond Homeostasis: Toward a Concept of Coherence," *Family Process*, 1982, 21(1), pp. 30–31, by permission of the author and publisher.)

In this light, unconditional positive regard is a reflection of the therapist's profound willingness and ability to accept the client family on their terms—that is, in terms of the system's basic organizational realilty or coherence. Can this be done? The only way to find out is to try it. Toward this end, I recommend to the reader the following exercise:

While having a conversation with someone—anyone, actually would be suitable for the purpose of this exercise—maintain the attitude within yourself that the person you are speaking with is your friend, can be trusted, is a psychologically healthy person, and in general is a beautiful representative of the human race by virtue of their uniqueness and idiosyncrasies. After a little while, develop and maintain an attitude that the person with whom you are speaking is phony, deceptive, psychologically disturbed in some way, however minor, and in general merits your sympathy as well as your watchfulness. After that, notice the various nuances in the attitude you actually do hold about that person. Notice how, depending upon the attitude you maintain, their words and tone and expression of feeling could be perceived and understood very differently, and very different conclusions could be reached about their meaning and intentions. Notice how totally different conversations might result depending on the attitude you might maintain about that person. Notice the power you have to determine your own perception. Notice which attitude you preferred to maintain; which felt most safe, most comfortable, most vulnerable, most exciting, most real, most productive. Notice how you felt about yourself while maintaining those different attitudes toward the other person. Practice this exercise a few times. Pretend you believe that the next person with whom you interact is just about ready to decompensate; after a little while, pretend you believe that he is a self-actualized person. Notice how much evidence you can accumulate for each belief, and how you can find ways to interpret their behavior according to your beliefs about them. Notice how each set of beliefs affects how you feel and behave in their presence. Spend a little time wondering how you arrived at the beliefs you actually do hold about that person and why you maintain those beliefs. (Reprinted from Paul Gron, *Freedom and Determinism in Gregory Bateson's Theory of Logical Levels of learning: An Application to Psychotherapy*, unpublished doctoral dissertation, Boston University, 1983, pp. 121–123. Reprinted by permission.)

SUMMARY

I have discussed two perspectives on the connection between person and system. The psychoanalytic view uses object relations theory as a bridge and derives a view of the family as an interlocking series of bilateral narcissistic relationships. Resistance is expected and found. Change tactics either take a very long time in psychodynamic family therapy or require tricky tactics to unbalance the system in the structural and strategic models of family therapy. The latter models are seemingly antagonistic to the psychodynamic perspective, but share basic assumptions about the family. The client-centered view, on the other hand, attempts to locate the family system in the set of persons who constitute the family. Seen in terms of the *family concept*, the family system is a subjective and lived phenomenon, and the family an emergent intersubjective entity capable of both change and stability and best able to determine when either process is most desirable. Therapy involves the facilitation of the family's intrinsic process through an attempt to understand this process accurately, to respect it as the meaningful product of a self-creating entity, and to interact, as an experiencing person, with the family members.

NOTES

1. Ronald F. Levant, *Family Therapy: A Comprehensive Overview,* © 1984, pp. 92–96. Reprinted by permission of Prentice-Hall, Inc., Englewood Cliffs, N.J.

2. Ronald F. Levant, "Family Therapy: A Client-Centered Perspective," *Journal of Marital and Family Therapy,* 2 (4). Copyright © 1978 American Association of Marriage and Family Therapy. Reprinted by permission.

**Contributions of Client-
Centered Therapy to Filial,
Marital, and Family Relationship
Enhancement Therapies**

Bernard G. Guerney, Jr.

This chapter will begin with a description of relationship enhancement (RE) therapies. Then, some of the research assessing the effectiveness of RE therapies will be briefly summarized. At that point it will be appropriate to show how the client-centered perspective has contributed to the development of RE. Finally, the theoretical integration of humanistic, psychodynamic, and behavioral perspectives and methods underlying RE will be described.

RE THERAPIES

Filial RE Therapy

Filial RE therapy was developed in the early 1960s. Filial methods may be seen on a videotape (Vogelsong, Guerney, & Guerney, 1978) and they are described in numerous publications, of which the following are representative: B. Guerney, 1964, 1969b; B. Guerney, L. Guerney, and Andronico, 1970; B. Guerney and Stover, 1971; L. Guerney, 1976, 1980. It is used with children up to the age of 10 and with modifications can be used with children up to 12 years of age. It has been used successfully with a very wide range of child pathologies. A parenting skills training program for prevention and enrichment has been adapted from it (Guerney, L., 1977, 1978).

In filial relationship enhancement therapy, the parent(s) of emotionally disturbed children are taught therapeutic attitudes and skills, including those necessary to conduct play therapy. Parents are taught primarily through demonstrations and constructive feedback and by supervision of the play sessions they conduct with their own children. Sessions held at the agency are supervised live. Home sessions are supervised on the basis of written and/or verbal parental report. Through this process the parents learn attitudes and skills of structuring, empathy/warmth/acceptance, allowing self-direction, and setting/enforcing limits. They are then taught principles and practices of learning and reinforcement, how to set priorities, and how to choose the most appropriate skills from among those they have learned in order to best promote their children's socialization and psychological adjustment. The goal is to establish mutually satisfying, growth-enhancing, day-to-day interactions between the parents and their children.

Filial RE may be conducted with one parent, both parents, or in one-parent groups, couples groups, or groups composed both of individual parents and couples. The parent meetings are generally held once a week. Time of treatment varies, of course, in accord with the case and the format. In the group format, significant reduction in symptoms occurs, on average, after eight sessions. But the goals of filial RE, resources permitting, go beyond elimination of pathology. They include transformation of the relationship into a strong, positive one in which gains will be *maintained* over time. For groups, an average of about 24–30 sessions are required for this level of success. Relatively few clients drop out of filial therapy. Filial therapy is not only a nonthreatening form of therapy, it is generally an *inspiring* form of therapy. This is especially the case in the group format, where enthusiasm and a strong spirit of mutual support almost invariably develops. The relatively few dropouts are usually due to time and money stresses and therefore have been greatest among parents without partners where such stresses are greatest.

A very wide range of degree of disturbance and of symptomatology has been successfully treated in filial RE over the past two decades. Filial RE works well with hyperactive and acting-out children as well as fearful, conflicted, or withdrawn children.

Marital and Family RE Therapies

In *family* RE therapy as many members of the family over 12 years of age whose presence is relevant and feasible are seen together. (They are also seen separately at intake and, if indicated, which is rare, later on as well.) In family RE—unlike filial RE in which the tasks of mastering skills and initiating changes are placed on the parents—children and parents are treated alike and have equal responsibilities for learning and initiating change almost from the beginning. Family RE methods may be seen on videotape (Vogelsong & Guerney, B., 1979).

Marital RE differs somewhat from family RE. For example, the frequency with which certain techniques are called for and the guidelines for mode-switching and facilitation are much simpler in marital RE therapy than they are in family RE therapy. However, the principles taught and the methods of instruction are basically the same.

As with filial RE therapy, marital and family RE therapies have also been successfully adapted for use as prevention/enrichment programs (Ginsberg & Vogelsong, 1977), and for training paraprofessionals in helping skills (e.g., Guerney, B., 1969a; Avery, 1978).

The Skills Taught

The children and parents are taught nine sets of skills and the attitudes underlying their usage. The skills may also be viewed as modes of behavior, each built around a set of guidelines. We have space here merely to list the skills, not to detail them. For a full description see *Relationship Enhancement* (Guerney, B., 1977a) and *Relationship Enhancement Skill Training* (Preston & Guerney, 1982).

The skills taught in marital/family RE are: (1) *expressive*—increasing self/feeling awareness and constructive assertiveness; (2) *empathic*; (3) *mode-switching* or *conversive*—using the skills in conversation; (4) *facilitative*—encouraging or teaching others to use the skills; (5) *problem/conflict resolution*—negotiating and interpersonal contracting; (6) *generalization*—practicing skills in daily life; (7) *self-changing*—implementing interpersonal contracts; (8) *other-changing*—helping others change so as to implement interpersonal contracts; (9) *maintenance skills*—making skill usage endure.

Formats

RE family therapy can be used in many formats. Two broad formats are *nongroup* and *group*. The sessions within each of these two broad formats can be either *extensive* (e.g., weekly 90-minute sessions) or *intensive* (e.g., four-hour sessions). Any of these formats can involve a basic unit as small as one person working on family relationships. We have termed this type of family representation *unilateral*. Another possibility is that a subunit of a family might attend. An example of this would be a father, a mother, and one daughter attending from a family with four children of appropriate age. We have termed this pattern of attendance *multilateral*. Or all appropriate family members might attend. We have termed this type of attendance *omnilateral* family therapy. Thus, there are $2 \times 2 \times 3$, or 12 basic formats. Still more formats consist of *combinations* of these basic formats: for example, intensive sessions at the beginning followed by extensive sessions. We have termed this particular variation the *front-loaded* format.

In *marital* RE therapy, the therapist may work with one or both spouses alone. In either case, a group may be comprised of either sole spouses or couples. The skills taught are the same as those taught in family RE. One type of group format used for enrichment may be seen on videotape (Figley & Guerney, 1974).

Methods of Teaching

The methods of teaching clients skills in filial, marital, and family RE are very systematic. The general procedure is first to carefully explain the rationale underlying the skill: why it is important; why it helps the individual to communicate better, to solve problems, and to create more trusting, intimate, harmonious relationships; and why it helps individuals achieve their interpersonal and personal goals. This procedure is followed by a demonstration of the skilled behavior. Next, the clients practice the skills, receiving word-by-word constructive feedback from the therapist. At all times, the therapist models the appropriate behaviors in his own interactions with the clients.

When clients have achieved some mastery of a skill, they are assigned the task of *practicing* the skills at home in specific situations. These situations are planned and structured as carefully as possible to maximize the probability that the practice will actually take place and prove successful. Common difficulties are anticipated by the therapist. Methods of avoiding or surmounting these difficulties are explained and/or demonstrated by the therapist and rehearsed by the clients under supervision. Performance of the skills at home is supervised by the therapist on the basis of the clients' verbal and written reports (brief questionnaires) and, whenever feasible, tape recordings.

The next step in teaching a given skill is showing the client how to use the skills more frequently in daily living, so that usage occurs with increasing spontaneity. This is encouraged, supervised, and reinforced with the aid of a log questionnaire completed by the clients. Methods of promoting continued use of the skills over the years is the final step. The skills are taught additively, and all previous skills are continuously supervised when a new one is being practiced.

Topic or Situation Selection

Topic or situation selection is also explained and closely supervised in an effort to maximize the chances for continuous success in acquiring and using the skills. Hence, when first acquiring the skills, clients are taught to select topics or situations that are not emotionally stressful. As the clients' mastery of skills increases, they are encouraged to make use of them in more and more emotionally difficult and important areas. Discussion of positive feelings and enrichment issues is always encouraged. With respect to problem or conflict resolution, when all the skills (except generalization and maintenance) have reached an appropriate level of proficiency, clients are encouraged to give priority to those issues that are most fundamental and important to improving their relationship and their personal well-being. Topics that are merely salient (e.g., "I am very upset with the way you were driving when we came here tonight") are eschewed by the therapist in favor of more fundamentally important topics (e.g., the wife's view that the husband is often unreasonably jealous). The clients select these fundamental topics with help from the therapist and write them down, usually in advance of the session, on a "Relationship Questionnaire" form.

This approach to topic selection is an abandonment of the "here-and-now," "all-roads-lead-to-Rome" orientation, not just of client-centered therapy, but of many other schools of therapy as well. We made this departure only after careful, systematic (albeit nonempirical) observation led us reluctantly to the conclusion that this new approach did indeed lead to more rapid and more reliable client progress. We hope that someone undertakes the task of conducting an empirical study to test the relative efficacy of these two different approaches to topic selection.

Research in RE Therapies

A number of studies have demonstrated the effectiveness of filial RE therapy (Guerney, B., & Stover, 1971; Guerney, B., 1976; Oxman, 1972; Stover & Guerney, 1967). Significant reductions in symptomatology and other improvements, even in the group format where therapeutic time must be divided among six to eight families, occur after two months (Sywulak, 1977). A three year follow-up showed the gains to be very well maintained (Sensué, 1981).

A controlled experiment using a randomly assigned waiting list group and also an own-control design has shown the group multilateral family RE approach to be effective in improving communication, the general quality of relationships, and self-concept. Where nonobtrusive behavioral measures of gain were used (in communication) this too showed improvement (Ginsberg, 1972). Another study of multilateral group family RE (Guerney, B., Coufal, & Vogelsong, 1981) showed it to be superior not only to a randomly assigned no-treatment group, but also to a randomly assigned traditional group treatment. This was true on nearly every one of the 18 different measures used to assess (1) communication behavior while discussing emotionally significant topics; (2) perception of general communication quality; (3) perceptions of general quality of the relationships. The same groups were followed up six months after termination (Guerney, B., Vogelsong, & Coufal, 1983). The superiority of the RE group over both other groups was maintained in all areas.

Group marital RE in an extensive format was first studied by comparing RE couples to a randomly assigned waiting-list control group, and also to the RE couples themselves during a no-treatment period comparable in length to the portion of the treatment period that was studied. Both comparisons showed that the couples in the RE treatment gained significantly more in their communication patterns and in the general quality of their relationship (Ely, Guerney, B., & Stover, 1973). Another study comparing couples in extensive-format group marital RE to a randomly assigned waiting-list control group showed that the RE couples gained more in marital communication and adjustment (Collins, 1977).

Intensive-format group marital RE was studied by Rappaport (1976). Clients in RE showed greater gains than they had during a waiting period of comparable duration. They gained more on measures assessing: communication behaviors assessed while they discussed emotionally significant topics; patterns of general communication; marital harmony; general quality of their relationship; trust and intimacy; and their perceptions of their ability to resolve problems.

A study by Wieman (1973) compared an extensive-format group marital RE abbreviated in duration to eight weeks with a reciprocal reinforcement approach. The gains on both treatment groups were superior (equally so) to those attained by a randomly assigned waiting-list group. The gains of both treatment groups were maintained through the 10-week follow-up period. The leaders of both groups were equivalent in age, sex, experience, etc. Yet on semantic differential scales, the RE couples, in comparison to the reciprocal reinforcement couples, perceived their treatment to have been significantly less light, safe, easy, cold, and calm, and more deep, good, worthwhile, exciting, strong, fair, important, comfortable, and professional.

Jessee and B. Guerney (1981) found an intensive-format group marital RE approach to be superior to a Gestalt-oriented group marital approach with respect to gains on variables reflecting communication, the general quality of the relationship, and ability to handle problems. Also, Ridley, Jorgensen, Morgan, and Avery (1982) found an intensive-format group marital RE approach to yield marital relationship gains superior to a discussion-oriented treatment.

Marital RE, in a dyadic format, has been studied by Ross, Baker, and B. Guerney (1982). Five therapists participated. During the (average) six years during which they had been practicing marital therapy, they had each developed flexible therapeutic approaches with which they felt most comfortable (termed here, *therapist's preferred therapy*). Therapists' preferences originated from a wide range of theoretical orientations. These therapists were jointly given a three-day training program in marital RE. After this, marital therapy cases assigned to them were randomly designated to receive either RE or the *therapist's preferred therapy*. Each therapist saw an equal number in each type of treatment. Measures taken after 10 weeks of treatment were compared to pretreatment measures. The couples who received RE gained significantly more on each of the variables: marital adjustment; quality of relationship; and quality of communication.

The results of this research indicate that RE is superior in process and outcome variables to any other treatment against which it has been compared so far, and that the effects of RE, including maintenance of gains, are treatment-specific effects and due neither to artifacts (e.g., repeated testing) or to generic treatment efforts (such as placebo, Hawthorne, thank-you, and experimenter-demand effects).

CONTRIBUTIONS OF CLIENT-CENTERED THERAPY TO RE THERAPIES

The Educational Model

RE therapies are deliberately built on an *educational* as opposed to a *medical* model (Authier, Gustafson, Guerney, B., & Kasdorf, 1975;

Guerney, B., 1977b, 1982, 1983; Joanning, Avery, Brock, & Coufal, 1980). The methods and procedures of delivering service chosen as models in developing RE therapy have not been those of the clinic but of the school. Likewise, when devising the therapist's functions and procedures, the professional role model for the RE therapist has been not the physician, who has served as the model for almost all non–client-centered approaches to the delivery of psychotherapeutic services, but the motivating, effective teacher.

The medical model functions as follows: illness or maladjustment→diagnosis→prescription→treatment→normality or cure. The educational model replaces that paradigm with this one: dissatisfaction or ambition→value clarification or goal selection→selection of attitude or skill-training program→teaching→goal attainment or satisfaction. We view the educational model as having very significant advantages over the medical model in terms of degree or depth of client gains, breadth of gains, durability of gains, cost effectiveness of service, development of sound measuring instruments to assess client personality and treatment gains, and research to advance therapeutic theory and practice.

Client-centered therapy played a pioneering and highly significant role in setting the stage for the replacement of the medical model by the educational model in the practice of psychotherapy, a process that is beginning to accelerate rapidly. One major contribution was Rogers's preeminent role in replacing the term *patient* with the term *client*. More important than the change in terminology itself, of course, was the shift in attitudes that this rephrasing represented. The implicit interpersonal contract between patient and healer is very different from that between a client and professional. The *patient* is in a "one-down," dependent position, placing herself in the hands of the healer and playing only a relatively passive role in the interaction. In contrast, generically speaking, the *client* hires the professional who serves at the client's discretion; the client plays an active role, using the professional as her expert guide.

Client-centered therapy made the contrast stronger yet, by holding that, although the therapist creates the necessary interpersonal environment for growth, it was the client who really should direct the course of the therapy. Gains were seen as the achievement of the client more than of the therapist. Without an attitudinal shift of this nature it is difficult to see how the educational, skill-training model of therapy could have emerged. At any rate, this Rogerian attitude was responsible for RE, the earliest of the programmatic, educational model approaches.

A second major contribution of client-centered therapy to RE and to the educational model concerns the replacement in the above-mentioned contrasting paradigms of *diagnosis*—so central to the medical model—by *value clarification and goal selection*. Within the medical model it is the professional who decides what is wrong with the patient: whether he is too depressed, too passive, too aggressive, too submissive, too competitive, not competitive enough, etc. For example, in the decades of the 1940s and 1950s possibly the most common diagnostic analysis made in child guidance clinics was that "the father is being emasculated, and the mother is not accepting her feminine role," meaning that the mother was playing too dominant a role in the family vis-à-vis the father. This was seen as leading to whatever "symptoms" the child was experiencing. Neither the father nor the mother (and certainly not the child!) was ever consulted—it was the professionals who decided who was or was not too dominant.

In contrast, from the perspective of the educational model, as in client-centered therapy, the client is viewed as being in the best position to balance appropriately the cultural experiences, personal needs, and feedback from his own present social milieu that enter into choosing what type of personality is desirable. Nor was it just client-centered theory and practice, but also research inspired by client-centered theory that contributed to this shift. We refer to the research demonstrating that successful psychotherapy appears not to be dependent upon therapists' use of diagnostic or analytic skills in planning psychotherapeutic strategy or outcome.

The replacement of *prescription*, in the contrasting paradigms presented above, by *choice of programmatic instruction* was also made possible in large measure by Rogerian theory, practice, and research. The psychotherapist who accepts the medical model feels free, on the basis of his diagnosis of the problem, to prescribe what type of experiences the patient should undergo—what medicine she should take, so to speak—for her own good. Such a therapist not only feels it is right to make such decisions for the client, but that it is his obligation to do so. This viewpoint has been carried further in the field of family therapy than most individual therapists would have dreamed of taking it, no matter how steeped they were in the medical model. To get the family-patient to take the right medicine (i.e., to experience what the therapist feels they need to experience to become "normal") the family therapist all too often feels free to deceive family members, telling them that he believes things that he does not believe, and instructing them to do things that he believes they really should not do. (Such deceptive techniques, euphemistically labeled *paradoxical techniques*, are essentially based on the same view that much of the public erroneously holds to represent "good child psychology"—if you want a resistant child to do something he should do for his own good, tell him to do the opposite.) In my view, such practices are both dangerous and unethical. The rejection by Rogerians of the notion that "therapist always knows best" when it comes to working out specific solutions to the client's problems, set the stage for therapists who follow the educational model also to reject that notion and to avoid the arrogance of power that accompanies it.

Rogerians have helped many therapists to recognize the limitations of any therapist's ability to know with certainty what solutions are best for the client and to recognize the lack of fruitfulness in the therapist's attempt to manipulate the client into insights and solutions. But the positive side of that viewpoint is even more important. We refer to the Rogerian position that, given the appropriate interpersonal climate, the client is likely to recognize and to achieve goals appropriate to and for himself. True, in the case of the educational model in general, and RE in particular, we add to the "appropriate interpersonal climate" the qualification, "and given the opportunity to master the requisite emotional and social skills." But the underlying faith in the client to set appropriate goals and to work out the specific ways of reaching them is central to the educational model and to RE. Rogerian theory, practice, and research have been the major forces in establishing and furthering that proposition.

Therapists' Attitudes

Most of the important attitudes RE therapists must hold derive in large measure from client-centered therapists' attitudes. The immediately preceding discussion states one of the RE therapists' attitudes that derives, not in full but in large measure, from the Rogerian perspective: faith that given the right environment and the right cognitive and emotional knowledge, attitudes and skills, it is a much more effective therapeutic strategy to trust the client to arrive at appropriate specific solutions than to trust the therapist to do so.

Stemming from trust in the client are certain other attitudes of RE therapists that were absorbed from the Rogerian tradition: openness, honesty, integrity, and straightforwardness with the client about therapeutic methods, strategies, and goals. As we have indicated above, in mentioning the so-called "paradoxical" techniques, such trusting attitudes are not as much the rule in the family therapy field as most nonfamily therapists probably suppose; rather, a desire for the power to manipulate clients effectively looms very large here.

Humility is still another attitude of RE therapists that has its origins in the client-centered tradition. Some humility is necessary when it comes to trusting the client more than oneself in the respects mentioned above. Without it, it becomes impossible to prevent oneself from jumping into (and muddying) the stream of possible solutions before the client has had the chance to catch his own fish there. This is an attitude acquired from seeing what clients, even including little children, can do for themselves that someone else never could have done as rapidly, or as well, for them. This type of education in the positive effects for clients of therapist humility probably comes more readily through the practice of client-centered therapy than from any other type of therapist schooling.

Contributions to the Therapeutic Environment

The rationale underlying RE incorporates the view that for most people skill learning is most rapidly and reliably acquired in an environment in which the teacher-therapist provides warmth, genuineness, integrity, trust, and empathic understanding and acceptance. The requisite attitudes and behaviors necessary for the therapist to provide this type of environment were first and most convincingly advocated by Rogers and his followers. Along with the corollary attitudes mentioned earlier, these are the attitudes and behaviors we try to impart to those studying to become RE therapists.

We also try to create for clients an environment that makes them feel that they are capable of success and, indeed, that they are succeeding in making progress toward the learning goals. We believe that it is essential for them to feel this way to sustain motivation and to acquire new and hard-to-master emotional and social skills. Therefore, we include knowledge and skills in social reinforcement in our training of RE therapists.

Understandably, this practice might be viewed by many as contrary, inconsistent, or at least ill-suited to client-centered theory. We do not view it that way. We consider the two key elements in learning successful reinforcement of clients' learning skills to be: (1) openly and genuinely *sharing one's positive views and feelings* about their progress and successes; and (2) *accepting clients where they now are.* Accepting clients "where they now are" allows the therapist to avoid judging them from the point of view of the therapist's final objectives. It also allows the therapist to avoid preconceived notions concerning the rate of progress the client "should" be making. These principles are very much in keeping with the client-centered orientation. But what about having goals in mind that you are helping the client to reach? Isn't that, in itself, inconsistent with the client-centered perspective?

While it is not a part of the client-centered tradition, we do not believe that it is fundamentally contradictory to the client-centered perspective for the therapist to have specific goals in mind for the client, provided a certain criterion is met. This might be considered the criterion of an *openly formulated teaching contract*. The criterion is that the client and therapist have openly and fully discussed and mutually agreed upon (1) what goals are to be sought, and (2) the straightforward methods the therapist will use to help the client achieve those goals. We view this open teaching contract as something quite different from what goes on in those types of therapy in which the therapist sets diagnostically based goals or subgoals that are not shared with the client or uses therapeutic methods not explained to the client. Because RE meets this criterion we view the use of goal setting and reinforcement principles alongside client-centered principles and methods as a genuine integration of the two approaches and not as a violation of either perspective. When a therapist shows genuine understanding and respect for the client regardless of his current status or progress and views "reinforcement" as sharing his own satisfaction with the client's efforts as well as the client's "successes," we believe such integration is successfully achieved.

The Skills Taught

What contribution has client-centered therapy made to the types of skills taught in RE therapies? A very significant one. In filial therapy, the core skills taught to parents are precisely the attitudes, principles, and techniques of a client-centered play therapist in the classic tradition of Dorfman, Axline, Ginott, and Moustakas.

In marital and family RE, one of the two behavioral modes (i.e., skill sets) that form the foundation for all the rest is composed of precisely the attitudes and techniques employed by the traditional client-centered therapist when he works with adolescents and adults. That skill set is called the *empathic mode*. In teaching clients this mode we are striving to teach them nothing more and, more important, nothing less, than the attitude or behaviors of the traditional client-centered therapist.

The second of the two foundation skills of RE—the *expressive mode*—while not based on traditional client-centered therapy, is certainly compatible with it. The expressive mode is, in part, the converse of the empathic mode. A key ingredient underlying the benefit to another of the empathic mode is that it shows understanding, respect, and positive regard for the views of the other. It diminishes the psychological challenge and defensiveness that accompany a threat to the other's self-concept as much as is feasible. The expressive mode endeavors to accomplish the same kind of minimization of threat to the other party. The difference is that in the empathic mode one is concentrating on the needs of the *other* person, whereas in the expressive mode the goal is to show understanding of the other and minimize unnecessary threat to the self-concept of the other, while expressing one's *own* thoughts, feelings, conflicts, and needs. The seven other skills currently taught in marital and family RE would not be nearly as effective as they are, were they not built on the foundation of these two skills.

CLIENT-CENTERED CONTRIBUTIONS IN THE CONTEXT OF OTHER CONTRIBUTING THEORIES AND METHODS

We have described the client-centered approach as having made a very significant contribution to RE therapies. To present a balanced picture, it seems necessary to consider what contributions non-Rogerian theories and psychotherapeutic methods or techniques have contributed to the development of RE.

In our view, RE therapies represent an integration in theory and practice of a very wide range of other psychotherapeutic theories and practices. We consider RE to be an integration of three major schools of psychotherapeutic thought: the humanistic, the psychodynamic, and the behavioral. We hasten to add that we do not see RE as being the only way in which such an integration might be constructed. Rather, RE represents one particular way of combining certain key elements of theory and practice from each of these major traditions into one new, coherent, and clearly defined whole.

It should be stated at the outset that we believe it is very important in considering the integration of diverse schools of psychotherapy to make a sharp distinction between two areas. One area is the underlying *theory*—defined here as the explanation of how people get to be the way they are and the processes by which they learn and grow. The other area includes the therapeutic *methods* or techniques that have been developed to put the theory into everyday practice with clients. Thus a Freudian therapist who faithfully follows the relatively nonintrusive therapeutic practices advocated by Freud himself and another who plays a much more active role in the therapeutic process might *both* be purely Freudian from the point of view of their fundamental theoretical position. Approaching this distinction between theory and methods from the opposite direction, it is possible to take the techniques of a therapist and explain why they are effective from a totally different theoretical perspective than the one that prompted that therapist to develop or to use those techniques.

As an example of the need for this conceptual separation, I'll cite something I recently saw on television. It was a report on a new method of psychotherapy. The fundamental theory that led to the development of the techniques used was *reincarnation*: the proposition that each of us has led innumerable past lives. Unresolved conflicts and traumas from these past lives may cause serious disturbances, impairments, and psychosomatic illnesses in our current lives. The method based on this theory rested mainly on hypnotic trances. Going back through the client's past lives in these trances makes it possible to locate the particular past-life person responsible for the client's current symptoms. Then, in repeated hypnotic sessions, the client, in his past-life person, is helped to work through his problems. When the problems of the past-life individual are resolved, the client becomes symptom-free in his current life.

In the particular case shown on television, the past-life person was a pianist possessed by rage over lack of professional and public recognition of his great talent. In repeated hypnotic sessions, with the encouragement of the therapist, this great anger toward his past-life contemporaries was given full vent. The client and the therapist also discussed all of this while the client was not in a trance. The client's headaches disappeared and had not returned at the time of the TV show, many months later.

I think most therapists would reject the underlying reincarnation theory and would explain the disappearance of the headaches differently: the client's "past-life person" was a fantasy reflecting an inability to express anger appropriately or to be assertive in the client's current life. The therapeutic sessions helped the client to recognize and accept anger as part of his current self and to become more appropriately assertive. Such a reinterpretation would be supported by the fact that the client did, in fact, report that his sessions made him much more aware of his angry feelings in his current life and more able to express them. This reinterpretation rejects completely the fundamental theory, but acknowledges that the method might nevertheless have psychotherapeutic merit.

Conversely, a theory might be completely valid, but the methods that have been based on it might be ineffective or inefficient. In our view, there are today few psychotherapeutically relevant theories so tightly and fully constructed that they automatically and unambiguously call for certain procedures and few therapeutic procedures so tightly constructed or implemented that they cannot be explained by more than one theory.

Consider now an example of very diverse techniques that can be explained on the basis of the same fundamental theory. Many practitioners of rational emotive therapy (RET) actively argue with and even berate their clients. (It seems to be part of the RET "technique" to do so, although it is not specifically prescribed by the theory.) Such nonacceptance or, indeed, outright rejection of the client's self-concept and internal frame of reference seems to be completely contrary to the thrust of client-centered therapy. Yet in my view there could be a positive therapeutic effect from such behavior on the part of the therapist based precisely on the *same* theoretical position taken by client-centered therapists. To see this, one must ask what aspect of the client's self-image the practitioner of rational emotive therapy rejects so forcefully. What the RET practitioner rejects—and what the client knows full well the therapist is rejecting—is anything the therapist believes is causing the client *himself* to be *less than fully self-accepting*. What the therapist rejects is anything that causes the client to refuse to accept and respect himself as a worthwhile human being.

What seems on the surface to be a technique diametrically opposed to client-centered theory is, in reality, an alternative technique for achieving the very thing that client-centered therapy, through very different techniques, also strives to achieve: helping the client to see that he should not reject himself, that he is a worthwhile person. Both RET and client-centered therapists take the theoretical position that the client's self-acceptance is a powerful force for positive change. They simply have very different *techniques* for convincing the client to view himself as worthwhile and fully capable of growth.

In drawing upon diverse theories and practices—often viewed as contradictory—to construct RE, I tried not to be merely eclectic, but integrative. I believe that the theories and techniques underlying RE represent not a hodge-podge but a consistent whole. To achieve this integration I chose techniques that, based on research and my personal experience, I believed to be most effective and then selectively drew upon theories to explain them. I also used theory to develop techniques that then had to stand the test of experience and research to prove their effectiveness. Space does not here permit an in-depth presentation of this integrated theory. However, we will attempt a very brief outline indicating what concepts we have accepted and rejected from major psychotherapeutic theories.

The theoretical formulation underlying RE includes the concepts of unconscious motivation, repression, the importance of defense mechanisms, and the positive role in growth sometimes played by catharsis—ideas first presented by Freud. However, the explanations concerning the ways in which many of these phenomena develop and function are viewed as being best explained by learning theorists, particularly the reinforcement-based explanations provided by Dollard and Miller (1950). Also, the Freudian view that defense mechanisms are triggered and resistance in therapy is generated largely to protect the individual from recognizing childhood conflict and traumas is rejected. Rather, the Rogerian view is accepted, that the major threats triggering defense mechanisms are threats to the self-concept.

The Freudian-based proposition that defenses are best overcome by such techniques as dream analysis, free association, and transference analysis is rejected as inefficient. Probing and interpretations are viewed as generally disruptive to the therapeutic process. Instead we adhere to the Rogerian proposition that defenses are best overcome and self-understanding and personal growth best promoted by providing an environment of respect and positive regard for the client.

Certain behavioral and social-learning methods and principles—especially social reinforcement and modeling—are viewed as significant concepts for understanding personal and interpersonal dynamics and for facilitating personal and interpersonal growth. However, in the Rogerian tradition, we believe that contingent social reinforcement cannot work very well in promoting growth unless it takes place in the context of noncontingent understanding, respect, and positive regard.

In RE theory, in the tradition of Harry Stack Sullivan, the importance of interpersonal relationship is stressed. Leary's (1957) elaborations of Sullivanian theory are central because they take the view that by teaching an individual how *interpersonal reflexes* work and by giving him conscious control over interpersonal responses that were previously reflexive, we place in the client's hands an extremely potent mechanism for personal and interpersonal growth.

CONCLUSION

From the perspectives of both theory and technique, client-centered therapy occupies a position of great importance in the genesis, development, and implementation of the RE therapies. Our experience and our research suggests to us that by adding other perspectives and methods to it we have strengthened rather than weakened its role on the on-going development of more effective strategies to assist individuals who are striving toward greater personal and interpersonal fulfillment.

14 Carl Rogers's Client-Centered Approach to Supervision[1]

Harold Hackney
Rodney K. Goodyear

Surprisingly little has been written about client-centered supervision. It is true that, until recently, there has been relatively little written from *any* perspective about supervisory models, practices, and processes. But this absence has seemed particularly notable in a tradition that, from its beginning, has been dedicated to the question of how one "learns" to be therapeutic (Rice, 1980).

In fact, Rogers and his colleagues seem to have employed supervisory interventions since the earliest years of client-centered therapy, and Rogers made several of the first statements on the training of clinicians (1951, 1955, 1957b). Moreover, as a pioneer in the use of audiotapes (Rogers, 1942a) and as the first to publish a transcript of an actual therapy session (Rogers, 1942b), Rogers provided an effective means for the close scrutiny of client-therapist interaction and of the therapeutic process:

> Here are the orderly sequences that were missed in the flow of experience. Here, too, are the nuances of inflection, the half-formed sentences, the pauses and the sighs, which were also partially missed. Then, if a transcript is laboriously produced, I have a microscope in which I can see... "the molecules of personality change." ...It is perhaps the most valuable and transparent window into the strange inner world of persons and relationships. (Rogers, 1974, p. 120)

That he used this new technology—which seems always to have been a central element in client-centered supervision—for early supervisory work is clear in a later statement about his work with students during the 1940s:

> I cannot describe the excitement of our learning as we clustered about the machine which enabled us to listen to ourselves, playing over and over some puzzling point at which the interview clearly went wrong, or those moments in which the client moved significantly forward. (Rogers, 1975b, p. 3)

But this description, unfortunately, gives no hint as to how Rogers viewed these early supervisory sessions. And while he had addressed training issues (1951, 1955, 1957b), those statements provide only limited information about his view of the supervisory process.

Patterson (1964) was one of the first writers to discuss the supervision process from a client-centered perspective. He concluded that clinical supervision is an influencing process that is neither teaching nor counseling, but that incorporates elements of both; while it should not be therapy, supervision is like all good human relationships and may be therapeutic to the supervisee. In an update almost 20 years later, Patterson (1983) maintained the essentials of his earlier position, but amplified it with more specific discussion of his supervisory procedures. Rice (1980), too, has written of client-centered supervision. Like Patterson, she has stressed the importance of the supervisor's attitude and also highlighted the process and relationship dimensions that she believes characterize client-centered supervision.

These several articles and book chapters virtually exhaust the client-centered literature on supervision. Yet the relative scarcity of these writings should not be taken as an index of the influence that Carl Rogers and his client-centered constructs and practices have had on supervision. For example, Rogers's introduction of audiotapes and typescripts into training and research established (in the face of strong resistance) a tradition that has carried through to the extensive use today of videotapes, live supervision, and even the computerized analysis of typescripts (Meara, Shannan, & Pepinsky, 1979). Almost *all* beginning counselors and clinicians are now taught basic responding skills that are really operationalized client-centered constructs and procedures (e.g., Carkhuff & Anthony, 1979; Ivey & Authier, 1978). Moreover, measures of such relationship qualities as empathic accuracy have been heavily represented in supervision research (e.g., Birk, 1972; Handley, 1982; Lambert, 1974; Pierce & Schauble, 1970, 1971), even by those who do not typically endorse client-centered constructs. But despite this pervasive client-centered influence in supervisory practice, more discussion of the model is needed by supervisors who work from a client-centered orientation.

IMPORTANCE OF THEORY IN SUPERVISION

The supervisor works from a theory that simultaneously serves as a guide for supervisory goals and behaviors *and* as a resource from which supervisees can draw upon for their own developing theories. That is, as the supervisee progresses, he or she draws upon the suspervisor's perspective to develop a more comprehensive base from which to conceptualize client problems and professional interventions. And even as the supervisor's theory is being transmitted to supervisees for their professional development, it also serves the more immediate purpose of guiding the supervisor's own work. The goals, content, and process of supervision are all governed by the supervisor's theory. In fact, data from recent studies indicates that supervisors' espoused theories closely correspond both to the standards by which they judge their supervisees (Peterson & Bry, 1980) and to their own supervisory behaviors (Friedlander & Ward, 1983; Goodyear, Abadie, & Efros, 1983; Goodyear & Robyak, 1982). In fact, Patterson (1983) states the case even more strongly, saying, "The supervisor has a commitment to a theory, and the supervisee must have at least a tentative commitment to a theory; it should be obvious that if learning is to occur, they must be committed to the same theory" (p. 22).

Supervisors were trained first as counselors or clinicians. To the extent that the models they first adopted for professional practice reflect enduring values and beliefs about human nature, then aspects of these models will be incorporated into their supervisory practice. Rogers himself has commented on ways that supervisors' theoretical orientations will affect their handling of supervision:

> If the therapist conducting the training holds an orientation which is interventive and interpretive, or one in which guidance and coaching play a prominent part, then he will guide and coach the trainee and interpret to him his own dynamics in the therapeutic relationships. If the therapeutic orientation of the supervisor is facilitative, endeavoring to permit the individual to gain insight into himself and to develop his own modes of meeting life, then the supervisory contacts will be primarily a listening, facilitative understanding. The attempt

will be to help the beginning therapist to become clearly aware of his own feelings in his therapeutic interviews so he can more adequately come to be himself in the relationship.... It is probably unnecessary to say that our experience runs much more along this facilitative line. (Rogers, 1957b, p. 86)

For supervisors from all theoretical orientations, supervision has a twofold purpose. It may function as a vehicle either for training or for case maintenance (though these are not mutually exclusive). The training function is probably the more prevalent. However, any evaluation of supervision must take both of these into account, for they undoubtedly affect the goals of supervision.

Bernard (1979) has proposed one framework for understanding supervision that is relevant both to training and case maintenance and that can be applied to the understanding of supervision from any theoretical orientation. Her "discrimination model" is two dimensional, defining three supervisory functions and three supervisory roles. Functions (or the supervisory foci) include *process* issues, concerned with the impact of the supervisee's skills and strategies on the counseling relationship; *conceptualization* issues, concerned with the supervisee's increased sophistication in understanding his or her client; and *personalization* issues, concerned with ways in which the supervisee's attitudes, values, and behaviors enhance or impede the counselor-client and the supervisor-supervisee relationships. Supervisory roles include those of *teacher*, in which the supervisor delivers information, suggestions, or strategies; *counselor*, in which the supervisor offers support, understanding, and acceptance; and *consultant*, in which the supervisor responds to identified counselor goals, needs, and the like. Although Bernard has argued that specific functions and roles should be employed in response to the supervisee's particular needs, it is clear that they may be prescribed by the supervisor's theoretical orientation. In the following section of this chapter, as Carl Rogers discusses and demonstrates his work as a supervisor, readers are invited to use Bernard's discrimination model as a framework for structuring their observations.

THE CLIENT-CENTERED SUPERVISION OF CARL ROGERS

Because he is the originator of client-centered therapy, it is important that supervisors have a current statement from Carl Rogers about how he regards supervision. Also, because no others are available, a transcript of Rogers actually functioning as supervisor should have unique value to both practitioners and theorists. These two sources together provide important information—both conceptual and behavioral—about how Rogers defines supervision, about the conditions he regards as necessary, and about the outcomes he regards as desirable. Following, then, are transcripts of (1) an interview with Dr. Rogers and (2) his supervisory work. So that the reader has a better context for understanding these materials, they are preceded by a description of their development.

Procedure

As a first step in developing these materials, a counseling session was videotaped, to be the basis for Dr. Rogers's supervision. Production of the videotaped session required several precautions. A primary concern was that the counseling session not violate the privacy or confidential nature of the actual client's therapeutic relationship. Of only slightly less importance was the objective that the session be representative of the counseling process and the counselor's style. It was determined that the best approach would be to create a facsimile of the actual counseling session, using a coached client, with the agreement of the actual client.

An advanced doctoral student in counseling at Purdue University was solicited to assume the client's role. She studied the progress of the case by reviewing audiotapes of the four preceding sessions and by discussing the case with the counselor. Then she was asked to project herself into the client's life story using her understanding of the case. This was the setting in which the "fifth" session occurred.

The 50-minute session was produced in a television studio at Purdue University using a counseling office "set." Initially, the "client" manifested nervousness and exaggerated facial and body movements, but began to become more comfortable after about 20 minutes. The content of the session was highly representative of the actual client's concerns, even including the types of "solutions" that the client would present for her problems. On the other hand, the coached client's nonverbal behavior differed considerably from that of the actual client, thus producing some initial dissonance for the counselor.

The content of the session dealt with the client's indecision regarding her marriage. She had been married four months, but already was considering separation. She entered counseling with presenting problems of situational depression and panic attacks that occurred primarily when she was at work. She was ambivalent about her future, at one moment wanting out of the marriage, at the next moment wanting to find a way to make it work.

The supervision session with Dr. Rogers occurred on August 22, 1981, at his home in La Jolla, California. The project in which he so generously agreed to participate also included supervision with four other theorists representing other theoretical orientations. The total project was intended to be a supervisory analog (Goodyear, 1982) to the "Gloria" films (Shostrom, 1964).

The format for each of the five supervision sessions, including that with Rogers, was as follows: presentation to the supervisor of a portion of the videotaped counseling session; the actual supervisory session; and a post hoc analysis of the process by the two authors and the supervisor. In each case, the supervisor was asked to discuss his supervision style, issues, and assumptions. (Note: the supervisee described his counseling style as a cognitive-behavioral approach using a family systems orientation.) For purposes of his chapter we shall reverse the order of the supervisory process and begin with a discussion of client-centered supervision that took place between Dr. Rogers and the authors.

The Process of Supervision: A Dialogue

Because client-centered supervision is not as well documented as client-centered therapy, Dr. Rogers was asked to discuss his approach to supervision and to compare it to his thoughts on therapy. The following is his response.

GOODYEAR: Dr. Rogers, I think it might be useful to have you speak to what your goals are in supervision, what it is you try to accomplish.

ROGERS: Well, I think my major goal is to help the therapist to grow in self-confidence and to grow in understanding of himself or herself, and to grow in understanding the therapeutic process. And to that end, I find it very fruitful to explore any difficulties the therapist may feel he or she is having working with the client. And I handle that this way: supervision for me becomes a modified form of the therapeutic interview. In other words, the therapist is saying "I'm having some problems with this client." So that I like to help the therapist explore his feelings in the relationship. Often, a therapist will be expressing feelings about the client: "I'm at an impasse." Or, "I don't really like this client." Or, "I find him boring."

My almost invariable response is to find out whether those feelings have been expressed in the relationship. And usually the response is sort of a startled, "No, of course not." And yet I think relationships are improved as they become more genuine. So if the therapist is afraid of the client or bored by the client or whatever, it is a very difficult thing to express feelings like that directly in the relationship. But it nearly always does some very enlivening thing to the relationship. And so that's one thing I try to do.

GOODYEAR: How would you differentiate, then, between psychotherapy and supervision? Is there any way to do that? At what point does supervision become therapy?

ROGERS: I think there is no *clean* way. I think it does exist on a continuum. Sometimes therapists starting in to discuss some of the problems they're having with a client will look deeply into themselves and it's straight therapy. Sometimes it is more concerned with problems of the relationship and that is clearly supervision. But in that sense, too, I will follow the lead, in this case, the lead of the therapist. The one difference is I might feel more free to express how I might have done it than I would if I were dealing with a client.

GOODYEAR: Related to that, would you handle a beginning therapist any differently than an experienced therapist? Would you fall back into the teacher mode at any point?

ROGERS: I think I would behave pretty much the same under either condition. Even the beginning counselor who may be doing objectively a pretty bad job can't make a full leap to the level of an experienced therapist. And so, what *can* be accomplished? Well, what can be accomplished is as much as they can achieve by being understood, by facing some of the things they recognize as bad. But if you get didactic about it, it is likely to make them more self-conscious the next time they see the client. So, teaching has to be pretty subtle. I might...I've never done this, but I might get the counselor to try to understand *me*. Give him some practice. I've often participated in a three-cornered way: therapist-person, client-person, and an observer.

That can be very profitable. But that would be training, not simply supervision.

GOODYEAR: This seems like an important distinction. Would you expand on it?

ROGERS: Well, I don't like to say, "You could do it thus and so" because I have no idea how you could do it. But I do like to perhaps stimulate the imagination some by saying how I would have handled it or how I see it: what some of my feelings are. And that's very easy for me to do because often when I try to see a tape of an interview, or even hear a tape, sometimes my feeling quite strongly is "Move out of that chair. Let me take over." Because I really do have a love of doing therapy. I try to avoid anything that seems like criticism... and I feel that way. I don't want to criticize because I feel each person does therapy in the best way that he or she can do in the moment. So in that sense there is usually nothing to criticize. I also avoid giving instruction. Just as with criticism, instructions can have a bad effect either way. If I decide, "Well, I certainly won't do that" then you are thinking about that instruction and you won't hear your client. You're not present, you're thinking, "Well, I should be doing this." So I guess at least one other way to state what I would like to happen is that I would like to help the therapist be totally present to the client. Here again my own bias comes in. I would like the therapist to be totally present to the client in a nonjudgemental way and a non–goal-seeking way. In other words, I think that when the therapist sets goals for the client, that tends to disrupt what I feel is the elegant flow of the client's movement as they follow their feelings. To me, that's kind of an aesthetic process that I don't like to see interfered with.

HACKNEY: It seems to me that preference to avoid goal-setting involves a leap of faith. I'd be interested to know if you experience it as a leap of faith also?

ROGERS: Yes, sometimes it's something that just comes quite naturally and I feel that. Other times... and I know there have been many times... when I've felt the client give some overwhelming picture of difficulties, I feel "My God! I wouldn't have any idea of what to do in that situation." Then it is a leap of faith to feel that perhaps if I stay with that person as a companion, maybe they can find their way through this ungodly mess. That faith is usually justified. The one thing that can throw me off on that, too, is if I get trapped in some diagnostic thinking. Sometimes if a person were to show very prominent paranoid behavior, it is difficult for me to really stay with their feelings and stay with them because I'm thinking, "My God, this is very paranoid." And I try to avoid that because I think I can make progress with a person only if I stay with them right where they are, whatever feelings they have.

GOODYEAR: How amenable are you to supervising people of other theoretical persuasions—for example, a behaviorist or a psychoanalytically oriented person? Is your style of supervision such that you would do that?

ROGERS: Well, I'm a brash person. I'd probably be willing to attempt it. However, I've never really had that opportunity. I've had supervisees whose ways of working were somewhat different from mine, but probably not that different. But I do find that anyone—analyst, behaviorist, or what-have-you—responds to being understood. If they view supervision as having to do with difficulties that they are experiencing in their therapy, if they were experiencing difficulties in therapy, then I think my responses to them would be helpful.

GOODYEAR: There is some discussion in the literature about when supervision should occur. When do you think is the optimal time for supervision? Is it immediately before a session, immediately after, or what is your experience about the optimal timing of supervision?

ROGERS: I would say that the optimal time is to me definitely after, because supervision *before* would seem almost invariably to get into instructions or "Why don't you do this?" or "Why don't you try that?" I also think the optimal time is when the therapist is having some problem in the relationship. I don't know that supervision is needed when the therapist and the client both feel things are going fine. I'm not really interested in supervision just to listen to a tape to see that progress is being made. But I don't think I would feel much like doing what you could call supervision. I

> think supervision is best when there are problems,
> when the therapist feels, "I'm not getting anywhere."
> (Goodyear, 1982.)

The Supervision Session

Bernard's (1979) discrimination model has already been introduced as a framework for examining Dr. Rogers's supervisory work. However, it is important also to acknowledge the two themes Rice (1980) has described as central to client-centered supervision. These themes are *process* and *relationship*. She observes that a creative tension often emerges as these themes are explored by the therapist and supervisor. The process theme is best represented by the "empathic process, attempting to stay in the client's internal frame of reference and to sense the client's awareness as it if were one's own" (p. 141). Presumably, this dimension is revealed as the therapist and supervisor review a recording of the session and manifests itself in the supervisor's and therapist's focus on client content and feeling.

The relationship dimension is captured in Rogers's conceptualization of *prizing* (prizing the client *and* prizing the therapist), and *congruence*, described by Rice as "the therapist's wholeness during the hour" (p. 138). Thus, if the therapist experiences an issue with the client but does not express it, a degree of incongruence is manifested. Within the supervisory context, such incongruent conditions would be quite important to discuss.

Because Rice has identified these themes as being specific to client-centered supervision, they are important in considering Dr. Rogers's work. At the same time, however, these two themes could easily be regarded as client-centered versions of two of Bernard's (1979) foci. That is, Rice's process theme seems to be Bernard's process focus limited to a client-centered perspective; Rice's relationship theme seems to be a specific version of Bernard's personalization focus. Thus the reader is again invited to consider Bernard's posited supervisory roles and foci in examining the following supervisory session. The session began after Rogers and Hackney together viewed the last 25 minutes from Hackney's videotaped counseling session.

HACKNEY: I'm not sure who should start this.
ROGERS: Well, I'd like you to start because I'm not sure what you'd like to learn.

HACKNEY: There are several things I've thought about while going over this case, but I think perhaps the thing that, that bothers me the most as I've worked with her, and I've seen her five times, uh....

ROGERS: This was the fifth time?

HACKNEY: This was the fifth time, yes. The thing that bothers me the most is that I'm unable to anticipate her motivation to change from one session to another. She comes in one session and, if there's been a crisis that week, then she's really motivated to try to work on that. When, if she's had a good week she doesn't have very much motivation and I really feel like I'm pulling teeth then. That's pretty much what it is. I work harder than she does.

ROGERS: You feel the responsibility for getting her to move.

HACKNEY: Right. I think I do...uh, I think related to that is some confusion in terms of what we're working toward because she originally came into counseling concerned about her marriage and her relationship to her husband. And the second session he came and joined her. He hasn't been able to make it since that time. And one week she's dealing with how she can adjust to being newly married; the next week she's saying "He's dragging me down.... I'm wondering if I'd be better off outside the marriage or not to be married." So I've been having some trouble in that regard too. Really, to know what to do; what, what focus to take in the therapy.

ROGERS: And the focus is really up to you?

HACKNEY: I've been assuming some responsibility for it, yes.

ROGERS: Did you ever express that to her?

HACKNEY: Not in so many words. I'm aware that on a couple of occasions I've asked her "What is it you'd like to be working on?" or "What is it you'd really like to see happen as a result of counseling?" But I think I've done that indirectly.

ROGERS: Almost as if you've been drawing the answers from her rather than expressing your own feeling of uncomfortableness.

HACKNEY: I think that's fair, yes. I think that *is* what I've been doing.

ROGERS: Sort of wish she would answer your questions for you.

HACKNEY: Probably that's part of it. I think a part of me also would like for her to discover some self-direction maybe. Maybe I'm believing in that too much at this point. But yes, I've been trying to pull it out of her rather than to express myself. I think what you're hitting on there may be one of the, the qualities of this relationship that we have—that, ah, that I'm removed in it, a bit.

ROGERS: In the portion we saw of the interview, any particular things trouble you there?

HACKNEY: I think she was working well, there, in that part, uh, I wish it were like that more often.

ROGERS: What do you feel about your own function?

HACKNEY: I felt pretty good about it, then. There were a couple of times when I thought I was putting words in her mouth. When she didn't seem to be, ah...they didn't ring true for her. But, uh, I felt pretty good about that particular segment.

ROGERS: I had the feeling as the interview went on that, ah, you were giving more and more direction to it.

HACKNEY: That's right, and I think that is part of my tendency. I think I...I will start out slowly in an interview and this, maybe this is an agenda that I have. But as a session wears on, I'm beginning to feel more and more of a need to have the client take something away that she can do during the week. There is a desire for some homework there, something for her to do to extend the therapy session with. I think that was the direction in which I was going.

ROGERS: What did you feel her response to that was?

HACKNEY: Well, I think she had...I think her interest was teased just a little bit with it, but I think she also had some fear of it. I think she was afraid to take a risk of trying to deal with her relationship with her husband.

ROGERS: It seems though, what you've succeeded in doing was teasing her a bit further than she might have gone otherwise.

HACKNEY: Yeah...(chuckles); it doesn't sound exactly like therapy. But I think you're right.

ROGERS: My estimate of her response was it was a fairly dubious response as to whether she could: "Yeah" (said tentatively).

HACKNEY: Right.

ROGERS: Any other comments of yours on that segment that we saw?

HACKNEY: I think that perhaps that the parts we didn't see, following that, were maybe an important point. It feels like all that was laying groundwork. Just a little bit later she said, "I'm not sure I can do it," and I said, "I'm not sure you could either." And she bristled when I said that and she said, "Well, I don't know, when I make up my mind to do something, I can usually do it." And my comment then was, uh, "Yes, I've seen that in you and I know you can do it when you make up your mind to do it." And she really looked at me suspiciously at that point because I think she felt trapped and she thought I had set her up. And I don't think I really meant to set her up, but that seemed to me to be the pivotal movement of the interview, because if there was anything that was going to be meaningful to her, it, maybe it came at that point.

ROGERS: Would you like me to say some of the things that I felt I saw?

HACKNEY: I would really like that, yes.

ROGERS: Some of the time I felt that, uh, you did well in responding to her feelings and understanding her as borne out by the fact that she feels that you're the only person who really listens to her and understands her. A few times I felt it would be possible to have gone more deeply, but that happens to all of us all of the time.

One thing that had meaning to me, because I look for metaphors—I feel people make more progress when they're dealing with metaphors—and when she spoke about the marriage and she couldn't move *this* way and she couldn't move *that* way, responded that she felt stuck. For whatever it's worth, my, my vision at that time was of prison bars. I would have responded: "You feel as if you're really in a prison, that you really can't get out." And that might have enabled her to use that metaphor more.

Then, then she seemed like a person, who as you say, has a hard time deciding what she wants: "It's sort of this way..." sort of a laid-back attitude, and, uh, I guess it seemed to me that you were, uh, fitting into the pattern. She wished...I don't know what she wished... she acted as though she didn't know quite what she wanted or where she wanted to go and then you began suggesting things as to directions she could go, and, uh,...I would have gambled on responding to her where she was, uh, with the possibility that that would lead her to take a firmer stand. As you say, when she makes up her own mind, then she did (words unintelligible).

HACKNEY: So I took that away from her.

ROGERS: Kind of a little bit, I feel. It interests me that she said, "When I make up my mind to do it, I'll go ahead and do it," and when you responded accurately to that, that threatened her. Which I think means that that *was* a very important statement to her. I've often noticed that if a person takes quite a positive step or expresses a feeling quite positively, and you understand it accurately, God that's almost too much for them! They tend to draw away from what they've just said.

HACKNEY: That was the reaction I got from her.

ROGERS: When you say that she has sort of different types of motivation, different degrees of motivation each time she comes in...that wouldn't bother me. I would go with whatever shred of feelings she would let me have at the time.

HACKNEY: I'd like to be able to do that (chuckle).

ROGERS: You realize I'm saying what I would do, and that doesn't mean it's necessarily what you should do.

HACKNEY: Well, I don't think what I'm doing is working for me...and I don't think it really is working for her either. So, I think it would be,...I think I would be better in this case if I could feel a little bit less responsible when she comes in with less motivation.

ROGERS: She came in of her own accord; she asked to see you.

HACKNEY: That's right, that's right. She's been *very* faithful, so far, in the case.

ROGERS: So, it would seem as though anything you do that takes any responsibility away from her is really quite unnecessary because she did decide to come, and she comes. (8-second pause.) An interesting and mixed-up modern young woman it seems like.

HACKNEY: Yes she is...and a delightful young woman too. She really is. She's the person I think I like the most among the people I'm working with.

ROGERS: O.K. That's one reason why you want it to go well.

HACKNEY: That's right.

ROGERS: Your liking her is a very good feeling and I like that. It means you will get somewhere with her. But if you like her enough to want her to go *your* way, that is a different matter.

HACKNEY: Yeah...well. That's especially true, because I'm not really sure what way to be if she's going my way. I'm not clear there either, so....

ROGERS: Well, you were somewhat clear toward the end of the interview as to a step you clearly thought was advisable for this coming week.

HACKNEY: Right. I had an agenda at that point. I was wanting to set up an opportunity for her and her husband to, uh, have a conversation. Whether that came off or not is another matter. But part of the sense that I was thinking of at that moment was that, because of the pace of their lives, they never even really had the opportunity. And then she felt ignored or missed.

ROGERS: And that's where you did feel a responsibility for helping set up something that would make that come about.

HACKNEY: Oh, I was taking care of it all, yes. (Pause.) Where do you think it might go if I were to...that's maybe an impossible question to ask...if I were to try to follow up what her inclinations were as far as her trying to find a moment with her husband, where do you think that would go? Do you think that would bring the initiation out of that?

ROGERS: I haven't *any* idea where it would go. But to me that's the fascination of therapy, is not knowing and yet connecting just as deeply as I can with the, in this case, the confusion, the "Maybe I will, maybe I won't; maybe I like John, maybe I like Don." Just connecting as deeply as possible with that feeling and following it wherever she leads me. Because she already feels your companionship in the relationship, that's important to this. And so she trusts you, and trusts you enough to be completely open. So that, I think her own feelings would move in some direction. When you ask, "What direction?" I don't know. To me that's the fascination of a relationship, that once in it I haven't any idea where to go. And yet...I'm more...in the way that *I* work, I would have less of an agenda than you do. My agenda could be, "Can I get so connected that I can feel every particle of what she's feeling whether it's her wishy-washy-ness or whatever?"...One thing I did notice that

I probably would have responded to is her eyes lit up twice in the interview. Once when John got a little angry. You responded to that, but I would have responded also to the gleam in her eye: "Boy, that really makes you light up!" And I've forgotten just what the other was but she lit up another time too. That's the kind of thing I like to do ... be so much with the person that their expression, their intimation, their words, their metaphors ... if they get excited and want to move further, that's. . . .

HACKNEY: Yeah, I think I know what you mean about letting them catch your excitement, too. I can see where that would work with her. . . . I don't mean that the way it sounds ... as a technique that when she does get excited is when she's being very good for herself. (Pause.) Well, I think I'll see what I can do about laying back just a little. But I think it's going to be hard to let go of some goals.

ROGERS: And I would say very sincerely that I was describing the way I would tend to go about it. You've got to be sure that that's the way you want to go about it, or else it will come across as a phony thing, of course.

HACKNEY: I'm aware of that. I guess that's where I'm testing myself a little bit, too. Because I'm not sure if that ... if that drive on my part is manufactured or if that *is* me too. Probably, uh, I suppose it could be me. At this point in time, maybe that's me.

ROGERS: At this moment in time you know that's the way you feel. Whether you'll feel that way the next time you see her, that's up to that moment. (Goodyear, 1982)

DISCUSSION

In their recent review of supervision research, Hansen, Robins, and Grimes (1982) concluded that "research in supervision continues to be a series of isolated studies that generally do not build on previous work" (p. 23). Holloway and Hosford (1983) have concurred with this and argued that, if there is to be a viable science of supervision, then research must proceed through stages. The first stage, and that which is currently most appropriate in supervision, should be devoted to descriptive observation. The transcripts presented here are well suited for that purpose, for they provide both Rogers's thoughts about supervision and an actual sample of his supervisory behaviors. It is also important that Rogers has affirmed that the recorded supervision session was typical of his client-centered supervision.

Even so, any supervision session is in some ways unique. Several factors that may have influenced both the content of this session and its supervisor-supervisee interactions should be acknowledged. Certainly the most obvious of these was the intrusion of the lights, camera, and technical crew. It was probably also relevant that Rogers was working with the demand (however covert) that this be a model session that would fairly depict in a short period his supervisory work. Moreover, this was understood to be a one-time encounter between two people who had not previously met and who seemed to hold theoretical orientations that are quite discrepant (as previously noted, Hackney works from a cognitive-behavioral family system perspective). Finally, it is perhaps also salient that Hackney had earlier that day received Gestalt-oriented supervision over the same material from Erving Polster in a rather intense session.

But even with these possible contaminants, the congruence between Rogers's stated model and his actual supervisory behaviors is notable. For example, while he makes a distinction between supervision and psychotherapy, it is clear that he perceives them as having parallel goals and processes. The supervisee's ability to prize the client is no more important than the supervisor's ability to prize the supervisee; the need for genuineness in the therapeutic relationship is no more an issue than the need for genuineness in the supervisory relationship. Further, while the client wears the mantle of responsibility and choice for change in therapy, the supervisee wears it in supervision.

At the same time, it was clear what client-centered supervision is *not*. For example, client-centered supervision does not impose tight controls on supervisees in order to shape them into pale versions of the supervisor. Moreover, Rogers makes a much sharper distinction between "teaching" and "supervision" than do proponents of other models such as rational-emotive therapy (e.g., Wessler & Ellis, 1983). Thus we would not expect to find Rogers directly teaching skills or using one-way glass to provide live supervision. And even though there is evidence that, in some circumstances, supervisees benefit from supervision that occurs immediately *prior* to the therapy session (Couchon & Bernard, 1982), Rogers shows a clear preference for supervision that follows the therapy session. To do otherwise would "get into instructions," as he puts it.

In considering Bernard's (1979) discrimination model of supervision, it becomes clear that Rogers prefers supervision to focus primarily on *personalization* by helping the supervisee explore and clarify his or her attitudes, beliefs, and feelings and to give a secondary emphasis to a *process* focus. Consistent with his long-standing aversion to diagnosis, *conceptualization* would be his least-preferred focus. While it is clear from what he said that Rogers would prefer the roles of counselor-consultant, he did function in a teaching role during the actual supervisory session—particularly during roughly the second half. We have wondered, however, about the extent to which this was a function of the context in which the session took place. That is, by being forced to watch the videotape of the therapy session before and separate from the supervisory session, Rogers may have felt obliged to make some pronouncement about it, assuming an expert role that he would not ordinarily have employed.

These observations are borne out in a study by Goodyear, Abadie, and Efros (1983) in which experienced supervisors evaluated videotapes either of this supervision session by Rogers or one of the parallel sessions by Rudolph Ekstein and Albert Ellis, or Erving Polster. Significantly, Rogers was perceived as the supervisor who most used the counselor role and least used the teacher role; he and Polster together were rated as focusing on personalization more than were Ekstein and Ellis. Additional findings from this study, using constructs from Apfelbaum (1958), were that Rogers functioned to a significantly greater extent than the others as a *model* (i.e., tolerant, accepting, and providing one model of adjustment), and that he and Polster were both less *critical* than Ekstein and Ellis; Ellis was perceived as least *nurturant* of the four supervisors. In a separate study based on these same videotapes, but using graduate students as judges who employed a different rating procedures, Friedlander and Ward (1983) obtained strikingly similar results.

While these issues of style and of relationship are central to client-centered supervision, there are some other issues that were not addressed by Rogers. For example, Cohen (1979) and Cormier and Bernard (1982) have suggested that vicarious liability is inherent in the process of clinical supervision and that "supervisors are ultimately responsible for the welfare of clients counseled by their supervisees" (Cormier & Bernard, 1982, p. 488). The much discussed case *Tarasoff v. Regents of University of California* (1974) has served to emphasize this legal dimension of clinical supervision as no theoretical statement could. Yet, in Rogers's discussion of supervision and in his actual work with Hackney it is clear that taking responsibility for the client from the supervisee under any circumstance would be repugnant to him. While we have no doubt that Rogers would safeguard the client's welfare, he provides no guidelines for other client-centered supervisors.

A similar issue arises with respect to evaluation. That is, while the client-centered supervisor is to provide an environment that is as nonthreatening as possible, supervision is inevitably evaluative. Client-centered supervisors looking for ways of resolving this dilemma are left to writings about supervision by other authors such as Patterson (1983).

That Rogers did not address these issues, however, detracts little from the overall contribution these transcripts make to the literature. Discussions of supervision by major interpreters of client-centered therapy (e.g., Patterson, 1964, 1983; Rice, 1980) have been invaluable. However, this discussion and demonstration of supervision by the originator of the theory has unique value.

NOTE

1. The videotape series from which the material for this chapter was developed (Goodyear, 1982) also includes the supervision of Dr. Hackney by Erving Polster (Gestalt), Rudolph Ekstein (psychoanalytic), Albert Ellis (rational emotive), and Norman Kagan (interpersonal process recall). In each case, the supervisor's work focused on Dr. Hackney's fifth session with the same client. The material is quoted by permission of Rodney K. Goodyear.

15 Communities for Learning: A Person-Centered Approach

John Keith Wood

The question, then, is how we are to summon up the will to survive—not perhaps in the distant future, where survival will call on those deep sources of imagined human unity, but in the present and near-term future, while we still enjoy and struggle with the heritage of our personal liberties, our atomistic existences.

(Robert Heilbroner, 1980, p. 165)

Group processes are vital to human life. Even in highly personalized societies like the United States, deliberations in work teams, classes, town meetings, conferences, juries, parliamentary bodies, and incalculable spontaneous collaborations brought about by common activity or thought determine much of individual possibility. The private person may be said to create her unique world, but is doubtless also created by the groups to which she belongs.

The critical problems facing humanity—the spoiling of air and water supplies, the threat of annihilation from nuclear weapons, starvation, contagious disease—are problems resulting from innumerable coordinated and uncoordinated individual acts. In a Club of Rome report, Botkin, Elmandjra, and Malitza (1979) draw up the radical alternatives:

At the same time that an era of scientific and technological advancement has brought us unparalleled knowledge and power...an enormous tangle of problems in sectors such as energy, population, and food...confront us with unexpected complexity. Unprecedented human fulfillment and ultimate catastrophe are both possible. What will actually happen, however, depends on another major—and decisive—factor: human understanding and action. (p. 1)

Individuals, although highly advanced, intelligent, and capable, have not been (and may not be) able successfully to manage the complicated patterns created by their isolated actions. The consequent predicament confronting the modern person is how to act intelligently in a coordinated and productive effort with others without forfeiting individual freedom. "The welfare of Humankind," Rene Dubos (1981) suggests, "may well depend upon our ability to create the equivalent of the tribal unity that existed at the beginning of the human adventure while continuing to nurture the individual diversity which is essential for the further development of civilization" (p. 251).

Given the complexity of the modern world, can informed, responsible individuals, despite their differences, act coherently in wise and effective groups to benefit themselves and humanity? It is a challenge, considering the poor reputation established by many group deliberations. Faculty meetings, committees, business conferences, formal social gatherings, and many other groups are notorious for their ineffectiveness and the facility with which they provoke alienation, boredom, frustration, confusion, and irritation in their members.

Large groups can be the most outrageously abrasive. The crowd, when emotionally aroused, convincingly demonstrates not only the large group's ability to act forcefully as one body, but also its destructive potentialities. William McDougall (1928) sums up the unflattering picture on *this* aspect of the large group as

> excessively emotional, impulsive, violent, fickle, inconsistent, irresolute and extreme in action, displaying only the coarser emotions and the less refined sentiments; extremely suggestible, careless in deliberation, hasty in judgement, ... devoid of self-respect and of a sense of responsibility, ... its behavior is like that of an unruly child or an untutored passionate savage ... and in the worst cases it is like that of a wild beast, rather than like that of human beings. (p. 64)

In spite of these discouraging aspects, observations of person-centered approaches to large group interaction suggest reasons to be hopeful about the large group's capacity for intelligent action. The intention of this chapter is to inform this optimism, rather than to

formulate specific intervention techniques, approaches, or even therapeutic attitudes for leaders to facilitate smoothly functioning group
meetings. Moreover, the goal is to explore the individual and collective
dimensions of wise and effective group functioning, not to promote the
merits of either an individualistic or collectivistic viewpoint. The
advantages to be gained from the perspective of the individual can be
matched by the often radically different perspective of the group. And,
a level of stupidity, impulsivity, and cruelty, equal to that found in a
collective, may also be found in the lone individual. On the superior of
the two viewpoints, the chapter reserves judgment.

BACKGROUND

During the late summer of 1973, a person-centered approach to
large group work—communities for learning—was casually conceived.[1]
One workshop was originally planned. To date, 40 or more such groups
in over 15 countries have been convened, not to mention scores of
subsequent events inspired by the initial series of programs. Participants
in these workshops, or large group meetings, have ranged in number
from 40 to 2,000. They have included persons from a wide range of
endeavors, but most were psychologists, educators, and helper-oriented
persons. The meetings, usually residential, have been held on a rambling
and dilapidated coffee plantation in South America, in a resort hotel in
Southeast Asia, in a European marbled monastery, in tree-lined university courtyards and college dormitory halls in North America, in television studios, retreat centers, and dozens of other settings. These
minimally structured events have lasted from 1 to 20 days, but most
often about 10 days.

The aim of these workshops was to explore those forms of social
interaction based on respect for the individual that might yield the
wisest collective action in a given predicament. An early theme of these
meetings was: "How can one function specifically, locally, and privately
in such a way that personal actions are not at odds with, but actually
contribute to, the welfare of humanity?"

Staff members did not wish to increase their personal incompeten-
cies by venturing into fields in which they were inexperienced, nor did
they intend to construct a new cosmology. Their goal was merely to
examine, through experience in large groups, the relevance of principles

developed from practice in client-centered therapy. The resulting large group workshops were called "person-centered," a term which was subsequently used to identify all such endeavors.

Since 1967 the La Jolla Program (Rogers, 1970b) had held an annual training program for encounter group leaders. To supplement the small group meetings, brief plenary sessions were held during each program. These meetings demonstrated that it was possible for over 100 persons to speak in one significant and intelligible conversation. Building on this knowledge, the person-centered workshops established the large group meeting as the core of activities rather than a peripheral aspect. In a significant departure from the structured encounter group program, the format of these person-centered workshops was designed by the participants themselves, who formulated the activities, scheduled events, and even established their own tuition fees. The staff members did not hold themselves apart from the group, but joined in as full-time participants. In theory and practice these workshops explored the question: "What could a client-centered approach teach us about community?"

STAFF—CONVENORS OF THE LARGE GROUP

In these large group workshops the primary function of the staff was to arrange the time and place, to state the purpose of the event, and to invite participants. Since it was not conceived primarily as a psychological event, the staff sought the participation of persons from a wide range of professions, economic classes, races, and styles of living. Most often a quiet private setting was selected for a workshop to be held during the summer months (Rogers, 1977).

Initially, the staff functioned as a central coordinating group: it fielded inquiries, collected deposits, and facilitated travel and lodging arrangements for participants. Staff members were attentive to small details in an effort to provide participants (with whom they counted themselves) with as much freedom as possible to regulate their own experience. Before deciding on behalf of the participants, staff members asked themselves, "Does making this decision oppress or empower the person?" The staff did not wish to make any decisions that might infringe on the person's freedom, no matter how trivial the issue might seem (for example, assigning people to rooms as opposed to allowing them to choose for themselves). On the other hand, because they did not wish to provoke confusion and inefficiency, the staff tried not to neglect simple decisions that would throw the large group into chaotic immobility if it were required to deal with them all.

When participants arrived and were finally face-to-face in one room, a group-centered process guided the workshop deliberations. The staff ceased to exist in any leadership role. They attempted to bring their influence to bear as separate, involved participants, although group members' perceptions may have been colored by previous associations with power.

The unwillingness of staff members to function as leaders brought many reactions. Participants sometimes felt abandoned, deceived, manipulated, and confused by this position. At other times, the staff's attitude was mistakenly perceived as an intervention, modeling: "I do my thing, *you* should do yours; that's the way to build community." But, in fact, it was simply the staff members' attempt to live according to their principles. The attribute that separated the convenors of these workshops from group leaders—even those who produced strikingly similar participant reactions with varying outcomes (Bion, 1959; Doob, 1970; Doob & Foltz, 1973)—was a willingness to enter into, and *be changed* by, the experience they were living with other participants in the large group.

It was soon accepted, sometimes after bitter encounters, that the staff members were not abdicating responsibility but were simply admitting that they were no better equipped than other participants to deal with the knotty issues of conflicting rights, interests, ethics, morals, and the complex crises that the community inevitably faced.

MODES OF GROUP LEARNING

"They're all from broken homes, you know, luv."
"Yeh, the poor dears, some have adjusted better than others, too."
[The housekeepers at a workshop]

Who knows how many voices these massive ceiling beams and mahogany-paneled walls have absorbed in their 75 years. Today nearly 150 persons fill the university's student lounge with sound. Perhaps one-third of the group sits on the floor, surrounding a Mexican jar filled with flowers; the remaining persons sprawl on overstuffed sofas, shift restlessly on hard-backed chairs, and spill over into an uneven circumference of standing "spectators."

It is only their second day here, yet many must strain to recover memories from beyond this room. The meeting has no leader to call it to order. A growing, yet hesitant, murmur fills the room. Several conversations are being held in clusters of twos and threes as people chat and wait.

At last someone says, in a high breathless voice, "I'd like to get started!"

An expectant hush falls quickly over the room.

The initial speaker (Mary is her name) shrugs her shoulders and adds, "I have nothing specific to say, really. I just want to make *space* for anyone, who has a *need*, to speak to the whole group."

Then Ralph, looking down at the floor, begins to speak. His slow words organize the group's nervousness into an interested stillness. Ralph is 60, slight of body. With only a hint of rehearsal he says, "I have been a physician for more than 30 years. I thought I had stopped learning. But last night I discovered a new appreciation for *feeling*, for experiencing my own emotions. I only regret that I have been closed up for so many years of my life." A silence follows.

"It's wonderful; everyone is so *open* here. I can just be my real self," someone finally says, in a tone of voice lacking conviction. "Everyone outside should have this experience."

A string of statements from different parts of the room unravels. The speakers are anonymous. Their remarks are directed to no one:

"It is okay for us to love one another here, but what about the *real* world?"

"I want to continue what is happening now."

"How am I going to apply what I learn here? I want to take something back to my work."

"I can't speak in large groups like this and really feel oppressed here. I would like to form a small group where I could really be myself."

To this seemingly unrelated lexicon of group members' thoughts is added the appeal for a schedule of activities to "maximize the experience" for everyone. Another person quickly opposes any structuring, favoring "letting it happen" as the best way to maximize the experience. Some wish the staff to make topical presentations. Others feel they can learn more if the staff stays out of the way. Some want more people to speak.

Others call for silence. Some wish to discuss ideas and theories. Others regard the discussions as already overly intellectual and wish that feelings would be expressed more. Someone objects to creating a "tyranny of emotions."

People speak their piece. Their words mark a now familiar, as yet unfathomable, stream of consciousness, of encounters that reveal disappointing relations with parents, miserable childhoods, sadness, anger, even rage, human suffering, and hope. These awkward communications characterize the early meetings of the large group. Once it begins, the stimulation of the group process is relentless, as if by one of the laws of nature.

The people gathered are not specially prepared for the enterprise. Surprisingly, in spite of being mostly from the helping professions, they are *not*, as a group, always skillful in facilitating human relations or problem-solving in this setting. They have come for personal growth, to alter a style of living, to benefit humanity, to become effective professionally, to feel good, to see what happens, to overcome the tedium of a dull marriage or unrewarding work, for attention, to have an adventure.

During the early days of the workshop, meetings generate emotions, rather than integrate feelings. Moralizing, chaotic expressions of opinions, provocative ideas, the threat of violence, all make reasoning difficult and issues seem rationally unresolvable.

At times the large group behaves no better than an unruly crowd, capable of expressing only radical emotion, simplistic thoughts, and (though there is seldom physical violence) senseless aggression. Misunderstandings widen the chasm between factions, and instead of clearing the air, personal expressions can end in unfair judgments and even insults. Out of frustration and exhaustion the group sometimes settles for hasty and arbitrary decisions.[2] Would anyone have suspected that sophisticated and well-intentioned persons, with a childlike desire to express their beliefs in front of one another, could create such an oppressive environment?

Though frustrating and confusing (giving intelligent, sensitive persons reason to be wary), the large group can also present an irresistible attraction. A participant put it this way:

I go to these meetings where nothing happens, really. Mostly confusion, frustration. Nothing is decided. And still, today when I went downtown, planning to have dinner and watch a movie, I could not stay away. When the time for the meeting was near, I was *compelled* to return. I could do nothing about it; even from my years as a psychiatrist, I could not resist. When it seemed like the community was about to gather, I was pulled back like a reluctant magnet.

Out of its characteristically awkward and graceless beginning, the large group confronts many of civilization's perennial concerns: power and authority, discovery and distribution of resources, violence and security, competition and fairness, sexuality, health care, education, freedom, leisure, alienation, and scarcity; and frequently—though not always—it develops elegant and equitable means of self-regulation and inventive resolutions to crises. Actions of the group can be humane and intelligent; they can reach beyond the proposals of any single participant. Out of initial confusion and conflict, significant encounters, wisdom, love, and beauty can flourish. The workskhop may be a puzzle, a spectacle, nurturance, learning, inspiration.

Individually , there were generally a few participants who reported disappointing personal experiences, a few whose experience was rapturous, and the vast majority—over 90 percent in Bozarth's study (1981)—who regarded their learning experience as personally beneficial.

This chapter focuses on the large group that is able to reach a constructive state whereby creativity and justice are afforded its members. Many groups, of course, fail in this regard. They stretch and squirm but never develop attributes superior to those of a crowd. The reader is doubtless familiar with such groups.

Presented here, to the contrary, are comments and examples related to large groups that reach a *creative state*: that is, a state in which the group functions coherently and effectively, with wisdom and efficiency. The members are intense, both autonomous and cooperative, sensitive to the subtle flow of consciousness and affect in each other *and* to the patterns created moment-by-moment in the group. The process is not bound by its own previous organization. It changes to accommodate every voice, both sensible and delinquent, will not compromise, and settles only for intelligent actions that are just, growth promoting, and healing to the individual and to the community. The individuals' awareness of the group's patterns—the coherent thoughts and actions of the group brought about by all the individual thoughts and actions— gives the group a self-consciousness. In the creative state the thoughts, sentiments, possibilities of the community and the isolated human consciousness may not be the same; they may not be *one*, but they are not *two*.

Crises

Crises are well-known for bringing out the best of human compassion and ingenuity. Though the large group can precipitate a crisis, it is also capable in its creative state of resolving it in a manner both intelligent and humane. Threats from within or without the group—the threat of violence, irresolvable conflict between members, and illness—are frequent crises that confront the large group.

The crisis precipitated when a member of the community "breaks down" emotionally is not uncommon. Person-centered workshops have demonstrated (though not always) that the group is capable of resolving this crisis while respecting the security, well-being, and dignity of both the individual *and* the group (Wood, 1982).

Anticipating the Future

In a morning's gathering of 150 persons, the question of how to organize time for meetings and other activities is raised.

"I think we need *more* structure than ordinary daily life," Terry proposes. "We want to have a definite plan whereby people can learn and solve problems arising in the course of our workshop. I envision breaking into small groups and reporting back to the large group according to a definite organizational pattern." Many people nod in sympathy.

Linda agrees: "We have a limited amount of time. We can't take a chance that nothing would happen and this entire venture would be a waste of time and money." Linda, Terry, and Paul volunteer to form a committee with others who work with organizational planning and business consulting in client-centered ways. The meeting adjourns with the committee promising to present a plan at the 2:00 P.M. meeting.

In the afternoon, the planning committee makes a compelling presentation to the large group. Through scheduled blocks of time, workshop participants will be able to "learn and meet personal needs in an orderly and efficient manner." The plan is accepted with apparent enthusiasm by the group.

As congratulations are being shared, a few small voices are heard objecting, not to the plan, or to the suggested topics, but to the very *idea of planning.* Julie, a shy young woman who has not spoken before in the meeting, and a soft-mannered middle-aged man, Anthony, manage to express a vague fear that something, perhaps an opportunity, is about to be lost. Was anything genuinely *new* being attempted in this workshop? Was this plan the most ingenious one the community was capable of envisioning?

Julie asks haltingly, "What would it be like to live for a while *with others in a community* in a truly new way, governed by our natural relationship, one to another, and our collective organic possibility, whatever that may be? What would it be like to be free to flow and connect with others with similar interests and perhaps discover our common purpose? Do we really need a schedule of activities to do this?"

People here and there nod in agreement.

"Adopting a schedule," Anthony adds thoughtfully, "would give us an efficient workshop. But those who did not fit into it would have to go their own way. Sure, the structure proposed allows them this freedom. If you don't like the society, you can always drop out. But can we all go our *own* ways *together*, wandering without a preconceived plan, but sensitive to the hidden purpose of this whole collection of persons?"

The meeting ends without setting a time or place for the next gathering. People will evidently try having no plan. Even the committee that had worked so hard to produce the schedule excitedly anticipates the outcome.

A participant's journal records the following:

> That evening, while reading in my room, a vague restlessness overcame me. "It must be time for a meeting," I whispered to myself. Unconvinced of my true motives, I left my room and headed toward the place where we met in the afternoon. Joining me were a half dozen others who were strolling down the hill. Entering the doorway we were surprised to find over half of the entire group, assembled and buzzing with excitement. In a few minutes nearly the complete community was present and someone was speaking of his incredulity that this "crazy scheme" might actually be working.

In the days that followed, a crude order was established. It did not obey a predetermined plan but nevertheless allowed the group to meet efficiently and satisfy its members' social and productive needs.

This example illustrates the fruit of patience and the willingness to be changed—not by novelty but by a new reality, in all of its complexity.

The persons in this community did not just exchange philosophies, but allowed themselves to organize in a fundamentally different way. Community members became aware of not only their individual patterns of behavior but also the pattern of the whole. A seemingly private impulse, for example, to go to the meeting room was shared by many. It was not only an isolated act but represented the group's volition.

The rejection of a member by the group, when individually many accept the person; the restlessness, humor, and moods that are contagious in meetings illustrate other such patterns. The ability to perceive the group's patterns decreases the likelihood of group members ignoring their responsibility for the consequences of collective actions. Moreover, this awareness may also contribute to more intelligent group actions.

Beyond Democracy: Participatory Intuition

The large group can and often does destroy every attempt at systematization. This can either debilitate or liberate the development of a creative state. The following episode illustrates an apparently chaotic experience that resulted in a liberating and precise democratic action—and, one could say, decision—using processes not ordinarily associated with democracy.

During the course of the workshop many participants wish to take a break, a day off from the busy, self-imposed schedule of activities. Many also oppose the idea.

"I am afraid," Lillian says. "Back home, I live alone. Next year I will be 70. All my best friends have passed on, and I spend a good deal of time by myself. I am afraid. I don't know. If we take a holiday, my new friends here... well, they might leave me. I couldn't bear to be dropped after feeling so much...love."

Some agree that the day off is as much a part of the workshop as other days. No one has to be alone. A time off can provide a learning opportunity also.

George objects: "We can take a day off anytime at home. I came here to work, not to loaf around."

"I don't want to legislate a day off," Chip remarks. "To legislate, to me, seems phony and structured. I want to just flow with it. When I feel like taking time off, I will do so."

"But you're not so free," replies Michael. "We are presently *flowing,* as you call it, to a lock-step schedule."

In the discussion it is also suggested (by some of the psychologically minded present) that "existential aloneness" may be behind the "resistance" to doing nothing on a day off.

Every dimension of the problem is aired. Every thought, opinion, relevant fact, possessed by any person who wishes to be heard is considered. The meeting ends without a stated decision.

Two days pass. Suddenly one morning the routine ceases. There are no morning small group meetings, no late morning general assemblies. A group of music-makers surrounds Lillian at the pool; people are going to town for shopping, some go on a picnic, some sleep late. The result of these accumulated independent acts is a day off!

Of course, whether or not the participants got their day off is of little consequence; but the process of resolving this question illustrates how informed intuition can bring about constructive, coherent action.

The collective action was *spontaneous but not impulsive.* It was not the "tyranny of spontaneity" in which people simply go their own way. This was a coordinated effort. Each knew the others' viewpoints from the exhaustive discussions. The final outcome was tempered by the thoughts and opinions expressed in the discussions. Thus the group was cognitively prepared for an informed choice.

The final action was *intelligent but not strictly logical.* It did not follow from a linear sequence of logical steps but included the participants' sentiments. Feelings and emotions were expressed and taken into consideration in the earlier deliberations. Every need, desire, feeling expressed was accepted as contributing to the eventual outcome.

Furthermore, the result was arrived at by a *democratic process but was not legislated.* In this process the power resided in and was executed by the people. Those whose lives would be affected were involved in the steps leading to the final action. Unlike most processes called "democractic," no compromise had to be made. The communal reality was not defined by a statistical summing of individual positions, but by unified action that respected both the interdependent relationships of individuals and the individuals themselves.

No plan was made, decision stated, or vote taken prior to the eventual action. There was no agreement regarding time, place, or conditions for acting. In workshops such as this, it is common for meetings to end in consensus but without a stated agreement. In fact, after debating an issue with diverse and strongly held sentiments and opinions, attempting to state any "decision" in words, to vote on an apparent consensus, or similar attempts at ratification, often leads to renewed disagreement and factions. The complexity of the group's sentiment, which can be expressed in a unified act, evidently cannot be captured in words like "yes" or "no."

In the foregoing example the process did not result in democractic policies but did result in wise action. The group did not adopt an "organic model of consensus management." Rather, each person expressed a unique individuality in an efficient collective effort that promoted the well-being of the whole and of the individual.

As one might suspect, when groups have *tried* to make decisions "intuitively" or by an "organic process," they have rarely succeeded. If individuality becomes the focus, self-preoccupation and chaos are the usual outcome; if individuals exhort one another to "work as a team" or to "build community," oppression or immobility often result. In the creative state, attention on the group process is alert but diffused.

Transformation of Group Culture

A participant confronts a large group with a furious need to "stage a happening." Members of the group are eager at first to support what they imagine to be a psychodramatic emotional display—beating pillows, kicking, screaming—a norm of behavior that has been established in this group. The man proposes an encounter. He will play the part of his wife. Another person will play the husband. The group will look on.

Though they cannot explain it, several persons in the group express discomfort with the man's proposal. Others grow impatient to "get on with it." A sensitive and profound dialogue ensues between members of the group and the protagonist. The play that takes place is not what the man had in mind. No one moves from their chairs. The group draws out of him an agonizing story of how he sadly witnessed his wife sink into an emotional breakdown over the death of a friend, which led to her eventual hospitalization. Step by step, as their understanding allows, the man and group members struggle through a drama of mutual invention.

"In doing this psychodrama, do you intend to live what your wife felt?" he is asked.

"Yes, in order to better understand her experience and my love for her," he answers.

"Do you intend to do something that could end in *your* hospitalization?"

"I don't know the outcome, but I am prepared."

"Could anyone be hurt in this play?"

"It is not my intention to hurt anyone."

To some his answers are reassuring, proving that he is "taking responsibility" for his actions. To others, his replies signal alarm. The tension builds steadily. Some urge him to "go ahead, dive in; the risks are worth it." Others want to support him but do not "feel right" about their involvement.

Minutes give way to hours and finally, an integration.

"I don't need to act out my wife's trauma. I *feel* what she felt and *you* feel it with me. I have gotten what I need already. I needed you to go with me. But I needed you to be strong, so I could be strong, so I could face myself. I needed you to care, in order to feel my caring. I've got what I needed, not what I thought I wanted. Suddenly, I understand the love of two strong people."

"What had your wife done?" someone asks as the group members shuffle from the room.

Passing through the swinging glass doorway, he replies, matter-of-factly:

"Exploding insanely, she threw loose objects at me and, tearing off her clothes, shattered a plate glass window with her naked body."

Somehow the group had sensed that the man's intention might be dangerous. Even if he assumed responsibility for his actions, the group would not accept a harmful outcome. Together, through mutual searching, members of the group (including the man himself) created a constructive alternative.

Conventional thinking might regard the change of direction as the "group will" putting "pressure" on the individual to conform his behavior to the group norm. But one must not forget that the man began with the intention of conforming to the cultural norm of explosive display of emotions and the group initially supported this approach, prepared to assist in the action.

Rather, the drama was one coherent act, during which the path, but not the destination, changed. The goal was accomplished through the transformation of the group culture. The person followed his desire to understand himself and it took him in a surprising direction—not toward violence but away from it. The community could have handled the crisis of an "emotional breakdown" if the man became a "problem." In this group, however, members of the group were sensitive to the pattern of the group and its consequence to the person. In a sense, they empathically "lived" the experience with him. They changed together.

The man related afterward that he understood more clearly the relationship with his wife, not only in the group but back home as well.

INDIVIDUAL FACTORS WHICH ACCOMPANY CREATIVE STATES IN LARGE GROUPS

One person alone is nothing; when two are together, you have a unity.

[from a small Brazilian village]

What a person-centered approach taught us about community was that a large group, in a creative state, can resolve crises, find solutions to complex problems, intelligently coordinate its activities without plans, legislation, or parliamentary procedures, and even transform its culture in a compassionate and efficient process that involves, respects, and benefits each of its members and itself. The question that remains is: What allows one group not only to surpass the accomplishments of individual members, but to reach a creative state, while others end without ever reaching the level of capability of one of their individual members?

Doubtless, the effects of setting, sunshine, summer leisure, the magic of beginnings, other romances, adventure, challenge, and many nonspecific factors play their part in forming a creative state. The composition of group membership is a critical factor. However, not being well understood, it is not developed in the following discussion. Suggested here are essential aspects of individual behavior and consciousness that seem to accompany the creative state.

Allowing Diffused Control

Though the organizers play a key role in convening the workshop, their actions alone do not predict a creative state. As soon as the preparatory tasks are accomplished, the staff relinquishes its institutionalized authority to the group. No leaders are elected, appointed, or otherwise designated, but they do emerge. They are many, and they are recognized as the persons who provide a significant fact, insight, or technical skill; an appropriate sentiment that others only vaguely sense; or a piece of information at exactly the right moment. It is as Xenophon described his comrades, 10,000 leaderless Greek soldiers, who made their way safely from Persia back to Greece. Drawing on individual intelligence and initiative, each one was a leader, "free individuals unified by a spontaneous service to the common life" (Hamilton, 1942, p. 226).

Autonomy and Humility

The creative state seems to be accompanied by what are usually regarded as contradictory aspects held concurrently in the group and eventually within the same person.

One aspect will be called *autonomy*. A person is capable of self-governance, independent thought and action, and expression of his or her unique thoughts, opinions, beliefs, and perceptions in reacting to the group. The person can maintain a separate identity by experiencing personal values, feelings, and thoughts in a larger context than merely the present moment. Thus, in the example related earlier, Julie and Anthony illustrate autonomy by confronting a movement toward unanimity with, "Wait a minute. This does not feel right to me as an individual."

Somewhat paradoxically the person is also able to live fully in the moment, abandoning pride, a sense of personal significance, to surrender to something that transcends himself or herself. This aspect will be called *humility*.

Those who put forward their best idea for a solution to a serious problem the group faces and then relinquish their idea, doctrine, belief, perception for one superior in that moment are expressing the convergence of autonomy and humility present in the creative state.

Humility. In order to further clarify this aspect it may be useful to define the notion of "trance states."

The usual state of consciousness is characterized by a frame of reference called the "generalized reality-orientation" that, in the background of attention, "supports, interprets, and gives meaning to all experiences" of the person (Shor, 1959). This orientation can temporarily fade or disintegrate in special states of mind and become nonfunctional. Sleep is the most common example of this condition. "Any state," Shor has stated, "in which the generalized reality-orientation has faded to relatively nonfunctional unawareness may be termed a trance state." In trance the person is highly suggestible and may come to experience reality in a totally different way. What was regarded as impossible becomes possible, even superhuman feats.

> The person no longer seems bound to the necessity for syllogistic reasoning, the distinctions between cause and effect may vanish, the notion of time may become more relative, opposites can coexist and

not seem contradictory.... A type of "perceptual cognitive restructuring" tends to occur in which the individual has available new avenues of experience and expression. (Ludwig, 1967, p. 13)

Trance can be induced by separation from routine daily life; emotional tension (Sargant, 1957); ambiguity and confusion (Frank, 1973); public confessions of feeling (Lifton, 1961); listening to music, singing and dancing (Deren, 1970); fatigue (Tyler, 1955); boredom (Heron, 1957); fasting (Field, 1960); and the use of alcohol, caffeine, and other mind-altering chemicals. These factors are all present to some extent in large group workshops as well as in the course of psychotherapy, psychic experiences, healing, religious conversion, spirit possession, and many other activities.

Persons in trance are able to extend their powers of physical agility and strength, concentration, perception, insight, and creativity—not only personally but also to guide and maintain the collective. Through trance and the developed tradition of the community (such as what witch doctors, healers, or psychotherapists may oversee):

The individual participates in the accumulated genius of the collective, and by such participation becomes himself a part of that genius— something more than himself. *His exaltation results from his participation*, it does not precede and compel it. (Deren, 1970, p. 229)

What we are calling humility allows the person to yield to the creative aspects of the trance: to relax the critical faculties and to surrender opinions, convictions, and perceptions by allowing the mind to bypass "the particularities of circumstances, the limitations and imprecisions of the senses" to arrive at "some common principled truth of the matter" (Deren, 1970, p. 22). This humility allows the surrender of impatience and easy answers for an attentive waiting—alert to follow *or* to lead *or* to remain still.

In this state, the individual is able to live unattached to a particular form. At one time, the absence of structured activities may bring about a creative state; at another time, the group may require a highly organized structure. Solutions that worked before or succeeded in other groups are not necessarily effective in a different situation. The individual may have to surrender even the understanding gained from past experience, to live with doubts, with fears, but without being governed by them.

Although not every person in the group is admired, or even liked, humility enables each person's existence to be *accepted*, as one accepts the world, without trying to decide if it is to be believed or not. People try to put themselves in the other's shoes, trying to sense the meaning of the person's expressions, both for the individual and for the group. Negative feelings are accepted as a reality and not *always* a prelude to destructive action. Different interpretations of the same event are used for invention. Without autonomy to express conflicting feelings, the group lacks the tension of creativity; without humility to transcend differences, it lacks the fact of creativity.

This creative state, it must be said, is fragile. It is so vulnerable that probably anyone, with the intention to do so, can prevent its appearance. This contention is supported by observations from other groups as well. Doob (1970) reports how the sensitive resolution of complex issues (through the development of a creative state) was sabotaged by "erratic and sometimes calculatedly disruptive behavior which seemed to manifest itself most when some progress or agreement was close to hand" (p. 109).

Sometimes, however, even well-intentioned people can do the same by lacking humility. As one person in a workshop put it, "We weren't mature enough to handle it." One need not be nice, agreeable, congenial, or even cordial; only good willed.

Autonomy. Without inner discipline, or a ritualized tradition to provide discipline, the trance state can also lead to the radical crowd behavior described by McDougall in the introduction to this chapter. The same conditions that result in relaxation of the generalized reality-orientation, opening the possibilities of creativity, can also, through weakening the critical judgment of group members, render participants prey to "group think." The person's self-transcending nature—humility—can be manipulated if he gives up a "dynamic, changing, viable and useful kind of cognitive response" for "certain kinds of routine and stock thoughts which he is unwilling to examine critically" (Schein, Schneier, & Barker, 1961, p. 262). The creative state needs self-directed persons to challenge mechanical thought and stock premises and to check the formation of mindless followers. Autonomy, with its isolated, personal viewpoint, can protect against the development of "true believers" and help to piece together a wise outcome for the group. It relentlessly challenges the objectives and fundamental values of the community.

By not abdicating responsibility and by exercising individual intelligence the individual is less likely to be "swallowed by efficiency," "sacrificed to the higher good," or pressured into becoming "the correct member of society."

Humility and autonomy are merely names given to the primary, yet inseparable, individual factors accompanying the creative state. They characterize one consciousness of the individuals. They are two sides of the same coin: The individual can be vigorously expressive, lucid, and delineated, while functioning in a spontaneous congruence, diffused with an intelligent and effective collective of persons. The conjunction is more than either face. It does not obey the private or the universal. This conjunction faces life with expectancy and without expectations. It is not interested in chaos or self-preoccupation. It is interested in *being* community, not "forming community," and will not tolerate oppression or immobility in the group. Contrary to conventional expectation, its autonomy functions for unity of the whole; its humility functions for individual growth.

Finally, good will, acceptance, and trust are not ends in themselves. They are likely an essential part of the provocation for wise and effective groups. Their role, as it may originally have been in religion, is probably as technical prerequisites to the transformation of group consciousness, not to anchor morality or a belief system.

In other eras autonomy and humility were part of this transformational consciousness. There were participants who, as oracles and prophets, provided leadership and wise counsel to the community in a state of consciousness that was also "a curious blend of gainfully directed hysteria and patient self-discipline" (Field, 1960, p. 65). In this regard, groups have probably always provided the means for altering the human consciousness to facilitate individual growth, make intelligent group decisions, and instruct the community.

Perhaps the group still provides such possibilities. At its best, the whole, the community, can be a teacher for the seeker, a therapist for the client, provider of alternatives for the problem-solver, inspiration for the artist. The essence of its creative state may come not from one person, with answers, but out of a group of persons with questions, not fully realizing that a wisdom may be hidden in their searching.

NOTES

1. The initiators of these large group interactions were Natalie Rogers, Carl Rogers, John K. Wood, Alan Nelson, and Betty Meador. After the first year's work Nelson and Meador undertook other pursuits and the staff was

reconstituted. In the next six years the most consistent staff group, working together on this approach to large group work, consisted of Natalie Rogers, Carl Rogers, John K. Wood, Maria Bowen, Jared Kass, Maureen Miller, and Joann Justyn. Since 1976 many other combinations of persons have also convened similar events in all corners of the world.

2. Doubtless, the tribal groups often envied for their harmonious functioning also failed to arrive at unity free from boredom, frustration, confusion, and aggravation.

16 Person-Centered Administration in Higher Education

William R. Rogers

With *decreases* in the purchasing power of higher education funds as well as in the number of students of traditional age, there appears to be a corollary *increase* in the number of writers who are ready with advice on how to manage our colleges and universities.[1] Central to the analysis of most of these writers is an awareness that higher education, unlike most businesses, has a "management dilemma" in the relatively autonomous spheres of influence maintained by faculty, trustees, staff, and students. Keller's thoughtful work in *Academic Strategy* (1983) outlines some of the political effects of our governance system, which is typically a "republic" of sorts, where faculty are partners with administration in setting academic policy, but in which actual faculty concerns often focus on individual research or departmental planning. The "dilemma" in this structure is poignantly, if accusingly, stated by Rourke and Brooks: "Faculties have put themselves in the indefensible position of being willing neither to assume the burden of guiding a university's academic development nor to concede to others the right to do so" (1966, p. 129).

Yet this description, which sounds so much like that of a beleaguered administrator, need not be the final word sealing an irresolvable dilemma. True, there are divergent points of view and self-interested claims for authority in universities and colleges. But this *could* be the basis for institutional creativity if one is imaginative enough to develop an educational "management style" that responds sensitively to the challenge of enabling diverse constituencies to find expression and fulfillment in an intentional community of learning.

Neither autocratic, hierarchical administrative control, nor weak resignation to factious interest groups is appropriate here. Rather it is my contention that a thoughtful incorporation of *person-centered* principles in higher education administration can open vistas of cooperation and productivity that move us well beyond the dilemma identified by Rourke and Brooks.

As in other chapters in this volume, a *person-centered* approach is here defined as the perspective that grows out of client-centered theory. It is not a way of reiterating the time-worn observation that the first act of effective administration is "human resource management" and the appointment of the "right person" for the job, important though that may be.

Interestingly enough, both higher education theorists like Keller (1983), Kerr (1979), and Boulding (1975) and organizational development and change theorists like Aldrich (1979) and Argyris and Schön (1978) have pointed to a desirable shift from hierarchical or centralized authority structures to collegial and consensual models. In many respects these organizational and problem-solving alternatives have "person-centered" components.

It is a challenging task to articulate a clear and specific set of *principles* by which person-centered values could be seen as guiding higher education administration. This chapter attempts to do just that.

Before developing 10 principles of this sort, however, it may be useful to give a homely but relevant illustration to which some of the principles might be attached. Additionally I will comment briefly on some of the historical changes in client-centered theory that make this present task both possible and urgent.

A CASE ILLUSTRATION AND COMMENTARY

Midafternoon on a Friday, the Budget and Planning Committee had gathered in the Board Room. It was time for a quarterly reassessment of the institutional operating budget, and first on the agenda was a request for almost double the Alumni Office expenditure authorization.

In a period of economic instability, sharp demographic downslides in the number of 18-year-olds entering college, inflationary increases in all costs, cutbacks in government support...how could a responsible administration even consider such expanded outlays?

Current wisdom from many management sources argues that there must be careful planning based on exact information systems, agility in strategic decision-making, adaptability, strict budgetary building processes, and firm budget control. Often this carries the implication that there should be a top-down structure of pyramidal authority in which the chief executive has the information, authority, and delegatory structure to manage the entire operation. And particularly in times of economic stress, the urgency of that impulse to control, and the concomitant anxieties of loss of control, seem more pronounced than ever.

I certainly would not dispute the importance of accurate data, clear planning, timely decision-making, and careful budgetary operation. But the *structure* in which that is carried on can be consensual, open, and interpersonally supportive, rather than authoritarian in its chain of command and pyramidally controlling in its impulse. I would argue that even in such critical areas as budget and planning, the most effective organizational structure must be one that is broadly inclusive of the wisdom and participation of persons whose personal, intellectual, and financial destinies will in some measure be affected by those organizational decisions. It is my contention that the information gathering, the priority setting, the budgeting allocations, and the fidelity to that budget are all *enhanced* in a structure that is *person-centered* and participatory, rather than protective of closely held prerogatives of a centralized authority.

The Friday Budget and Planning session in our illustration involved a committee consisting of representatives from the student body, the faculty, the administration, and the trustees. They had previously set planning priorities together in both long-range and strategic planning sessions. These had included, among other things, increased recognition of alumni achievement and educational services for alumni, coupled with increased volunteer training for alumni participation in the annual giving program. Midway through the year these dimensions of the college program had proven to be so successful that further support for phone, postage, special events, and staff coordination was essential. The success had come about largely through participatory processes of volunteer work and fresh enthusiasm among both alumni and staff members. The heightened cooperative activity was demonstrated in increased percentages of alumni involved both in Alumni Board activities and in annual giving. This record, coupled with other improvements in the college—especially in enrollment, attractive new educational programs, sound investments, and conservative budgeting—created a climate in which committee members could look favorably on a budget increase request.

The real debate, as one might expect, involved the concomitant expression of felt needs from other departments within the college, especially in personnel areas. It was only in the airing of competing claims, the reassessment of some educational and program priorities, the attentiveness to personal feelings and ideas, and the willingness to rise above self-interest to view more balanced institutional needs, that concurrence was eventually given to the Alumni Office request.

The personal characteristics of a person-centered administrator who could lead effectively in this situation would include the following:

1. Thoroughness and openness in systematically sharing data relevant to the issues under discussion.

2. A genuine belief that the emerging judgment of a group of knowledgeable and concerned persons will show greater wisdom than the single-handed decision of even the chief administrator.

3. Patience in attending to the diverse perspectives represented in the institution, including feelings as well as ideas.

4. Willingness to lay aside temporarily the compulsion for task-completion when unresolved policy or personal conflicts demand immediate attention.

5. Intuitive sensitivity to feelings of hesitation, ego-investment, ambivalence, anger, withdrawal, displacement, etc., as well as to feelings of *esprit de corps* and support.

6. Keen discernment of the positive meeting points and areas of agreement as a group moves toward consensus, and an ability to articulate that emerging center while recognizing the residual divergence of opinion.

7. Appreciation of the support and creativity contributed by others within the organization.

8. Willingness for self-scrutiny and evaluation in broadening one's own perspective and in assessing the relative fulfillment of the criteria for success or accomplishment within the institution.

It could certainly be argued that such characteristics, and the related person-centered procedures, are not for everyone. They clearly involve an investment of time, trust, and often of risk. Yet they may also actually generate greater long-term effectiveness in decision-making insofar as they facilitate a unity of movement and a minimum of disgruntled foot-dragging following a consensus—especially in matters of budget.

CLIENT-CENTERED THEORY IN TRANSITION

The impact of client-centered theory in higher education has been pronounced in student services. Direct counseling of both individuals and groups has been influenced on campus after campus by the insights and style of client-centered therapy. Moving away from the older counseling modes of history-taking, advice, interpretation, pledges, moral remonstrance, and the like, the counselors influenced by Carl Rogers paid special attention to principles of careful listening, empathic understanding, clarification of feeling, exploration of felt ambivalences, and nurturance of the internal resources of the "organismic valuing process." Their aim was to enable students to grow with a sense of self-worth and focused self-direction.

This emphasis was "student centered" and in many respects individualistic. But both client-centered theory and its relation to higher education have changed in some important respects since the mid-1970s. The essence of this change has been increased attention to the *structural* or *organizational* patterns that are critical in enabling full human development. Briefly stated, it became increasingly evident *that efforts to help individuals in a therapeutic mode would always remain limited and merely remedial if the oppressive social and institutional realities surrounding life remained untouched.* The "client" was no longer seen as the lone individual caught in a painful confusion of intrapsychic conflicts, though such feelings continued to be taken seriously. Rather, the broader economic, political, institutional, and value context of the culture could be seen as client-centered—in the interest of changes that would enhance opportunities for "full-functioning" personal life. The fact that a number of client-centered therapists have moved into positions of responsibility for administrative planning in colleges and universities makes this shift all the more tangible and direct.[2]

In an effort to make more specific the guidelines that animate person-centered educational leadership, I offer the following principles. In each case some countervailing concerns will also be identified. Following the statement of principles, several illustrative areas of higher education administration, in addition to our budget example, will be highlighted.

PRINCIPLES OF PERSON-CENTERED ADMINISTRATION

1. Facilitating Clarity of a Shared Vision

Without a sense of common purpose, the strivings of individuals often languish in isolation and lost momentum or get entangled in competition, frustration, and defeat. Especially in academia where the traditions of graduate training and scholarship emphasize autonomy, individuality, private research, self-discipline, and self-reliance, it is a special challenge to nurture an environment that is conducive of a sense of belonging and shared destiny.

There are at least two major components in such an environment. One is the provision for regular and systematic forums involving representatives of the entire learning community to focus on goals, long-range plans, basic purposes, and strategic adaptations. The other is a daily climate that encourages attentiveness to the hopes and frustrations of each person in the community. The informal as well as formal aim should be the inclusion of individual concerns in the broader vision of the institution. Such recognition may also facilitate voluntary relinquishment of privatistic dissonant interests.

The first component often entails a committee structure attentive to priorities in long-range and strategic planning. It may also involve periodic gatherings of the entire community to address the basic philosophical and value dimensions of the total enterprise. The second component involves encouragement of a personal transition from what Maccoby (1977) terms the "craftsman" orientation to that of a team player or "gamesman" who enjoys participating in the growth and change of the institution and who can bring into healthy balance both competition and cooperation.[3]

The *countervailing principle* that must be maintained alongside an emphasis on shared vision is *clarity of personal responsibility* and *distinctness of function.* Everyone who thinks that he or she should be involved in everyone else's business must foster a sense of caution. Shared vision does not mean a mushy uniformity of function. Nor should it dilute the specific energy necessary to carry out particular tasks, even though these are in pursuit of commonly agreed-upon goals. The quest of a common vision could be devastating if it were simply a mask for either mistrust or the shirking of individual accountability.

2. Assessment of Individual Interests in Curriculum and Educational Planning

One important mission of a college must be to formulate exciting, meaningful, and personally relevant educational experiences for individual students. It is particularly crucial to a person-centered perspective that educational opportunities be designed in such a way as to meet the individual needs, interests, and talents of students rather than simply providing large classes with routinized assignments and monolithic requirements.

In a sense, it is every faculty member's responsibility to attend to the individual student's interests and capabilities, as well as to the demands of a particular academic discipline. Frequently, the degrees of latitude in required readings and in special research and writing projects reflect such an individualized approach. But it is the continuing responsibility of the administrator to provide *structural* mechanisms to ensure freedom and initiative for individual students in designing particular patterns of study and growth. It is also the administrator's responsibility to provide encouragement, incentives, and resources for faculty initiatives related to person-centered teaching.

Some schools, such as Hampshire College, do this by stimulating faculty to develop a "modes of inquiry" sequence that helps a student from the very begining of the freshman year to design a focused and manageable problem for investigation from a variety of methodological and theoretical perspectives. In a number of other schools special options for a self-designed major are provided. At Guilford that option is structured in such a way that the student may choose to work with three faculty members as a special advisory committee in designing a set of courses and research projects constructed along the lines of a student's personal intellectual interests.

The concern for individual student initiative gets expressed not only in curriculum and degree requirements but also in the area of student activities planning. To ensure that a wide variety of student interests are taken seriously in the planning process, it is important that groups involved in student governance and activities include broad representation. Artistic, recreational, political, and creative programs can be designed that meet both competitive and noncompetitive interests, as well as the array of minority and international sensibilities within the campus student body.

The *countervailing principle* that must be taken seriously in juxtaposition to individual electives and self-designed educational programs is the need for a specific *core of basic studies* that will ensure breadth of *comprehension in major areas of humanistic, scientific, and social thought.* We have witnessed disappointing institutional experiences and floundering students when entire programs become elective. At Harvard College, where the idea of individually designed electives was vigorously established, there has been a return over the last decade to a greater balance with the core curriculum.

However, respect for disciplinary integrity, as well as thoroughness in the study of fundamental academic material, need not be in opposition to the person-centered perspective. Certainly most students are seeking to develop intellectual competence, a secure grasp of particular areas of knowledge, and confidence in utilizing appropriate methods of inquiry in approaching new problems. It is partially in response to such interests that the rigorous pursuit of historical, literary, cultural, and scientific studies has its rationale.

3. Consultation with Persons Affected by Decisions

Probably one of the most important differentiations between a hierarchical and consensual form of governance occurs in the degree to which broad consultation occurs in the decision-making process. "Consultation" could easily be misread to mean simply asking a person how he or she feels about a conclusion that has already been reached. Genuine consultation in decision-making, however, means working carefully and thoroughly enough with all affected parties so that there is both understanding and consensus in the final determination. This does not mean, of course, that there will never be times when people are disappointed or feel that their particular perspective has been waived in the interests of the broader group. However, it does mean that, even when such disappointments occur, they will be in the context of a broader comprehension of the goals and well-being of the entire institution.

Consultation and the building of consensual decision-making become especially difficult in such matters as office space assignment, budgeting, and staffing allocations. The space in which professional lives are lived is a matter of considerable personal consequence. Too often such decisions are made at the Dean's drawing board where matters of logistics and space utilization coupled with questions of economy may govern in mechanical ways. Instead of this, it is possible and desirable to have a facilities committee that examines the needs and wishes of individuals and works with them in the development of a plan that mediates their interests and the needs of the institution. Patterns of communication flow, contiguity and availability of space, cost, etc. must also be weighed.

The Budget and Planning Committee example given earlier demonstrated a procedure in which representatives from major departments had a hand in expressing their needs and in weighing the priority decisions that had to be made in allocating limited resources across a number of competing programs. To have such a process work effectively takes time. The calendar of budget preparation needs to reflect that fact by spreading annual budget discussions over a period of up to one year. Multi-year programs projections, line item justifications on a zero-based model, and personal conversations between the budget committee members and representatives of each department can help make this process more fair and more person-centered.

Staffing decisions have the potential for great conflict, especially during a time when many schools face the necessity of retrenchment and staff cuts. Problems of personal destiny, perhaps even dismissal, make it essential that there be consultation with people who may be affected. It is exactly at such points, however, that the subtle attraction of a certain kind of cowardice emerges in which administrators shy away from direct consultation. They are confronted with the simultaneous needs to care for people for whom they have respect and affection and to deal with issues of performance and institutional necessity. To succumb to cowardice would not only represent a failure of nerve in maintaining fidelity to a person-centered approach but could lead to serious feelings of betrayal and loss of morale among staff.

One of the ways this situation might be handled wisely is through a committee structure like a faculty senate or an administrative council where questions of position allocations are carefully weighed in terms of the individual needs as well as information concerning such things as instructional costs analyses and program cost-effectiveness studies. When planning can be done on a schedule of timely deliberation and thorough consultation, providing all interested parties full access to the discussion, the conclusions and the actions taken have a greater likelihood of being understood and of gaining the confidence and consent of the community.

The *countervailing factors* that must be weighed against this principle of broad consultation include matters of *confidentiality* and *efficiency*. There are times when individuals would like to have such things as performance evaluations kept confidential. In decisions involving staff dismissals, for instance, there may be a need to have consultation only with the administrator and the staff person involved, even though the broader questions of replacement and planning for future program needs could be carried on in committee deliberations. In my judgment, fidelity to a person-centered approach means respect for such confidentiality as it pertains to individual needs.

Individual or institution? What if one has to choose? In a sense this is a false dichotomy, since without strength in the institution there is little or no support for the individual (perhaps no job!), and without strong individuals there would not be a viable institution. Attention to both is necessary! Where one *must* choose between protecting the confidentiality of an individual and protecting the institution from incompetent or unethical behavior, there is similarly the possibility of a "both-and" resolution. Both the appropriate disciplinary action can be taken in the interest of strengthening the institution, *and* care can be given in hearing the individual's concerns, both before and after a decision has been reached. Specific aspects of the individual's feelings for which confidentiality might be requested can be kept out of the arena of public discourse.

Efficiency or effectiveness? Questions are often raised by those who think that a streamlined process of executive decision-making is more desirable than complex patterns of consultation. Such a concern with efficiency is short-term and contains a hidden pitfall, so camouflaged as to be devastating. Decisions *can* be made more quickly when one administrator, or even a small elite group, sends a policy on to subordinates. The pitfall, however, is that when such decisions are made without consultation, the remnants of "unheard" concerns, felt betrayal, mistrust of the deliberative process, and most especially well-reasoned evidence on the opposite side of the conclusion will conspire to create the lead weight of resistance against cooperation with those administrators. More radically, there might be outright defiance not only of the procedures but of the institutional goals that those administrators are presumably defending. In the long run, I would argue that it is far more *effective* to spend the time necessary to include the concerned opinions and judgments that bear on a decision. Once such a decision is made, unanimity of support ensures a kind of success and institutional movement that is usually impossible when there are alienated factions left from the failure to consult and deliberate fully on the significant issues.

4. Openness of Procedures

Related to the concern for broad consultation in decision-making is a corollary principle of openness in the procedure by which such consultation is undertaken. It is not enough simply to have a dedication to broad, consensus-building objectives. One must also establish *how* that procedure takes place and follow the procedure with consistency.

Openness of procedures in decision-making involves two components. One is a pattern of communication that announces publicly and in advance the issues, committees, responsibility flow, and agenda that will be followed in shaping policy. The second involves clarity in articulating the timetable, the points of reference and the criteria of judgment used in deliberations. Both the structure and the process should be spelled out, including modes for reconsideration and re-evaluation of the adequacy of judgments that have been made.

Perhaps one of the best ways to ensure that procedures within an institution of higher education are openly visible is to outline both narratively and graphically in a handbook the procedures relating to all areas of a person's involvement in the institution's life. The process needs to be explicit in hiring and promotion, in salary and benefit negotiations, in research and leave policies, in dismissal proceedings, in new program development, in committee assignments, in financial aid decision-making, in student discipline, in athletic planning, in facilities utilization, in retirement, and in strategic planning. Models for such handbooks as well as for the more official bylaws of institutions are available from such groups as the American Council on Education and the Association of American Colleges, or from specific institutions that have taken care in the formulation of these matters. Such guidelines and handbooks, of course, need frequent revision; and it should be the responsibility of at least one member of the college or university staff to be sure that these procedures are kept current and available.

The *countervailing factor* to this principle of openness of procedure is the *need for clear accountability*. Definitions of project responsibility and staff supervision need clarity in order to prevent a dilution of energy and productivity. When others feel included and know that they have an opportunity for an expression of concern at appropriate points within decision-making processes, they tend to have a greater trust in the people responsible for institutional administration, and they become more accountable themselves. There is also less worry about the machinations of backroom politics that abound when closed or veiled procedures prevail.

5. Inclusion of Broad Constituencies in Institutional Development

Many of the remarks in the discussion of the preceding two principles have implied internal institutional deliberation and procedures involving students, faculty, and administrative staff. But a person-centered administration would also take seriously the importance of informing and including other constituencies such as trustees or regents, alumni, emeriti faculty, and affiliated boards (such as Boards of Advisors or Boards of Visitors) in discussing issues and initiatives within the institution. It is, of course, typical that such groups that have interest in the institution and historic or personal connections with it are consulted in matters of institutional advancement or development (which most often means fund-raising). But such groups can provide an important source of new ideas as well as feedback on emerging internal operations when timely presentations can be made by the administration concerning matters of consequence to the institution. What I am suggesting is that these related constituencies are important not only for purposes of "cultivation." Personal attention to these constituencies can yield not just good will, but good ideas.

For example, in planning new initiatives in lifelong education, in making decisions about plant renovation or expansion, or in the acquisition and utilization of new facilities, knowledgeable friends of a college could have important contributions to make. Most often this contribution is institutionalized through committees and subcommittees of the Board of Trustees. It can easily extend to discussions with groups of alumni and concerned community leaders not daily involved in the life of the institution.

Even in fund-raising, importance must be given to the personal concerns and family needs of individual donors, not just to the needs of the institution. This is to suggest a person-centered approach to financial appeals on behalf of the college or university. There are many ways in which charitable contributions can bring both the intrinsic satisfaction of a joy of giving, and personal benefits such as increased income from annuity trusts and pooled life income funds. It is often a pleasure to discover the dual benefit that can be provided both to the individual and to the institution in such gift arrangements.

The *countervailing factor* that must be weighed in including the personal interests of broader constituencies surrounding the institution involves *caution in creating expectations for ongoing involvement in policy formulation.* Clearly individuals and groups who are only partially related to the daily insitutional life cannot be held seriously accountable for a very full range of decisions and responsibilities within the institution. To use their judgment wisely, administrators must clearly define the parameters of the problems and initiatives in which their contributions can be made. Such areas must be limited in number, thoughtfully timed, and clearly explained within the procedural systems that were discussed earlier. When those matters are tended to carefully, the contributions of the broader constituencies are usually focused, supportive, and creative—not demanding or entangling.

6. Availability

Just as one of the important features of student-centered teaching is availability to students, so within person-centered administration, a central principle must also be that of availability. In the case of administration, the network of people responding to that availability includes students, faculty, staff, alumni, and a multitude of external constituencies. This may lead an administrator to feel overwhelmed. The tendency for many is to retreat to an inner office, frequent travel, or the protective deflections of an efficient administrative assistant.

Clearly the *countervailing concern* in this case is effective *time management.* Most administrators regard the unscheduled interruptions that occur with an "open door policy" to be the most debilitating feature of a time management plan.

However, effective time management and availability on a personal level do not have to be incompatible. Calendar organization that includes both closed periods for policy planning, writing, correspondence, etc., and open periods for responsiveness to scheduled and unscheduled personal conversations is one of the keys. But that is not enough. To sit in one's office surrounded by a deluge of mail, committee papers, and special reports hardly portrays an accessible administrative style. Availability is conveyed in the small, repeated experiences of personal extension that occur in conversations on the walkways, time spent before and after meetings, and participation in campus events. In literally every exchange, the qualities of a "willingness to be known" and "empathic understanding" can be actualized. These are important to one's *genuine* availability. They can be conveyed as well in relatively brief encounters—even over the phone—as in lengthy relationships. We are available only within the "limits of time." For an administrator or teacher the limits simply have to be managed more carefully.

7. Empathic Understanding

While there is a vast body of research on the importance and function of empathy in client-centered therapy, there is a converse lacuna of any suggestion of its importance in administration. Administrators, after all, have to look at the facts, at the overall institutional structure, at the budget, at the multiple needs of many departments that must be weighed judiciously. How could one afford to be empathically involved with a single person?

I wish to argue that this principle of empathy is just as essential in administration as it is in psychotherapy. True, there are limits to the number of people we can know well; but the attitude of clear receptivity, openness, readiness to understand, and empathy with the intent and feeling of another is crucial in the daily work of administration. It marks the difference between comprehending the concerns of others in the institution and merely riding over them; the difference between including people collegially and simply using their ideas; the difference between a caring community and a conglomerate of relatively autonomous individuals who are functionally together but personally isolated. Empathy, like availability, is conveyed in a number of small ways, but it is essential to the ethos of an institution because it frees individuals to be expressive and creative within it.

The *countervailing feature* in the case of empathy may be the need for *firmness of institutional decision* and for willingness to articulate decisions with clarity, albeit compassion, even when they appear to go against the feelings and interest of a particular individual.

Yet the very willingness to listen empathically and patiently to the feelings and needs of individuals, particularly in cases where there may be misunderstanding, disappointment, or pain, can make the difference between the genuinely humane institution and one that functions simply with a hard-headed momentum of a power elite.

The examples of cases in which empathy proves to be a critical factor are quite numerous. Working with students who have appealed disciplinary decisions often involves close attention to their personal and educational needs as well as to the behaviorial standards of the institution. Working with a faculty member or administrator who has received a negative performance evaluation calls for empathic concern. Empathy is also called for when working with someone who has dealt insensitively with a situation that has ethical or legal consequences. At times the processes of promotion, salary, or tenure call for a similar empathy as well as the ability to interpret the needs of the institution.

Empathy in such cases is not to be confused with manipulative ways of softening a blow or of deceitfully tricking someone in negotiations. That would blatantly be the antithesis of a person-centered approach! Decisions must be made clearly, reasoned openly, and presented straightforwardly. But in the process of decision-making, and in its aftermath, the administrator has the responsibility to attend caringly to the feelings and responses of the other.

It is particularly this subtle interweaving of concern for the individual and concern for the institution that marks a strong administrator: one who is willing to rethink issues when deeper understandings emerge; one who is able to be clear about the real and perceived needs of a variety of individuals and groups; one who uses the capacity for understanding not to manipulate but to genuinely include; one who can wear authority lightly; one who is able to take a stand while having that quality of kindness and compassion which reflects genuine individual concern even in situations involving the definition of limits.

8. Alertness to Hidden Agendas

In working both with individuals and with committees, diligence in pursuing the explicit agenda should never obscure the more subtle feelings, needs, and private ambitions of people engaged in that interaction at that time. Research in group dynamics and in organizational structure has amply identified the importance of such hidden agendas. Without acknowledging them, an administrator can easily misgauge the priorities being expressed and could, over time, develop policies that would deny some of the most important values and personal strivings of people within the institution.

In actual practice, this sensitivity sometimes calls for explicit articulation of unexpressed concerns. Often it involves stepping back from the discussion of an agenda item to gain some understanding of areas of reluctance or misunderstanding, ambiguity or skepticism. At times such agendas are strictly personal in nature (e.g., displaced anger from a conflict at home, frustration over an incomplete project, or jealousy of the achievements or advantage of another). At other times the administrator may discover a more broadly held hidden sentiment that is important and powerful but unarticulated. Hidden agendas may emerge when the specific departmental or program priorities of the institution get buried or garbled beneath larger projects. They may emerge when programs get coupled with needs for self-esteem and felt significance. If the confluence of psychological needs and programmatic loyalties is not taken seriously, then it is more likely that decisions made about broader matters will eventually be undermined by resentful counterproductivity or apathy on the part of those whose hidden concerns have not been acknowledged.

The *countervailing concern* is a need for *specific task completion.* The inevitable pressures of time, expansion of responsibilities, and limitations on personal and physical resources could easily lead to a compelling task orientation. However, task completion, like the formulation of policy decisions, cannot be taken as an end in itself, but must be balanced with the patience needed to deal with human concerns. Even when one looks at task completion as instrumental to the efficient running of the organization, that efficiency would not be long-lived in cases where unarticulated material had been ignored, only to rear its head with subtle insistence in the sabotaging of the presumed agreements reached in the "completion" of the task. Real task completion involves the open and mutually confirmed assurance that all the significant issues and persons have been taken into account in reaching a decision or in completing the task.

9. Creation of Forums for the Transformation of Multiple Individual Concerns into Group Consensus

The crucial need, in institutions of higher learning, for an understanding of empathy and hidden agendas, taken together with the pressing everyday concerns of resource allocation, curriculum, priorities, and value choices, inevitably creates the organizational imperative that a series of open forums be provided in which multiple and potentially conflicting perspectives can be brought together. Often such a forum can be provided in the committee structure of the faculty and administration or in the more general gatherings of the entire faculty and/or staff. The latter, of course, could easily be ineffective if the proponents of apparently incompatible positions had not come together first for both informal and formal exchanges in smaller, more supportive settings.

Current examples of the kinds of issues on which there may be conflicting policies might include the following: continuation or alteration of tenure policies in a period of retrenchment and extended retirement ages; relative balance of general education requirements and the need for concentrations of study within a major academic discipline; the extent and style of special curricula in areas like women's studies, international studies, or minority studies; or the expectations for mastery of new skills in computer sciences. With regard to the latter, for instance, the utility of such skills in mathematics and the sciences may seem a deviation of purpose for persons concerned with literature and the arts. Others may seize the opportunity to talk about social policy implications and the ethical issues related to computers. Still others may wish to deal with "literacy" issues in the direct application of skills, or even with the implications of computer problem-solving analogs of human intelligence. The point is that genuine interest in differing perspectives calls for a climate of sensitivity to individual concerns and the gradual formulation of a perspective that will unite these concerns in an operating consensus.

The earlier example of the budget meeting illustrated an instutionalized forum that *anticipated* debate over budget allocations—not just at the beginning of the fiscal year but throughout it. The committee also anticipated changing contingencies of program that might call for budget readjustment. Most of all, it anticipated that some departments might resent having to "hold the line" on budget control while others might be expanding operations and increasing costs. Having a place where both the facts and the feelings could be discussed, and discussed before simmering for months, was essential in congealing a unified and reasonable perspective on the level of need for the alumni programs in question.

The *countervailing principle* in this case must be *discretion and parsimony in the proliferation of committees*. An institution cannot have mediating committees in every area of potentially divergent opinion. On many issues a simple administrative relationship may provide the necessary sounding board or mechanism for requesting reconsideration. Careful organizational decisions need to be made about the key areas in which broadly based judgments must be welded into an operational policy. Most typically these areas are personnel and resource distribution, long-range goals and programs, and curriculum design and marketing.

10. Faithfulness to Individual Value Sensitivities

Beneath the specific issues of curriculum, degree requirements, organizational structure, athletic and artistic participation, there is a level of personal concern with the sometimes ineffable, but profoundly meaningful, value commitments that guide both individual lifestyles and a broader sense of mission in the institution. Such value commitments may have relatively universal components, as for example: candor, honesty, fidelity to promises, respect for individuals, justice and fair treatment for all within the community. But there may also be particular value concerns of some whose orientations are rooted in philosophical or religious traditions less common to the mainstream of the institution, and perhaps even idiosyncratic.

While it is in some ways desirable that a meeting of minds emerge within an institution at this level of fundamental values, the *countervailing concern* must be a *respect for pluralism* within the culture generally and within institutions in particular. Such respect for pluralism, however, is made possible only by a deeper, shared concern with the basic integrity of individual human rights and with a dedication to their just protection. Dedication to free inquiry and to respect for individual differences may be rooted in beliefs that are more transcendent and universal. This sense of universality could also extend to a more humble awareness of the structures of time and of meaningfulness that go well beyond the particularity of one's own life or institution. Such an affirmation will differ in its exact interpretation with the religious and philosophical sensibilities of people in various institutions. My point is not that such meanings or interpretations are the same or should be the same for people within an institution, but rather that such matters be taken seriously and dealt with respectfully by administrators seeking to understand the profound reaches of value commitments, for values deeply held always have a bearing on matters of education and human worth so essential to the central task of higher education.

CONCLUSION

This set of 10 principles is intended as a cluster of guidelines for administrative work based on the person-centered model in higher education. Within contemporary discussions of organizational theory these principles tend to be more compatible with "type B" or "Theory Z" institutional styles (McQuillen, 1982). They emphasize collegial or democratically organized structures rather than pyramidal or hierarchically organized models. In my own experience these principles grow directly from central convictions within person-centered theory as it has been applied in psychotherapy and in teaching. They are also a natural extension of my work with two Quaker colleges, Earlham College and Guilford College, where the value structure as well as the historical traditions support a thoroughly consensual style of governance. Such experiences, of course, leave me with the vivid assurance that such principles are important not only theoretically but in the practical organization of lively, inventive, and high-quality educational institutions. This is not to say that such principles are easy to put into practice. I have tried to express some of the ambiguity by indicating those countervailing concerns that call for creative and judicious discrimination. It is in the creative handling of such ambiguity that the finest quality of educational administration may emerge (Cohen & March, 1974).

Finally, a person-centered approach has two levels of meaning. On *one level*, the level given most attention in this essay, are those structural elements that ensure attention to personal needs throughout an institution by allowing a "coming together" within a gathered community where shared goals and operating procedures are clear. On the *second level* are the immediate and individual interactions with people in the moment-to-moment exchanges of daily life. I believe that it is finally within these small exchanges, multiplied a hundred times, that the style of person-centered administration is ultimately established. For it is in the quality of compassion, understanding, openness, and integrity experienced directly in the leadership style of an administrator or a faculty member that the worth and satisfaction of such a perspective is vividly fulfilled.

NOTES

1. I would draw to the readers' attention several important volumes on academic administration. Richard Quay (1976), who published *Research in Higher Education: A Guide to Source Bibliographies*, has noted that there are some 9,000 bibliographic references to administrative issues in higher education. The following citations include some that the reader may find significant and contemporary: Balderston, 1974; Carnegie Commission on Higher Education,

1973; Carnegie Council on Policy Studies in Higher Education, 1980; Corson, 1975; Grant & Riesman, 1978; Kerr, 1982; Mayhew, 1978; Millett, 1978; and Walker, 1979.

2. Some therapists who have taken such positions are John Shlien at Harvard, Laura Rice at York, Samuel Banks at Dickensen, and myself at Guilford.

3. Madeline Green (1982), Director of the Center for Leadership Development at the American Council on Education, has developed this idea further in an illuminating way, especially as it pertains to individuals emerging from a tradition of solo scholarship and teaching into positions of leadership in higher education.

17 The Personal Meaning of Illness: Client-Centered Dimensions of Medicine and Health Care

David Barnard

Since the early 1960s some major shifts have occurred in the relations between health professionals and the lay public. Medical practice and health policy, long assumed to be the province of professional experts, have become the focus of public scrutiny and—to an unprecedented degree—public decision-making. Through the influence of third-party payors, physicians' clinical judgments have been affected by demands for economic accountability. Through legislative action and judicial review, medical research and day-to-day practice have been subjected to strict standards of informed consent and patient participation. "Patients rights" movements have affected hospital policies regarding accessibility of the medical record, information about alternatives to recommended therapy, and the patient's right to refuse even life-saving medical treatment. The concerns of women and minorities about sensitively delivered, knowledgeable care have led to the emergence of health organizations, clinics, and advocacy groups both inside and outside the official medical care system.

In addition to these social and political shifts, there have begun to emerge a number of conceptual changes as well. The way physicians and other health professionals view disease—and the person *with* the disease—has come under strong criticism, with implications for a more genuinely person-centered approach to illness and its medical treatment. This chapter will draw together various strands of this critique which converge in an emphasis on *the personal meaning of illness in the life of the individual.* It will delineate an emerging unified perspective within medicine on the nature of human illness and the goals of medical care. Central to this perspective are attitudes toward the doctor-patient relationship and the shape of the clinical encounter that embody several dimensions of a client-centered approach.

The common starting point for many critiques of medical practice and its dominant concepts is dissatisfaction with what has come to be known as "the biomedical model." This model assumes a direct (even though frequently masked) correspondence between a person's subjective distress and underlying physiochemical bodily changes. From this perspective, the task of medical treatment is to translate the patient's subjective language of distress into the corresponding physical pathology, thus opening the way for appropriate intervention to return the physiochemical properties of the body to their premorbid state. In this account, "illness" begins with the disruption in the physiochemical status of the body and ends when that status is returned to normal. The "meaning" of illness resides in the physician's categories for interpreting subjective distress in terms of underlying physiochemical conditions. These categories, when imposed on the patient's experience, lead to treatment recommendations which it is then the patient's responsibility to follow.

Many have argued that the biomedical model, when uncritically applied, carries several implications that detract from optimal medical care. First, the patient's own *explanations and attributions* concerning his or her distress are secondary in importance to the physician's, if they are even elicited or acknowledged at all. Indeed, the physician must substitute his or her explanations for the patient's as quickly as possible to ensure rational therapy.

Second, the *significance* of the patient's symptoms is determined by the physician according to the inherent seriousness of the condition and the requirements of treatment. The biomedical model directs the physician's attention to the problem of accurate diagnosis and therapy, and not to personal or cultural meanings or associations that patients may attach to their distress.

Third, because illness consists in disturbed physiochemical processes, social and cultural factors are irrelevant in identifying and treating bodily disorders. There is no room in the strict biomedical model for the *cultural patterning of illness,* in which bodily complaints may express or represent culturally appropriate forms of coping with personal or social stress.

Fourth, patients are assumed to consult the physician for the treatment of bodily complaints. In the absence of identifiable organic disease, patients' *requests and agendas in the consulting room* are considered illegitimate, and the physician does not feel compelled to address them.

Fifth, since presumably it is the physician and not the patient who understands the biomedical model and must apply it to solve the patient's problem, *expertise, power, and authority* in the doctor-patient relationship are inherently and appropriately unequal. The physician diagnoses and recommends; the patient answers questions accurately and follows advice.

Research in these five areas points to an emerging theoretical framework for a person-centered approach to everyday medical practice which addresses the following issues: (1) patients' attributions and explanatory models for interpreting their own distress; (2) the varied significance that patients attach to bodily distress and disability; (3) the cultural patterning of illness that affects the experiencing and presentation of bodily distress through complex symbolic processes; (4) patients' requests and hidden agendas that underlie visits to the medical clinic in both serious and benign ("nonsickness") situations; (5) patterns of doctor-patient interaction that contrast traditional authoritarian models with strategies for the negotiation of conflicting perceptions and values.

The concept of negotiation as an optimal strategy for medical practice is the natural outcome of emphasis on the first four issues. Each suggests the need for suspending uncritical allegiance to the biomedical model in favor of greater respect for the patient's own reality and individual experience of illness. A review of some major perspectives within each of these areas will thus lay a foundation for the client-centered attitudes and behaviors of the negotiated approach to doctor-patient interaction.

PATIENTS' ATTRIBUTIONS AND EXPLANATORY MODELS

Eisenberg construes the encounter between physician and patient as essentially a process of interpretation and the construction of meaning:

> The patient who consults a doctor because he has experienced discomfort or dysfunction seeks more than remission of his symptoms; his quest is for relief from the fears aroused by the disruption in the continuity of his accustomed self. Beset by distress, he searches

for an interpretation of the meaning of the misfortune which has befallen him. (1981, p. 239)

Patients frequently enter the physician's office with their own interpretations of what is wrong with them. These interpretations may be derived from family or cultural traditions, media dissemination of health information, or personal fears. Patients' *illness attributions* are usually directed at what is "wrong"—what the patient "has"—and what has caused the problem (its etiology) (Stoeckle & Barsky, 1981). These attributions may coincide only partially, if at all, with scientific interpretations.

In this setting, *eliciting the patient's attributions* becomes a crucial dimension of the physician's effectiveness in carrying out the "tasks of care": diagnosis and treatment, personal support, communication of information about illness, maintenance and rehabilitation of the chronically ill, and prevention and education (Stoeckle, 1979). One of the most common functions of physicians, for example, is providing reassurance that the patient's symptoms are benign and not evidence of serious disease. Such reassurance is likely to be much more effective when it addresses the patient's own interpretations, rather than simply conveying the physician's scientific views. The physician's interpretations may fail to reassure unless the patient is convinced that the physician has heard and accounted for all the patient's concerns (Sapira, 1972). "Reassurance that does not take into account the patient's assessment of the threat that he faces might serve only to mystify him and to undermine his confidence in the physician" (Mechanic, 1972).

The physician's lack of awareness of patients' explanatory models for understanding pathophysiology and etiology can complicate therapy. It can also lead to harmful assumptions about patients' ignorance or lack of cooperativeness, when, in fact, the fundamental problem is a difference in interpretive framework. Stoeckle and Barsky (1981) cite several studies to illustrate these problems of "compliance." Roth (1962) observed that some peptic ulcer patients, believing that stomach acid comes from food itself, will avoid recommended between-meal snacks and antacids. Harwood (1971) describes Puerto Rican patients' reluctance to take orange juice to supplement their potassium intake during diuretic treatment for heart failure, on the grounds that oranges upset the desirable balance between "hot" and "cold" that is central to Puerto Rican understandings of health and disease.

Pfifferling (1981) refers to the belief that the scientific interpretation of experience is reality, and that all other interpretations are inaccurate or fantastic, as "medicocentrism." Similarly, Dingwall (1976) argues that research into patient "compliance" too often places the blame for the patient's failure to follow medical advice on the supposedly ignorant or recalcitrant patient. He advocates an approach that begins with the assumption that patients are rational people, motivated by their beliefs about what constitutes reality, who make decisions about what is best for them on the basis of available information. In this view, "noncompliance" may reflect a failure of the medical system to communicate information that is acceptable, logical, and convincing from the patient's point of view. More effective communication, and therapy, depend on a process of *negotiation* that is based on the acknowledgment of the internal logic and cogency of both the scientific and lay frames of reference.

THE PERSONAL SIGNIFICANCE OF ILLNESS

Cassell (1979) distinguishes *curing* from *healing* and *disease* from *illness*. He argues that while physicians attempt to cure diseases (the physical and chemical processes that disrupt organ function) patients suffer illnesses that are the challenges to the sense of identity and meaning that often accompany physical distress: "illness" is the personal experience of disease. Thus, while the physician's concentration on physical processes may cure the disease, it may not heal the illness.

Cassell's concept of illness includes four main elements: loss of control; heightened dependency; increased sense of vulnerability; and loss of the sense of omnipotence. Loss of control may be experienced with reference to one's own body or to the medical system itself, whose procedures and institutions impose their own rules, agendas, and requirements on the patient, regardless of individual preferences. With loss of control and disability comes heightened dependency: on technical experts for knowledge and skills necessary for treatment; and on family, friends, and others for assistance in carrying on the business of life during the illness and recovery periods.

The more profound existential threats are to the sense of invulnerability and immortality. Illness is an encounter with limitation and finitude. In particular, chronic incurable conditions require major adjustments in personal identity. Patients must assimilate *the fact of imperfection,* of impairment and constraint, as much as they must adjust lifestyle or habits to incorporate palliative and rehabilitative regimens (Bergsma & Thomasma, 1982; Strauss & Glaser, 1975). Even acute conditions that are either self-limiting or responsive to medical cure can easily leave their mark as they penetrate the illusion of indestructability. This is well expressed in the conclusion to a personal account of an episode of thyroid disease:

> It was not a run-of-the mill summer: not like any I ever had before, not one I would care to repeat. What was out of the ordinary about it except a few doctor's office calls? —nothing dramatic, nothing devastating, nothing dangerous, much less fatal or life-threatening. And yet I am left with the feeling that life is no longer what it was, and that it never will be—that it was in some sense threatened, after all. There was a time not so long ago when I felt—not immortal, of course, but at least for the present invulnerable: comparatively young and strong, and inwardly scornful of those who fell behind. That confidence is now gone. Is it the beginning of age, the first day of the rest of my life, in a different sense from the usual saccharine one? What has happened to others may happen to me; I never used to believe that. (Smith, 1980, pp. 288–289)

The "healing function" of the doctor (Cassell, 1979) includes the tasks of eliciting from the patient these existential dimensions of illness, acting to restore control and autonomy, and helping the patient reconstitute a sense of wholeness and confidence in the face of infirmity or an uncertain, limited future.

Lipowski (1970) outlines a range of personal meanings that patients commonly attribute to illness: illness as challenge, as enemy, as punishment, as weakness, as relief, as strategy, as loss or damage, as value. He suggests that individual coping styles and the nature of doctor-patient relationships are significantly determined by the meaning the patient attaches to his or her experience. Thus, while a patient who perceives illness as a challenge may behave cooperatively and, from the physician's perspective, appropriately, a patient for whom illness is evidence of weakness or culpability may display unexpected anger, guilt, or passivity in the treatment relationship. Patients for whom illness has become a reliable strategy for manipulating an otherwise unresponsive social environment may frustrate physicians by an apparent unwillingness to pursue or accept health (cf. Kahana & Bibring, 1964; Pfifferling, 1981, pp. 215–218).

Another set of issues that accompany physical illness but may escape the awareness of physicians solely focused on "cure" are the social, familial, and economic problems that patients face during illness and recovery. Just as an "ecological" view of illness calls attention to the potential etiological significance of social, environmental, and interpersonal factors, this view acknowledges that a person's illness has ramifications throughout the social networks of which he or she is a part (Engel, 1980). Within the family, for example, illness can result in the rearrangement of power relationships, roles and responsibilities, and attention. Economic security and social status can be threatened for the family as a whole (Katon & Kleinman, 1981; Litman, 1979). A regimen that, from the physician's point of view, is a straightforward and routine approach to disease management, may present to the patient intimidating and seemingly insoluble social and interpersonal dilemmas. Failure to attend to these may result in added anxiety and anguish for the patient, or outright resistance to "rational" medical treatment (Barnard, 1980, Chapter 1).

THE CULTURAL PATTERNING OF ILLNESS

It was suggested above that discrepancies between patients' and professionals' explanatory models can complicate therapy. The following case illustrates this process in a way that emphasizes the role of *cultural differences*.

A 26-year-old Guatemalan woman who had resided in the U.S. for 10 years and who was being treated for severe regional enteritis with intravenous hyperalimentation and restriction of oral intake had become angry, withdrawn, and uncooperative. She believed her problem to be caused by the witchcraft of her fiance's sister. She also believed that because she was no longer receiving food by mouth, and especially because she could no longer regulate her hot/cold balance of nutrients, the basis of the traditional health beliefs of the folk medical system she grew up in, she had been written off by her doctors as unlikely to live. Her behavior followed directly from this mistaken belief. She was unable to talk about her ideas because of her fear of ridicule, and her doctors were totally unaware of this problem except as manifested in her difficult behavior. When the psychiatric consultant encouraged the patient to express her own ideas about the illness, she was visibly relieved to find her ideas treated with respect, although the doctor indicated he did not share them. Her hostile and withdrawn behavior disappeared and she cooperated with the treatment regimen when she was reassured that the doctors had not given up on her. (Kleinman, Eisenberg, & Good, 1978, pp. 254–255)

Culture and ethnicity have been found to affect a wide range of health behaviors (Harwood, 1981). Recent cross-cultural and anthropological research has emphasized what Kleinman, Eisenberg, and Good (1978) call "the cultural construction of clinical reality." Good and Good suggest that "A meaning-centered or interpretive medical anthropology approaches sickness not as a reflection or causal product of somatic processes but as a meaningful human reality" (1981, p. 174).

In this perspective, the human experience of illness is shaped by cognitive categories and social behavior sanctioned by particular cultures. Categories available to sufferers and healers for handling disease will reflect dominant or socially acceptable forms of thinking and ways of viewing reality. The encounter between sufferer and healer is thus culturally conditioned, and the effectiveness of therapy is in large part the result of the congruence between the healer's language for naming distress and the sufferer's expectations (Fabrega, 1974; Frank, 1973; Kleinman, 1973, 1980).

Kleinman (1980) presents data from the Chinese culture that indicate that numerous physical sensations—including dizziness, faintness, general weakness, insomnia—are presented to physicians as specific disease entities requiring treatment. When asked if emotional factors may be involved in the onset of these symptoms, patients usually deny this emphatically. In fact, Kleinman argues, mental illness is stigmatized in Chinese culture. Somatic complaints, on the other hand, are culturally acceptable forms of help-seeking at times of personal or social stress. Similarly, Good (1977) reports that Iranian patients frequently report heart palpitations to physicians. These complaints are seen to be expressions of a complex network of personal and social meanings that may include loss and grief, anxieties about old age, and family conflict.

These data reinforce the idea that the physician functions as an interpreter (Eisenberg, 1981). It is misleading, however, to assume that the only form this interpretation takes is the translation of the patient's subjective language of distress into the biophysical processes that are presumed to account for the patient's experience—a process of "decoding" the patient's language, substituting for it a picture of the "somatic referents of a patient's discourse" (Good & Good, 1981). Rather, an essential aspect of this interpretation is the appreciation of the personal, cultural, and social meanings that are carried by particular forms of distress when they are presented to a healer in particular life contexts. Good and Good conclude:

> An important part of the data interpreted by the clinician consists of reports by patients of their experiences of sickness. The patient's experience does not reflect simply underlying biochemical or psychophysiological processes. Consciousness of suffering is meaningful; all symptoms have personal significance and are inherently "culturally patterned." Thus the clinician is not merely engaged in the interpretation of objective data; all clinical practice involves the understanding and translation of subjective realities. (1981, pp. 177–178)

PATIENTS' REQUESTS AND HIDDEN AGENDAS

The proportion of patients presenting themselves to ambulatory medical services who are without serious physical disorders has been estimated to be from 68 percent to 92 percent. Moreover, the most common diagnosis made in general practice is "nonsickness." Reflecting on these data, Barsky observes,

> When...symptoms are mild, chronic, and common...other non-biomedical factors influence the decision to visit a doctor; thus many patients come seeking something other than palliation or cure of physical disease. Other factors motivate them, and the clinical encounter becomes more intelligible if the physician can diagnose these other reasons for coming. (1981, p. 492)

Barksy suggests four principal nonbiomedical agendas that account for these contacts with the medical system: concurrent life stress, psychiatric disorder, social isolation, and the need for information. A common thread is the role of the physician as a source of social contact and interpersonal support. Emphasis on physical complaints may be the opening gambit in a visit to the clinic, because that is presumed to legitimate the physician's time and attention. The real purpose of the visit, however, may be unrelated to the symptom that is presented.

Bereavement, conflicts in the family, or job-related stress are common background situations that may be elicited during the medical interview.

Similarly, as noted in a previous section, physicians may serve a crucial reassuring function by correcting patients' misattributions of benign or mild symptoms to serious causes. Thus providing accurate information may be the most important transaction in many medical encounters.

The correct diagnosis of the presence or absence of organic pathology and the institution of appropriate therapy may meet only a part of the patient's agenda in these interactions. Unsatisfied needs for reassurance, consolation, sympathy, or information may result in "doctor-shopping," repeat visits for mild or asymptomatic conditions, or the presentation of a string of complaints with no apparent organic basis (Balint, 1964). The pejorative labels "hypochondriac" or "crock" may be attached to such patients as physicians become frustrated at having to deal with problems of living that fall outside the strictly biomedical domain (Barsky & Klerman, 1983).

Though most studies of patients' hidden agendas in medical encounters emphasize psychological factors, another significant factor is more religious or philosophical: the patient's efforts at *the construction of meaning*. The construction of meaning may be defined as the process of imagining and maintaining dependable structures of order and significance in life—structures that endow particular actions, ideas, or motivations with value and constitute the basis for continued human striving. The process of meaning construction is one in which people are engaged at all times, with varying degrees of conscious awareness. As such, it is an activity that people bring with them into their encounters with the medical system. On the one hand, illness is an event that often severely challenges current life meanings or interpretations of reality, provoking a process of reinterpretation and a search for new meanings (or, conversely, a tenacious clinging to familiar—though outmoded—old meanings). On the other hand, the construction of meaning is an ongoing process that proceeds independently of illness experiences and is thus a background dimension to all medical interactions, whether they directly concern serious illness or not.

In this perspective, physicians encounter their patients in the midst of the ongoing stream of life, and part of what transpires in the doctor's office is that patients renew their energies, hopes, and courage for the tasks of living. Physicians are in a position to communicate recognition, respect, and solidarity with the patient in his or her engagement with life. And through the tasks of listening, supporting, and educating, physicians can assist patients in building a picture of their world that is compatible with continuing human effort. Whether conceptualized in primarily psychological or religiophilosophical terms, these aspects of medical practice lend weight and importance to many nonbiomedical agendas in the consulting room.

NEGOTIATION AND THE CLIENT-CENTERED ASPECTS OF MEDICAL PRACTICE

In their discussion of "clinical social science" as a component of the physicians's approach to patient care, Katon and Kleinman make the following comment on resolving conflicts in the doctor-patient relationship:

> The physician skill required is the ability to negotiate between differing perceptions of illness, goals of treatment, and conflicts. The objective is neither to dominate patients nor convert them to the physician's value orientation, but to enlist the patient as a therapeutic ally and provide care for problems patients regard as important in ways patients desire. That is to say, these clinical social science interventions aim at making care less doctor-centered and more patient-centered. Crucial to this shift in the structure of clinical relationships is recognition that clinical care should involve a genuine negotiation between physician and patient. (1981, p. 262)

Lazare, Eisenthal, Frank, and Stoeckle observe:

> The optimal goal of negotiation is to resolve conflict so that the clinician feels that he has done what he believes to be professionally appropriate while the patient feels he has received that which is in his best physical and psychological interest. Compromises are acceptable so long as they still provide enough satisfaction to make the relationship worthwhile and do not breach professional standards. (1978, p. 127)

The concepts of *negotiation* and *compromise* in the doctor-patient relationship run counter to the model that asssumes the physician's unilateral exercise of authority and expertise. The latter view, in fact, is consistent with strict adherence to the biomedical model, in which the physician defines both the relevance and significance of the patient's experiences of distress. The preceding sections have attempted to suggest some limitations to the strict biomedical model. These include obstacles to the formation of a therapeutic alliance between physician and patient; ignorance of the frame of reference within which a patient is likely to interpret and evaluate medical explanations and advice; misunderstanding and misdiagnosis of psychologically and culturally influenced forms of illness behavior; and inattention to central but frequently masked motivations for patients' contacts with the medical system.

Katon and Kleinman (1981) present a model for clinical negotiation that attempts to avoid these obstacles. Their model comprises the following principal elements: the physician's elicitation of the patient's attributions, explanatory models, and illness problems; the physician's offering of professional interpretation of the patient's situation; the physician's invitation to the patient to respond to the professional view from the patient's perspective; and, finally, efforts to reconcile differences, in some cases through the patient adjusting to the physician's view and, in other cases, the physician adjusting explanations or recommendations to take greater account of the patient's perspective. In cases of serious and lasting conflict, Katon and Kleinman recommend that the physician strongly advocate a course of action with the added reminder that the ultimate decision rests with the patient. Referral to another physician remains a final option if conflict is irresolvable.

The clinical negotiation model thus emerges from and synthesizes a response to the various aspects of medical practice that have been discussed in preceding sections. The model also embodies several presuppositions and commitments that are central to the *client-centered* approach to helping relationships (Rogers, 1951, 1961). This essay will conclude by mentioning these under three headings: (1) interpersonal process, (2) attitudes toward professional authority, and (3) a view of healing.

1. The key interpersonal factor in the negotiation model is *empathy.* (For an eloquent description of empathy as an element of healing relationships, see Rogers, 1961, p. 53.) Again, Katon and Kleinman provide a succinct formulation:

> In order to carry out a negotiation the fundamental characteristics of
> an effective doctor-patient relationship are essential. These include
> setting up and establishing a milieu that is warm and accepting and in

which the patient can express troublesome feelings. Perhaps the central feature of this milieu is physician empathy. Indeed, we regard empathy as so crucial to the negotiation model that it is unlikely that the elicitation of the patient's model and subsequent negotiation is possible without an affective bond between doctor and patient. We also believe that the negotiation model itself (by validating the importance of the patient's feelings and beliefs) will function to increase affective bonds between doctor and patient. (1981, p. 266)

Empathy, warmth, and acceptance facilitate the patient's expression of personal, subjective realities by removing the fear of ridicule or denigration by the physician. Thus, in addition to the support and reassurance that empathy can provide to the patient directly, it encourages disclosure of data that the physician needs in order to formulate an accurate, person- and culture-sensitive impression of the patient's true beliefs, expectations, and needs.

2.   A second client-centered feature of the negotiation model is its implied attitude toward professional authority. In order to encourage patients to reveal their own explanatory models, physicians must suspend their automatic, unequivocal allegiance to the scientific, technical categories of the biomedical model. It is crucial that patients not conclude that they are being humored or that the physician listens to their beliefs only as a prelude to smothering them beneath categories and interpretations that are seen as the only "true" or relevant ones. This is the force behind the principle of genuinely appreciating the logic, cogency, and integrity of the patient's model. As Katon and Kleinman, and Lazare and his colleagues observe, physicians remain ethically bound not to breach their own professional standards. Yet, to take the findings and perspectives of clinical social science seriously is to recognize that a truly scientific—as opposed to "scientistic"—medical practice will attend carefully to the personal and cultural variability of the presentation of distress and to the wide range of options for construing and treating illness within a culturally determined medical system (Engel, 1977; Kleinman, Eisenberg, & Good, 1978; Stoeckle, 1979).

The negotiation model is consistent with what Szasz and Hollender (1956) call the "mutual participation model" of the doctor-patient relationship. "Mutual participation" stresses a relationship between two autonomous, rational adults collaborating in pursuit of a common goal—the patient's improved health and well-being. It minimizes the hierarchical distancing and asymmetry of the professional-client relationship, emphasizing instead the positive strengths and autonomy of the client that complement the special expertise and dedication to service of the professional. Szasz and Hollender contrast this model with the "activity-passivity model," in which all power and initiative rest with the physician and the patient's desires and perceptions are either absent or irrelevant, and the "guidance-cooperation model," in which the physician-expert dispenses advice and treatment and the patient dutifully obeys.

From the perspective of the client-centered approach both the negotiation and "mutual participation" models safeguard autonomy and minimize dependency in the healing process. The locus of healing remains within the client-patient and his or her resources and energies, rather than shifting to the expert's esoteric knowledge and technique. Carl Rogers repeatedly warns against this shift in his elaboration of client-centered therapy. His comments on the relative value of psychological diagnosis to the therapeutic process are both typical and instructive:

> Our experience has led to the tentative conclusion that a diagnosis of the psychological dynamics is not only unnecessary but in some ways detrimental or unwise.... In the first place, the very process of psychological diagnosis places the locus of evaluation so definitely in the expert that it may increase any dependent tendencies in the client, and cause him to feel that the responsibility for understanding and improving his situation lies in the hands of another. When the client perceives the locus of judgment and responsibility as clearly resting in the hands of the clinician, he is, in our judgment, further from therapeutic progress than when he came in. (1951, p. 223)

3. These aspects of the negotiation model are related to a fundamental view of the healing process. The model embodies the client-centered hypothesis that persons themselves possess decisive healing resources (Rogers, 1951, esp. Chapter 2). In the medical context, patients possess a positive potential for growth and health. Medical interventions and knowledge, in this perspective, are only one among many determinants of personal health. A major role of the physician is to assist the patient to reclaim or renew his or her own strengths and tendencies toward growth. In certain circumstances this may entail the application of technical modes of healing. In all cases, however, it will require the effort of helping the patient to clarify personal needs and

goals, and to select, with the help of the physician, plans and actions consistent with and supportive of personal values.

The negotiation model cultivates the subjective realities of the patient and bases healing on the affective bond between doctor and patient. It thus asserts that healing is essentially a *personal* rather than a *technical* process (cf. Cassell, 1979). Technique and the categories of biomedical analysis are applied only in the context of personal understanding. This is a different view from the claim that biomedical categories refer to universal, immutable entities that exist apart from personality or culture and that technical healing processes function independently of the subjective realities of sufferer or healer. To construe healing as essentially personal does not eliminate technical interventions or scientific understanding. Rather, it locates them within the broader, richer context of illness as a *meaningful human reality* (Good & Good, 1981). Moreover, emphasis on healing as personal rather than technical upholds the personhood of the physician as well as that of the patient.

Robert C. Fuller

One of the most receptive audiences for client-centered therapy has been the field of pastoral counseling and pastoral theology. And for good reason. For not only did Rogers's work chronologically dovetail with the emergence of the pastoral counseling movement, it also resonated almost perfectly with the deeper intellectual and cultural forces that have shaped the "therapeutic" thrust of much of American Protestant thought over the past 40 years. A critical overview of Rogers's influence upon American religious thought and practice would appear to be central to any understanding of the wider applications of client-centered principles. Such a review is important because, in the first place, it will clarify some of the deeper philosophical and metaphysical assumptions embedded in the client-centered approach to psychotherapy. And, second, it will also help focus attention upon the extent to which Rogers's writings contain important theological implications that have, for the most part, eluded those professionally committed to the task of spiritual care and guidance.

EMERGENCE OF THE PASTORAL COUNSELING MOVEMENT

Pastoral guidance and counseling activities are the practical or concrete expression of pastoral theology. It should be noted that pastoral theology is concerned with the nature and tasks of the ministry and therefore is distinct from dogmatic or fundamental theology. Pastoral theology represents the attempt to build upon the foundations of fundamental theology in such a way as to articulate the rationale and methods by which pastors might assist persons in handling the crises and conflicts that arise in the developmental, interpersonal, and existential dimensions of human life. Throughout the history of Christianity, the activities that comprise the religious "cure of souls" have assumed many forms (Clebsch & Jaekle, 1975; McNeil, 1951). Exorcism, devil-craft, annointing, and confession would be but a few of the techniques employed by those entrusted with the healing and guiding of their religious constituencies.

Since World War II, however, pastoral theology has become almost exclusively concerned with both the theory and application of counseling psychology. The reasons for the surging popularity of pastoral counseling in the past several decades are not difficult to ascertain. Modernizing forces such as urbanization and industrialization thrust individuals back upon their inner resources and in so doing fostered the emergence of academic psychology and encouraged the "privatization" of spiritual life (Berger, 1967; Mannheim, 1968). The increasingly complex and pluralistic character of modern American society has also made it difficult for church spokesmen to confidently identify the Christian message with any one social, political, or economic cause. Hence, much of the enthusiasm that progressively minded theological movements such as the Social Gospel had generated for establishing a "practical ministry" has been forced to seek new channels of expression. At the same time, the 1930s and 1940s produced a theological climate that encouraged attempts to seek rapprochement with the so-called "secular" academic disciplines. It was, in fact, a principal objective of both the liberal and neo-orthodox theologies that dominated university and seminary thinking between 1920 and 1960 to create a dialogue between the theological and secular perspectives concerning man's estranged condition. Whatever their differences, liberal and neo-orthodox theologians agreed that the root cause of mankind's broken condition was not so much specific behavioral "sin" as it was a more general orientation to life that is not clearly grounded upon the ultimate source of authentic life. It was natural, then, that their solutions to this estrangement placed primary emphasis upon the individual, the private, the psychological.

Thus, by the late 1940s, both the social and theological environments had become especially conducive to identifying psychological counseling as a necessary ingredient in a relevant ministry. Faced with the urgent task of finding new ways for meeting the needs of troubled persons, seminaries began to give explicit attention to pastoral education in the field of counseling psychology. The University of Chicago, Garrett Theological Seminary, Iliff School of Theology, Andover Newton, and the Southern Baptist Theological Seminary were among the leaders in equipping their students with practical skills garnered from the burgeoning field of psychotherapy. Not surprisingly, by the 1950s a vast array of literature had already emerged to give the pastoral counseling movement focus and a common core of commitments.

PASTORAL COUNSELING'S APPROPRIATION OF ROGERS

Seward Hiltner's *Pastoral Counseling* (1949) and *Preface to Pastoral Theology* (1958) placed him at the forefront of those seeking to articulate the theological rationale for pastoral counseling activities. According to Hiltner, pastoral theology should be concerned with giving substantive direction to the three main tasks or functions of Christian "shepherding": healing, sustaining, and guiding. Hiltner reasoned that, given "the peculiarly psychological intellectual climate of our time," pastoral theology must formally draw upon the theory and methods of scientific psychotherapy in defining its objective (1958, p. 26). He passionately argued that the single most important lesson that psychotherapy had to teach pastors about their counseling responsibilities was that lecturing individuals about morality abets, rather than assuages, mental and emotional difficulties. Hiltner insisted that "counseling involves clarification on ethical issues, but not coercion" (1949, p. 22). That is, the pastor must come to grips with the psychological discovery that personal and moral growth cannot be commanded from without, but must rather emerge from the patient's inner capacities for responsible living.

> Guiding, if it is part of shepherding, is eductive in character—that is, it "leads out" something that can be regarded as either within the person or potentially available to him (through resources other than our own selves). (Hiltner, 1958, p. 151)

Hiltner further explained that, "As I use the word 'eductive' to give a thumbnail description of my approach, I believe it to be in the same general direction as Rogers's 'nondirective' or client-centered' approach" (1949, p. 255). Indeed, Hiltner time and again cited Rogers at critical junctures in his argument that pastoral counseling should suppress the tendency to give moralistic advice and instead focus on the client's inner frame of reference so as to strengthen his or her natural sense of moral direction.

> Does this mean that pastoral guiding is nondirective and client-centered? In the sense of the purpose for which these terms were coined by Carl R. Rogers, the answer is YES. (Hiltner, 1958, p. 154)

Hiltner's predilection toward client-centered principles was grounded in his commitment to the process theology or metaphysics found in the writings of Alfred North Whitehead and Charles Hartshorne. As a "fundamental theology," process thought helped reduce notions of the spiritual forces that "transcend" human experience to categories of both theological and psychological immanence. Process theology articulates what is often called a panentheistic view of the world in which God is conceptualized as an immanent spiritual energy that propels an evolving universe toward the realization of its inner potentials or possibilities. As such, God is potentially present and active within each and every moment of experience as that directional force urging each entity or "occasion" of life toward the fulfillment of its unique potentials.

The theoretical categories of process thought prompted theologians such as Hiltner to equate pastoral theology with the attempt to align individuals with an immanent spiritual force. Putting estranged individuals back into touch or harmony with this progressive life-tendency requires methods that open persons up to a more complete experience of their inner natures. What is more, process thought made it unnecessary for the pastoral counselor to make any hard and fast distinction between psychological (originating within the personal center) and theological (emanating from beyond the personal center) perspectives of God's presence in human experience. Indeed, psychological factors that increase our sensitivity to prerational levels of experience could be considered necessary and even sufficient causes for realigning individuals with an immanent divinity. Rogers's articulation of such psychological concepts as "organismic valuing process," the "self-actualizing tendency," and the therapeutic value of "unconditional positive regard" obviously fits closely with Hiltner's process thought.

Hiltner was hardly alone in his recognition that modern psychotherapy had a great deal to contribute to Christian understandings of human authenticity (Outler, 1954; Roberts, 1950). Caroll A. Wise, first in his *Pastoral Counseling* and later in *Pastoral Psychotherapy*, argued that "any movement which professes goals so closely related to religion as psychotherapy, and aims at the increase of the quality of human existence, cannot be avoided by the pastor" (1980, p. ix). Interestingly, Wise believed that his point of view was not so much derived from Rogers as it was a simultaneous and parallel development.

> There is a similarity between the approach of Rogers and that presented in this book. However, the main lines and development were laid down long before the appearance of Rogers' work, and were influenced largely by psychologists who were psychoanalytically oriented. (Wise, 1951, p. 205)

Whether the influence was direct or mediated through a certain *Zeitgeist* in liberal Protestant thought, Wise's appropriation of "psychoanalytically oriented" insights for the purpose of pastoral counseling had an unmistakably Rogerian character. "The role of the pastor," he wrote, "is not to be defined primarily in areas of beliefs or morals or social action as some do. Persons, their growth, enhancement, creativity, and fulfillment are the fundamental concern" (1980, p. x).

The nondirective or client-centered approach to pastoral counseling advocated by Hiltner, Wise, and others proved to be eminently congenial to the burgeoning field. By the mid-1960s Rogers's work had, according to historians William Clebsch and Charles Jaekle, "exerted an almost normative influence upon pastoral counseling in American Protestant circles" (Clebsch & Jaekle, 1975, p. 9; see also Oates, 1962, pp. 13, 44). There are, moreover, clearly identifiable reasons for this ready assimilation of Rogerian thought as opposed to other psychotherapeutic models. First of all, client-centered therapy requires considerably less formal training than other psychotherapeutic models such as, for instance, psychoanalysis (Hall & Lindzey, 1970, p. 524). It can, therefore, be more easily introduced to seminary students and even full-time ministers whose schedules do not permit extensive psychological training. Secondly, Rogers's writings employ less jargon and are thus more accessible to a general reading audience. And, more importantly, the Rogerian perspective is decidedly nonreductionist and thus permits readers to graft the tenets of client-centered therapy onto a variety of philosophical or theological interpretations of the nature and meaning of human fulfillment.

Among the first to correlate Rogers's writing with specific ontological and theological positions were Thomas Oden and Don Browning. Their works were expressions of a theological climate inspired by Paul Tillich's method of establishing a "correlation" between secular analyses of the human condition and theological symbols as well as the highly influential "Chicago school," which insisted upon "doing" theology in an empiricist, inductive manner. Tillich had, for example, written extensively concerning the ability of psychology to substantially inform theological discussions of man's spiritual life. In an article entitled "The Impact of Pastoral Psychology on Theological Thought," Tillich observed that "the general and rather empty notion of the divine Spirit must be filled with concrete material taken from man's existence under many dimensions and in many realms of life" (Tillich, 1960, p. 19). Similarly, Daniel Day Williams of the University of Chicago noted that Rogers's work shed important light on the "personal channel of grace" and illuminated the "universal elements in our experience" (Williams, 1961, p. 59).

Browning's exploration of the relationship between psychological theory and theology was more systematic than either Tillich's or Williams's. In a volume entitled *Atonement and Psychotherapy* (1966) he argued that Rogerian theory provides useful conceptual tools with which the contemporary theologian might describe the Christian message of salvation. Steeped in the Chicago school of empirical theology as well as the categories of process thought, Browning expounded Rogers's writings in such a way as to show how they help us to understand the way in which God's atoning nature is mediated to, and received by, human awareness. He contended that there is a fundamental proportionality "between any finite healing-producing structure and God's infinite healing activity" (p. 94). It follows that Rogers's description of psychological processes such as "organismic valuing" and "innate actualizing tendencies" can, by analogy, help clarify theological language concerning man's intended nature; descriptions of "disturbed functioning" and "experience denied to awareness" give vivid testimony to our estranged condition; and knowledge concerning the necessary and sufficient role of empathy and "unconditional positive regard" in fostering personality growth helps clarify the ontological structures of divine acceptance.

Browning also believed that client-centered therapy invited theological interpretation. Its methods and techniques presuppose an ontology that is never fully articulated in Rogers's writings. According to Browning "the client's acceptance in therapy is predicated upon an ontological acceptance that transcends the therapeutic situation to which the therapist's acceptance witnesses" (p. 149). Similarly, the very possibility of providing unconditional acceptance, let alone its integral role in producing human wholeness, would seem to presuppose the existence of "a prior or *a priori* ground with reference to which the client is actually ontologically accepted" (p. 153). At a deeper level of analysis, then, client-centered therapy could be argued to be the anthropological correlate or expression of the Christian scheme of salvation.

Oden, too, believed that there is a religious dimension to Rogerian psychotherapy. He explained that "if we mean by theology a deliberate and systematic attempt to speak self-consistently of man's predicament, redemption, and authenticity, then the therapeutic work of Carl Rogers has deep theological concerns, even though he has little to say formally about God" (1966, p. 83). Oden further contended that Rogers's description of man's self-actualizing tendencies, the role of introjected values in disturbing the organism's innate valuing process, and the freeing quality of unconditional acceptance represented a secular witness to the Christian message. Oden's central point was that an "adequate theory of therapy must not only understand therapeutic growth as a product of human self-disclosure, but authentic human self-disclosure as a response to the self-disclosure of God in being itself" (p. 43). Arguing in a syllogistic fashion, Oden observed that

> (a) If, in order to be effective, psychotherapy must mediate an accepting reality which is grounded in being itself; (b) if the accepting reality in being itself has disclosed itself in an event to which the Christian proclamation explicitly witnesses; then (c) the implicit ontological assumption of all effective psychotherapy is made explicit in the Christian proclamation. (Oden, 1966, p. 24)

Oden's syllogism, of course, belies his firm commitment to a theological position in which divine revelation supervenes the kinds of insights discerned by Rogers and other humanistically inclined thinkers. Whereas Hiltner and Browning had turned to Rogers for the actual substance of their theological reflections, Oden was methodologically bound to restrict Rogers's insights to a penultimate status. Since Rogers failed to understand the vast extent to which man's brokenness can ultimately be attributed to his disobedience to God's will, his thought was ultimately fated to fall short of fully redeeming human nature or restraining our errant tendencies. In short, Rogers's view of the "saving" process was theologically ill-suited to the task of reconciling persons either to God or to the moral structures of responsible human community.

TENSIONS BETWEEN THEOLOGICAL AND CLIENT-CENTERED VIEWS OF GUIDANCE

Oden's theological criticisms of Rogerian thought testify to the uneasy alliance between the aims and methods of humanistic psychology and those of the ministry. The pastoral counselor, in adopting the strategies of client-centered therapy, risked blurring his or her distinct identity as a representative of the Christian church. Particularly troublesome was the extent to which psychology is itself antithetical to the wider concerns of pastoral theology. After all, how can a theoretical outlook inherently skewed to the personal, existential, and nonjudgmental not help but undermine the larger religious community whose very existence is predicated upon the experience of the transcendent, the universal, and the morally righteous? And, furthermore, to what extent can a pastoral counselor methodologically bracket any concern with the existence or relevance of an extra-mundane reality and still be considered to be offering religious guidance? As Clebsch and Jaekle noted in their review of contemporary pastoral care,

> [Modern] men and women have increasingly viewed personal problems and decisions in ways which do not reflect or derive from traditional Christian notions of life and action. Increasingly the proximate concerns of prudence rather than the ultimate concern of salvation have set the context for ethical decision. This circumstance has raised important questions of identity for the pastoral function of guiding. When men understand themselves in an intramundane context, traditional forms of pastoral guidance seem almost always irrelevant, often oppressive, and at best quaint. (Clebsch & Jaekle, 1975, p. 56)

Clebsch and Jaekle, while recognizing that Christian pastoral care has always availed itself of the psychology of its particular epoch, point out that secular models of healing and guidance must be selectively appropriated so as not to detract from the churches' primary function of addressing human difficulties "in the context of ultimate meanings and concerns" (pp. 68, 4). The danger is that the church would become co-opted by the prevailing intellectual climate and thereby lose sight of any transcendent perspective from which to interpret human existence. The exclusive use of client-centered or "eductive" counseling techniques would, for example, appear to be a complete abdication of responsibility for confronting persons with the demands of moral and spiritual existence. A further concern, pointedly raised by Kenneth Leech in his highy respected *Soul Friend: The Practice of Christian Spirituality* (1980), is that nondirective approaches to pastoral care and guidance ultimately lead to the impoverishment of the sacramental, mystical, and contemplative elements of Christian spirituality. The utterly optimistic view of human nature upon which Rogers's theory rests is, in Leech's opinion, inconducive to fostering attitudes that orient individuals to look beyond themselves in their search for meaningful existence. From the standpoint of Christian spirituality, pastoral care requires a psychological model that will directly link the quest for personal fulfillment with the quest for establishing interior harmony with God.

Howard J. Clinebell typified the more cautious appropriation of client-centered principles by the pastoral counseling movement as it began to mature and become a more integral part of seminary education during the late 1960s. His *Basic Types of Pastoral Counseling* is, to this day, "the" standard textbook of pastoral counseling. Clinebell's relatively liberal theological stance naturally inclined him to understand the essential task of the ministry as similar to that of humanistic psychotherapy.

> Pastoral counseling is the utilization, by a minister, of a one-to-one or small group relationship to help people handle their problems of living more adequately and grow toward fulfilling their potentialities. This is achieved by helping them reduce the inner blocks which prevent them from relating in need-satisfying ways. (Clinebell, 1966, p. 20)

The theory and methods of client-centered therapy were thus tailor-made for pastoral counseling. By teaching theological students to "discipline their mouths," Rogerian techniques could help check the tendency to proffer moralistic advice at the expense of establishing a nurturing therapeutic atmosphere (p. 29). Yet, as Clinebell forcefully pointed out, after more than 20 years of pastoral counseling he had found himself "forced to modify [his] Rogerian-psychoanalytic assumptions and methods in order to meet the obvious needs of parishioner-counselors" (p. 7).

The Rogerian method provides a firm foundation but not the entire edifice of an adequate approach to counseling.... The Rogerian model has tended to make the minister feel that he should strenuously avoid the use of his authority.... In contrast, the revised model [which I propose] is based on the conviction that it is often constructive, even essential, for the pastor to use his authority selectively in sustaining, guiding, feeding (emotionally), inspiring, confronting, teaching, and encouraging persons to function responsibly. (Clinebell, 1966, p. 30)

Clinebell's "revised model" of pastoral counseling broadened and modified Rogers's system to include an element of what he called "confrontation." While retaining the Rogerian insistence upon the counselor's adoption of a person-centered attitude, Clinebell went on to argue that pastors cannot exercise the full scope of their duties within the confines of the client-centered model. That is, pastoral counseling must also utilize instructional techniques that help equip the parishioner with an ego-adaptive, reality-oriented set of personality skills. In presenting his case for including instructional and even confrontational strategies in pastoral counseling, Clinebell reasoned that

Rogers was reacting to an older approach to counseling consisting of exhorting, advising, and persuading. He retained the either-or, feeling-knowing dichotomy of that approach, but opted for feeling instead of knowing. Educative counseling seeks to move beyond the either-or to a both-and position. (Clinebell, 1966, p. 194)

Clinebell was not alone in giving voice to the need for pastoral counselors to clearly recognize the difference between their therapeutic responsibilities and those of their secular counterparts. In a volume written approximately 10 years after his *Atonement and Psychotherapy*, Don Browning offered a thoughtful reassessment of the merits of Rogerian psychotherapy as a foundation for both pastoral counseling and pastoral theology.

Whatever the virtues of [client-centered] counseling as a model for pastoral care (and there are many), its overemphasis signals a default on the part of the Protestant community. It is unwilling to tackle the hard problems of reconstructing the normative moral and cultural value symbols by which the church and its members should live. (Browning, 1976, p. 25)

Browning sensitizes us to the importance of the moral dimension of pastoral counseling by drawing our attention to an often-overlooked aspect of Max Weber's sociological analysis of religion. Weber's entire thesis of the Protestant ethic is, Browning correctly observes, a brilliant testimony to the long-term impact that various types of pastoral counseling have in shaping the orientation of an entire culture. According to Weber, the rational-ascetic image of the responsible individual that has guided Western culture was, in fact, fashioned in the workshop of pastoral counselors as they tried to channel the energies of anxious souls into more productive activities.

It is with this larger sociocultural perspective in mind that Browning calls critical attention to the question of whether client-centered techniques are an appropriate tool for the ministry.

> Pastoral care should never be understood simply as a matter of "loosening people up," helping them to become "more open" or more "spontaneous and flexible".... Pastoral care must first be concerned to give a person a structure, a character, an identity, a religiocultural value system out of which to live. It must first be concerned to help people discover these things and become incorporated into them. Then it should concern itself...with actually attempting to live the life that moral inquiry has found to be good. (Browning, 1976, p. 103)

Browning contends that the most pressing issue in contemporary pastoral theology is that of countering the widespread narcissistic tendencies of our culture and to help reestablish concern for the requirements of moral community. Unfortunately, pastoral counseling activities have generally ignored or even undermined this task. Insofar as client-centered principles serve pastors in their healing and guidance capacities, the church has been giving insufficient attention to helping individuals become responsible bearers of an identifiable moral outlook.

ROGERS'S IMPACT UPON CONTEMPORARY RELIGIOUS THOUGHT

The reservations that Oden, Clinebell, Leech, Browning, and others have expressed concerning the applicability of Rogerian thought to the full range of issues related to pastoral counseling would appear to have considerable theological merit. Indeed, the distinctive character of the religious cure-of-souls tradition is that it entails sensitizing individuals to ultimate meanings and ultimate concerns. Yet, I believe that to dismiss Rogers as a resource for contemporary religious thought and practice due to the nontheological and perhaps even amoral character of his writings reveals a certain insensitivity to the deeper significance of his work. I would even go so far as to state that the vast majority of theologians who have studied Rogers's works have either misread or distorted the fundamental character of what might be labeled the broadly religious and spiritual thrust of his psychological writings. Oden's insistence that Rogers is on the one hand "a theologian of considerable merit" and yet on the other hand guilty of espousing a non-Christocentric view of salvation would appear to be a prime example of the way in which Rogers's interpreters have allowed their own theological biases to color their estimation of his work. True, Rogers's thought does not fully or adequately address the concerns of the moral or ascetic strain of Protestant theology. But it is helpful here to keep in mind the fact that theology is itself but one style or mode of religious thought. While theology seeks to justify and interrelate the major symbols of a particular religious traditon, religious thought entails any intellectual activity that probes the ways in which our experience partakes of something that might be considered central to existence. As such, religious thinking permeates almost every area of human inquiry—art, the natural sciences, mathematics, and, of course, psychology. Thus to refer to Rogers's psychology as containing a religious dimension is not to infer that it is merely disguised or incomplete theology. Nor does the fact that Rogers's psychology displays this religious depth to a greater extent than many other psychological systems imply that it is any less psychological. But drawing explicit attention to the religious—although decidedly nontheological—character of Rogers's thought makes possible a reconsideration of its relevance to contemporary religious reflection.

Over the past few decades theological discourse has centered on the possibility of speaking meaningfully about the existence or reality of God. In previous eras, debates of this type were waged between believers and those who championed agnosticism or atheism. What distinguishes the current religious climate is that even the self-identified believer is honestly facing up to a very real element of unbelief within himself. Scientific reasoning has so eroded the intellectual credibility of Biblical literalism (at least among the educated public) as to force individuals to re-examine their own experience and to search out new grounds upon which they might subscribe to the hypothesis that their lives are engulfed by any sort of supersensible reality whatsoever. "The" religious question is no longer whether or not there is such a thing as a first cause. The question around which religious commitment currently revolves is whether human nature is even capable of genuinely experiencing a deeper order of reality from which it might derive its ultimate meaning or significance.

It is to this crisis in the contemporary religious climate that Rogers's personal and professional lines of thought have most forcefully responded. By doing so within the context of academic psychology, he has forged both for himself and for his contemporaries a new and intellectually compelling means of locating the self within a larger spiritual universe. And it is for this reason that one of the most significant contributions of client-centered psychotherapy has been its ability to help dispel the spiritual disquietude characteristic of modern secular culture.

Rogers has been especially candid about the extent to which his psychological viewpoints emerged in response to a religious tradition that to him had become both emotionally and intellectually untenable (Rogers, 1961, 1967, 1980). Raised in what he describes as a "highly conservative and almost fundamentalist Protestant family," Rogers was from his earliest years taught the normative importance of understanding individual human life within a larger religious or metaphysical perspective. Yet the narrowness of his parents' beliefs made them incapable of guiding him in his initial encounters with the wider world. Throughout his youth and young adulthood Rogers became increasingly disenchanted with the stern and rigid piety anchored in Biblical absolutism. As he left home and for the first time became exposed to the socially and intellectually pluralistic character of modern American culture, he became keenly aware that his inherited faith no longer commanded authority or compelling power for him. In a college term paper on "The Source of Authority in Martin Luther" he concluded "that man's ultimate reliance is upon his own experience—a theme which has stayed with me." It was but one more step for him to arrive at the more radical conclusion that "perhaps Jesus was a man like other men—not divine."

As the supranaturalisms of his inherited world view became less and less tenable, Rogers eventually rejected the notion of "transcendence" as a category in which to locate those laws or principles central to all existence. His deconversion from theological orthodoxy did not, however, diminish his spiritual sensibilities. Upon graduating from college he enrolled in Union Theological Seminary in hopes of pursuing a career in religious leadership. Union, then known for its liberal leanings and tendency to equate religious conviction with commitment to concrete social action, offered Rogers the intellectual freedom in which to pursue his abiding interest in "the meaning of life and the possibility of the constructive improvement of life for individuals."

It was at Union that Rogers first became acquainted with the methods and goals of counseling psychology. He had by this time reached a personal, theological, and professional crossroads. Constitutionally disposed to consider it "a horrible thing to have to profess a set of beliefs in order to remain in one's profession," Rogers finally decided to quit Union and to pursue a career in counseling psychology. What should be resisted in interpreting Rogers's exodus from the ministry, however, is the temptation to view it as but one more example of the "secularization of theology" scenario through which so many of the pioneers of American social science abandoned the ministry for work in an objective, positivistic intellectual discipline. True, Rogers had shifted his quest for "the meaning of life and the constructive improvement of life for individuals" away from what he had come to believe were outmoded categories of thinking. Yet, in retrospect, his career has been devoted less to the secularization of theology as it has to what might be called the spiritualization of psychology. That is, the humanistic psychology for which he has been the preeminent spokesman has never been humanistic in the strictest sense. Far from contending that human nature can be exhaustively explained or manipulated through the exercise of technical reason, Rogers's conviction that "our organisms as a whole have a wisdom and purpose which goes well beyond our conscious thought" makes a strict psychological determinism impossible (1980, p. 106). Thus, in contrast to both behaviorism and psychoanalysis, which use the language of material and efficient causation, Rogers speaks of an actualizing tendency said to be intrinsic to the life process. Forward-moving or normative behavior is therefore ultimately not reducible to either environmental reinforcement contingencies or prudent, ego-dominated sublimations but rather derives from "a flood of experiencing at a level far beyond that of everyday life" (1980, p. 123).

Rogers's affirmation of a preconscious, biologically-based actualizing tendency makes it possible for him to speak of our psychological natures as in some fundamental way rooted in a drive or tendency central to the universe. His often-quoted observation that "what is most personal is most universal" is thus not simply a heuristic clinical hypothesis. It is also, and more fundamentally, a metaphysical doctrine. Attuning ourselves to the psyche's deeper laws is to be simultaneously aligning ourselves with the deeper ontological structures through which being emerges over nonbeing. Of note is the fact that Rogers likens the act of fully and deeply entering into another's inner frame of reference to

> listening to the music of the spheres, because beyond the immediate message of the person, no matter what that might be, there is the universal. Hidden in all of the personal communications which I really hear there seems to be orderly psychological laws, aspects of the same order we find in the universe as a whole. So there is both the satisfaction of hearing this person and also the satisfaction of feeling one's self in touch with what is universally true. (Rogers, 1980, p. 8)

Rogers's aesthetic feel for the self's universal depths is suggestive of Ralph Waldo Emerson's ability to see in nature the presence of a universal spirit that constitutes the fundamental reality out of which our individual lives evolve. What is more, Rogers's metaphysic of self-actualization is predicated upon a remarkably Emersonian view of the "correspondence" between various levels or orders of the wider, spiritual universe.

> My main thesis is this: There appears to be a formative tendency at work in the universe, which can be observed at every level. (Rogers, 1980, p. 124)

And, just as Emerson's philosophy of correspondence bespoke the ability of individuals to become inwardly receptive to the influx of guiding energies that flowed from higher ontological levels and thereby become empowered for authentic "self-reliance," so does Rogers's philosophy of self-actualization. Self-actualization, as with especially insightful moments in the therapeutic process, requires opening ourselves up in such a way as to permit "the powers of the universe to be present and operative in a very special way." By expanding our awareness to include this point of contact with a transpersonal creative drive we are able at last to assume our rightful place in the cosmic scheme of things.

> The greater this awareness the more surely the person will float in a direction consonant with the directional evolutionary flow...moving

in the direction of wholeness, integration, a unified life. Consciousness is participating in this larger, creative, formative tendency. (Rogers, 1980, pp. 127–128)

Rogers is, thus, not offering a simplistically romanticized view of Nature as the theoretical basis for humanistic psychology. Rather, Rogers shares with many Eastern metaphysical systems an expressed belief in the potential fusing of the psychological realm with the wider spiritual universe. One might, in this sense, describe Rogerian thought as entailing a sacramental dimension insofar as it envisions the possibility of aligning the individual psyche with an immanent spiritual presence.

> Thus, when we provide a psychological climate that permits persons to *be*. . . we are tapping into a tendency which permeates all of organic life—a tendency to become all the complexity of which the organism is capable. And on an even larger scale, I believe we are tuning in to a potent creative tendency which has formed our universe. . . . And perhaps we are touching the cutting edge of our ability to transcend ourselves, to create new and more spiritual directions in human evolution.
>
> This kind of formulation is, for me, a philosophical base for a person-centered approach. It justifies me in engaging in a life-affirming way of being. (Rogers, 1980, p. 134)

It should be evident that Rogers's psychology provides modern Americans with a new set of terms and procedures with which they might understand themselves to be inwardly harmonizing with the ultimate nature of things. To this extent it would also appear that Rogers has been a significant voice in what historian William McLoughlin has termed the "Fourth Great Awakening" of American culture (McLoughlin, 1978). By using the term *awakening*, McLoughlin refers to those identifiable "periods of cultural revitalization that begin in a general crisis of beliefs and values and extend over a period of a generation or so, during which time a profound reorientation of beliefs and values takes place" (p. xiii). McLoughlin believes that we are currently engaged in such an awakening. This awakening, like the three other major periods of cultural revitalization that took place before it, is giving new expression to a core of beliefs that has shaped the American experience since its inception. Among those core conceptions of American cultural life are belief in the existence of a covenant or relationship between the divine and human orders, faith in the free and morally responsible individual, the Protestant work ethic promising success and inner exaltation to all who conscientiously order their lives, and faith in the progressive movement of both nature and history toward some ultimate or utopian telos.

According to McLoughlin, older formulations of these fundamental values had, by the early 1960s, become culturally dysfunctional. Social, ecological, and economic changes had created a jarring disjunction between official norms and personal experience, old beliefs and new realities, dying and emerging patterns of interpersonal interaction. Slowly but surely a host of disparate voices have begun to form a new vision of American culture that McLoughlin believes will enable us to "maintain faith in ourselves, our ideals, and our 'covenant with God' even while they compel us to reinterpret that covenant in the light of new experience" (1978, p. 2). McLoughlin further observes that the consensus that is beginning to emerge from our current ideological reorientation

> will most likely include a new sense of the mystical unity of all mankind and of the vital power or harmony between man and nature. The godhead will be defined in less dualistic terms, and its power will be understood less in terms of an absolutist, sin-hating, death-dealing "Almighty Father in Heaven" and more in terms of a life-support, nurturing, empathetic, easygoing parental (Motherly as well as Fatherly) image. (McLoughlin, 1978, p. 214)

Rogers has undoubtedly been one of the most eloquent spokespersons of this cultural awakening (Fuller, 1982). By offering new, non-theological understandings on our personal relationship to the "formative tendency of the universe," he has articulated a psychological perspective well tuned to his contemporaries' needs for a more spiritually nourishing world view. In the process he has also given poignant new expression to the aesthetic or harmonic strain of American religious thought. Aesthetic spirituality, as found in the writings of such luminaries as Jonathan Edwards, Ralph Waldo Emerson, and William James, proclaims that by opening ourselves to the depths of nature we simultaneously behold the spiritual energies of an immanent divinity. The Rogerian notion of authenticity, no less than those of Edwards, Emerson, or James, gives voice to what William Clebsch describes as the belief that "the person who accepts nature's invitation to live in harmony with it personifies deity in himself" (1973, p. 94). In this sense psychological congruence is to Rogers what "consent to Being in general" was for Edwards, what "divine influx" was for Emerson, and what incursions from the "subliminal self" were for James. In each case, an almost pantheistic emphasis upon God's immanence supports the view that "'Getting right with God' and 'being your own person'...are one and the same act of self-reliance" (Clebsch, 1973, p. 94).

The fact that Rogers—perhaps even more so than James—went from Nature to psychological nature in his identification of the spiritual character or true self-reliance bespeaks the general drift of our culture away from traditional theological terminology. Thus, while Rogerian thought is, as Oden, Clinebell, and Browning have observed, in itself an insufficient model for pastoral counseling and pastoral theology, it is not for that reason to be lightly regarded as a source for contemporary religious thought. The methods for client-centered therapy have proven to be effective tools for transforming personal consciousness in a way that enables individuals to "feel they are in touch with, and grasp the meaning of, this evolutionary flow" (Rogers, 1980, p. 228). As Rogers himself points out, his psychological work with others has been intended to "liberate their nature and their destiny...to release the Tao in them" (p. 42). Rogers has, in other words, directly responded to the religious crisis of our time by helping individuals to acquire a felt sense of their participation in a supersensible order of reality. And while a religious sensibility of this sort is not a moral achievement per se, it is certainly the precondition of feeling intrinsically, rather than superficially, identified with others. Rogers's focal concern with the aesthetic foundations of moral awareness is thus in perfect keeping with the Edwardsian, Emersonian, and Jamesian insistence that authentic moral action is a direct function of our inner identification with being itself.

The "way of being" to which Rogers calls us is, then, one which makes the religious hypothesis central to all other issues concerning the fully functioning life. To Rogers, the secret to psychological well-being is in the last analysis that of opening up to deeper ontological or metaphysical orders from which our personal lives acquire both meaning and vitality. It is thus one of the most enduring of his contributions that Rogers has provided the conceptual resources for countless numbers of Americans to revive an aesthetic outlook that makes possible what Clebsch describes as the "consciousness of the beauty of living in harmony with divine things—in a word, being at home in the universe" (1973, p. xvi).

19

A Person-Centered Approach to Research

Dave Mearns
John McLeod

Historically, most researchers seeking to investigate psychological or small-scale social phenomena have attempted to retain tight control of the processes they study by placing people in standardized laboratory settings; by using measuring techniques such as questionnaires, inventories, and rating scales; by deceiving people; or by selecting the aspects of behavior they choose to observe. Psychologists and social researchers have adopted this particular type of research strategy for a variety of complex reasons (Shotter, 1975) rooted in the social and political context within which social science has developed and the philosophical ideas, such as logical positivism, that have influenced it in its growth. Nevertheless, one important consequence of this model of research has been to keep the researcher at a safe distance from the person or group being researched. Typically, subjects are not given the opportunity to communicate directly with researchers. They may be required to speak through the medium of a questionnaire or rating scale, or the researcher may be merely an unseen audience to their performance in some contrived situation. In either case, the individual or group is intended to be experienced by researchers as an object of study rather than as a person or persons with whom they must relate (Macmurray, 1961). This denial of the fact that researchers and those they study are people relating to each other has been widely recognized as contributing to a number of fundamental methodological problems in behavioral research (Rosenthal, 1967; Orne, 1962).

In contrast to this dominant positivist tradition in social science, various researchers have over the years constructed alternative approaches that emphasize and draw upon close contact with the lived experience of research participants and explicitly focus on the relationship between the researcher and researched. In the USA the work of Lewin and his colleagues in the field of action research (Marrow, 1969) can be seen as an early attempt to carry out research that seriously takes into account the ways that people themselves make sense of the situations in which they find themselves. Also the Duquesne University School of Phenomenological Psychology (Giorgi, 1970; Valle & King, 1978) has published a series of studies in which classic topics in psychology— learning, motivation, emotion, intelligence—have been explored from the point of view of what the person experiences while learning, taking an intelligence test, or being anxious. In Britain, Laing and Esterson (1964), in studying disturbed families, and the ethogenic social psychologists (Harré & Secord, 1972), in looking at topics such as youth violence (Marsh, Rosser, & Harré, 1978), have introduced the notion of research as a process or dialectic centered on negotiation between researchers and informants regarding the meaning of events experienced by the latter. All these alternative approaches, while differing in their areas of application, are more or less phenomenological in nature. They aim to produce sensitive and thorough accounts of the manner in which people experience and make sense of their worlds, as distinct from the traditional research methodologies, which attempt to identify the environmental or internal variables that determine that experience.

These phenomenological and action-based approaches to research have developed largely in isolation from humanistic psychology, which has tended to concentrate more on fields of practice such as counseling, therapy, group work, and education than on theory and research (Farson, 1978). Paradoxically, however, the reputations of influential figures in humanistic psychology such as Carl Rogers and Sidney Jourard have rested in some degree on published research employing quasi-experimental design, measurement, and control of variables. In addition, reviewers of research on such characteristically humanistic phenomena as growth groups (for example, P. Smith, 1980) evaluate the methodological adequacy of studies by the criteria of experimental psychology. Phenomenological and humanistic practitioners, therefore, view research with some ambivalence—although they suspect that conventional research methods may deny what is essentially human, they realize that the results of this type of research can help achieve a wider audience for the humanistic enterprises being studied.

There are, nevertheless, strong themes running in parallel through the work of both phenomenological researchers and writers on counseling,

.therapy, and groups: the primacy of experiencing; respect for the beliefs and values of others; an emphasis on relationship and process factors; and a search for authenticity. In the field of humanistic practice these themes are most clearly articulated in the philosophy of the person-centered approach (Rogers, 1961; Gendlin, 1962; Hart & Tomlinson, 1970). This philosophy can be seen as offering a set of ideas and values that can be as usefully applied to research as to therapy. The purpose of this chapter is to elaborate the ways in which person-centered philosophy can provide not so much a set of methodological techniques or rules as a general framework for understanding persons within which existing research practices can be located and assessed. Throughout this chapter, the application of person-centered ideas to the research process will be illustrated by examples of research currently being conducted by one of the authors. This work consists of an evaluation of an experiment in flexible schooling within one Scottish Comprehensive School (Mearns, 1982) and an investigation of social education provision in a range of other schools in Scotland (McBeath, Mearns, Thompson, & Rodger, 1981). The research is sponsored by local education authorities, and the methods being used include interviews with teachers and students (ages 11 to 16 years) and participant observation. We do not in any way intend, however, to give the impression that a person-centered approach to research is appropriate only within educational settings; examples of other research conducted within a broadly person-centered perspective can be found in Reason and Rowan (1981).

Reflection on the experience of doing this research, together with analysis of taped interviews and reports from research participants, suggests that a set of key characteristics is associated with a person-centered approach to research. While these aspects inevitably overlap and relate in different ways, for the sake of clarity they will be discussed separately. The first characteristic we have identified is central to the approach to a client or research participant taken by any person-centered practitioner: the other person is met as an equal; a partner in whatever enterprise is being pursued; a person with his or her own perceptions, feelings, and preferences. The second basic feature reflects the phenomenological nature of person-centered philosophy in emphasizing that the goal of research is to explore, as sensitively and accurately as possible, the frame of reference of the other. Third, the reality of this other person or group of persons, and the relationship existing between them and the researcher, is conceptualized as being always in process, with movement and direction. Fourth, the researcher seeks to maintain congruence and a sense of authenticity in self and other. The fifth and final characteristic concerns the value orientation of the researcher. In particular, it is important that the researcher be prepared to accept the values of others in a nonjudgmental fashion. We believe that these characteristics, when taken as a whole, define a distinctive and powerful perspective on the research act.

MEETING THE PARTICIPANT AS AN EQUAL

The choice of the term *participant* rather than *subject* or *client* is not just a question of splitting hairs: it reflects a fundamental attitude underlying person-centered research. The term *client* is too closely associated with the therapeutic domain, while the term *subject* carries such dictionary definitions as "person owing allegiance to," "person to be treated or dealt with." *Participant*, with its denotative meaning of "person having a share in" and "being a part of" indicates that the person is sharing in the research process and as such has an equivalent status to the researcher.

This is a radical departure from the classical view of the "subject" as servant of the researcher. Traditionally, the importance of the "subject" lies not in the person she is, but in the extent to which she fits the preset criteria of her selection and may be regarded as a representative of her population. The fact that she is a multifaceted individual is important only in terms of the nuisance value this individuality creates for the researcher intent on focusing on particular facets while controlling the rest. In this social context, when one person defines the relevance of another, an authority relationship is present from the outset.

Although this authority relationship is likely to affect the outcome of any research, that effect will often be acceptable to the researcher. For instance, the researcher examining the influence of the elimination of head movements on visual perception might be expected to create a controlling research environment in which the authority of the researcher is obeyed. Even in social research there is much work, usually of a deductive nature, for which an authority relationship is accepted. However, for inductive social research and studies that demand considerable trust in the researcher or long-term contact with participants, the authority relationship may be contraindicated.

Participants often expect to be lower in status than the researcher. If the researcher is not aware of this possibility and clear about his "contract" with participants, he may find that he is maneuvered into this dominant role. As one of the schools researchers reported:

I am really blowing it in that school. I wanted to be able to work with them on the things *they* wished to do and evaluate those things together. Instead, the way it has developed is that they see my regular visit as the time when I will tell them what to do and make pronouncements on how good or bad they are. Added to that, of course, is the fact that they resent me for this power they have given me.

I have failed through my own insecurity and lack of appreciation of the strength of their expectations. Instead of establishing the research question: "What is the nature of the job we are doing?", I am evaluating the distorted question: "How well or badly are you doing the tasks which I set you?"

These comments illustrate another derivation of authority relationships. Instead of recognizing the researcher for his abilities in research alone, the subjects generalized his "authority" role to their own world and work. Because the researcher felt "insecure" about his position, he found it difficult to decline the "authority" role when it was offered.

Maintaining and communicating the attitude that the participant is the authority in his own world and as such is equivalent in status, can have dramatic effects even within a single research interview. In the schools project the researcher notes:

In analyzing taped interviews with participants who were school students, it is noticeable how the student usually adopted a submissive role at the beginning. But when the interviewer maintained a genuine interest in learning *from* the students, and declined to make assumptions about what life was like for them, their responses became longer, more reflective, included more statements about feelings, and sometimes even contradicted responses made earlier in the one hour interviews. For example:

1. Interviewer to tenth-grade pupil: "Do you like school?"
Answer when question was presented *early* in interview: "It's alright I suppose."
Answer to same question *later* in the interview: "Well, I don't mind *this* school—most of the teachers are pretty fair with you. What I don't like is having to come to school at all. I have got six months to serve before I can leave—but that's not the school's fault."

2. Interviewer to seventh-grade pupil: "How is secondary school (high school) different from primary (elementary) school?"
Answer early in interview: "It's bigger."
Interviewer's supplementary: "Are there any other ways you find it different?"

Pupil: "Don't know."
Answer later in interview: "It's a bit frightening, . . . it's so big. . . . You
don't get to know any of the teachers and they don't get to know
you, so they treat you all the same. . . unless you cause trouble!"

Even more disrespectful of the world of the participant is the
researcher who, far from trying to break an authority relationship,
actually establishes it by "talking-down" in a domineering or patronizing
way to the participant. Young people particularly have a ready-made
stock of standard responses for such authority figures:

RESEARCHER: So you want to join the Air Force, Smith. . . . That
appeals to you? . . . The thought of flying big fast
aeroplanes
STUDENT: S'pose so Sir

By speaking down to this ninth-grade, academically average student, the
researcher got a low-level response from him. In a subsequent interview
with the student it was discovered that he had put a great deal of thought
and investigation into his wish to become a *navigator*. He described the
exam scores he would have to obtain in great detail and also what would
be expected of him in early training. All this thought and investigation
had been denied to the first researcher who had failed to respect the
equality of the participant.

The researcher who remains detached and seemingly aloof from
his participants on the grounds that he must remain "objective" may
succeed in retaining that objectivity of view, but is likely to be given
little to view. The researcher who is more participative might lose some
objectivity, but is more likely to be trusted, seen as less threatening, and
admitted to the participants' experience. With this in mind one of the
schools researchers wrote:

It is important at times to roll up your sleeves and give concrete
support. For me this has meant things like: now and again taking a
class for an absent teacher; team teaching where my knowledge was
relevant; helping on a school committee; being a listening ear for an
isolated student or teacher; and actively working with students and
teachers on a camping trip. While these activities seemed at first to
be temporary deviations from my role as investigator, I now realize
how important they have been to my long-term relationships with
teachers and students. More than anything else they have fostered
equality in our relationships: equality in the sense that we are both

able to help each other, rather than the participants helping me without reciprocation. Also there is equality in the sense that we have both seen each other failing. So the myth of the "omnipotence" of the researcher was quite quickly destroyed!

This notion of meeting the participant as an equal is not new to social research: the "participant observer" approach emphasizes the relevance of the researcher's involvement in the process under investigation. But while many workers in action research have found it to be a more viable procedure than detached observation, it has never attained theoretical respectability. There has always been a tendency to view such involvement as a "necessary evil." However, in the context of the person-centered approach, this involvement is an important part of a practical and theoretical framework, from which can develop such processes as acceptance, congruence, and empathic understanding.

EMPHASIS ON THE FRAME OF REFERENCE OF THE PARTICIPANTS

Understanding the participant's frame of reference and how that changes involves empathic ability on the part of the researcher. Rogers (1977) has written at length on the centrality of empathy in the person-centered approach. Similarly in person-centered research the expression of empathy has far-reaching effects. Empathy shows understanding and hence advances trust. Even inaccurate attempts at empathy can communicate a *desire* to understand and consequently advance trust. Mutual trust is particularly important when the researcher must work with the participant over a long period of time or be allowed access to the private conscious experience of the participant.

Empathy encourages further exploration by the participant. In the following extract from a one-and-a-half-hour interview the researcher is exploring what "glue sniffing" had meant in the life of a 15-year-old student (formerly a chronic user).

> STUDENT: Well it was no big deal really—teachers make a lot of fuss about it.
>
> INTERVIEWER: Like adults might see it as a problem, but not necessarily yourself?
>
> STUDENT: Well it's a problem to give it up, but it's not like heroin.

INTERVIEWER: You found it difficult to give up?
     STUDENT: Yeah, I'd be screaming for it—and screaming at myself not to take it. I'd be lying there on the floor screaming and crying.
INTERVIEWER: That sounds like it was incredibly difficult....I mean it wasn't just "difficult," it sounds like it was breaking you up.
     STUDENT: Yeah it was a fight every minute of the day. I'd get down...you know...crying...crying for myself I suppose. That was when I always used to buzz. But now I couldn't.... I had no escape.

It is difficult to see how a phenomenological study such as this could proceed in the absence of empathic sensitivity on the part of the interviewer. Even during this short dialogue the reflection of both superficial and deep feelings has been sufficiently supportive to the participant for him to lead the researcher into very personal parts of his world.

Willingness to empathize increases the likelihood that the researcher will make new discoveries. Since it deflects from any inclination she may have to interpret on the basis of her own assumptions about what is happening, it maximizes the possibility that the researcher's view of the topic may change and develop. The following extract, taken from the notes of one of the schools researchers reflects this process:

I had always assumed that young people didn't spend much time, or weren't able to "think about the nature of their existence." But by really listening to this group and not making assumptions about what they were saying, they tentatively opened out and gave me their deeper thoughts about themselves and others. I didn't realize that young people were so mature. We're going to have to radically rethink our educational objectives.... Maybe they [the young people] were saying they were bored with the course because we were indeed aiming too low.

THE PROCESS ORIENTATION OF PERSON-CENTERED RESEARCH

A common criticism that humanistic psychologists have of research is that it is too *static* or too concerned with *product* to be useful in the humanistic domain. But research from a person-centered framework is inevitably more dynamically responsive to its products. The product is not an endpoint, but a temporary, individualized construction that in turn is thrown back into the process. In the schools research, participants were given a copy of everything written by the researcher during his investigation. The initial reason for this was to try to reduce that source of great suspicion and distrust: "What is he writing about us?" This practice not only relieved much of the suspicion, but it forced the researcher into examining and being prepared to justify his assertions. Often this involved him in rechecking loosely supported conclusions. An additional gain, since this research was linked to on-going development, was that the participants had the opportunity to make adjustments in the light of the researcher's observations. The following is a small example of this process of reflexive evaluation:

> From my interview with Sally [a student] it was clear that she was confused about what her two teachers expected her to do. It seems that this confusion was as much a contributor to her recent "delinquency" as anything else. On bringing this up with Peter and Jane [the teachers], we soon found that they had very strongly held, but quite *different* views of Sally. Both saw her as "turned off," but one interpreted this as her "basic laziness," and the other as a temporary result of "the way she had been treated by others." It seems clear that this difference was at least contributing to Sally's confusion. The upshot is that the teachers are surprised at the strength with which they held these different impressions, and both have determined to see what happens when they suspend their judgments.

For a brief moment the teachers' different views were "product" in the classical sense, but it was inevitably put back into the process by the teachers' increased consciousness of the relativity of their personal views in their future dealings with the student.

Another significant aspect of all stages of the research process is the development of the collaborative relationship between researcher and participants. Usually this is recognized in research only to the extent that the importance of "rapport" is acknowledged. However, the person-centered approach goes much further than this in emphasizing the paramount importance of the development of trust within the research relationship. Hence deception is inappropriate to the person-centered approach, as is the avoidance of difficulties within the relationship. Rogers (1969) has suggested that experiencing and dealing constructively with conflict is a necessary element in any deepening relationship. This is as applicable to the research relationship as to any other kind of relationship. Persistently avoiding or stepping back from conflict may be expedient in short-term relationships, but it is not appropriate when the researcher is dependent on those relationships over the years of his work. When a therapist experiences *persistent* feelings of disagreement, irritation, or dislike, she would want to ask herself some questions, but would also want to bring these out into the open lest they fester and destroy the therapeutic relationship. Similarly the person-centered researcher wants to show such responsibility to the relationship. Hence anger, disagreement, annoyance, can and should be voiced in a situation in which it has a chance of at least being clarified or resolved. This willingness to handle difficult material and to clarify differences early not only helps to deal with those particular issues, but also communicates the importance that the researcher attaches to the relationship as a fundamental aspect of the research process.

The process orientation of person-centered research not only recognizes that the participant is in process, but that the relationship between researcher and participant is in process. Also, the research study as a whole is an evolving process that is immediately influenced by its products. This process orientation is analogous to a moving picture show. At any time what is available to practitioners (e.g., educators, therapists) is a large number of "still photographs." Taken individually these are "findings" in the traditional sense and can be acted upon. However, if they are run together an added dimension is available to the practitioner: the moving process.

RESEARCH BASED ON A PERSON-CENTERED PHILOSOPHY SEEKS AUTHENTICITY

As in therapy, the "congruence" of the researcher is an important aspect of the research process. Researcher congruence is defined as *the accurate transmission of the feelings of the researcher in his behavior in relation to a participant.* Incongruence represents a discontinuity between underlying feelings and outward expression at either of two points (A and B):

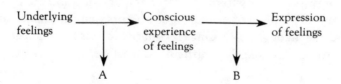

Discontinuity at A implies that the researcher is not aware of his underlying feelings, nor is he conscious of being incongruent, though he may feel "uncomfortable." For example the following is taken from notes made by the researcher after an interview with a teacher:

> Throughout the interview with Mary I felt uncomfortable. I couldn't concentrate, and I couldn't focus for any length of time on what she was saying. I am not surprised that she behaved pretty defensively and didn't explore things very deeply.... My empathy must have been pretty close to zero. It was only later, on listening to the tape, that I was aware of how *angry* I had been early in the interview. It had started when she talked about "researchers not really being involved." Instead of being aware of that anger and dealing with it, I was polite-and-put-on-the-pretense-of-listening. No wonder she didn't trust me.

Discontinuity at B is quite different. In this case the researcher is fully aware of his underlying feelings, but consciously chooses to hide or misrepresent them through lying, concealing, defensive avoidance, or a polite change of subject. One of the most frequent examples of this lack of genuineness in research occurs when the researcher asks a question in which he is not really interested. It may be that he has become bored with the research or with the participant, or maybe he is trying to ask a "clever" but irrelevant question, or a time-filling question (*"If I ask her this it will give me time to think of a better question!"*). Young people seem particularly adept at discriminating between the genuine question and its opposite, as in this example:

> RESEARCHER: and what do you think you will get into once you leave school?
>
> STUDENT: ha!... Every adult asks you that. Usually they're not really interested—they just want to make polite conversation or hint that you are not working hard enough!...

Congruence in the researcher emphasizes his full involvement *with* the participant in an interested, attentive way. It communicates his feeling of responsibility to the research relationship and the process of investigation. None of us are such good actors that the participant fails to detect our incongruence. Once incongruence has been detected, trust is likely to be damaged: It is difficult to trust deception in any form.

Congruence in the researcher is particularly important when he is seeking congruence in the participant. For instance, in research in humanistic psychology, we may want to discover the participant's more personal and deeper responses to a particular issue. It is quite common to find several different layers of response in one participant: a publicly expressed attitude (sometimes two or three for different social situations); a private view; a more personal view seldom expressed even to himself; and also the needs or fears related to these different views. An example of this "layering" of responses came out in an interview with a senior teacher who was reputed to be antagonistic to the "alternative school" under investigation:

> I've said some pretty harsh things about the Alternative School—particularly within the department, and sometimes even in the staffroom. But...you know...that is only *part* of the story. I really am a bit envious about the freedom which John and Sue [the teachers] have—and I think I am also a bit jealous...because I don't think I could handle kids in their way.... Basically I'd like them to succeed.

This short extract brings out various layers of response: the teacher's public hostility, his private interest, his jealousy, and his deeper feeling of insecurity. In an example like this it is important not to assume that "deeper is best." The "truth" lies in the totality of all the layers. When the continuation of this innovation comes to public vote by the school staff, this teacher is likely to vote against: hence his most superficial attitude is important to the researcher. However, if it transpired that the innovators invited him to help with their work, he might well become their strongest advocate: that is, the deeper level is also important to the researcher.

THE PERSON-CENTERED APPROACH TO VALUES

Researchers should refrain from proselytizing their own value systems. However, it is a more complex question whether researchers should endeavor to conceal their values. Traditionally, researchers have tended to favor concealment in the fear that participants will select responses to reflect the researcher's values. This policy of concealment fits the model of researcher as "authority" and is consistent with the illusion of value-freedom in research (Polanyi, 1958). Indeed concealment encourages a perception of the researcher as authority figure, for secretiveness about values is a powerful social strategy. Concealment does not fit the person-centered approach. It would be impossible to be actively involved in the work of participants and to maintain congruence while concealing one's values.

If there is any one value that would be central to the values system of the person-centered researcher, it is an *acceptance of other value systems*. In research as in therapy, acceptance of the values of the participant does not necessarily mean approval of his actions. In the following extract from a taped interview with a teacher, the researcher is far from approving of that participant's actions:

> TEACHER: I usually let a new class know where they stand right away. I make sure that I am late for the first class, then by the time I walk in they're usually making a noise—so I tell them that they're nothing more than a bunch of utter TRASH—fit only for the dustbin of society. That lets them know exactly where they stand. What do you think of that?
>
> RESEARCHER: I can't see me handle a class that way—it wouldn't fit me at all. But then, maybe we all have our own ways of trying to get the "climate" we want. I mean what do you want them to think?
>
> TEACHER: I want them to feel secure—more than anything else I want to fit in with what they expect and what they feel *safe* with. They understand a firm line—they know where they stand—they feel safe. I can't stand these wishy-washy liberals who mess kids about— they try to let them think they've got power—and then eventually they come down on them like a ton of bricks. I hate that—it's so damned unfair on the poor kids—they don't know where the hell they are with a teacher like that.... Are you one of them? (Smiles.)
>
> RESEARCHER: Well...let's say I recognize some of the symptoms...though I might disagree with the prognosis! (Both laugh.)

The key point in this interaction occurs when the researcher acknowledges his different views while still indicating an acceptance of the other person. This openness and acceptance allowed the participant to explore the values that lay behind her behavior: It was these values that made her behavior intelligible.

In terms of the schools research this episode represented an important step toward understanding the decision-making processes within the school. The school was run through democratic management whereby every teacher had one vote on the policy-making staff meeting. However, decision-making was particularly difficult because there were two distinct and opposed "camps" within the school. Clarifying these differences and their effects on the students involved the researcher in seeking to understand both camps. One camp was easy to understand since it reflected values and attitudes similar to those of the researcher, but the other involved him in 12 long interviews with teachers who held quite different views. Following 11 of these interviews, the researcher wrote:

> I feel pretty humble. These teachers have taught me how relative and how restricted is my own value system, and more important: how my value system carries no more absolute veracity than theirs— something I already knew cognitively, but had never *felt* so strongly before.

The twelfth teacher brings up another important point about acceptance of the participant's values—sometimes it is not possible. In the words of the researcher:

> I came out of this interview feeling that I didn't understand this teacher any more than I had at the beginning. I was not able to empathize at all—I was too threatened by what I regarded as the "violence" of his views toward students and education.

This kind of experience reminds us that each researcher is likely to have personal "limits" in the extent to which he can genuinely accept participants' values. The broader these limits are, the more able the researcher will be to work closely with a wider range of participants. However, there will always be occasions when these limits will be exceeded and the researcher will not be able to function.

In the context of the person-centered approach to research, acceptance of other value systems can be seen as a basic prerequisite to entering the frame of reference of the participant. Without it, empathy is a shallow "technique" that will meet more blocks than breakthroughs. If the researcher is not genuinely accepting of other value systems he cannot discover the data that are intimately or exclusively related to them. This acceptance is not seen as a "skill," or even an "attitude," but a basic *value* in itself.

THE FIELD OF RESEARCH FROM A PERSON-CENTERED FRAMEWORK

Some of the early research into client-centered therapy focused on the question of whether the approach was particularly suited to certain categories of client or problem. While this is still a relatively unanswered question for therapy (Smith, Glass, & Miller, 1980), we would like to suggest that a person-centered approach to research methodology is clearly more appropriate in certain research contexts than in others. We definitely do not regard this approach as the new panacea for all behavioral researchers. There are many research questions for which a positivist, experimental approach is more economical and more effective.

The person-centered approach can be seen to offer distinct advantages when the full cooperation of research participants is necessary, and particularly when the researcher aims to probe deeply and personally into the conscious experience of participants. One example of this type of research is the study carried out by Cohen and Taylor (1972) into the experience of long-term imprisonment. In their study it is clear that the trust, openness, and flexibility of their generally person-centered approach was effective in encouraging a group of tough lifetime criminals to explore areas of feeling and vulnerability in a way that would have been impossible with more structured measurement-oriented methods. In addition, the person-centered approach fulfills the requirements of research that involves, or may lead to, a *developmental* aspect. The open-ended nature of person-centered investigations increases the likelihood that new perspectives will be identified that can then be assimilated into the developmental process.

This open-endedness is also consistent with broadly inductive rather than deductive research, with "How?" and "What?" rather than hypothesis-testing types of initial questions. For example, with questions such as "How do these students experience the flexible schooling option?" or "What is happening in the classroom?" rather than "Are students high in need for achievement more successful in obtaining employment?" This latter type of specific and limited question is often well answered by positivist methods, whereas the more process-oriented questions, which demand answers at different levels of experiencing, require considerable trust, cooperation, and openness in both researcher and participants.

A person-centered approach to research is a powerful method in research settings that are likely to evoke a strong reaction in terms of the values held by the investigator: for example, with questions such as "What is the impact of high unemployment on student attitudes toward school?" or "What is the impact of rape upon its victims?" The person-centered framework supports researcher behaviors and attitudes that will minimize the chances of distortion and bias. The person-centered researcher will be expected to empathize with participants, be aware of differences between projection and empathy, be prepared to accept different value positions, and give equal weight to different perspectives. The research process as a whole is also one in which participants can check whether their views are being accurately represented.

Adopting a person-centered framework for research carries three implications that can be particularly difficult for the researcher. First, the careful building and maintenance of collaborative research relationships require a lot of time. When there is a large number of research participants the amount of time required rises, but not in direct proportion. However, this is not to say that the person-centered approach is applicable *only* to small-sample research. For instance, the schools research involved 30 principal participants and over 100 second-line participants.

Second, the person-centered approach is quite demanding in terms of the depth of personal commitment that the researcher is making, not just to the research process, but also to the participants as persons. This can be quite draining, but it is also offset by the fact that this personal commitment tends to be reciprocated. On many occasions the principal schools researcher gained energy from the participants' understanding and caring.

The third implication for the researcher concerns the process orientation of person-centered research. It is impossible to define tightly the research strategy or even the research field in advance. As one avenue is explored, others open up. The researcher, with due regard to his proposal, must make choices as to which should be explored during this "unpredictable journey."

THE OUTCOME OF PERSON-CENTERED RESEARCH

The criteria by which the adequacy or success of a piece of person-centered research may be judged are quite distinct from those relevant to traditional, positivist research. Within the philosophy of the person already outlined, criteria such as statistical significance and the use of psychometrically validated measures or matched control groups are not appropriate indicators of the value of a piece of research. Instead, researchers seeking to remain consistent with a person-centered approach need to make reference to criteria that are personal rather than impersonal, and negotiated equally between participants rather than exclusively laid down by an external authority.

An important criterion for person-centered researchers is their sense of the authenticity of the material they are gathering. Rogers (1961) and Gendlin (1962) have argued that the individual responds most fully and completely to the world through her "organismic" processes or "felt sense" of what is happening, and that it is through symbolizing in some way this flow of feelings that the authentic meaning of things becomes apparent. Gendlin (1966) in particular suggests that the truth of any statement lies in the extent to which it accurately captures, and thus carries forward, the felt sense the person has in relation to the situation or issue being confronted. From this point of view, the validity or truth of interview or any other kind of research material lies in its having resulted from a process that includes frequent reference to the feeling level. The example given earlier of the teacher who began by denouncing a change in the school, but who later in a private interview with the researcher was able to articulate other feelings of interest and jealousy, as well as issues of security, illustrates well this type of process. The research participant is being given an opportunity to express fully every aspect of his felt sense of the topic being discussed, and consequently the researcher, or any reader of the interview transcript, will be very likely to accept the authenticity of what he has said. The researcher, in this case, must be nondefensive enough to accept whatever will emerge from the interview, skilled enough to facilitate the other person in her exploration of feeling, and willing to be a participant in an encounter in which personal change may take place.

Another important source of validation in person-centered research lies in the judgments of research participants. Rogers (1961), writing about therapy, suggested that it is the client who knows what is right and which direction to go in; similarly, in research, it is the participant who knows whether the selection the researcher makes of the mass of information obtained is one that is meaningful and powerful. The process of negotiation that is at the heart of person-centered research therefore includes negotiation concerning what will be published. In the flexible-schooling study, for example, the teachers involved were asked to read a draft of a report written by the researcher and then to write a chapter based on their comments. At other times participants may insist on radical changes in reports, and their disagreements with the researcher will bring to light items of significance that have been missed or key differences in emphasis. The researcher must be willing to learn from negotiations over what will be included in the research report.

In drawing attention to the manner by which validity or accuracy in research reports emerges from collective decision-making, the person-centered approach is extending a line of argument that has its roots in contemporary philosophy of science. Philosophers such as Kuhn (1962), Polanyi (1958), and Horton (1967) have found increasing acceptance for their view that science is a communal enterprise and that the truth of scientific theories is determined not only by the extent to which predictions derived from these theories are confirmed by nature, but by agreements among scientists about how research is to be conducted, what counts as evidence, or what is an acceptable level of accuracy. The person-centered approach extends these arguments by suggesting that in research on people not only are the people themselves quite capable of making such judgments and should be encouraged to do so, but their judgments may lead to conclusions and directions as valuable as or more so than those prescribed for them.

A further issue in person-centered research concerns ways of transmitting the knowledge generated by the research to new audiences. Often the depth of detail required to characterize with any accuracy the lived experience of research participants precludes the use of journal articles. In addition, many people who might be interested in the research may have difficulty gaining access to professional journals. Another consideration is that other forms of communication may be more consistent with the aims of the research than would a written report. In the social education project conducted by one of the authors, it was thought that workshop sessions involving role playing would impart better to teachers the student experience than would either written articles or conference papers.

Finally, any discussion of the outcome of person-centered research— of the nature of the product constructed through this type of research process—must consider the ways in which the researcher molds, filters, or analyzes the raw materials that she gathers. The primary objective of the person-centered researcher is to give an account of the frames of reference or perspectives of research participants. In practical terms this objective will often be fulfilled by constructing detailed descriptions of these perspectives. In many instances description will constitute an adequate conclusion to the research process, since merely opening out the frame of reference of a person or group can be an informative, useful, and powerful end in itself. At times, however, the researcher, as an individual trained in the social sciences, will develop her own perspective on the material and will wish to present this analysis alongside the accounts of participants. What is important, from a person-centered stance, is that the researcher's "theory" has no special status as regards validity: it is one of many possible perspectives on a series of events. Meeting the participant as an equal involves not claiming to be able to explain his actions more adequately than he can himself.

IMPLICATIONS FOR THE TRAINING OF RESEARCHERS

The primary intention of this chapter has been to open debate on the contribution of person-centered ideas to research in the behavioral sciences. While elaboration on training for research in this mode might be in danger of pre-empting that debate, it is worth mentioning some of the implications for training, if only to illustrate the differences between person-centered and traditional approaches to training for research. Implicit in the previous discussion have been a set of skills (ability to make empathic contact, ability to monitor congruence); attitudes (meeting the participant as an equal, openness); and values (mainly an acceptance of the values of the other) that are seldom if ever mentioned in texts on research methodology. Along with these skills, attitudes, and values researchers must, of course, have knowledge in the field of their research. Knowledge presents few problems for researchers trained and located within academic institutions. But adequate treatment of skills, attitudes, and values demands experientially based training, for example role play, exercises in empathy and values clarification, or supervised experience in the field. It is difficult to see how acceptance of other value systems could develop unless the trainee researcher actually put himself into situations in which his prejudices in this respect could be identified and worked through.

A further important issue in training for person-centered research, but one that cannot be fully explored here, concerns the ethics of this type of work. Researchers who are seeking to enter deeply into the lives of participants, and who may assist in developmental processes within these lives, have a responsibility to be available, or to have someone else available, to assist participants to assimilate and use their own personal "findings." This is at least important in the initial stages of this process. The moral nature of person-centered research therefore involves wider issues of responsibility and authenticity than are usually considered in research training.

To the best knowledge of the authors, few training courses in the methodology of the social sciences have ever expected students to become more aware of their own values or their own areas of vulnerability and defensiveness. Yet it is just these issues that are central to the conduct of person-centered research. There are no specific skills or techniques associated with the person-centered approach to research, but rather a philosophy of the person, or attitude toward life, that can be expressed in the research act. The ways in which this attitude can be most effectively introduced into training programs and the many forms of research that may result from doing so remain to be discovered.

20

Secrets and the Psychology of Secrecy[1]

John M. Shlien

All secrecy corrupts; semisecrecy corrupts absolutely.

This paraphrase of Lord Acton's famous dictum, "All power corrupts; absolute power corrupts absolutely,"[2] connects us at once with the idea that secrets and secrecy are related to power. Absolutely true. The paraphrase (from the British statesman R.H.S. Crossman) further tells us that there is danger and destruction inherent in secrecy. It is not the total falsehood but the half-truth that corrupts completely. The half-true lie captures all available energy for its disentangling. Things do not fit as a whole, but neither can the right and wrong parts be separated from the intentionally sticky wrappings. The mind-numbing outcome is "learned ignorance."

Crossman's paraphrase was developed after World War II, during a period of obsession with "security" and "intelligence" that extends to the present. Interestingly, those two words, "security" and "intelligence," tell us something about the alluring but false meanings of secrecy. Strong, honorable, and humane security and intelligence do not come from secrecy, but we are misled to think that they do, and we are weakened (corrupted) thereby. Documents are stamped "Secret," "Top Secret," "Read and Destroy," so that merely "Secret" is a mild classification. Moreover, everything is "leaked," sometimes deliberately. Thus the atmosphere of semisecrecy, the worst.

In such an atmosphere, everything is suspect. That is one illustration of the difference between secrets and secrecy. When everything is suspect, most people seek safety in a conspiracy, for reasons they do not

quite know or fully inquire into, and thereby become outsiders supporting a secret society—which, if it actually exists, may have some
secrets (rituals, documents, symbols). Even if so, and if these secrets
become known surreptitiously, the society is still surrounded by secrecy.
That is the real source of its power. Secrets and secrecy are separate
concepts, and our true intelligence is sapped by the search for the
secrets, leaving us victim of and co-conspirator in secrecy. Meanwhile,
there are countervailing forces pressing for public exposure of all
information, but we do not know whether these are true libertarians
("open covenants, openly arrived at") or enemies from another
unfriendly secret society. The cross-currents from this uncertainty
further paralyze and imbed us in secrecy.

Much of our lifetime is geared to the production of excuses,
defenses, masking images, to contend with our own and each other's
unwanted realities or to create desired appearances that we wish might
become realities. That is how we actually live. Then there is the other
side of the ambivalence—how we (sometimes) want to live. In the
psychic (and perhaps neurological) economy of the individual there is
an urge for "cleanliness," the wish for straight and clear passage without
delay and confusion. If constant cleanliness is not the wish—because
there is also an urge for disguise, adventure, intricacy as an art form—
people at least seek occasional "purification" in forms of confession
and psychotherapy. (Failing that, there are the deathbed confessions,
those sad final clearance sales for which the owner paid the price and
lived the worse for it.)

Secrets and secrecy have always been a force in the history and
literature of psychotherapy. In fact, it seems that secrets have been the
main currency in the commerce between therapist and patient since
Freud developed the psychoanalytic method and described his early
case studies, setting the tone for a long tradition. "Dora" is an example.
"I believe that Dora only wanted to play 'Secrets' with me, and to hint
that she was on the verge of allowing her secret to be torn from her by
the physician" (Freud, 1959, p. 94). In the same study he presents a
description of symbolic behavior: "a very entertaining episode," he
calls it, when another patient opens and closes a little box she always
carries, leading to the now predictable conclusion that it, "like the
reticule and jewel-case, was once again only a substitute for the shell of
Venus, for female genitals" (p. 94). The clever detective, the amused
and powerful physician, the disclosure of "private parts" to the curious
public, and the unmistakable fact that anxious neurotics do want both

to hide and reveal—all these combine to make psychotherapy a study of secrets. Secrets appear to be the hidden treasure (buried, repressed), and the quest for the "keys"—the techniques of uncovering—is the central objective of practice. How different it might be if practices could enable clients to feel safe enough to reveal more willingly what they quite well know.

The atmosphere of secrecy is enhanced by the pseudorespectful air of "confidentiality," such as postponement of publication of personal material and the reasonable ethical concern that guarantees should attend personal revelations confided in good faith. That is, there should be secrecy about secrets. It is important to mention three points here. Keeping other people's secrets is not the same as keeping one's own, so confidentiality should not be mistaken for a secret. Second, the somewhat-abused and often-honored-in-the-breach concept of confidentiality tends to draw a curtain of deferential inhibition around the phenomenon of secrecy, leaving the focus on techniques of uncovering secrets. Third and most important, secrecy is a separate layer, over and above content, therefore not the same as secrets. Secrets may be negative, positive, or neutral in social value, but secrecy is *always* ominous.

To illustrate: A child goes for a walk with her mother and aunt. "I heard the F-word at school today. What does it mean?" Mother to child: "Nothing." Mother to aunt, audibly but over the child's head: "How can you tell a child a thing like that?"

The child has just learned that there are secrets, and there is also secrecy. About that latter she does not quite know, or what to ask. She will learn the meaning (content) of the secret, overcome that particular ignorance, but how will she ever completely "unlearn" (overcome) secrecy and the sense of it? The secret has captured her attention. When she solves that, she thinks she has solved the whole—except for that half-sensed knowledge that there is always something still more forbidden in the world, in the air, like a cloud, almost nameless. Call it secrecy. Secrecy is the whisper in which the secret is told or hidden. This is how "learned ignorance" comes into being.

A black student once told me, "They [white parents] tell their children something about not playing with us, and I don't know what it is."[3] He isn't supposed to know. Even the white parents aren't supposed to know, nor are their children. It just "happens," and how it happens they hope will be forgotten because they did not intend an open instruction. That might have been questioned. Even if presented as a secret ("I'll tell you this, but don't tell"), it can, though with difficulty, be questioned. Secrecy, on the other hand, would have you believe that you thought of this yourself, even if ashamed, even if you can't account for or justify it.

CLIENT-CENTERED APPROACH TO SECRETS

I first heard of Carl Rogers (during World War II) when a fellow soldier-psychologist characterized the Rogerian position as, "Let the patient keep his secret until the pain of bearing it is greater than the shame of revealing it." It was unfriendly, it was wrong, but it was the prevailing image of the cold-hearted "brass-instrument" American psychologist turned to therapeutic endeavors. Such ruthless patience made the "probe" seem relatively benign, and the symbolic analysis of dreams as the "royal road to the unconscious" seemed a warm and sunny passage by comparison.

That statement ("Let the patient keep his secret until...") left me with a considerable prejudice against Carl Rogers. When we first met, I was interviewing him from the standpoint of the sociology of knowledge. He surprised me. He was not cold and implacable. Still, I was not a client, but an inquisitive and somewhat bumptious student, and might not be seeing him at his ruthless worst. Later, I came to know him well, have been a close observer of his work and a friend to him and his family for 30 years. I can say with certainty: *he is not very interested in secrets.* Interested in privacy, self-discovery, expressions of hidden feelings and thought, yes, but as for searching out secrets as key events or hidden traumatic episodes, no. The client will hardly have her secret "torn from her." Rogers does not play the game.

Here are some excerpts (around the thirty-fourth interview) from the well-known case of Mrs. Oak—a case filmed and reported in detail in Rogers and Dymond, *Psychotherapy and Personality Change:*

1C.: And then, of course, I've come to...to see and to feel that over this...see, I've covered it up. (*Weeps.*) But...and...I've covered it up with so much *bitterness*, which in turn I had to cover up. (*Weeps.*) That's what I want to get rid of! I almost don't *care* if I hurt.

1T.: (*Gently.*) You feel that here at the basis of it, as you experienced it, is a feeling of real tears for yourself. But that you *can't* show, mustn't show, so that's been covered by bitterness that you don't like, that you'd like to be rid of. You almost feel you'd rather absorb the hurt than to...than to feel the bitterness. (*Pause.*) And what you seem to be saying quite strongly is, "I do *hurt*, and I've tried to cover it up."

2C.: I didn't *know* it.

2T.: M-hm. Like a new discovery really.

3C.: (*Speaking at the same time.*) *I never really did know. But it's...you know, it's almost a physical thing. It's...it's sort of as though I–I–I were looking within myself at all kinds of...nerve endings and–and bits of–of...things that have been sort of mashed.* (*Weeping.*) [emphasis added]

3T.: As though some of the most delicate aspects of you— physically almost—have been crushed or hurt.

4C.: Yes. And you know, I do get the feeling, oh, you poor thing. (*Pause.*)

4T.: Just can't help but feel very deeply sorry for the person that is you.

(C.R. Rogers & R.E. Dymond, Eds., *Psychotherapy and Personality Change*, pp. 326–327. Chicago: University of Chicago Press, 1954. Copyright © 1954 by the University of Chicago Press. Reprinted by permission.)

This case was important to Rogers. He was fully invested in understanding this sometimes vague and poetic woman. He was anything but inattentive. For years after her therapy ended, I had many opportunities to talk with Mrs. Oak about her family, work, and pleasures, as a friend. (She is, sorry to say, no longer alive.) At the point (3C above, italicized for emphasis), she had been thinking, among several simultaneous thoughts, of a secret, an experience she had never wanted to tell anyone. It was about the awkward, painful, disillusioning first sexual experience and the rupture of her hymen. The shock and disappointment lasted for months. She knew it need not be so, had not been so for some other women ("It's just a little piece of skin"), but it had been for her.

Perhaps without much stretch of the imagination you can read it in her words, "within myself at all kinds of...nerve endings and bits of...things that have been sort of mashed." It is not that Rogers missed the delicacy, the almost physical quality of the hurt. Nor had the two of them failed to explore her sexual feelings. But he did not probe. He did not dart, alert for the secret.

Mrs. Oak laughed when she told me about it. It was no longer a "secret." Though she hadn't told anyone, though she easily could, she no longer feared to tell it. It was a matter of indifference. She said that she could have told Carl the explicit details—there was plenty of opportunity both in his response and later—but "he heard me then as he heard me always, in terms of my feelings and my whole self." In a most fascinating way, she felt that she *had* told it.[4] It was explicitly included in her mind, though not in her words, and his understanding seemed to her to cover that. At any rate, if it was just a little piece of skin, then it was just a little bit of journalism lost, but at stake was a big broken dream. Life was supposed to have been beautiful. Did they then discuss broken dreams? To judge that, you must read the whole case. (Yes.) The practical point here is that Rogers was not waiting for and did not pursue typical secrets in typical ways.

LINES OF INQUIRY ON SECRETS AND SECRECY

Prompted by the significance of secrets and secrecy in this field, and the contrast in ways of dealing with such material, I have joined in an attempt to investigate the subject, which has become a matter of keen interest to scholars from many fields (Bok, 1982). What can be briefly mentioned in these pages does not have the status of proven facts, only of tentatively supported opinion.

From informants in dozens of interviews and from reflection upon the topic and its literature, there are many interesting leads for research underway. In material from psychotherapy, it appears that secrets, however dramatic or titillating, are reported *by the therapist* as (1) intimate disclosures; (2) tiny in their social significance; (3) about someone *else's* (the client's or patient's) demeanor. The secrets themselves are large to the withholder but make almost no difference to anyone else. (A hidden blemish, wicked thoughts of personal deeds or intentions.) The therapist is usually impressed by the content *only because of the difficulty the client has in exposing it.* Therapists are also impressed by their own status as receivers—that is, exceptionally trusted and trustworthy. The effect is to turn attention away from science and toward journalism. It leads the therapist to the role of "investigative reporter." The allure of tracking secrets keeps the focus on the other. Secret collecting is almost entirely "the psychology of other people," when the best source of knowledge is, in this topic especially, oneself. Obviously, the material does not lend itself readily to the researcher. That being its nature, inquiry is difficult. That difficulty should drive investigators to self-examination and disclosure rather than the torture of recalcitrant subjects.

It is well-known that secrecy is judged by a double standard. Secrets and lies play a positive part in the development of ego boundaries or the sense of individuality during childhood.[5] Later in life these same behaviors may be socially corrosive and psychologically deadly. The ambivalence continues. While it may be healthy to live openly and honestly, it would, however, be dreadful—indeed, a condition of realized paranoia—to be totally transparent against one's will.

In our studies, lies do not clearly or necessarily at all qualify as secrets. Secrets have to do with shame. Privacy has to do with dignity. Lies may be used to cover secrets, but lies do not fit well with maintenance of privacy and the desired sense of dignity.

Secrets and lies have an odd relation to the truth. Secrets—when they have content—are phenomenologically true, and may never have been lied about, simply not revealed. Curiously, the audience for a revealed secret tends overwhelmingly to take it for the truth, simply because it had been hidden. The lie, however, starts with factually known truth, departs from that base, and is often then supported by a network of subsidiary lies so far from the original truth that the connection grows dim, and the most recent lies are for the sake of the just previous ones, rather than the departed truth (which may, by this time, be forgotten).

Secrets are mistakenly described as undiscovered facts of nature (the location of the lost Atlantis, etc.), but no, secrets are only human. They are the property of persons who do not want someone else to know something. The secret must have some value to the withholder. Secrets told anonymously have relatively little effect on the teller. To have full effect the secret should not fall on deaf or indifferent ears. The receivers of secrets have their own problems as containers, a subject of great complexity and of considerable interest to therapists.

Informants believe that they can recollect their first lie, and usually their first secret. They seldom feel sure that they can recall the points at which they learned the concept or sense of secrecy.

Secret-having tends at an early age to become a content-empty, abstract form. Children frequently manipulate others by claiming, "I know something you don't know," when in fact all they know is that this is a source of power and attraction on an inclusion-exclusion basis. (This is, of course, the basis of the elementary "secret society.")

In the psychological economy, many secrets are kept as treasures, but the keeper pays the interest. Keeping secrets prevents change. This may be valuable if it is a good thing to hold the personality in place, even though very expensive to support.

On the other hand, revealing secrets has at least two powerful effects. One is the initiation of change. In therapy, it is of enormous importance, a *giant* step in moving out of a frozen pattern. *The act of revelation seems to be more significant than the content of the secret.*

The second effect of revealing is the investment of your personal power in the guardianship of the receiver. Depending somewhat upon the nature of your secret, one tends to think better of (to attribute goodwill and trustworthiness to) the recipient after than before telling the secret.

Often those who have told secrets feel empty and depressed, since secrets are exciting property. Finding secrets is as exciting as holding; therefore two or more parties often agree to share secrets by way of recompense.

Every informant knows or recognizes at once these three features of secret giving and taking: (1) the power of the secret in bonding; (2) the dread of isolation; and (3) the artifice of making something valuable by making it rare. Each is of enormous significance, a chapter in itself.

Daydreams may be more important than night dreams. Certainly informants are more cautious and secretive about daydreams. Most feel more responsible for them, as if waking production of a fantasy is more deliberate, calculated, and therefore more revealing.

There are five main classes of people to whom secrets are told: (1) The Stranger—perhaps a chance meeting with someone not to be seen again; (2) The Confidante—a friend, priest, a hired or furnished professional; (3) The Loved One—a relationship of intimacy, probably reciprocal, in which they not only exchange secrets but create secrets; (4) The Captive—a harmless prisoner, unable to betray, could even be scheduled for death; (5) The Fellow—a recognized covert or "closet" kinship, matching stigmata, dangerous but in the same danger. The psychotherapists who see these five categories believe that they are involved in at least three, sometimes all, at various stages.

So far, this is largely about secrets. The psychology of secrecy is about that next layer, secrecy. No one tells us how it is brought about, and we are not to expose its existence, though no one told us that, either. That is what the psychology of secrecy must be about. In terms of modern systems theory, it is *recursive*. The task for a psychology of secrecy is to describe the phenomenon, and to explain (1) the *motives* that keep secrecy alive, and (2) the *purposes* it serves, both well and poorly.

One of those purposes is to preserve the reciprocal infliction of mixed pain and pleasure called "the tyranny of the neurosis." There are some, and I am one, who think that the tyranny of neuroses is the most powerful thing on earth. You have seen it many times. It starts with some content, and a mutual agreement not to acknowledge that content. You might think this an "agreement to disagree," but no, it is an "agreement to agree"! That may seem unnecessary, but no, they must have the agreement to agree because (1) it is secret, and (2) they know that there are also reasons why they should *not* agree (cf. Chapter 8, p. 162, for example). Then follows a forever expanding collaboration of reverberating deceit and self-deceit which in fact *both parties know* well but dare not admit to themselves or each other.

For example, a woman gradually entices her adolescent son to turn with her against his shy and inoffensive father, who later kills himself. No, this one: a professor, out of jealously, dislike, or possessiveness, ruins a brilliant, effeminate student. Then, out of some guilt and much fear of criticism, he rescues the student. The student knows that he should hate the professor, but cannot afford to, and is also grateful, as he is supposed to be. The professor knows he is hated and should be, but the gratitude, real and pretended, is a balance he seeks. They need each other. They invent intricate and, to observers, preposterous affectations, defenses of each other (to just short of the point of real clearance). Soon they are quite dependent upon one another. They play off third parties, who are also aware but pretend not to be. They bind one another in renewed ways until they become both slave and master to each other. Each makes the other pay heavily by further elevating, then humiliating. Both know the process all too well. Both are so ashamed of it and gratified by some aspects that they cannot bear to acknowledge it, much less make public confession of their *semisecret* relationship, and now the process (of secrecy) takes control.

From this process, as always happens in the analysis of secrecy, a new and this time a socially significant secret emerges. In this instance, the secret is: slavery is not dead. It may be outlawed in the social system, but it is alive and unwell in the individuals. The masking "agreement to agree" constitutes a culture in which this neurosis can develop. Some people want to be masters. Others are willing to be slaves, at least temporarily, knowing dimly or more clearly that they may later enslave their erstwhile masters and again at least temporarily reverse the roles. Or the roles become intermingled in what some call *complementary neuroses*, which then produce the tyranny from which escape is no more likely than revolution.

That is the danger in the game of secrets. If it would only stay that game; but it becomes secrecy, and very much needs a psychology.

NOTES

1.   Version of a paper presented at APA Symposium, "Client-Centered Therapy in the 1980's" (Shlien, 1981).

2.   It may not be absolute power for that is seldom if ever achieved, but it is the striving for absolute power that we see so often corrupting so many.

3.   This could happen to any child of another local minority—Jewish, Catholic, Protestant, poor—in some way frightening or despised and arousing both a need for self-protection and shame at the injustice.

4.   What is so fascinating? First, that understanding of the general seems to the client to include understanding of the particulars! Second, it is damned fortunate that is so, since we all have simultaneous thoughts in awareness, but only one voice to express them. That is a comment on the nature of consciousness, levels of awareness, problems of selection and retrieval—all of the greatest importance in themselves, and as related to secrecy, but beyond the scope of this chapter.

5.   Standard examples: "I did not take the cookie," "I did have a bowel movement," when neither is true. The discovery that a parent cannot with certainty know otherwise is a source of separate identity. The trouble is, it is confused with guilt, and we must wonder, is there not a better way to assure individual development of autonomy *and* integrity?

21   One Alternative to Nuclear Planetary Suicide[1]

Carl R. Rogers
David Ryback

It is certainly not news that our planet and all the people on it are threatened by the incredible build-up of nuclear arms. This threat has led to vigorous efforts in a great many countries to halt the arms race—the production, testing, and deployment of the increasingly deadly missiles. It seems strange and tragic that we may destroy our global culture and most of life on the planet at the very moment when technologically and psychologically we have the capability of moving into a new era in which we could all live richer lives.

It needs to be recognized that in the last analysis it is not nuclear arms that pose the threat. A missile resting in its silo is not the main threat. It is the intercultural and international feuds, the hatreds between groups, the religious animosities, the interracial bitterness, the hostile feelings of the "have-nots" toward the "haves"—it is these social tensions that endanger us, since any one of them might trigger a nuclear war.

In my own country, and in others as well, it seems that the primary method of dealing with these tensions at the international level is through force or the threat of force. Intimidation appears to be the mode most commonly used in our diplomacy. It is the escalation of such threats that has led to increasing possibility of all-out nuclear war.

Is there, then, any hope, or are we on a collision course leading to our own destruction? It is the purpose of this presentation to say that there is a body of knowledge and there are ways of being and acting which can reduce or even resolve these fundamental situations of social tension. This body of knowledge, these skills, these attitudes, need to be developed, to be promoted, enlarged, researched, and improved. It is vital to our very survival that we learn how to deal constructively with hatreds and competition between groups.

In this chapter I present several personal experiences with such feuding or antagonistic factions. I would like to try to draw from my experience some principles that might guide us in handling other conflictual situations. Then I use the Camp David experience, where the leaders of Egypt, Israel, and the United States met for 13 days, to show that the principles that we have learned in smaller groups are evident in the Camp David meetings and hence seem definitely applicable at the international level. I would like to point to the fact that there are alternatives to our present form of diplomacy by armed threat. A person-centered approach to intergroup hostility is one such alternative.

The Pattern

It is important to recognize that in any serious dispute between groups, the underlying pattern is exceedingly simple. Group A is convinced of the fact that "We are right and you are wrong. We are good and you are bad." Unfortunately, Group B has the identical point of view. They firmly believe that, "We are right and you are wrong. We are good and you are bad." This simple pattern holds true at the level of the neighborhood squabble and also holds true at the highest international level. A recent striking example is the statement by President Reagan that the govenment of the Soviet Union is "the incarnation of evil." The Soviet leaders, for their part, see the U.S. government as a diabolical enemy, intent on nuclear war, and concentrating on first-strike missiles.

If we are to achieve reduction in tension or any resolution of differences, the existence of this pattern must be recognized, at least dimly, by both sides. Group A must recognize that the certainty with which they believe in their own rightness and goodness is equaled by the certainty with which Group B believes in its own rightness and goodness. By what process can this recognition be achieved? Here I will turn to some personal examples, describing them at sufficient length to indicate something of the process that takes place.

Health "Providers" versus Health "Consumers"[2]

The National Health Council is an organization made up of representatives of the American Medical Association, the American Dental

Association, nurses' organizations, health insurance companies, health-oriented agencies, and many other similar groups. A few years ago these "health providers," as they termed themselves, decided to include in their annual conference a group of "health consumers" from the urban ghettos and the rural underprivileged. They should receive full credit for this humane and courageous decision, which clearly involved risk to themselves. The health consumers were elected or selected by local groups in their own areas. They were all poor persons, many black, some Mexican-American. As the time of the conference approached, the planners became uneasy and invited the staff of the Center for Studies of the Person to act as facilitators of groups at the conference. The invitation was accepted.

When the conference opened, the hostility of the "consumers" was so thick it was palpable. After the usual bland opening events, the conference threatened to split wide open. The "consumers" were going to withdraw. The conference was seen as just another attempt by the establishment group to give a meaningless token representation to the poor. They would have none of it. Only the statements of the facilitators that they had come all the way across the country, for no fee, simply to make certain that *everyone* in the conference would be *heard*, that everyone would have a truly representative voice, held the conference together temporarily.

Twenty groups of 20–25 each were formed, with "providers" and "consumers" in each group. I remember the group I facilitated. The bitterness of the poor erupted in full force. Their anger at white professionals, at the lack of health services, at the lack of any voice in their own health care was so strong that some of the professionals were frightened, while others were self-righteously angry in response. The value of a facilitator, who could truly understand and clarify the feelings expressed, was most clearly demonstrated. Without the facilitators there is no doubt the conference would have blown apart. Voicing his hatred of oppression, one black man said that the Marines had trained him to kill, and if need be he would use that training against the people and institutions that were holding him down. A black woman with little formal education was undoubtedly the most influential person in the group. Highly skeptical of everyone's motives, including mine, she spoke out of a long and terrible personal struggle against poverty, prejudice, and oppression. Whenever she spoke, everyone listened—and learned.

As the group sessions continued, there was a small but significant growth in understanding. The white professionals began really to see their functioning as it appeared to the recipients. A ghetto member who hated health insurance companies realized that the insurance company executive in our group was not all bad, and that they could communicate. A white social worker finally gained the courage to tell how she had constructed a "cover story" for herself as an unemployed worker needing health care, and how, playing this role, she had approached various health-oriented "helping" agencies. The appalling treatment she had received had disillusioned her about her own profession, but now she could begin to see some hope. Some blacks began to differ with others of their color, to their great embarrassment, because they felt they should keep a united front against whites. A Mexican-American woman finally told tearfully of how she felt totally scorned and uncared for by *both* blacks and whites.

To put the process in more general terms, the existing conflicts, such as those between haves and have-nots, between blacks and whites, between professionals and recipients, between establishment and radicals, burst into the open. But these violent outpourings occurred in a climate in which each person was respected and permitted to state his or her feelings without interruption; a climate in which the facilitators showed that their caring concern was for the dignity of each person, and their primary purpose was to foster open communication. In this atmosphere the issues became greatly clarified, and, what is perhaps equally important, persons emerged as separate, unique individuals, each with his or her own perception of those issues. Little by little real interpersonal communication began. This is the essence of the process that a person-centered approach puts in motion.

At this point, some radicals will say, "See, what you are accomplishing is better, less angry communication! You are destroying the possibility of revolutionary change! You are defusing the hatred and bitterness which alone can spark any real change for the oppressed!" I would only ask such readers to hear the rest of the story.

Although the "health consumers" had never known one another before, they quickly coalesced and began to formulate resolutions that were circulated to the various groups, where they were discussed, revised, amended. Then we were all told that it was "the established policy" of the National Health Council to be a forum only, and that it did not take stands on health issues, so no resolutions could be adopted. Undaunted, the "consumers" waited until the final meeting of the whole conference, which was scheduled to be a series of talks "summarizing" the conference, though some of the speakers had not even attended. A "consumer" spokesman immediately moved that the whole program be dropped and that the time be spent considering and voting on the resolutions that had been circulating. Excitement was high, and the pros and cons emotional. The motion carried by a large majority, and the scheduled speakers were thanked and dismissed. The conference ended with highly affirmative feelings, not only on the part of the "consumers" but on the part of most of the establishment members as well.

During the following year, a surprising thing happened. A very large number of these resolutions were carried out. The power of the "consumers" continued to have its effect (Rogers, 1977, pp. 110–112).

What are some of the principles that emerged from this experience—some of the lessons from which we might profit? Here are a few.

It is important that a person with facilitative attitudes and a facilitative way of being be present in such a dispute and that this person be sensitively empathic to the whole range of feelings and opinions expressed by members of each group. It is equally important that this empathic understanding is nonjudgmental and acceptant. When group members experience themselves as being truly heard—and accepted—in their bitterness, their yearnings, whatever—they are able to view themselves and their feelings more objectively, with less irrationality.

When the facilitator hears and understands the feelings of Group A, members of Group B can gradually take somewhat the same understanding stance, and when he is empathically sensitive to members of Group B, Group A can begin to hear them too. They begin to recognize that there are two sides to the dispute, two ways of seeing the situation.

In an atmosphere that contains more mutual understanding, steps can be taken toward dealing with the issues on a more realistic basis, with consideration of all the interests involved.

A particularly important lesson is that the facilitator is able to give equality to the groups, even though normally one is a low-status group and the other a high-status group. The equality provided by the facilitator grows out of the fact that he or she treats each individual as a person of dignity and worth and shows as much respect for the feelings and attitudes of low-status members as of high-status members. Thus, often for the first time, people who normally cannot talk to each other can communicate as equals, temporarily equal in power.

What the facilitator does *not* do is perhaps as important as what he or she does do. A facilitator committed to a person-centered way of being does not guide or push or prod. He or she is content to go with the process of the group, whether rapid or slow. He or she does not persuade or take sides. The facilitator does not offer solutions. His basic trust is in the wisdom that he knows from experience resides in the group, if he can only create the psychological climate in which it can emerge.

Dealing with Longstanding Enmities[3]

I experienced a deep feud when I worked with a group from Belfast, Northern Ireland. It was possible to observe what happens in a group where the bitterness involves generations of economic, religious, and cultural hatred. There were five Protestants—including one Englishman— and four Catholics in the group. The nine were carefully chosen to include extremists and moderates on both sides, men and women, older and younger. The Englishman was a retired army colonel. We wanted to facilitate straightforward communication and to film this interaction.

In the early sessions the bitterness, horror, and despair of everyday life in Belfast was abundantly clear. Tom's sister was blown to bits by a bomb that might have been thrown by terrorists of either side. Dennis and his family have hidden behind mattresses as bullets struck their home during a wild burst of shooting on their street. Dennis has on several occasions had to help carry away the torn bodies, living and dead, from bomb explosions. Becky spoke repeatedly of the brutality of the British army patrols to her teenaged sons. After one episode when the boy was made to believe he would be shot, "That child came in and I never saw fear like it on anybody's face in my whole life."

Gilda, young and attractive, spoke of the hopelessness. "I just get so full of despair. I just give up, you know." Becky said, "I really feel hopeless. . . . If something is not done the bitterness is just going to keep eating away at those kids and eventually they could become IRA men."

The bitterness was on both sides. Pretty Protestant Gilda said, "If I seen an IRA man lying on the ground—this is the wrong thing I suppose in your eyes—I would *step* on him, because to me he has just went out and taken the lives of innocent people."

All the violent feelings leave their mark. Sean, a sensitive young Catholic teacher, told how he had been forced to pull down a "steel shutter" between his functioning self and the seething feelings within. Otherwise he would go berserk. In a very quiet, soft voice he spoke of this inner wild beast:

Yeah, I know myself. I'm quite aware of this kind of thing, and it scares me to know that it is there. 'Cause it is violent and emotional and daft. . . . I take long walks and let this thing inside of me talk. It isn't quite the same as human feelings—it isn't quite the same as having a beast inside you—some sort of animal feelings, you know—

The whole mixed stream of hatred and violence, of fear and despair, seems so powerful that to think one weekend could possibly make *any* difference seems incredibly quixotic. Yet changes did occur. One small example composed of two interchanges between Dennis, a Protestant, and Becky, a Catholic:

DENNIS: (speaking about Becky) The general impression back in Belfast is, if she is a Catholic she is a Catholic and you just put her in a wee box and that is the end of it. But you just can't do that. She has communicated to me that she is in a worse position than what I am.... I would hate to be sitting in Becky's chair... because I feel that she feels the absolute despair that I would feel. I don't know how I would react if I were one of her lads. I would probably go out and get a gun and finish up doing something radical and end up dead.

BECKY: (later) Words couldn't describe what I feel towards Dennis from the discussion we had at dinner time. We spoke quietly for about 10 minutes and I felt that here I have got a friend and that was it.

DENNIS: We sat here at dinner time and had a wee bit of a yarn quietly when you were all away for your dinner—

BECKY: I think he fully understands me as a person.

DENNIS: I do, there is no question about that—

BECKY: And for that reason I am very grateful and I think I have found a friend.

During our sessions the hatreds, the suspicions, the mistrusts of the two feuding groups were very evident, sometimes in covert form, gradually becoming more open in their expression. The individuals were speaking not only for themselves but for generations of resentment and prejudice. There were only 16 hours of group interaction, yet during that incredibly short period these centuries-old hatreds were not only softened but in some instances deeply changed. It is evident that facilitative attitudes can create an atmosphere in which open expression can occur. Open expression, in this kind of a climate, leads to communication. Better communication very often leads to understanding, and understanding washes away many of the ancient barriers. So rapid was the progress, so significant the changes, that some of the statements I have quoted here had to be deleted from the film. To show such understanding of the opposition would have endangered the lives of the speakers when it was shown in Belfast.

When the group returned to Belfast, almost all of them continued to meet at the home of the British colonel, whose neighborhood was the safest. After the film was completed they formed teams—one Protestant, one Catholic—and showed the film to many church groups of both sects, and led discussions. None of this had been planned. There were no funds to help out. It was done on their own spontaneous initiative.

For one group to make progress toward reconciliation has not ended the killings in Belfast. True, but suppose there had been a thousand or two thousand groups? The expense would be a fraction of what private Catholic armies, the British occupation army, and private Protestant armies have cost. As for facilitators, there are hundreds already sufficiently trained, and with three months' notice, they could be on the job.

This whole view is thoroughly confirmed in a recent interview with two Belfast men, very knowledgeable in the community, who have been acquainted with the project and who have seen the impact of the film on small audiences. They are all for training large numbers of Irish as facilitators. "We've got to get thousands of people involved. Once we do, it gets harder for the two percent of paramilitary gunmen [to control the public mind]. The whole idea of encounter groups—this is it! Encounter groups need to be done at a street-by-street level."

When will all this come about? It will happen when the concerned public makes up its mind that the problem is so serious that something *must* be done. It is not experience or personnel or solid evidence that is lacking. It is the public will. The public is not yet sufficiently informed or convinced that there are any possible solutions, and even if there were, it is not willing—yet—to take the risk. When it is, a humanistic, person-centered approach has something to offer, even in situations of deadly antagonism (Rogers, 1977, pp. 129–133).

When can we learn from this experience? It seems evident that, even in the space of 16 hours, centuries-old feuds can be modified and reduced. This comes about in a situation in which both factions are entirely removed from their own locale, meeting in a residential retreat setting. The informality encouraged by the facilitators is another factor in the process. One striking outcome is that even in this short space of time people can move so far from their own constituency, from the beliefs of their own group, that their lives may be endangered. This is a problem that needs to be recognized.

Other Experiences

I have described these two experiences at some length, but I could add a number of others. At various international conferences, conflicting groups have made progress in understanding each other. At Escorial in Spain, 177 people from 22 different countries gathered for a workshop and during the 10-day period began to form a genuine community—this, in spite of the fact that the group contained Marxists and conservative businessmen, Catholic priests and atheists, members of national and cultural groups that hated each other.

I could also cite a brief experience with a black-white encounter group in South Africa, where, though the time was very short, some progress was made in mutual understanding in a most complex and difficult and tragic situation. In short, we have a very considerable body of experience on which to build.

DEALING WITH AN INTERNATIONAL SITUATION— THE CAMP DAVID EXPERIENCE

You may feel that what has been presented is all very well with small groups—conferences, workshops, encounter groups—but such a process could not possibly help with international issues where we are dealing with large political entities. In this connection it is of great value to consider the Camp David experience. I wish to discuss the dynamics of the process that occurred at the Camp David meetings in September, 1978. I will not go into the political aspect or the complexity of the specific issues involved. I will not consider the enormous amount of groundwork that preceded the conference. I will focus primarily on what I see as the similarities and the differences between the Camp David experience and the groups I have described. I will endeavor to indicate the way in which this examination of the process points toward future steps.

Some Significant Similarities

In a number of important ways, the experience at Camp David was definitely parallel to what we have experienced in intensive group meetings in which there were tensions and hostilities between antagonistic groups. I will endeavor to list these similarities, later pointing up some of the significant differences.

1. The sessions were held in a residential retreat setting. This is a highly important fact. None of the factions were on their own conventional turf. They were free from the distractions of their ordinary offices or meeting places. It helps to be faced with a new environment in which fresh perceptions crowd in upon one. It is important that the meeting was residential, because this means that the participants were in daily casual contact with members of the other groups. They saw them at meals. They saw them as they took walks, played tennis, or whatever. There need not necessarily be communication in these casual contacts, but there is at least the chance to observe the others in a variety of situations. Camp David showed, as we have found, that a residential retreat setting is most conducive to a positive group process.

2. The meetings were highly informal. The accommodations were comfortable but not pretentious. The three leaders lived in neighboring cabins, and their staff members in other cabins not too far away. Informality of dress was encouraged. A zippered jacket was given to each person upon arrival. Whether they were worn or not is inconsequential. It signified that casual dress was quite satisfactory. It was informal in manner of speech. Though titles were sometimes used, they were not regarded as necessary. One aspect of the informality was certainly sharply different from the usual diplomatic gatherings. Individuals sat wherever they wished at meals. There was no protocol; there were no special tables.

Beyond the informality of the setting, President Carter bravely encouraged an informality of interpersonal interaction that allowed for more genuine and sincere expression on the part of the dialoguing factions.

The three major participants responded somewhat differently to this informality.

Prime Minister Begin was the soul of propriety. He preferred to wear a tie and coat and strictly observed protocol, always reminding President Sadat and me that he was not a head of state and therefore did not rank as an equal with us. (Carter, 1982, p. 331)

Sadat tended to dress rather formally also.

A most unusual feature of the conference was that the wives were invited. Sadat did not bring his wife, but Carter says of Rosalynn and Mrs. Begin, "...the two wives were, in effect, an integral part of their own national delegations" (Carter, 1982, p. 346).

One example, reported by Dayan, shows that informality was not only encouraged, but existed. Aharon Barak, of the Israeli delegation, had been asked by Carter one night, after a joint session, to reformulate a particular memorandum and to bring it to him, no matter how late. Barak completed his task at 1:00 A.M. There was no phone in his cabin, so he went looking for one. He saw a barefooted woman, presumably a secretary, sitting on the steps of the Camp David cinema. He approached her and asked if she could help him get in touch with the president by phone. "Certainly," she answered. "Follow me. There's an office with a telephone in a nearby hut." Only when the lights were switched on did he find that his guide was Rosalynn Carter. She cut off his apologies, saying, "I'd better connect you with the President myself. The operator would hesitate to ring him at this hour" (Dayan, p. 156). Can one imagine such an incident at a conventional diplomatic conference? The incident helps to point up the tremendous contrast between the Camp David attitudes and those of the usual formal diplomacy.

In many of these informal respects the meetings resembled intensive groups that we have known, where people tend to be on a first-name basis and the whole atmosphere has a cordial informality.

3. Partly because of this informality the three leaders were able to be present as persons and to meet as persons. They could, of course, withdraw into their roles and into their status positions, but the opportunity was there for them to meet simply as three individuals. Carter and Sadat, according to the best information, frequently did meet as persons without any facade. Begin was more rigid in his role, with one very crucial and important exception, which will be mentioned later.

Another important aspect of their meeting as persons was that they could speak with authority. It was not necessary for them to consult with their superiors or to follow a party line. They could speak for themselves and in general could speak for their constituents, even though their final decisions needed to be ratified by parliaments back home.

In the intensive groups of which I have spoken, it was simply natural for people to meet as persons and to speak for themselves. However, this aspect of Camp David is most unusual in diplomatic conferences, where ordinarily a delegate must consult the home office or the party central committee before expressing any position or point of view.

4. The conference was self-contained and private. There was no press or TV coverage. Members of the media were not admitted. The one important exception to this shows how devastating it would have been to the conference had reporters been present.

At the very outset, President Sadat insisted on reading an 11-page paper to the other two leaders. It purportedly set forth the Egyptian position. It was a shocking document, to which the Israelis especially listened with some horror. It showed none of the conciliatory attitudes that had brought Sadat to Camp David. It presented a position that the Israelis could not possibly accept. Carter, too, was astonished at the belligerent and rigid stand that it took.

The silence was long and heavy. Carter "tried to break the tension by telling Begin that if he would sign the document as written, it would save all of us a lot of time.... [He] was surprised when everyone broke into gales of genuine laughter" (Carter, 1982, p. 345). It later developed that Sadat had given this document to the Arab newspapers in order to prove to the Arab countries that he was adopting a very hard line in dealing with the Israelis. Had each portion of the conference been reported in the press, it would, of course, have been necessary for the leaders to take very conservative and rigid stands.

As it was, however, it was possible for the leaders to make tentative, and even uncertain, statements. It was possible to change one's mind. It was at least possible to move away from the pattern of "I am right and good and you are wrong and bad."

We, too, have found that the most progress is made when an intensive group is similarly self-contained and private. When such a group is not in a residential setting and members talk with others between sessions, often they find it necessary to retreat to more rigid or conservative positions, influenced by the attitudes of those to whom they have spoken.,

5. There was no set agenda for the meetings. This is unheard of in a diplomatic conference. There was, of course, a profound and well-understood general purpose—that of arriving at some sort of formulation that would advance the peace—but the steps toward that goal were not rigidly outlined in advance. Problems were taken up and dealt with and discussed as they arose, not in some preset order. There were no regular working hours—another contrast with the usual diplomatic conference, with meeting times carefully set and agreed upon.

Similarly, there were no preconditions to the meeting, no rules that had been set up in advance. Sadat, prior to the conference, had formulated certain preconditions, but after discussing the matter with Cyrus Vance, he dropped his insistence on such conditions.

In our experience in situations of social tension, the agendaless meetings are far more fruitful than those that attempt to follow an agenda. In this respect, our experience coincides with that of Camp David.

6. The meetings were basically very emotional. Statements were often made that were very intemperate and full of feeling. The differences between Israel and Egypt ran very deep and had lasted for many years. From the beginning Sadat and Begin had difficulty communicating. "There was no compatibility between the two men, and almost every discussion of any subject deteriorated into an unproductive argument, reopening the old wounds of past political or military battles" (Carter, 1982, p. 355). (That these "shouting matches" might have been better handled will be discussed later.)

On the third day, Carter says of himself,

> I became angry, and almost shouted, "What do you actually want for Israel if peace is signed? How many refugees and what kind can come back? I need to know whether you need to monitor the border, what military outposts are necessary to guard your security. What else do you want? If I know the facts, then I can take them to Sadat and try to satisfy both you and him. My problem is with the issues that do not really relate to Israel's security. I must have your frank assessment. My greatest strength here is your confidence—but I don't feel that I have your trust. What do you really need for your defense? It is ridiculous to speak of Jordan overrunning Israel! I believe I can get from Sadat what you really need, but I just do not have your confidence."
>
> Weizman replied, "We wouldn't be here if we didn't have confidence in you." (Carter, 1982, p. 349)

Cyrus Vance, who was perhaps the most calm individual in the whole conference, had his breaking point. In a meeting with Begin in regard to the second draft of an American proposal, "Vance was very angry. This time, unlike his demeanor on earlier occasions, he failed to preserve his calm. He became red in the face, gesticulated with his hands, and raised his voice." Later in that same meeting, "The mood of anger gave way to sadness and disappointment," as they realized that the conference might well fail (Dayan, 1981, p. 174).

In any sessions with antagonistic or hostile groups, there is bound to be a high degree of feeling, and emotional, even irrational, statements are not uncommon. If handled well, these often serve a positive purpose in releasing tension.

7. President Carter made many facilitative efforts. Though he was at times a persuader rather than a facilitator, he nonetheless was able to take a more neutral stance than either of the other two and to bend his efforts toward increasing understanding. In one of the early meetings of the three leaders, Begin and Sadat were arguing bitterly over a whole range of issues. Carter said practically nothing, but continued to take notes, which he frequently did in the meetings. At the end of the session he simply read from his notes the issues that had divided them and the stand of each party in regard to the issues. This certainly served a most facilitative function since in stating the issues calmly and clearly, those present could understand them better and could see the issues in a more rational light.

President Carter consciously endeavored to be a mediator and facilitator. When mistrust deepened between the other two,

I acted as a referee and put them back on track, and on occasion explained what was meant when there was an obvious misinterpretation. Strangely enough, every so often laughter broke out. Once, for instance, one of them referred to kissing Barbara Walters, the television journalist, and wondered if the cameras were on and what his wife might think. (Carter, 1982, p. 353)

As the tension heightened and Begin and Sadat frequently refused to meet with each other, Carter served a facilitative function by talking first with one and then with the other, presenting to each leader in a calm and cool way the views and positions taken by the other.

Sometimes he could not quiet the turmoil, and simply had to wait for it to die down. In one situation,

All restraint was now gone. Their faces were flushed, and the niceties of diplomatic language and protocol were stripped away. They had almost forgotten that I was there, and there was nothing to distract me from recording this fascinating debate....

Begin had touched a raw nerve, and I thought Sadat would explode. He pounded the table.... (Carter, 1982, p. 351)

Eventually, the discussion cooled down of its own accord.

In our experience, it is rare that people have refused for any length of time to meet with others. But certainly Carter's role as a more neutral party, able to understand and voice the views of the contending leaders, was a major facilitative help.

8.   There was a "pressure cooker" aspect of the conference. In every intensive group lasting over a number of days, feelings become intensified, the group process becomes more dynamic, because persons are in contact or potential contact all day, every day, with just one focus in mind. It has been our experience that the highs and lows of feelings become much more marked. This was very evident at Camp David. In describing this aspect, Dayan says that they were "cooped up in the high pressure chamber of the Camp David Conference" (Dayan, 1981, p. 169).

To be continually in face-to-face contact for 13 days with a person with whom you violently disagree, together with a person who seems to understand each of you, is a powerful dynamic that leads toward better understanding. There is no doubt that Carter helped to keep this high-pressure aspect from exploding and turned it into a positive force.

9.   It is of interest that there were separate times when each of the three leaders experienced the conference as a complete failure. Sadat and his entourage packed up their bags and were ready to leave the morning of the eleventh day. It was only a very intense plea on the part of President Carter that led Sadat to say that he would stay to the end. Begin, even on the last day of the conference, decided that he would not sign anything, that no agreement was possible, and that the conference was a failure. Carter's experience came on Day 11, when he learned that Sadat was leaving. In this "terrible moment," he recognized that the conference was a failure and "prayed fervently for a few minutes that somehow we could find peace" (Carter, 1982, p. 392).

This is an aspect with which I (Rogers) am very familiar. It has sometimes seemed to me that in intensive group sessions with hostile groups it is only when I recognize that no progress can be made, that the cause is hopeless, that somehow a turning point is reached. I have no explanation of the reasons for this. I simply know that it has happened on several occasions that only when I have felt that the sessions had come to a dead end has there come a turn toward the positive.

10.   The incident that seems to have turned the Camp David conference from a complete failure to a significant success was a highly personal one, involving none of the issues relevant to the conference. President Carter describes this incident, and it is a very moving one. On

the last day of the conference, when it seemed that all efforts were failing and when Begin was adamant about not signing anything, Carter took a very personal step. Photographs had been taken of the three leaders together and Sadat had autographed all of these photographs. Begin had requested that three be autographed for his grandchildren. Susan Clough, Carter's secretary, suggested that she obtain the names of the grandchildren, so that President Carter could personalize the inscriptions. This was done. He went to Begin's cabin. He found Begin

> sitting on the front porch, very distraught and nervous because the talks had finally broken down at the last minute.
>
> I handed him the photographs. He took them and thanked me. Then he happened to look down and saw that his granddaughter's name was on the top one. He spoke it aloud and then looked at each photograph individually, repeating the name of the grandchild I had written on it. His lips trembled and tears welled up in his eyes. He told me a little about each child and especially about the one who seemed to be his favorite. We were both emotional as we talked quietly for a few minutes about grandchildren and about war. (Carter, 1982, p. 399)

It is worth pausing for a moment to consider the message that was contained in Carter's behavior. He was saying, mostly nonverbally, "I know the conference has failed, as far as you are concerned. Yet I want you to know that I care for you as a person, and I value those whom you love. I think of their future in the world we are creating. I think of the possibility of war and its effect on them." Certainly he touched not the prime minister, but the man. They connected as persons with common concerns.

Although there was further conversation, Begin objecting to the statement about Jerusalem, his attitude was changing. Within the hour he phoned to say that the just-drafted new letter about Jerusalem was acceptable to him. Then he took an unprecedented step. He went to Sadat's cabin. Carter, being told of this, went over, determined to interrupt if they were arguing. He arrived as Begin was leaving Sadat's cabin. "He was quite happy as he told me they had had a love feast and that Sadat had agreed to Begin's language on the Knesset vote" (Carter, 1982, p. 400).

To some it may seem very strange that the turning point of an international conference of great significance was based on a tearful discussion of grandchildren rather than the issues of the conference. Yet to us who have experienced intensive groups this seems quite natural. It is when the deepest personal feelings are touched that change takes place in the individual's attitude. This definitely seems to have been the case here.

11. All three of the leaders experienced an intense emotional "high" when the agreements were finally reached, after the conference had been so perilously close to failure. "All three of us were flushed with pride and good will toward one another because of our unexpected success" (Carter, 1982, p. 403). It is convincing evidence of this heightened feeling that Sadat and Begin, who had for so long been violent enemies and who even at Camp David had difficulty in communicating with each other without anger, embraced each other warmly on public television at the signing ceremony. There can be no doubt of the sincerity of this feeling at the moment, even though it undoubtedly had existed very recently and probably would fade in the days to come.

Such intensive emotional highs are common indeed in the closing moments of an intensive group. They are even more marked when tensions have been reduced and there is a feeling of great relief as well as great pleasure. They certainly do not last with this intensity. They are in part possible because of the limited nature of the experience. Whether or not they continue to exist as close bonds depends on the situation and the people involved.

Some Differences—With Comments

There are a number of ways in which the experience of Camp David differed, sometimes rather sharply, from the intensive groups described earlier. Some of these differences will be pointed out and comments made as to ways in which the situation might have been handled differently. These suggestions are certainly not given in any presumptuous way. The achievements at Camp David were outstanding and speak for themselves. The suggestions are simply to induce thoughtful consideration if other similar diplomatic conferences are held.

1. Although President Carter's facilitative efforts were unusual and often effective, there was no attempt to understand the leaders at a more profound emotional level. Some might feel that this would be inappropriate, but this was not the opinion of Dayan, who was one of the major participants. He says, after speaking favorably of the attitudes of both Carter and Vance,

But there were times—and that evening was one of them—when I felt that neither the President nor the Secretary of State had sufficiently penetrated the core of the problems of the Middle East. They did not put themselves in the shoes—or rather the hearts—of either side. They knew what the Israeli and the Arab representatives were saying, but they did not always distinguish between what was being uttered for bargaining purposes and external consumption and what was the profound expression of the spirit and the yearning of a nation. (Dayan, 1981, p. 183)

The task of the experienced facilitator is to do exactly what Dayan describes—to step into the shoes, and into the hearts, of the antagonists, to be thus sensitively empathic and to voice this deep understanding. Equally important, he would be nonjudgmental. He would understand, in a profound and acceptant way, the spirit and the yearnings of each of the contending parties. He would not be concerned with solving the complex issues, but solely with clarifying and bringing into the open the feelings, attitudes, concepts, and opinions of the participants. It is our experience that this delicate "indwelling" in the inner world of each person leads most rapidly to improved communication, and gradually to improved relationships and movement toward reduction of tension.

But, one may ask, even if such a facilitator could be found, would he be acceptable to the leaders and their delegations? I believe there are people with training and experience who would be capable of the task, though they might not be acceptable to the particular participants. However, we have seen that persons like Dag Hammarskjold or U Thant showed many of the sensitivities of a good facilitator and with some additional experience could very well have served such a function. In other words, a high-level person not directly involved with any of the three countries or the three leaders could have served a deeply facilitative function, which might have enhanced the negotiations by removing some of the obstacles.

Could such a facilitator have handled the "shouting matches" that sometimes erupted? Probably not always, but experience shows that to recognize, accept, and bring into the open the underlying feelings on both sides of such a violent verbal encounter often reduces the tension and makes it more possible for each individual to see, at least partially, the point of view of the other.

It seems quite possible that an experienced person-centered facilitator could have increased the likelihood that Begin and Sadat would have met together more often than they did, in face-to-face contact rather than sending each other messages through Carter.

2. There was no attempt to hold continuing meetings that included the three delegations. It seems reasonable that the primary meetings were among the big three, since their status was sharply different from that of the other members of the delegations. However, it is interesting to speculate what might have happened if the remaining 24 members of the delegations had met together with experienced facilitators. Since 24 is a rather large group, it would have been well to divide them into two groups of twelve each, with four members of each delegation participating in each group. Their meetings would have had much the same intensity and the sharp differences that we observed between the big three. They would have resembled the intensive groups described earlier in this chapter. It would have been understood that their meetings did not have official weight, but I believe they could have served as very good breeding grounds for innovative and stimulating ideas that could have been communicated to their leaders. Such meetings would have served several important purposes. The members of the delegations would have gone through much the same kind of experiences as Sadat, Begin, and Carter. Consequently they would be aware, within themselves, of the kind of mutual understandings that had been achieved. Thus they would have constituted an important support group when the leaders returned to their respective countries. The leaders paid a large price for not having such sensitively understanding support groups. Even before the conference ended, two of Sadat's major delegates resigned because they did not approve of what they saw as concessions that he had made. Likewise, Begin met a storm of criticism when he returned to Israel, as did Sadat.

It is recognized that this suggestion of unofficial meetings of the total delegations is an innovative and "far-out" suggestion, yet it seems worthy of consideration. It would not have been difficult to have selected facilitators for such sessions. Carter quite frequently met with individual members of the Israeli and Egyptian delegations, sometimes meeting with two or three of them at the same time. It is believed that the other leaders also met with individual members of the American delegation. Such meetings were usually to thrash out difficult points. I believe they would have been improved had the delegates already been involved in facilitated encounters with members of the other delegations. It is recognized that such meetings might have negative as well as positive aspects, as was found in the "Fermeda experience," which will be mentioned later.

3. Partly because the conference was touch-and-go right up to the last moment, there was little opportunity for consideration of "back-

home" problems. It has frequently been found that in the intense emotional interaction of such a group the participants tend to forget the distance they have come from their constituents. It is very fruitful for them to become aware of the attitudes of those they will meet on their return and to be more ready to cope with the differences, the criticisms, the lack of understanding that they will meet when they are again with their constituents. It is unfortunate that there was no such opportunity for these considerations.

4. It would seem that all parties could have profited from more consultation with people in various fields—group dynamics, labor negotiations, and the like—to learn more of what was already known about the handling of frictional situations. It is known that Carter, through Cyrus Vance, did consult the Harvard Negotiation Center and, whether because of their advice or spontaneously, followed a "one text procedure," which was part of their counsel (Fisher & Ury, 1981, pp. 118–122). Very simply put, it meant that when Sadat had stated his position in extreme terms and the Israelis had responded with a position paper of their own, the only avenue to peace seemed to be through making concessions, which neither side would be willing to make. Carter then introduced an American proposal—the single-document strategy—which came as close as possible to meeting the demands of both sides and in which there was no investment. It was a document made to be improved upon, and it meant that both sides were working to improve a single document rather than standing by their own separate documents. This is simply one example of the help that might have been obtained through consultation with those persons, outside the diplomatic world, with long experience in handling disputatious groups.

WHAT OF THE FUTURE?

I have presented a way of working with antagonistic factions that has proven effective in my experience. Looking through the prism of this viewpoint, I have examined the negotiations at Camp David. The similarities in the process are striking. But where does this lead us?

Research and Development

There are many people with wide experience working in the field of conflict resolution. I have spoken of my experience, working in a person-centered way, but that is only one view. What is needed is to recognize this as an important field of study and fund deeper and broader investigations into all the ways in which intergroup tensions may be resolved. In the United States, the proposed Peace Academy (to be on equal terms with the military academies) would be an excellent base for such studies. Internationally, the new University for Peace, established by the United Nations (and aided by its first million-dollar gift from Japan) would be an ideal place for the intellectual and experiential pursuit of pathways to peace. We can hope that similar institutions will be established in other countries.

At present we spend billions on research and development leading to new and more destructive weapons of war. We spend almost nothing on research and development of new and more effective means of moving two feuding parties toward peace. Such funding is essential.

At present only a small amount of research and experimentation is going on, usually with inadequate funding. Such an experiment is the "Fermeda experience" (Doob, 1970), in which unofficial representatives of two African nations were brought together to see if they could find solutions (unofficial, of course) to an important border dispute. In many ways, they implemented the techniqes that have been pointed out as being effective in our experience and in the Camp David experience. In the philosophy and manner of leadership, the experiment differed considerably from a person-centered approach. The process appeared positive up to a point, but due to special frustrating circumstances the final outcome was disappointing. The investigators are to be congratulated on conducting this experiment and on reporting what they have learned so fully. There should, however, be dozens of such studies and experiments going forward with generous funding from national and international sources. There is much we could learn about new and more effective ways of reducing intergroup hostilities and resolving intergroup problems.

A Proposal

As an immediate step, which could be taken without such massive support, a seminar or workshop might be held for diplomats, executives of multinational corporations, international labor leaders, and others with influence in international affairs. The purposes of this workshop would be: (1) for such individuals to *experience*, during a period of 10 days or more, the reduction in their own intercultural and interpersonal prejudices and animosities and the building of a sense of community;

(2) to contribute from their own backgrounds new ways of working with tensions; (3) to plan a suitable long-term training program for persons such as themselves, to sharpen and improve understanding of and skills in dealing with feuding groups. Such a workshop could be carried out with international sponsorship.

CONCLUDING COMMENTS

We have endeavored to make clear that a person-centered approach is one way, a unique way, of increasing communication and reducing tension in situations "bristling with malice." A process is initiated in a pervasive psychological environment springing from the special way of being of the facilitator or facilitators. This process leads to improved understanding, more mutual trust, and progressive steps toward the resolution of differences.

We have pointed to the Camp David experience as having many similarities to this approach. Camp David indicates that this kind of approach may be effective, not only with small groups, but at an international level.

We have called for national and international sponsorship of well-funded centers for research and development of this and every other promising approach to peaceful settlement of the tensions that now plague our planet and may lead to its destruction. We have pointed out that it is high time that we invest in the means of bringing peace and not only invest in the means of making war. We need to enlarge the knowledge, develop the appropriate attitudes and skills so necessary in resolving hostilities.

We have suggested one step that could be taken now—an extended seminar or workshop for those working with international issues, where they might experience a person-centered approach and determine whether it would improve their own abilities to work toward peaceful solutions.

Finally, we know of no more critical area for study and practice than the expansion of ways of resolving bitterness and animosity. Our modern world will perish in a holocaust unless we learn new and more effective means of reducing and resolving the competitions, hatreds, and enmities that are leading us toward our doom. But the purpose of this chapter is to say—there is hope.

NOTES

1. The first part of this paper is the work of the senior author. The second portion, regarding Camp David, is a joint effort.

2. Adapted from *Carl Rogers on Personal Power: Inner Strength and Its Revolutionary Impact* by Carl Rogers. Copyright © 1977 by Carl R. Rogers. Reprinted by permission of Delacorte Press.

3. Adapted from *Carl Rogers on Personal Power: Inner Strength and Its Revolutionary Impact* by Carl Rogers. Copyright © 1977 by Carl R. Rogers. Reprinted by permission of Delacorte Press.

Afterword

Because excerpts from the interview with "Gloria" are used in this book, and because rumors developed in ignorance of her real life and circumstances, we invited Carl Rogers to publish a brief statement of the sequel as he knows the facts.

The Editors.

GLORIA—A HISTORICAL NOTE

Carl Rogers

For years students and professionals from all parts of the country and abroad have been asking me "Do you have any further information about Gloria?" They have been much moved and stimulated by viewing the three interviews held with Gloria in 1964 by myself, Fritz Perls, and Albert Ellis. The three therapists interviewed her, in that order, all in one day.

I have answered this question dozens, perhaps hundreds of times. But since the film, to my surprise, continues to be heavily used in teaching, I should like to give a more public answer.

Gloria kept in touch with me by letters—usually one or two a year—for a period of at least ten years. The last letter I had from her, shortly before her untimely death, was written fifteen years after the filmed interview.

Without quoting her, or giving the private details, I should like to present a few of the highlights of our intermittent yet close relationship, which showed so clearly her increasing maturity and ability to cope, and to be her true self.

A year or more after the interview was filmed, the Western Behavioral Sciences Institute, of which I was a member, was organizing a weekend conference where I was to be the leader. The person handling the registrations came to me and said, "Here is a Gloria, applying for the workshop. Would it be *the* Gloria?" I looked at the application and found that it was. I wrote her, telling her that we were planning to use the three films as a rather central part of the weekend. Personally, I would be delighted to have her attend, but she might find it somewhat uncomfortable to be talked about by so many people. She came, and I believe the experience with the group *was* somewhat uncomfortable for her. There were two experiences which occurred during that weekend which are worthy of note.

After the showing of the Fritz Perls interview with her, Gloria stood up in the group of more than a hundred people, obviously wanting to speak. Her face was flushed and it was soon evident that she was furious. "Why did I *do* all those things that he asked me to do! Why did I let him do that to me!" She felt that she had somehow given over her power and this enraged her. She made it very clear that she did not like the interview at all.

This reaction was of special interest to the group since at the conclusion of the original filming she had expressed quite a different view. At that time she had been asked whether she had any comments about the three therapists. She said that if she were beginning therapy she would like to work with me. She thought that in her present situation the challenging ways of Dr. Perls might be the best for her. So it was somewhat surprising to find that when she relived the experience by watching the film, she was repelled by Dr. Perl's domination of her and her acquiescence in surrendering her power.

The second aspect of the weekend which I wish to report is the luncheon she shared with me and my wife. I had wanted to learn how life was going for her and I invited her to take lunch with us. She and Helen formed a very quick contact (Helen's interest in people was like a magnet) and we had a lively and enjoyable luncheon. As we were about to leave, she said she had a question she wanted to ask. Would we object if, in her thinking, she regarded us as her parents in spirit? We both understood her to mean that she wished to see us as parents she would have liked to have had. We each replied that we would be pleased and honored to have that status in her life. Her warm feelings for us were reciprocated.

In the ensuing years she wrote me about many things in her life, but

I do not feel free to reveal the content. I will only say that there were very good times, and there were tragic times, especially of family illness, and she showed sensitivity, wisdom, and courage in meeting the different aspects of her experience. I felt enriched by knowing the open way in which she met difficult issues. I was often touched by her letters.

I believe that those who view (or read*) the interview will gain more from it by knowing a small part of my later interaction with Gloria. I am awed by the fact that this fifteen-year association grew out of the quality of the relationship we formed in one thirty-minute period in which we truly met as persons. It is good to know that even one half-hour can make a difference in a life.

---

*A transcription of the interview is contained in Rogers & Wood, 1974, 237–254.

References

Aldrich, H. *Organizations and environments.* Englewood Cliffs, N.J.: Prentice-Hall, 1979.

Anderson, W. Personal growth and client-centered therapy: An information-processing view. In D.A. Wexler & L.N. Rice (Eds.), *Innovations in client-centered therapy.* New York: Wiley, 1974.

Angyal, A. *Foundations for a science of personality.* New York: The Commonwealth Fund, 1941.

Angyal, A. *Neurosis and treatment: A holistic theory.* New York: Viking, 1973.

Anthony, J.J. A comparison of measured and perceived conditions of empathy, warmth, and genuineness in secondary school counseling. (Doctoral dissertation, University of Florida, 1971.) *Dissertation Abstracts International,* 1972, *33,* 562A. (University Microfilms No. 72-21, 040)

Apfelbaum, B. *Dimensions of transference in psychotherapy.* Berkeley: University of California Press, 1958.

Argyris, C., & Schön, D. *Organizational learning.* Boston: Addison Wesley, 1978.

Association for Humanistic Psychology. *Resource directory.* San Francisco: Author, 1980.

Athay, A.L. The relationship between counselor self-concept, empathy, warmth, and genuineness, and client rated improvement. (Doctoral dissertation, University of Utah, 1973.) *Dissertation Abstracts International,* 1974, *34,* 3976A. (University Microfilms No. 73-31, 254)

Authier, J., Gustafson, K., Guerney, B.G., Jr., & Kasdorf, J.A. The psychological practitioner as teacher: A theoretical-historical practical review. *The Counseling Psychologist,* 1975, *5* (2), 31–50.

Avery, A.W. Communication skills training for paraprofessional helpers. *American Journal of Community Psychology,* 1978, *6,* 203–209.

Balderston, F.E. *Managing today's university.* San Francisco: Jossey-Bass, 1974.

Balint, M. *The doctor, his patient, and the illness.* New York: International Universities Press, 1964.

Barnard, D. *Psychological and theological perspectives on the practice of medicine:*

An *analysis of competence and limitation.* Unpublished doctoral dissertation, Harvard University, 1980.

Barrett-Lennard, G.T. Dimensions of therapist response as causal factors in therapeutic change. *Psychological Monographs,* 1962, *76* (43, Whole No. 562).

Barrett-Lennard, G.T. The Relationship Inventory: Later developments and applications. JSAS *Catalog of Selected Documents in Psychology,* 1978, *8,* 68. (Ms. No. 1732, p. 55)

Barrett-Lennard, G.T. The client-centered system unfolding. In F.J. Turner (Ed.), *Social work treatment: Interlocking theoretical approaches* (2nd ed.). New York: Free Press, 1979. (a)

Barrett-Lennard, G.T. A model of communical-relationship systems in intensive groups. *Human Relations,* 1979, *32,* 841–849. (b)

Barrett-Lennard, G.T. The Relationship Inventory now: Issues and advances in theory, method, and use. In L.S. Greenberg & W.M. Pinsoff (Eds.), *The psychotherapeutic process: A research handbook.* New York: Guilford, in press.

Barron, F. *Personal soundness in university graduate students.* Berkeley: University of California Press, 1954.

Barsky, A.J. Hidden reasons some patients visit doctors. *Annals of Internal Medicine,* 1981, *94* (Part 1), 492–498.

Barsky, A.J., & Klerman, G.L. Overview: Hypochondriasis, bodily complaints, and somatic styles. *American Journal of Psychiatry,* 1983, *140* (3), 273–283.

Bateson, G. *Steps to an ecology of mind.* New York: Chandler, 1972.

Bebout, J. It takes one to know one: Existential-Rogerian concepts in encounter groups. In D.A. Wexler & L.N. Rice (Eds.), *Innovations in client-centered therapy.* New York: Wiley, 1974.

Beck, A.P. Phases in the development of structure in therapy and encounter groups. In D.A. Wexler & L.N. Rice (Eds.), *Innovations in client-centered therapy.* New York: Wiley, 1974.

Behrends, R.S., & Seeman, J. Personality integration and maximal use of biofeedback information. *American Journal of Clinical Biofeedback,* 1982, *5,* 110–122.

Bereiter, C. Some persisting dilemmas in measuring change. In C. Harris (Ed.), *Problems in measuring change.* Madison: University of Wisconsin Press, 1963.

Berger, P. *The sacred canopy.* New York: Doubleday, 1967.

Bergin, A.E. Some implications of psychotherapy research for therapeutic practice. *Journal of Abnormal Psychology,* 1966, *71,* 235–246.

Bergin, A.E. The evaluation of therapeutic outcomes. In A.E. Bergin & S.L. Garfield (Eds.), *Handbook of psychotherapy and behavior change.* New York: Wiley, 1971.

Bergin, A.E., & Lambert, M.J. The evaluation of therapeutic outcomes. In S.L. Garfield & A.E. Bergin (Eds.), *Handbook of psychotherapy and behavior change* (2nd ed.). New York: Wiley, 1978.

Bergsma, J., & Thomasma, D. *Health care: Its psychosocial dimensions.* Pittsburgh: Duquesne University Press, 1982.

Bernard, J.M. Supervisor training: A discrimination model. *Counselor Education and Supervision*, 1979, *19*, 60–68.

Bion, W. *Experiences in groups.* New York: Basic Books, 1959.

Birk, J.M. Effects of counseling supervision method and preference of empathic understanding. *Journal of Counseling Psychology*, 1972, *19*, 542–546.

Block, J. *Lives through time.* Berkeley, Calif.: Bancroft, 1971.

Blumenthal, A.L. *The process of cognition.* Englewood Cliffs, N.J.: Prentice-Hall, 1977.

Board, F.A. Patients' and physicians' judgments of outcome of psychotherapy in an outpatient clinic. *Archives of General Psychiatry*, 1959, *1*, 185–196.

Bok, S. Secrets. *On the ethics of concealment and revelation.* New York: Pantheon, 1982.

Boszormenyi-Nagy, I. A theory of relationships: Experience and transaction. In I. Boszormenyi-Nagy & J.L. Framo (Eds.), *Intensive family therapy: Theoretical and practical aspects.* Hagerstown, Md.: Harper & Row, 1965.

Botkin, J.W., Elmandjra, M., & Malitza, M. *No limits to learning: Bridging the human gap.* New York: Pergamon, 1979.

Boukydis, K.N. Caring and confronting. *Voices: The Art and Science of Psychotherapy*, 1979, *15*, 31–34.

Boulding, K.E. The management of decline. *Change*, 1975, *7* (5), 8–64.

Bourne, L.E. Typicality effects in logically defined categories. *Memory and Cognition*, 1981, *10*, 3–9.

Bowen, M. A family concept of schizophrenia. In D.D. Jackson (Ed.), *The etiology of schizophrenia.* New York: Basic Books, 1960.

Bown, O.H. *An investigation of therapeutic relationships in client-centered psychotherapy.* Unpublished doctoral dissertation, University of Chicago, 1954.

Bozarth, J.D. The person centered approach in the large community group. In G. Gazda (Ed.), *Innovations to group psychotherapy* (2nd ed.). Springfield, Ill.: Thomas, 1981.

Bozarth, J.D., & Grace, D.P. Objective ratings and client perception of therapeutic conditions with university counseling center clients. *Journal of Clinical Psychology*, 1970, *26*, 117–118.

Bozarth, J.D., Mitchell, K.M., & Krauft, C.C. Empirical observations of antecedents to psychotherapeutic outcome: Some implications. *Rehabilitation Counseling Bulletin*, September, 1976, *20* (1), 28–36.

Breuer, J., & Freud, S. *Studies on hysteria.* New York: Basic Books, 1957.

Brodey, W.M. Some family operations and schizophrenia: A study of five hospitalized families each with a schizophrenic mother. *Archives of General Psychiatry*, 1959, *1*, 379–402.

Brody, H. The systems view of man: Implications for medicine, science, and ethics. *Perspectives in Biology and Medicine,* Autumn 1973, *17,* 71–92.

Browning, D. *Atonement and psychotherapy.* Philadelphia: Westminster, 1966.

Browning, D. *Moral context of pastoral care.* Philadelphia: Westminster, 1976.

Bruner, J.S. On perceptual readiness. *Psychological Review,* 1957, 64, 123–152.

Burstein, J.W., & Carkhuff, R.R. Objective, therapist and client ratings of therapist offered facilitative conditions of moderate to low functioning therapists. *Journal of Clinical Psychology,* 1968, 24, 240–241.

Butler, J.M. Self concept change in psychotherapy. In S.R. Brown & D.J. Brenner (Eds.), *Science, psychology, and communication: Essays honoring William Stephenson.* New York: Teachers College Press, 1972.

Butler, J.M. & Haigh, G.V. Changes in the relation between self-concepts and ideal concepts consequent upon client-centered counseling. In C.R. Rogers & R.F. Dymond (Eds.), *Psychotherapy and personality change.* Chicago: University of Chicago Press, 1954.

Cain, D.J. The therapists' and clients' perceptions of therapeutic conditions in relation to perceived interview outcome. (Doctoral dissertation, University of Wyoming, 1972.) *Dissertation Abstracts International,* 1973, *33,* 6071B. (University Microfilms No. 73-14, 271)

Campbell, D.T., & Stanley, J.C. *Experimental and quasi-experimental designs for research.* Chicago: Rand McNally, 1963.

Cantor, N., & Kihlstrom, J.F. *Personality, cognition and social interaction.* Hillsdale, N.H.: Erlbaum, 1981.

Caracena, P.F., & Victory, J.R. Correlates of phenomenological and judged empathy. *Journal of Counseling Psychology,* 1969, *16,* 510–515.

Carkhuff, R.R. *The development of human resources.* New York: Holt, Rinehart & Winston, 1971.

Carkhuff, R.R., & Anthony, W.A. *The skills of helping: An introduction to counseling.* Amherst, Mass.: Human Resource Development Press, 1979.

Carkhuff, R.R., & Berenson, B.G. In search of an honest experience: Confrontation in counseling and life. In R.R. Carkhuff & B.G. Berenson (Eds.), *Beyond counseling and therapy.* New York: Holt, Rinehart & Winston, 1977.

Carmichael, J.A. *Perception of self-as-object as a consequence of systematic disensitization and client-centered therapy.* Unpublished master's thesis, University of Victoria (British Columbia), 1970.

Carnegie Commission on Higher Education. *Governance of higher education: Six priority problems.* New York: McGraw-Hill, 1973.

Carnegie Council on Policy Studies in Higher Education. *3000 futures: The next twenty years for higher education.* San Francisco: Jossey-Bass, 1980.

Carter, J. *Keeping faith.* New York: Bantam, 1982.

Cartwright, D.S. Annotated bibliography of research and theory construction in client-centered therapy. *Journal of Counseling Psychology,* 1957, *4,* 82–100.

Cartwright, D.S. *Theories and models of personality.* Dubuque, Iowa: Brown, 1979.

Cartwright, D.S. Exploratory analysis of verbally stimulated imagery of the self. *Journal of Mental Imagery,* 1980, *4,* 1–21.

Cartwright, D.W., & Harary, F. Structural balance: A generalization of Heider's theory. *Psychological Review,* 1956, *63,* 277–293.

Cartwright, D.W., Jenkins, J.L., Chavez, R., & Peckar, H. Studies in imagery and identity. *Journal of Personality and Social Psychology,* 1983, *44,* 376–384.

Carver, C.S., & Scheier, M.F. *Attention and self-regulation: A control-theory approach to human behavior.* New York: Springer-Verlag, 1981.

Cassell, E.J. *The healer's art: A new approach to the doctor-patient relationship.* Baltimore: Penguin, 1979.

Clebsch, W. *American religious thought.* Chicago: University of Chicago Press, 1973.

Clebsch, W., & Jaekle, C. *Pastoral care in historical perspective.* New York: Aronson, 1975.

Clinebell, H . *Basic types of pastoral counseling.* New York: Abingdon, 1966.

Cochrane, C.T., & Holloway, A.J. Client-centered therapy and Gestalt therapy: In search of a merger. In D.A. Wexler & L.N. Rice (Eds.), *Innovations in client-centered therapy.* New York: Wiley, 1974.

Cohen, C.E. Goals and schemata in person perception: Making sense from the stream of behavior. In N. Cantor & J.R. Kihlstrom (Eds.), *Personality, cognition, and social interaction.* Hillsdale, N.J.: Erlbaum, 1981.

Cohen, M.D., & March, J.G. *Leadership and ambiguity: The American college president.* New York: McGraw-Hill, 1974.

Cohen, R.J. *Malpractice: A guide for mental health professionals.* New York: Free Press, 1979.

Cohen, S., & Taylor, L. *Psychological survival: The experience of long-term imprisonment.* Harmondsworth: Penguin, 1972.

Colistro, F.P. Empathy, client depth of experiencing, and goal-attainment scaling: A within-session examination of the client centered therapy process. (Doctoral dissertation, University of British Columbia, 1978.) *Dissertation Abstracts International,* 1979, *39,* 5405A–5406A. (University Microfilms No. not listed)

Collins, J.D. Experimental evaluation of a six-month conjugal therapy and relationship enhancement program. In B.G. Guerney, Jr. (Ed.), *Relationship enhancement: Skill-training programs for therapy, problem prevention, and enrichment.* San Francisco: Jossey-Bass, 1977.

Constantinople, A. An Eriksonian measure of personality development in college students. *Developmental Psychology,* 1969, *1,* 357–372.

Cooley, R.S., & Seeman, J. Personality integration and social schemata. *Journal of Personality,* 1979, *47,* 288–304.

Corcoran, K.J. Experiential empathy: A theory of felt-level experience. *Journal of Humanistic Psychology*, 1981, *21* (1), 29–38.

Cormier, L.S., & Bernard, J.M. Ethical and legal responsibilities of clinical supervisors. *Personnel and Guidance Journal*, 1982, *60*, 486–491.

Corson, J.J. *The governance of colleges and universities: Modernizing structure and processes.* New York: McGraw-Hill, 1975.

Couchon, W.D., & Bernard, J.M. *Effect of timing of supervision on supervisor and counselor performance.* Unpublished manuscript, Purdue University, 1982.

Craik, F., & Tulving, E. Depth of processing and the selection of words in episodic memory. *Journal of Experimental Psychology: General*, 1975, *104*, 268–294.

Dayan, M. *Breakthrough: A personal account of the Egypt-Israel peace negotiations.* New York: Knopf, 1981.

Dell, P.F. Beyond homeostasis: Toward a concept of coherence. *Family Process*, 1982, *21* (1), 21–41.

Deren, M. *The divine horsemen.* New York: Chelsea House, 1970.

DeRyck, P. Observations on Rogers as therapist. *Journey*, 1982, *4*.

Dicks, H.V. *Marital tensions.* New York: Basic Books, 1967.

Dingwall, R. *Aspects of illness.* London: Martin Robertson, 1976.

Dollard, J., & Miller, N.E. *Personality and psychotherapy.* New York: McGraw-Hill, 1950.

Doob, L.W. (Ed.). *Resolving conflict in Africa: The Fermeda workshop.* New Haven/London: Yale University Press, 1970.

Doob, L.W., & Foltz, W.J. The Belfast workshop. *Journal of Conflict Resolution*, 1973, *17*, 489–512.

Dubos, R. *Celebrating life.* New York: McGraw-Hill, 1981.

Duncan, C.B. A reputation test of personality integration. *Journal of Personality and Social Psychology*, 1966, *3* (5) 516–524.

Eisenberg, L. The physician as interpreter: Ascribing meaning to the illness experience. *Comprehensive Psychiatry*, 1981, *22* (3), 239–248.

Ely, A.L., Guerney, B.G., Jr., & Stover, L. Efficacy of the training phase of conjugal therapy. *Psychotherapy: Theory, Research, and Practice*, 1973, *10* (3), 201–207.

Engel, G.L. The need for a new medical model: A challenge for biomedicine. *Science*, 1977, *196* (4286), 129–136.

Engel, G.L. The clinical application of the biopsychosocial model. *American Journal of Psychiatry*, 1980, *137* (5), 535–544.

Epstein, L., & Feiner, A. *Countertransference.* New York: Aronson, 1974.

Erikson, E.H. *Childhood and society* (2nd ed.). New York: Norton, 1963.

Erikson, E.H. *Insight and responsibility.* New York: Norton, 1964.

Fabrega, H. *Disease and social behavior: An interdisciplinary perspective.* Cambridge, Mass.: MIT Press, 1974.

Fairbairn, W.R.D. An *object relations theory of personality*. New York: Basic Books, 1954.

Farson, R. The technology of humanism. *Journal of Humanistic Psychology*, 1978, *18*, 5–35.

Feitel, B.S. Feeling understood as a function of a variety of therapist activities. (Doctoral dissertation, Teachers College, Columbia University, 1968.) *Dissertation Abstracts*, 1968, *29*, 1170B. (University Microfilms No. 68-12, 933)

Fenichel, O. *Problems of psychoanalytic technique*. Albany, N.Y.: Psychoanalytic Quarterly, Inc., 1941.

Field, M.J. *Search for security*. Evanston, Ill.: Northwestern University Press, 1960.

Figley, C., & Guerney, B.G., Jr. (Producers). *The conjugal relationship enhancement program*. University Park, Penn.: Individual and Family Consultation Center of The Pennsylvania State University, 1974. (Videotape)

Fish, J.M. Empathy and the reported emotional experiences of beginning psychotherapists. *Journal of Consulting and Clinical Psychology*, 1970, *35*, 64–69.

Fisher, R., & Ury, W. *Getting to yes: Negotiating agreement without giving in*. Boston: Houghton Mifflin, 1981.

Fiske, D.W. The shaky evidence is slowly put together. *Journal of Consulting and Clinical Psychology*, 1971, *37*, 314–315.

Fiske, S.T. Social cognition and affect. In J.H. Harvey (Ed.), *Cognition, social behavior and the environment*. Hillsdale, N.J.: Erlbaum, 1981.

Framo, J.L. Rationale and techniques of intensive family therapy. In I. Boszormenyi-Nagy & J.L. Framo (Eds.), *Intensive family therapy: Theoretical and practical aspects*. Hagerstown, Md.: Harper & Row, 1965.

Framo, J.L. Symptoms from a family transactional viewpoint. In N.W. Ackerman (Ed.), *Family therapy in transition*. Boston: Little, Brown, 1970.

Frank, J. *Persuasion and healing*. Baltimore: Johns Hopkins University Press, 1973.

Freeman, L. *The story of Anna O.* New York: Walker, 1972.

Fretz, B.R. Postural movements in a counseling dyad. *Journal of Counseling Psychology*, 1966, *13*, 335–343.

Friedlander, M.L., & Ward, L.G. *Dimensions of supervisory style*. Unpublished manuscript, State University of New York, Albany, 1983.

Freud, A. *The ego and the mechanisms of defense*. New York: International Universities Press, 1966.

Freud, S. The future prospects of psychoanalytic theory. In J. Strachey (Ed. and trans.), *The standard edition of the complete psychological works of Sigmund Freud* (Vol. 7, pp. 3–122). London: Hogarth, 1910.

Freud, S. *The ego and the id*. London: Hogarth, 1923.

Freud, S. *The problem of lay analysis.* New York: Brentano, 1927.

Freud, S. *A general introduction to psychoanalysis* (Vol. 1). New York: Liveright, 1935.

Freud, S. *An autobiographical study.* London: Hogarth, 1948.

Freud, S. *Collected papers* (Vol. 3). New York: Basic Books, 1959.

Fuller, R. Carl Rogers, religion, and the role of psychology in American culture. *Journal of Humanistic Psychology,* 1982, 22, 21–32.

Garfield, S.L. *Psychotherapy: An eclectic approach.* New York: Wiley, 1980.

Gendlin, E.T. *Experiencing and the creation of meaning.* New York: The Free Press of Glencoe, 1962.

Gendlin, E.T. A theory of personality change. In P. Worchel & D. Byrne (Eds.), *Personality change.* New York: Wiley, 1964.

Gendlin, E.T. Experiential explication and truth. *Journal of Existentialism,* 1966, 6, 131–146.

Gendlin, E.T. Therapeutic procedures in dealing with schizophrenics. In C.R. Rogers, E.T. Gendlin, D.J. Kiesler, & C.B. Truax (Eds.), *The therapeutic relationship and its impact: A study of psychotherapy with schizophrenics.* Madison: University of Wisconsin Press, 1967.

Gendlin, E.T. The experiential response. In E.F. Hammer (Ed.), *Use of interpretation in therapy: Technique and art.* New York: Grune & Stratton, 1968.

Gendlin, E.T. A short summary and some long predictions. In J.T. Hart & T.M. Tomlinson (Eds.), *New directions in client-centered therapy.* Boston: Houghton Mifflin, 1970.

Gendlin, E.T. Experiential phenomenology. In M. Natanson (Ed.), *Phenomenology and the social sciences.* Evanston, Ill.: Northwestern University Press, 1973.

Gendlin, E.T. Client-centered and experiential psychotherapy. In D.A. Wexler & L.N. Rice (Eds.), *Innovations in client-centered therapy.* New York: Wiley, 1974.

Gendlin, E.T. "Befindlichkeit": Heidegger's philosophy of psychology. *Review of Existential Psychology and Psychiatry,* 1978–9, 16 (1–3), 43–71.

Gendlin, E.T. *Focusing.* New York: Bantam, 1981. (a)

Gendlin, E.T. *A process model.* Unpublished manuscript, University of Chicago, 1981. (b)

Gendlin, E.T. The politics of giving therapy away. In D.G. Larson (Ed.), *Teaching psychological skills: Models for giving psychology away.* Monterey, Calif.: Brooks/Cole, 1984.

Gendlin, E.G, Beebe, J., III, Cassens, J., Klein, M., & Oberlander, M. Focusing ability in psychotherapy, personality, and creativity. In J.M. Shlien (Ed.), *Research in psychotherapy* (Vol. 3). Washington, D.C.: American Psychological Association, 1968.

Gendlin, E.T., Grindler, D., & McGuire, M. Body and space in focusing. In A.A. Sheikh (Ed.), *Imagination and healing.* New York: Baywood, 1984.

Gendlin, E.T., & Lemke, J. A critique of relativity and localization. *Mathematical Modeling*, 1983, 4 (1), 61–72.

Gilligan, C. *In a different voice.* Cambridge, Mass.: Harvard University Press, 1982.

Ginsberg, B.G. Parent-adolescent relationship development: A therapeutic and a preventive mental health program. (Doctoral dissertation, Pennsylvania State University, 1971.) *Dissertation Abstracts International*, 1972, 33, 426–427A. (University Microfilms No. 72-19, 3-6)

Ginsberg, B.G., & Vogelsong, E.L. Premarital relationship improvement by maximizing empathy and self-disclosure: The PRIMES Program. In B.G. Guerney, Jr. (Ed.), *Relationship enhancement: Skill-training programs for therapy, problem prevention, and enrichment.* San Francisco: Jossey-Bass, 1977.

Giorgi, A. *Psychology as a human science.* New York: Harper & Row, 1970.

Goldfried, J.R., & Robins, C. Self-schemas, cognitive bias, and the processing of therapeutic experiences. In P.C. Kendall (Ed.), *Advances in cognitive-behavioral research and therapy* (Vol. 2). New York: Academic Press, 1983.

Goldstein, K. *The organism.* New York: American Book Co., 1939.

Gomes, W.G. *The communicational-relational system in two forms of family group composition.* Unpublished master's thesis, Southern Illinois University, 1981.

Good, B.J. The heart of what's the matter: The semantics of illness in Iran. *Culture, Medicine, and Psychiatry*, 1977, 1, 25–58.

Good, B.J., & Good, M.D. The meaning of symptoms: A cultural hermeneutic model for clinical practice. In L. Eisenberg & A. Kleinman (Eds.), *The relevance of social science for medicine.* Dordrecht, Holland: Reidel, 1981.

Goodyear, R.K. (Producer). *Psychotherapy supervision by major theorists.* Manhattan, Kan.: Instructional Media Center, Kansas State University, 1982. (Videotape series)

Goodyear, R.K., Abadie, P.D., & Efros, F. *Supervisory models in practice: Comparisons of Ekstein, Ellis, Polster, and Rogers.* Unpublished manuscript, Kansas State University, 1983.

Goodyear, R.K., & Robyak, J.E. Supervisors' theory and experience level in supervisory focus. *Psychological Reports*, 1982, 51, 978.

Gordon, T. A theory of healthy relationships and a program of parent effectiveness training. In J.T. Hart & T.M. Tomlinson (Eds.), *New directions in client-centered therapy.* Boston: Houghton Mifflin, 1970.

Grant, G., & Riesman, D. *The perpetual dream: Reform and experiment in American education.* Chicago: University of Chicago Press, 1978.

Green, M. Humanists as managers in higher education and business. *Liberal Education*, 1982, 68 (3), 221–231.

Greenberg, L.S., & Safran, J.D. Encoding, information processing and the cognitive behavioral therapies. *Canadian Psychology*, 1980, 21, 59–66.

Greenberg, L.S., & Safran, J.D. Integrating affect and cognition: A perspective on the process of therapeutic change. *Cognitive Therapy and Research,* in press.

Grigg, A.E., & Goodstein, L.D. The use of clients as judges of the counselor's performance. *Journal of Counseling Psychology,* 1957, *4,* 31–36.

Gron, P. *Freedom and determinism in Gregory Bateson's theory of logical levels of learning: An appliction to psychotherapy.* Unpublished doctoral dissertation, Boston University, 1983.

GAP (Group for the Advancement of Psychiatry). *Treatment of families in conflict: The clinical study of family process.* New York: Basic Books, 1970.

Guerney, B.G., Jr. Filial therapy: Description and rationale. *Journal of Consulting Psychology,* 1964, *28* (4), 303–310.

Guerney, B.G., Jr. (Ed.). *Psychotherapeutic agents: New roles for nonprofessionals, parents, and teachers.* New York: Holt, Rinehart & Winston, 1969. (a)

Guerney, B.G., Jr. Filial therapy as a logical extension of current trends in psychotherapy. In B.G. Guerney, Jr. (Ed.), *Psychotherapeutic agents: New roles for nonprofessionals, parents, and teachers.* New York: Holt, Rinehart, & Winston, 1969, 47–56. (b)

Guerney, B.G., Jr. Filial therapy used as a treatment method for disturbed children. *Evaluation,* 1976, *3,* 34–35.

Guerney, B.G., Jr. *Relationship enhancement: Skill training programs for therapy, problem prevention, and enrichment.* San Francisco: Jossey-Bass, 1977. (a)

Guerney, B.G., Jr. Should teachers treat illiteracy, hypocalligraphy, and dysmathematica? *Canadian Counsellor,* 1977, *12* (1), 9–14. (b)

Guerney, B.G., Jr. The delivery of mental health services: Spiritual versus medical versus educational models. In T.R. Vallance & R.U. Sabre (Eds.), *Society's stepchildren: Mental health services in transition.* New York: Human Sciences Press, 1982.

Guerney, B.G., Jr. Establishing a school for living cooperative: A proposal. In N. Stinnett et al. (Eds.), *Building family strengths* (Volume 4). Lincoln: University of Nebraska Press, 1983.

Guerney, B.G., Jr., Coufal, J., & Vogelsong, E.L. Relationship enhancement versus a traditional approach to therapeutic/preventive/enrichment parent-adolescent programs. *Journal of Consulting & Clinical Psychology,* 1981, *49,* 927–939.

Guerney, B.G., Jr., Guerney, L.F., & Andronico, M.P. Filial therapy. In J.T. Hart & T.M. Tomlinson (Eds.), *New directions in client-centered therapy.* Boston: Houghton Mifflin, 1970.

Guerney, B.G., Jr., & Stover, L. *Filial therapy: Final report on MH 1826401.* Unpublished manuscript, Pennsylvania State University, 1971.

Guerney, B.G., Jr., Vogelsong, E.L., & Coufal, J. Relationship enhancement versus a traditional treatment: Follow-up and booster effects. In D.H. Olson & B.C. Miller (Eds.), *Family studies review yearbook.* Beverly Hills:

Sage, 1983.

Guerney, L.F. Filial therapy program. In D.H. Olson (Ed.), *Treating relationships*. Lake Mills, Iowa: Graphic Publishing Co., 1976, 67–91.

Guerney, L.F. A description and evaluation of a skills training program for foster parents. *American Journal of Community Psychology*, 1977, 5 (3), 361–371.

Guerney, L.F. *Parenting: A skills training manual*. State College, Penn.: IDEALS, 1978.

Guerney, L.F. Filial therapy. In R. Herink (Ed.), *The psychotherapy handbook*. New York: The New American Library, 1980.

Guntrip, J.J. *Psychoanalytic theory, therapy, and the self*. New York: Basic Books, 1971.

Gurman, A.S. The patient's perception of the therapeutic relationship. In A.S. Gurman & A.M. Razin (Eds.), *Effective psychotherapy: A handbook of research*. New York: Pergamon, 1977.

Hackney, H. The evolution of empathy. *Personnel & Guidance Journal*, 1978, 57, 35–38.

Haley, J. *Problem solving therapy*. San Francisco: Jossey-Bass, 1976.

Halkides, G. *An investigation of therapeutic success as a function of four variables*. Unpublished doctoral dissertation, University of Chicago, 1958.

Hall, C., & Lindzey, G. *Theories of personality*. New York: Wiley, 1970.

Hamilton, E. *The Greek way*. New York: Norton, 1942.

Handley, P. Relationship between supervisors' and trainees' cognitive styles and the supervision process. *Journal of Counseling Psychology*, 1982, 29, 508–525.

Hansen, J.C., Moore, G.D., & Carkhuff, R.R. The differential relationships of objective and client perceptions of counseling. *Journal of Clinical Psychology*, 1968, 24, 244–246.

Hansen, J.C., Robins, T.H., & Grimes, J. Review of research on practicum supervision. *Counselor Education and Supervision*, 1982, 22, 15–24.

Harré, R., & Secord, P. *The explanation of social behaviour*. Oxford: Blackwell, 1972.

Harwood, A. The hot-cold theory of disease: Implications for treatment of Puerto Rican patients. *Journal of the American Medical Association*, 1971, 216, 1153–1168.

Harwood, A. (Ed.). *Ethnicity and medical care*. Cambridge, Mass.: Harvard University Press, 1981.

Hart, J.T., & Tomlinson, T.M. (Eds.). *New directions in client-centered therapy*. Boston: Houghton Mifflin, 1970.

Hartmann, H. *Ego psychology and the problem of adaptation*. New York: International Universities Press, 1939.

Hartmann, H. Comments on the scientific aspects of psychoanalysis. *The Psychoanalytic Study of the Child*, 1958, 13, 127–146.

Heath, D.H. *Explorations of maturity.* New York: Appleton-Century-Crofts, 1965.

Heath, D.H. *Maturity and competence: A trans-cultural view.* New York: Gardner, 1977.

Heilbroner, R.L. *An inquiry into the human prospect.* New York/London: Norton, 1980.

Heron, W. The pathology of boredom. *Scientific American,* 1957, *196,* 52–56.

Hill, C.E. A comparison of the perceptions of a therapy session by clients, therapists, and objective judges. JSAS *Catalog of Selected Documents in Psychology,* 1974, *4,* 16. (Ms. No. 564)

Hill, C.E., Snyder, J.F., & Schill, T.R. An analogue study of standard client perceptions of A and B therapists. *Journal of Clinical Psychology,* 1974, *30,* 94–96.

Hiltner, S. *Pastoral counseling.* New York: Abingdon-Cokesbury, 1949.

Hiltner, S. *Preface to pastoral theology.* New York: Abingdon, 1958.

Holloway, E.L., & Hosford, R.E. Towards developing a prescriptive technology of counselor supervision. *The Counseling Psychologist,* 1983, *11* (1), 73–78.

Horton, R. African traditional thought and Western science. *Africa,* 1967, *37,* 50–71.

Ivey, A.E., & Authier, J. *Microcounseling* (2nd ed.). Springfield, Ill.: Thomas, 1978.

Jahoda, M. *Current concepts of positive mental health.* New York: Basic Books, 1958.

James, W. *The principles of psychology* (Vol. 1). New York: Dover, 1950. (Originally published, 1890.)

Jenkins, J.L., & Cartwright, D. A mental imagery approach to id, ego, and superego evaluation: Diagnostic and treatment implications. *Academic Psychology Bulletin,* 1982, *3,* 47–60.

Jennen, M. *Onvoorwaardelijke positieve gezindheid. Reflectie over de beleving en communicatie van deze therapeutische grondhouding.* Unpublished paper, Catholic University of Leuven, 1974.

Jessee, R., & Guerney, B.G., Jr. A comparison of Gestalt and relationship enhancement treatments with married couples. *The American Journal of Family Therapy,* 1981, *9,* 31–41.

Joanning, H., Avery, A.W., Brock, G.W., & Coufal, J. The educational approach to social skills training in marriage and family intervention. In W.T. Singleton, P. Spurgeon, & R.B. Stammers (Eds.), *Analysis of social skills.* London: Plenum, 1980.

Jones, E. *The life and work of Sigmund Freud* (Vol. 1). New York: Basic Books, 1953.

Jones, E. *The life and work of Sigmund Freud* (Vol. 3). New York: Basic Books, 1957.

Jones, H.T. The relationship of counselor-client personality similarity to counseling process and outcome. (Doctoral dissertation, University of Missouri, 1968.) *Dissertation Abstracts*, 1969, 29, 2962A. (University Microfilms No. 69-3390)

Judge, B. On reflection. *Psychotherapy: Theory, Research, and Practice*, 1979, 16 (1), 22–29.

Jung, C.G. *Man and his symbols.* New York: Doubleday, 1964.

Kahana, R.J., & Bibring, G.L. Personality types in medical management. In N.E. Zinberg (Ed.), *Psychiatry and medical practice in a general hospital.* New York: International Universities Press, 1964.

Kalfas, N.S. Client-perceived therapist empathy as a correlate of outcome. (Doctoral dissertation, University of Arizona, 1973.) *Dissertation Abstracts International*, 1974, 34, 5633A. (University Microfilms No. 74-7696)

Kanter, M. Clearing a space with four cancer patients. *Focusing Folio*, 1982, 2 (4).

Kantor, D., & Lehr, W. *Inside the family: Toward a theory of family process.* San Francisco: Jossey-Bass, 1975.

Kaslow, F., Cooper, B., & Linsenberg, B. Family therapist authenticity as a key factor in outcome. *International Journal of Family Therapy*, 1979, 1 (2), 184–189.

Katon, W., & Kleinman, A. Doctor-patient negotiation and other social science strategies in patient care. In L. Eisenberg & A. Kleinman (Eds.), *The relevance of social science for medicine.* Dordrecht, Holland: Reidel, 1981.

Keeney, B.P., & Sprenkle, D.H. Ecosystemic epistemology: Critical implications for the aesthetics and pragmatics of family therapy. *Family Process*, 1982, 21 (1), 1–19.

Keller, G. *Academic strategy: The management revolution in higher education.* Baltimore: Johns Hopkins Press, 1983.

Kemper, T. *A social interactional theory of emotions.* New York: Wiley, 1978.

Kerr, C. Administration of higher education in an era of change and conflict. In C. Kerr (Ed.), *Conflict, retrenchment and reappraisal: The administration of higher education.* Chicago: University of Chicago Press, 1979.

Kerr, C. *The uses of the university.* Cambridge, Mass.: Harvard University Press, 1982.

Kiesler, D.J., Klein, M.H., Mathieu, P.L. & Schoeninger, D. Constructive personality change for therapy and control patients. In C.R. Rogers, E.T. Gendlin, D.J. Kiesler, & C.B. Truax (Eds.), *The therapeutic relationship and its impact: A study of psychotherapy with schizophrenics.* Madison: University of Wisconsin Press, 1967.

Kirschenbaum, H. *On becoming Carl Rogers.* New York: Dell, 1979.

Klein, M. Notes on some schizoid mechanisms. *International Journal of Psycho-*

analysis, 1946, *27*, 99–110.

Klein, M. *Our adult world and other essays.* New York: Basic Books, 1963.

Klein, M.H., Mathieu, P.L., Kiesler, D.J., & Gendlin, E.T. *The experiencing scale: A research and training manual.* Madison: Wisconsin Psychiatric Institute, The University of Wisconsin, 1969.

Kleinman, A. Medicine's symbolic reality. *Inquiry*, 1973, *16*, 203–216.

Kleinman, A. *Patients and healers in the context of culture.* Berkeley: University of California Press, 1980.

Kleinman, A., Eisenberg, L., & Good, B. Culture, illness, and care: Clinical lessons from anthropologic and cross-cultural research. *Annals of Internal Medicine*, 1978, 88 (2), 251–258.

Koestler, A. *Janus: A summing up.* New York: Random House, 1978.

Krull, T.K., & Wyer, R.S., Jr. Category accessibility and social perception: Some implications for the study of person memory and interpersonal judgments. *Journal of Personality & Social Psychology*, 1980, *38*, 841–856.

Kuhn, T. *The structure of scientific revolutions.* Chicago: Chicago University Press, 1962.

Kurtz, R.R., & Grummon, D.L. Different approaches to the measurement of therapist empathy and their relationship to therapy outcomes. *Journal of Consulting and Clinical Psychology*, 1972, *39*, 106–115.

Laing, R.D. *The self and others: Further studies in sanity and madness.* Chicago: Quadrangle Books, 1962.

Laing, R.D. *The politics of the family and other essays.* New York: Pantheon, 1969, 1971.

Laing, R.D., & Esterson, A. *Sanity, madness and the family.* Harmondsworth: Penguin, 1964.

Lambert, M.J. Supervisory and counseling process: A comparative study. *Counselor Education and Supervision*, 1974, *14*, 54–60.

Lambert, M.J., De Julio, S.S., & Stein, D.M. Therapist interpersonal skills: Process, outcome, methodological considerations, and recommendations for future research. *Psychological Bulletin*, 1978, *85*, 467–489.

Lasch, C. *The culture of narcissism: American life in an age of diminishing expectations.* New York: Norton, 1979.

Lazare, A., Eisenthal, S., Frank, A., & Stoeckle, J.D. Studies on a negotiated approach to patient-hood. In E. Gallagher (Ed.), *The doctor-patient relationship in the changing health scene.* Washington, D.C.: U.S. Department of Health, Education, and Welfare, 1978. (Pub. No. NIH 78-183)

Leary, T. *Interpersonal diagnosis of personality.* New York: Ronald, 1957.

Lecker, S. Family therapies. In B. Wolman (Ed.), *The therapists' handbook.* New York: Van Nostrand, 1976.

Leech, K. *Soul friend: The practice of Christian spirituality.* San Francisco: Harper & Row, 1980.

Lehmann, B. Enkele gedachten over afstand en nabijheid in de psychotherapis.

Tijdschrift voor Psychotherapie, 1975, 1, 95–101.

Lesser, W.M. The relationship between counseling progress and empathic understanding. *Journal of Counseling Psychology*, 1961, 8, 330–336.

Levant, R.F. Client-centered approaches to working with the family: An ovrview of new developments in therapeutic, educational, and preventive methods. *International Journal of Family Counseling*, 1978, 6, 31–44. (a)

Levant, R.F. Family therapy: A client-centered perspective. *Journal of Marriage and Family Counseling*, 1978, 4, 35–42. (b)

Levant, R.F. Client-centered family therapy. *American Journal of Family Therapy*, 1982, 10 (2), 72–75.

Levant, R.F. Client-centered skills training programs for the family: A review of the literature. *The Counseling Psychologist*, 1983, 11 (3), 29–46.

Leventhal, H. A perceptual-motor processing model of emotion. In P. Pliner, K.R. Blankstein, & I.M. Spigel (Eds.), *Advances in the study of communication and affect* (Vol. 5). New York: Plenum, 1979.

Lewis, W.W. *The construct validation of a reputation test*. Unpublished doctoral dissertation, George Peabody College for Teachers, 1959.

Libo, L.M. The projective expression of a patient therapist attraction. *Journal of Clinical Psychology*, 1957, 13, 33–36.

Lieberman, L.R. Reinforcement and non-reinforcement in Rogerian psychotherapy: A critique. *Perceptual and Motor Skills*, 1969, 28, 559–565. (a)

Lieberman, L.R. Reinforcement in Rogerian psychotherapy: Rejoinder. *Perceptual and Motor Skills*, 1969, 29, 861–862. (b)

Lietaer, G. Niderlandstalige revisie van Barrett-Lennard's Relationship Inventory voor individueel-therapeutische relaties. *Psychologica Belgica*, 1976, 6, 73–94.

Lietaer, G. Onvoorwaardelijke aanvaarding: Een omstreden grondhouding in client-centered therapie. In J.R. Nuttin (Ed.), *Gedrag, dynamische relatie en betekeniswereld*. Leuvense Universitaire Pers, 1980, 145–159. (a)

Lietaer, G. Goals of personal therapy for trainees, considered from a client-centered or existential viewpoint. In W. De Moore & H.R. Wijngaarden (Eds.), *Psychotherapy: Research and training. Proceedings of the XIth International Congress of Psychotherapy*. Amsterdam: Elsevier/North-Holland Biomedical Press, 1980, 305–308. (b)

Lietaer, G. The client-centered approach in the seventies. Part I: A structured review of the literature. *Tijdschrift voor Psychotherapie*, 1981, 7, 81–102.

Lifton, R.J. *Thought reform and the psychology of totalism*. New York: Norton, 1961.

Lindsay, J.S. Balance theory: Possible consequences of number of family members. *Family Process*, 1976, 15, 245–249.

Lipowski, Z.J. Physical illness, the individual, and the coping process. *Psychiatry in Medicine*, 1970, 1 (April), 91–102.

Litman, T.J. The family in health and health care: A social-behavioral overview. In E.G. Jaco (Ed.), *Patients, physicians, and illness: A sourcebook in behavioral science and health.* New York: Free Press, 1979.

Loevinger, J. *Ego development.* San Francisco: Jossey-Bass, 1976.

Loevinger, J., & Wessler, R. *Measuring ego development* (Vol. 1). San Francisco: Jossey-Bass, 1970.

Lorr, M. Client perceptions of therapists: A study of therapeutic relation. *Journal of Consulting Psychology,* 1965, *29,* 146–149.

Ludwig, A.M. The trance. *Comprehensive Psychiatry,* 1967, *8* (1), 7–15.

McBeath, J., Mearns, D., Thomson, W., & Rodger, H. *Social education: The Scottish approach.* Glasgow: Jordanhill College Press, 1981.

Macalpine, I. The development of the transference. *Psychoanalytic Quarterly,* 1950, *19,* 501–539.

Maccoby, M. *The gamesman.* New York: Bantam, 1977.

McClanahan, L.D. A comparison of counseling techniques and attitudes with client evaluations of the counseling relationship. (Doctoral dissertation, Ohio University, 1973.) *Dissertation Abstracts International,* 1974, *34,* 5637A. (University Microfilms No. 74-7649)

McDougall, W. *The group mind.* New York: Putnam, 1928.

McGuire, W. (Ed.). *The Freud-Jung letters.* Princeton, N.J.: Princeton University Press, 1974.

McLoughlin, W. *Revivals, awakenings, and reform.* Chicago: University of Chicago Press, 1978.

Macmurray, J. *Persons in relation.* London: Faber, 1961.

McNeil, J. *A history of the cure of souls.* New York: Harper & Brothers, 1951.

McQuillen, C.C. Universities as "Theory Z" organizations. *AGB Reports,* 1982, *24* (6), 20–23.

McWhirter, J.J. Two measures of the facilitative conditions: A correlation study. *Journal of Counseling Psychology,* 1973, *20,* 317–320.

Mahoney, M.J. Cognitive and self-control therapies. In S.L. Garfield & A.E. Bergin (Eds.), *Handbook of psychotherapy and behavior change.* New York: Wiley, 1978.

Malcolm, J. Annals of scholarship. Trouble in the Archives—I. *The New Yorker,* December 5, 1983, pp. 59–152.

Mannheim, K. *Ideology and utopia.* New York: Harcourt, Brace & World, 1968.

Marcia, J.E. Development and validation of ego-identity status. *Journal of Personality and Social Psychology,* 1966, *3,* 551–558.

Markus, H. Self-schemata and processing information about the self. *Journal of Personality and Social Psychology,* 1977, *35,* 63–78.

Markus, H ., & Smith, J. The influence of self-schema on the perception of others. In N. Cantor & J.F. Kihlstrom (Eds.), *Personality, cognition, and social interaction.* Hillsdale, N.J.: Erlbaum, 1981.

Marrow, A. *The practical theorist.* New York: Basic Books, 1969.

Marsh, P., Rosser, E., & Harré, R. *The rules of disorder*. London: Routledge Kegan Paul, 1978.

Marshall, K.A. Empathy, genuineness, and regard: Determinants of successful therapy with schizophrenics? A critical review. *Psychotherapy: Theory, Research, and Practice*, 1977, *14*, 57–64.

Martin, D.G. *Learning-based client-centered therapy*. Monterrey, Calif.: Brooks/Cole, 1972.

Martin, D.G. *Counseling and therapy skills*. Belmont, Calif.: Brooks/Cole, 1983.

Martin, P.J., & Sterne, A.L. Post-hospital adjustment as related to therapists' in-therapy behavior. *Psychotherapy: Theory, Research, and Practice*, 1976, *13*, 267–273.

Maslow, A.H. *Motivation and personality*. New York: Harper Brothers, 1954.

Mathieu-Coughlan, P., & Klein, M.H. Experiential psychotherapy: Key events in client-therapist interaction. In L.N. Rice & L.S. Greenberg (Eds.), *Patterns of change: Intensive analysis of psychotherapy process*. New York: Guilford, 1984.

Maturana, H.R., & Varela, F.J. *Autopoiesis and cognition: The realization of the living*. Dordrecht, Holland: Reidel, 1980.

Mayhew, L.B. *Surviving the eighties: Strategies and procedures for solving fiscal and enrollment problems*. San Francisco: Jossey-Bass, 1978.

Mead, G.H. *Mind, self, and society from the standpoint of a social behaviorist*. Chicago: University of Chicago Press, 1967. (Originally published, 1934.)

Meara, N.M., Shannon, J.W., & Pepinsky, H.B. Comparison of the stylistic complexity of the language of counselor and client across three theoretical orientations. *Journal of Counseling Psychology*, 1979, *26*, 181–189.

Mearns, D. *Inveralmond Alternative School: Phase I evaluation*. Glasgow: Jordanhill College Press, 1982.

Mechanic, D. Social psychological factors affecting the presentation of bodily complaints. *New England Journal of Medicine*, 1972, *286* (21), 1132–1139.

Meltzoff, J., & Kornreich, M. *Research in psychotherapy*. New York: Atherton, 1970.

Menninger, K. *The theory of psychoanalytic technique*. New York: Basic Books, 1958.

Millett, J.D. *New structures of campus power: Success and failures of emerging forms of institutional governance*. San Francisco: Jossey-Bass, 1978.

Minuchin, S. *Families and family therapy*. Cambridge, Mass.: Harvard University Press, 1979.

Mitchell, K.M., Bozarth, J.D., & Krauft, C.C. A reappraisal of the therapeutic effectiveness of accurate empathy, non-possessive warmth and genuineness. In A.S. Gurman & A.M. Razin, *Effective psychotherapy: A handbook of research*. New York: Pergamon, 1977.

Mowrer, O.H. (Ed.). *Morality and mental health.* Chicago: Rand McNally, 1967.

Murray, E.J. A content-analysis method for studying psychotherapy. *Psychological Monographs*, 1956, *70* (13, Whole No. 420).

Neisser, U. *Cognition and reality: Principles and implications of cognitive psychology.* New York: Freeman, 1976.

Oates, W. *Protestant pastoral counseling.* Philadelphia: Westminster Press, 1962.

Oden, T. *Kerygma and counseling: Toward a covenant ontology for secular psychotherapy.* Philadelphia: Westminster Press, 1966.

Orlinsky, D.E., & Howard, K.I. The relation of process to outcome in psychotherapy. In S.L. Garfield & A.E. Bergin (Eds.), *Handbook of psychotherapy and behavior change* (2nd ed.). New York: Wiley, 1978.

Orne, M. On the social psychology of the psychological experiment: With particular reference to demand characteristics and their implications. *American Psychologist*, 1962, *17*, 776–783.

Orr, D. Transference and countertransference: An historical survey. *Journal of the American Psychoanalytic Association*, 1954, *2*, 621–670.

Ostrom, T.M., Lingle, J.H., Pryor, J.B., & Geva, N. Cognitive organization of person impressions. In R. Hastie (Ed.), *Person memory: The cognitive basis of social perception.* Hillsdale, N.J.: Erlbaum, 1980.

Outler, A. *Psychotherapy and the Christian message.* New York: Harper & Brothers, 1954.

Oxman, L.K. The effectiveness of filial therapy: A controlled study. (Doctoral dissertation, Rutgers University, 1971.) *Dissertation Abstracts International*, 1972, *32*, 6656-B. (University Microfilms No. 72-16, 093)

Palazzoli, M.S., Cecchin, G., Prata, G., & Boscolo, L. *Paradox and counterparadox: A new model in the therapy of the family in schizophrenic transaction.* New York: Aronson, 1978.

Parloff, M.B., Waskow, I.E., & Wolfe, B.E. Research on therapist variables in relation to process and outcome. In S.L. Garfield & A.E. Bergin (Eds.), *Handbook of psychotherapy and behavior change* (2nd ed.). New York: Wiley, 1978.

Patterson, C.H. Supervising students in the counseling practicum. *Journal of Counseling Psychology*, 1964, *11*, 47–53.

Patterson, C.H. A client-centered approach to supervision. *The Counseling Psychologist*, 1983, *11* (1), 21–26.

Perls, F., Hefferline, R., & Goodman, P. *Gestalt therapy: Excitement and growth in the human personality.* New York: Dell, 1951.

Peterson, D.R., & Bry, B. Dimensions of perceived competence in professional psychology. *Professional Psychology*, 1980, *11*, 965–971.

Pierce, R.M., & Schauble, P.G. Graduate training of facilitative counselors: The effect of individual supervision. *Journal of Counseling Psychology*,

1970, *17*, 210–215.

Pierce, R.M., & Schauble, P.G. Toward the development of facilitative counselors: The effects of practicum instruction and individual supervision. *Counselor Education and Supervision*, 1971, *11*, 83–89.

Pfifferling, J.H. A cultural prescription for medicocentrism. In L. Eisenberg & A. Kleinman (Eds.), *The relevance of social science for medicine*. Dordrecht, Holland: Reidel, 1981.

Plum, A. Communication as skill: A critique and alternative proposal. *Journal of Humanistic Psychology*, 1981, *21* (4), 3–19.

Polanyi, M. *Personal knowledge*. London: Routledge Kegan Paul, 1958.

Polster, E., & Polster, M. *Gestalt therapy integrated*. New York: Brunner/Mazel, 1973.

Posner, M.I. Abstraction and the process of recognition. In G.H. Bower & J.T. Spence (Eds.), *The psychology of learning and motivation* (Vol. 3). New York: Academic Press, 1969.

Preston, J., & Guerney, B.G., Jr. *Relationship enhancement skill training*. Unpublished manuscript, Pennsylvania State University, 1982.

Quay, R. *Research in higher education: A guide to source bibliographies*. New York: College Entrance Examination Board, 1976.

Rachman, S.J., & Wilson, G.T. *The effects of psychological therapy* (2nd ed.). New York: Pergamon, 1980.

Rappaport, A.F. Conjugal relationship enhancement program. In D. Olson (Ed.), *Treating relationships*. Lake Mills, Iowa: Graphic Publishing Co., 1976.

Raskin, N. *The concept of the self in client-centered and person-centered approach, 1970–1980*. Paper presented at Grand Rounds Conference, Northwestern University Medical School, Chicago, September 1980.

Raskin, N.J., & van der Veen, F. Client-centered family therapy: Some clinical and research perspectives. In J.T. Hart & T.M. Tomlinson (Eds.), *New directions in client-centered therapy*. Boston: Houghton Mifflin, 1970.

Reason, P., & Rowan, J. (Eds.). *Human inquiry: A source book of new paradigm research*. London: Wiley, 1981.

Rice, L.N. The evocative function of the therapist. In D.A. Wexler & L.N. Rice (Eds.), *Innovations in client-centered therapy*. New York: Wiley, 1974.

Rice, L.N. A client-centered approach to the supervision of psychotherapy. In A.K. Hess (Ed.), *Psychotherapy supervision: Theory, research, and practice*. New York: Wiley, 1980.

Rice, L.N. The relationship in client-centered therapy. In M.J. Lambert (Ed.), *Psychotherapy and patient relationships*. Homewood, Ill.: Dow Jones-Irwin, 1983.

Rice, L.N., & Greenberg, L.S. The new research paradigm. In L.N. Rice & L.S. Greenberg (Eds.), *Patterns of change: Intensive analysis of psychotherapy process*. New York: Guilford, 1984.

Rice, L.N., & Saperia, E. Task analysis of the resolution of problematic reactions. In L.N. Rice & L.S. Greenberg (Eds.), *Patterns of change: Intensive analysis of psychotherapy process.* New York: Guilford, 1984.

Ridley, C.A., Jorgensen, S.R., Morgan, A.C., & Avery, A.W. Relationship enhancement with premarital couples: An assessment of effects on relationship adjustment. *American Journal of Family Therapy*, 1982, 10 (3), 41-48.

Roberts, D. *Psychotherapy and a Christian view of man.* New York: Scribner's, 1950.

Rogers, C.R. The use of electrically recorded interviews in improving psychotherapeutic techniques. *American Journal of Orthopsychiatry*, 1942, 12, 329-434. (a)

Rogers, C.R. *Counseling and psychotherapy.* Boston: Houghton Mifflin, 1942. (b)

Rogers, C.R. *Client-centered therapy.* Boston: Houghton Mifflin, 1951.

Rogers, C.R. *The implications of client-centered therapy for family life.* Paper presented to the International Society for General Semantics, Chicago Chapter, April 1953.

Rogers, C.R. The case of Mrs. Oak. In C.R. Rogers & R.F. Dymond (Eds.), *Psychotherapy and personality change.* Chicago: University of Chicago Press, 1954.

Rogers, C.R. Comment. *Journal of Counseling Psychology*, 1955, 2, 196.

Rogers, C.R. The necessary and sufficient conditions of therapeutic personality change. *Journal of Consulting Psychology*, 1957, 21, 95-103. (a)

Rogers, C.R. Training individuals to engage in the therapeutic process. In C.R. Strother (Ed.), *Psychology and mental health.* Washington, D.C.: American Psychological Association, 1957, 76-92. (b)

Rogers, C.R. Client-centered therapy. In S. Arieti (Ed.), *American Handbook of Psychiatry* (Vol. 3). New York: Basic Books, 1959. (a)

Rogers, C.R. A theory of therapy, personality, and interpersonal relationships as developed in the client-centered framework. In S. Koch (Ed.), *Psychology: The study of a science* (Vol. III). New York: McGraw Hill, 1959. (b)

Rogers, C.R. *On becoming a person.* Boston: Houghton Mifflin, 1961.

Rogers, C.R. The interpersonal relationship: The core of guidance. *Harvard Educational Review*, 1962, 32, 416-429.

Rogers, C.R. The actualizing tendency in relation to "motives" and to consciousness. In M. Jones (Ed.), *Nebraska Symposium on Motivation.* Lincoln: University of Nebraska Press, 1963. (a)

Rogers, C.R. The concept of the fully functioning person. *Psychotherapy: Theory, Research, and Practice*, 1963, 1, 17-26. (b)

Rogers, C.R. Toward a modern approach to values: The valuing process in the mature person. *Journal of Abnormal and Social Psychology*, 1964, 68, 160-167.

Rogers, C.R. *Three approaches to psychotherapy I.* Psychological Films, 1965. (Film)

Rogers, C.R. Autobiographical essay. In E.B. Boring & G. Lindzey, A history of psychology in autobiography (Vol. 5). New York: Appleton-Century-Crofts, 1967.

Rogers, C.R. Freedom to learn. Columbus, Oh.: Merrill, 1969.

Rogers, C.R. Can I be a facilitative person in a group. In C.R. Rogers, On encounter groups. New York: Harper & Row, 1970. (a)

Rogers, C.R. On encounter groups. New York: Harper & Row, 1970. (b)

Rogers, C.R. Becoming partners. New York: Dell, 1972.

Rogers, C.R. In retrospect: Forty-six years. American Psychologist, 1974, 29, 115–123.

Rogers, C.R. Client-centered psychotherapy. In A.M. Freedman, H.I. Kaplan, & B.J. Sadock (Eds.), Comprehensive textbook of psychiatry (Vol. 2). Baltimore: Williams & Wilkins, 1975. (a)

Rogers, C.R. Empathic: An unappreciated way of being. The Counseling Psychologist, 1975, 5, 209. (b)

Rogers, C.R. Three approaches to psychotherapy II. Psychological Films, 1975. (Film) (c)

Rogers, C.R. Carl Rogers on personal power: Inner strength and its revolutionary impact. New York: Delacorte, 1977.

Rogers, C.R. The foundations of the person-centered approach. Education, 1979, 100, 98–107.

Rogers, C.R. A way of being. Boston: Houghton Mifflin, 1980.

Rogers, C.R., & Dymond, R.F. (Eds.). Psychotherapy and personality change. Chicago: University of Chicago Press, 1954.

Rogers, C.R., Gendlin, E.T., Kiesler, D.J., & Truax, C.B. The therapeutic relationship and its impact: A study of psychotherapy with schizophrenics. Madison: University of Wisconsin Press, 1967.

Rogers, C.R., & Segel, R.H. Psychotherapy in process: The case of Miss Mun. Pennsylvania State University Psychological Cinema Register, 1955. (Film)

Rogers, C.R., & Skinner, B.F. Some issues concerning the control of human behavior. Science, 1956, 124, 1057–1066.

Rogers, C.R., & Truax, C.B. The therapeutic conditions antecedent to change: A theoretical view. In C.R. Rogers, E.T. Gendlin, D.J. Kiesler, & C.B. Truax (Eds.), The therapeutic relationship and its impact: A study of psychotherapy with schizophrenics. Madison: University of Wisconsin Press, 1967.

Rogers, C.R., & Wood, J.K. The changing theory of client-centered therapy. In A. Burton (Ed.), Operational theories of personality. New York: Brunner/Mazel, 1974.

Rosch, E. On the internal structure of perceptual and semantic categories. In T.E. Moore (Ed.), Cognitive development and the acquisition of language. New York: Academic Press, 1973.

Rosch, E. Principles of categorization. In E. Rosch & B.B. Lloyd (Eds.), *Cognition and categorization.* Hillsdale, N.J.: Erlbaum, 1978.

Rosenthal, R. Covert communication in the psychological experiment. *Psychological Bulletin,* 1967, *67,* 356–367.

Ross, E.R., Baker, S.B., & Guerney, B.G., Jr. *Effectiveness of relationship enhancement therapy versus therapist's preferred therapy.* Unpublished manuscript, Pennsylvania State University, 1982.

Roth, H.P. Patients' beliefs about peptic ulcer and its treatment. *Annals of Internal Medicine,* 1962, *56,* 72–80.

Rourke, F., & Brooks, G. *The managerial revolution in higher education.* Baltimore: Johns Hopkins Press, 1966.

Roustang, F. *Dire mastery.* Baltimore: Johns Hopkins Press, 1982.

Saltzman, C., Luetgert, M.J., Roth, C.H., Creaser, J., & Howard, L. Formation of a therapeutic relationship: Experiences during the initial phase of psychotherapy as predictors of treatment duration and outcome. *Journal of Consulting and Clinical Psychology,* 1976, *44,* 546–555.

Sapira, J.D. Reassurance therapy: What to say to symptomatic patients with benign diseases. *Annals of Internal Medicine,* 1972, *77,* 603–604.

Sapolsky, A. Relationship between patient-doctor compatibility, mutual perception, and outcome of treatment. *Journal of Abnormal Psychology,* 1965, *70,* 70–76.

Sargant, W. *Battle for the mind.* New York: Doubleday, 1957.

Schein, E.H., Schneier, I., & Barker, C.H. *Coercive persuasion.* New York: Norton, 1961.

Schmitt, J.P. Unconditional positive regard. *Psychotherapy: Theory, Research, and Practice,* 1980, *17,* 237–245.

Seeman, J. Client-centered therapy. In D. Brower & L. Abt (Eds.), *Progress in clinical psychology.* New York: Grune & Stratton, 1956.

Seeman, J. Toward a concept of personality integration. *American Psychologist,* 1959, *14,* 633–637.

Seeman, J. Teacher judgments of high and low adjustment. *Journal of Educational Research,* 1963, *57,* 213–216.

Seeman, J. *Personality integration: Studies and reflections.* New York: Human Sciences Press, 1983.

Seeman, J., Barry, E., & Ellinwood, C. Personality integration as a criterion of therapy outcome. *Psychotherapy: Theory, Research, and Practice,* 1963, *1,* 14–17.

Sensué, M.E. *Filial therapy follow-up study: Effects on parental acceptance and child adjustment.* Unpublished doctoral dissertation, Pennsylvania State University, 1981.

Shapiro, D.A. The effects of therapeutic conditions: Positive results revisited. *British Journal of Medical Psychology,* 1976, *49,* 315–323.

Shlien, J.M. *Erotic feelings in psychotherapy relationships: Origins, influences, and resolutions.* Paper presented at Annual Meeting of the American Psychological Association, Philadelphia, August 1963.

Shlien, J.M. The literal-intuitive axis and other thoughts. In J.T. Hart & T.M. Tomlinson (Eds.), *New directions in client-centered therapy.* Boston: Houghton Mifflin, 1970.

Shlien, J.M. The psychology of secrecy and another generation of best kept secrets. In C.R. Rogers (Chair), *Client-centered therapy in the 1980's.* Symposium presented at the Annual Meeting of the American Psychological Association, Los Angeles, 1981.

Shor, R.E. Hypnosis and the concept of the generalized reality-orientation. *American Journal of Psychotherapy,* 1959, *13,* 582–602.

Shostrom, E. (Producer). *Three approaches to psychotherapy.* Santa Ana, Calif.: Psychological Films, 1964. (Film)

Shotter, J. *Images of man in psychological research.* London: Methuen, 1975.

Shweder, R., & Bourne, E.J. Does the concept of the person vary cross culturally? In A.J. Marsella & G.M. White (Eds.), *Cultural conceptions of mental health and therapy.* Boston: Kluwer, 1982.

Sloane, R.B., Staples, F.R., Cristol, A.H., Yorkston, N.J., & Whipple, K. *Psychotherapy versus behavior therapy.* Cambridge, Mass.: Harvard University Press, 1975.

Smith, D.J. How I spent my summer. *Soundings,* 1980, *63* (3), 257–289.

Smith, M., Glass, G., & Miller, I. *The benefits of psychotherapy.* Baltimore: Johns Hopkins University Press, 1980.

Smith, M.B. Optima of mental health: A general frame of reference. *Psychiatry,* 1950, *13,* 503–510.

Smith, M.B. Research strategies toward a conception of positive mental health. *American Psychologist,* 1959, *14,* 673–681.

Smith, M.B. Explorations in competence: A study of Peace Corps teachers in Ghana. *American Psychologist,* 1966, *21,* 555–566.

Smith, M.B. Competence and socialization. In J.A. Clausen (Ed.), *Socialization and society.* Boston: Little, Brown, 1968.

Smith, M.B. *Social psychology and human values.* Chicago: Aldine, 1969.

Smith, M.B. Psychology and values. *Journal of Social Issues,* 1978, *34* (4), 181–199.

Smith, P. *Group processes and personal change.* London: Harper & Row, 1980.

Sprenkle, D.H., Keeney, B.P., & Sutton, P.M. Theorists who influence clinical members of AAMFT: A research note. *Journal of Marital and Family Therapy,* 1982, *8* (3), 367–369.

Standal, S.W. *The need for positive regard: A contribution to client-centered theory.* Unpublished doctoral dissertation, University of Chicago, 1954.

Stanley, C.L. "Relationship orientation" of counselor-trainees as related to client perception of the counseling relationship and client change in connotative meanings. (Doctoral dissertation, University of Southern California, 1966.) *Dissertation Abstracts,* 1967, *27,* 3699A–3700A. (University Microfilms No. 67-5311)

Stanley, C.S., & Cooker, P.G. Gestalt therapy and the core conditions of communication facilitation. A synergistic approach. In E.W.L. Smith (Ed.), *The growing edge of Gestalt therapy*. New York: Brunner/Mazel, 1976.

Steier, F. The American Society for Cybernetics: Interest group on the cybernetics of helping. *International Network of Family Therapy Newsletter*, 1983, *1* (4), A.

Stoeckle, J.D. The tasks of care: Humanistic dimensions of medical education. In W.R. Rogers & D. Barnard (Eds.), *Nourishing the humanistic in medicine: Interactions with the social sciences*. Pittsburgh: University of Pittsburgh Press, 1979.

Stoeckle, J.D., & Barsky, A.J. Attributions: Uses of social science knowledge in the "doctoring" of primary care. In L. Eisenberg & A. Kleinman (Eds.), *The relevance of social science for medicine*. Dordrecht, Holland: Reidel, 1981.

Stolorow, R.O. Psychoanalytic reflections on client-centered therapy in the light of modern conceptions of narcissism. *Psychotherapy: Theory, Research and Practice*, 1976, *13*, 26–29.

Stover, L., & Guerney, B.G., Jr. The efficacy of training procedures for mothers in filial therapy. *Psychotherapy: Theory, Research and Practice*, 1967, *4* (3), 110–115.

Strupp, H.H., Fox, R.E., & Lessler, K. *Patients view their psychotherapy*. Baltimore: Johns Hopkins Press, 1969.

Strauss, A.L., & Glaser, B.G. *Chronic illness and the quality of life*. St. Louis, Mo.: Mosby, 1975.

Sullivan, H.S. *The interpersonal theory of psychiatry*. New York: Norton, 1953.

Swann, W.B., Jr., & Read, S.J. Acquiring self-knowledge: The search for feedback that fits. *Journal of Personality and Social Psychology*, 1981, *41*, 1119–1128.

Sywulak, A.E. *The effect of filial therapy on parental acceptance and child adjustment*. Unpublished doctoral dissertation, Pennsylvania State University, 1977.

Szasz, T., & Hollender, M. A contribution to the philosophy of medicine. *Archives of Internal Medicine*, 1956, *97*, 585–592.

Tarasoff v. Regents of University of California, 529 P. 2d, 342, 118 Cal. Rptr. 129, vacated, 17 Cal. 3d 425, 551 P. 2d 334, 31 Cal. Rptr. 141 (1974).

Taylor, S.E., & Crocker, J. Schematic bases of social information processing. In E.T. Higgins, P. Herman, & M.P. Zanna (Eds.), *The Ontario symposium on social psychology* (Vol. 11). New York: Academic Press, 1981.

Taylor, S.E., & Fiske, S.T. Salience, attention, and attribution: Top of the head phenomena. In L. Berkowitz (Ed.), *Advances in experimental social psychology* (Vol. 11). New York: Academic Press, 1978.

Taylor, W.R. Research on family interaction: Static and dynamic models.

Family Process, 1970, 9, 221–232.

Tiedemann, J. Angst in de therapeutische relatie. *Tijdschrift voor Psychotherapie*, 1975, 1, 167–171.

Tillich, P. The impact of pastoral psychology on theological thought. *Pastoral Theology*, 1960, 11, 17–23.

Toman, W. *Family constellation: Its effects on personality and social behavior* (3rd ed.). New York: Springer, 1976.

Toukmanian, S.G. A perceptual-cognitive model for counseling and psychotherapy. In W.M. Pinsoff & L.S. Greenberg (Eds.), *The psychotherapeutic process: A research handbook*. New York: Guilford, in press.

Troemel-Ploetz, F. "I'd come to you for therapy": Interpretation, redefinition and paradox in Rogerian therapy. *Psychotherapy: Theory, Research and Practice*, 1980, 17, 246–257.

Truax, C.B. A scale for the measurement of accurate empathy. *Psychiatric Institute Bulletin*, 1961, 1 (12).

Truax, C.B. Reinforcement and nonreinforcement in Rogerian psychotherapy. *Journal of Abnormal Psychology*, 1966, 71, 1–9. (a)

Truax, C.B. Therapist empathy, warmth, and genuineness and patient personality change in group psychotherapy: A comparison between interaction unit measures, time sample measures, and patient perception measures. *Journal of Clinical Psychology*, 1966, 22, 225–229. (b)

Truax, C.B. Therapist interpersonal reinforcement of client self-exploration and therapeutic outcome in group psychotherapy. *Journal of Counseling Psychology*, 1968, 15, 225–231.

Truax, C.B. Reinforcement and nonreinforcement in Rogerian psychotherapy: "A reply." *Perception and Motor Skills*, 1969, 29, 701–702.

Truax, C.B., Altman, H., Wright, L., & Mitchell, K.M. Effects of therapeutic conditions in child therapy. *Journal of Community Psychology*, 1973, 1, 313–318.

Truax, C.B., & Carkhuff, R.R. *Toward effective counseling and psychotherapy*. Chicago: Aldine, 1967. (a)

Truax, C.B., & Carkhuff, R.R. The client-centered process as viewed by other therapists. In C.R. Rogers, E.T. Gendlin, D.J. Kiesler, & C.B. Truax (Eds.), *The therapeutic relationship and its impact: A study of psychotherapy with schizophrenics*. Madison: University of Wisconsin Press, 1967. (b)

Truax, C.B., & Kiesler, D.J. A tentative scale for the rating of unconditional positive regard. In C.R. Rogers, E.T. Gendlin, D.J. Kiesler, & C.B. Truax (Eds.), *The therapeutic relationship and its impact: A study of psychotherapy with schizophrenics*. Madison: University of Wisconsin Press, 1967.

Truax, C.B., & Mitchell, K.M. Research on certain therapist interpersonal skills in relation to process and outcome. In A.E. Bergin & S.L. Garfield (Eds.), *Handbook of psychotherapy and behavior change*. New York: Wiley, 1971.

Truax, C.B., Wittmer, J., & Wargo, D.G. Effects of the therapeutic conditions of accurate empathy, nonpossessive warmth, and genuineness on hospitalized mental patients during group therapy. *Journal of Clinical Psychology*, 1971, 27, 137–142.

Tulving, E. Episodic and semantic memory. In E. Tulving & W. Donaldson (Eds.), *Organization of memory*. New York: Academic Press, 1974.

Tyler, D.B. Psychological changes during experimental sleep deprivation. *Diseases of the Nervous System*, 1955, 16 (10), 293.

Valle, R., & King, M. (Eds.). *Existential-phenomenological alternatives for psychology*. New York: Oxford University Press, 1978.

Van Kaam, A. Phenomenal analysis: Exemplified by a study of the experience of "really feeling understood." *Journal of Individual Psychology*, 1959, 15, 66–72.

van der Veen, F. Family psychotherapy and a person's concept of the family: Some clinical and research formulations. *Institute for Juvenile Research Reports*, 1969, 6 (16).

van der Veen, F. Client perception of therapist conditions as a factor in psychotherapy. In J.T. Hart & T.M. Tomlinson (Eds.), *New directions in client-centered therapy*. Boston: Houghton Mifflin, 1970.

Vandevelde, V. *Het koncept onvoorwaardelijke positieve gezindheid in de client-centered terapie.* Unpublished master's thesis, Catholic University of Leuven, 1977.

Vogelsong, E., & Guerney, B.G., Jr. *The Relationship Enhancement Program for Family Therapy and Enrichment.* University Park, Penn.: Individual and Family Consultation Center of the Pennsylvania State University, 1979. (Videotape)

Vogelsong, E., Guerney, B.G., Jr., & Guerney, L.F. *Filial therapy.* University Park, Penn.: Individual and Family Consultation Center of The Pennsylvania State University, 1978. (Videotape)

Wachtel, P.L. Contingent and non-contingent therapist response. *Psychotherapy: Theory, Research and Practice*, 1979, 16, 30–35.

Waelder, R. Introduction to the discussion on problems of transference. *International Journal of Psychoanalysis*, 1956, 37, 369–384.

Walker, D.E. *The effective administrator: A practical approach to problem solving, decision making, and campus leadership.* San Francisco: Jossey-Bass, 1979.

Watzlawick, P., Beavin, J.R., & Jackson, D.D. *Pragmatics of human communication.* New York: Norton, 1967.

Watzlawick, P., Weakland, J., & Fisch, R. *Change: Principles of problem formation and problem resolution.* New York: Norton, 1974.

Wessler, R.L., & Ellis, A. Supervision in counseling: Rational-emotive therapy. *The Counseling Psychologist*, 1983, 11 (1), 43–50.

Wexler, D.A. A cognitive theory of experiencing, self-actualization, and therapeutic process. In D.A. Wexler & L.N. Rice (Eds.), *Innovations in* client-centered therapy. New York: Wiley, 1974.

Wexler, D.A., & Rice, L.N. (Eds.). *Innovations in client-centered therapy*. New York: Wiley, 1974.

White, R.W. Motivation reconsidered: The concept of competence. *Psychological Review*, 1959, 66, 297–333.

White, R.W. Competence and psychosexual states of development. In M.R. Jones (Ed.), *Nebraska Symposium on Motivation*. Lincoln: University of Nebraska Press, 1960.

Wieman, R.J. *Conjugal relationship modification and reciprocal reinforcement: A comparison of treatments for marital discord*. Unpublished doctoral dissertation, Pennsylvania State University, 1973.

Williams, D. *The minister and the care of souls*. New York: Harper & Brothers, 1961.

Winnicott, D.W. *The maturational process and the facilitating environment*. New York: International Universities Press, 1965.

Wise, C. *Pastoral counseling*. New York: Harper & Brothers, 1951.

Wise, C. *Pastoral psychotherapy: Theory and practice*. New York: Aronson, 1980.

Wood, J.K. Person-centered group therapy. In G. Gazda (Ed.), *Basic approaches to group psychotherapy and group counseling*. Springfield, Ill.: Thomas, 1982.

Zajonc, R.B. Feeling and thinking: Preferences need no inferences. *American Psychologist*, 1980, 35, 151–175.

Zauderer, E.S. The relationship of some counselor characteristics to revealingness in clients. (Doctoral dissertation, Ohio State University, 1967.) *Dissertation Abstracts*, 1968, 28, 3889B. (University Microfilms No. 68-3095)

Zimring, F.M. Theory and practice of client-centered therapy: A cognitive view. In D.A. Wexler & L.N. Rice (Eds.), *Innovations in client-centered therapy*. New York: Wiley, 1974.

Zinker, J.C. *The creative process in Gestalt therapy*. New York: Brunner/Mazel, 1977.

Zinner, J., & Shapiro, R. Projective identification as a mode of perception and behavior in families of adolescents. *International Journal of Psychoanalysis*, 1972, 53, 523–530.

Zuk, G.H. Family therapy: 1964–1970. *Psychotherapy: Theory, Research and Practice*, 1971, 8, 90–97.

Index

About the Editors

Ronald F. Levant, Clinical Associate Professor of the Program in Counseling Psychology at Boston University, is best known for his work in the field of family therapy, to which he has contributed numerous articles and a book (*Family Therapy: A Comprehensive Overview,* Prentice-Hall, 1984). He was a former student of John Shlien at Harvard in the early 1970s, and is thus one of the "third generation" of client-centered therapists. His interests lie in the integration of phenomenology with systems theory, and in the development and evaluation of preventive psychoeducational family programs.

John M. Shlien, Professor and former Chair of the Program in Counseling and Consulting Psychology at Harvard University, is well known for his contributions to the development of the client-centered approach. A former student of Carl Rogers, he later succeeded Rogers as chair of the clinical psychology program and director of the counseling center at the University of Chicago. Dr. Shlien is a friend, colleague, and/or former teacher of many of the researchers and theoreticians in this tradition.